D1535461

THE TWENTIETH CENTURY
IN THE FAR EAST

' Within the four seas all are brothers.'
—*Saying of Confucius.*

THE TWENTIETH CENTURY
IN THE FAR EAST

*A Perspective of Events, Cultural
Influences and Policies*

BY

P. H. B. KENT

KENNIKAT PRESS
Port Washington, N. Y./London

THE TWENTIETH CENTURY IN THE FAR EAST

First published in 1937
Reissued in 1970 by Kennikat Press
Library of Congress Catalog Card No: 77-115203
ISBN 0-8046-1096-7

Manufactured by Taylor Publishing Company   Dallas, Texas

ACKNOWLEDGEMENT

This book is based on personal observation, personal experience, personal records and such study over a period of thirty-five years as has been possible in a busy professional life. To all past and contemporary writers on Far Eastern subjects, on whose work I may have drawn unconsciously without making specific acknowledgement, I convey my sense of obligation. I thank my Chinese and Japanese friends who have extended to me their confidence. In this connection I recall in appreciative memory many such friends of an older generation, since dead.

I thank my friend Mr. W. O. Leitch, M.Inst.C.E., late General Manager and Chief Engineer of the Peiping–Liaoning railway, under whose direction the maps have been prepared. I am also indebted to many other friends for encouragement and assistance, to whom I make grateful acknowledgement.

P. H. B. K.

GUARDS CLUB,
December 31, 1936.

CONTENTS

9

CONTENTS

PART III

*The Foreign Contribution to the Economic Fabric of China
and in the Cultural Field*

PART IV

Japan and the Mainland of Asia

CONTENTS

CONTENTS

MAPS

The Far East
China
Manchoukuo

FOREWORD

The Western World has been forced to realize, however contrary to its inclination, that the Far East is more than a purely cultural and commercial field. Reflecting men and women are beginning to understand that its problems are world problems having a direct and vital interest for them. They ask to be told something of how the present situation has come about ; of the prospects of stable and effective government in China ; of the strength of Communism ; of the aims and policies of Japan and Russia. Anxious thought is being directed towards our own position. Other matters arousing attention are economic reactions, the possibility of war in the Far East, American policy and other aspects of the Pacific Problem.

Such questions, covering a wide range, do not for the most part admit of direct answer. Certainly in the course of casual conversation on occasions of short visits from the Far East to England but little more can be done than suggest lines of thought.

It may be pointed out, for example, that those who believe in China do not think that her story running through the ages is nearing an inglorious close. Despite her present critical condition, internationally speaking, they see her with weight in world affairs still to come. The question arises, how far are we in a position to influence its direction ?

Regarded from other points of view, the ' King's Writ,' as we understand it, does not run through her vast territories ; the bulk of her people live and die on the edge of economic disaster, victims of the stark realities of banditry, flood and famine ; her internal problems, not least the problems of personal ambition and party control of government, are so immense as to seem at times insoluble.

Again, the system of extra-territorial jurisdiction was designed to protect foreigners from the consequences of strange conceptions of responsibility and law, and different methods of judicial administration. Its maintenance is still necessary in spite of progress. Meanwhile, by a curious paradox, it has become one of China's chief political bulwarks, although her statesmen could not admit it and perforce must try to destroy it.

Suggesting thought in another direction, the West has not been altogether just to Japan. It has tended to ignore history and psychology, which is a dangerous thing to do. It is especially dangerous in the present case since the future of East Asia and of the Pacific present far-away problems difficult to cope with. On the other hand, Japan has spoilt a good case. It is not to be supposed that Russia, America and Great Britain will accept dictation at her hands, or that the latent strength of the Chinese race will not assert itself.

Passing into more philosophic regions the proposition may be advanced that the souls of peoples are little changed by changes in forms of government or by study of political theories. In East Asia nearly a third of the human race has its home. Trends of far-eastern thought and aspiration are therefore matters of deep concern.

Finally, reference may be made to the material for opinion provided by many and admirable books.

The demand, however, is not for abstract ideas but for the essence of these matters in concrete form. As regards books, the criticism is often made that the books on China (for the giant frame of China, swaying indeterminately in the fierce blasts of internal and international policies, is the inspiration for most of them) are too many, too long, and too loaded with unpronounceable names.

Such criticism is unfair to the labourers in a peculiarly difficult field. But it is not unintelligible. The Great War cut a deep dividing line through the world of average men. In the comparatively leisured days of the early part of the present century, and the days that went before, there were fewer books and more time. The appearance of a book on a far-eastern subject was then something of an event. Now it is difficult to make a choice. To-day only the historically and politically minded, or those with some special interest or a duty, find time or perhaps inclination to seek understanding from the past or to try to unravel the complications of the present.

I ask myself, may it not be possible to state the matter sufficiently for general purposes in simple terms, at the length of a medium length novel, without involving any great assumption of knowledge on the reader's part, even though this should involve the offence of yet another book ? Could not the attempt be made with some hope of success to sketch something in the nature of a swiftly moving picture, with some ' close-ups ' to reality ? Could not one try to suggest something of the contrast, and the meaning of the difference, between the pleasant land of China as some of us first knew it, ' the land of the blue-gown,' and the scarred face we know to-day ; something of the spirit of old Japan and the Japan of modern times ; and of the new Russia which at bottom perhaps is still so much the old ?

Those who live in the midst of some of the more striking events which go to make up history receive impressions of fundamental things. It may not be easy to record them. Nevertheless it seems to me worth trying to outline the picture as I have seen it gradually spreading out over more than thirty-five years. For it was my fate to arrive in China a few days before the Boxer Protocol was signed in September 1901 in Peking, with which I propose this book should begin. Even if out of drawing in places, with gaps which to some may seem serious or matter that to others may seem unnecessary, such a picture at least would be conceived in sympathy and I hope not unfairly executed. Few men spend their working lives on the China coast without affection for the country of their exile. Few men know Japan without falling to her charm. They may be credited even with a little understanding. They may be allowed to claim, perhaps, a sense of proportion and be acquitted of any unreasoning bias in favour of their country's interests.

The course of events in the Far East since the beginning of the century, told in a series of short chapters each based on some outstanding event like a chain, as it were, of telegraph posts carrying the thread of the story, giving a glimpse of the fierce elemental forces which have been let loose and of their development in explanation of present conditions, recording sufficiently the contribution made for good or evil by the western world, might be of use and interest to the men and women to whom these pages have been dedicated, on whose shoulders rest the responsibility of the future.

The need for understanding of the East by the West is more

pressing to-day than it ever was. The problems of Europe have obscured far-away processes of evolution charged with Fate. Europe has led the world too long to see before her any other destiny. National rivalries are sapping her strength. She forgets that she invaded the seclusion of Eastern Asia, however inevitably, with world consequences which can neither be avoided nor delayed.

PART I

FIRST YEARS OF THE TWENTIETH CENTURY—1901–11

Chapter 1

The Protocol

September 7, 1901

Few diplomatic instruments have provided more interesting material for reflection than the ' Final Protocol for the settlement of the disturbances of 1900 ' which was signed in Peking on September 7, 1901. Among the signatories were envoys of the New World, of the last of the Hapsburgs, of Bismarck's Germany. The rising Empire of Japan stood beside Great Britain. It included Republican France, still surrounded by ancient dynasties ; Italy, in the main the Italy of Garibaldi ; Belgium, soon to become again a battlefield of Europe ; the Netherlands and Spain, recalling the glorious age of discovery and conquest ; and, last but not least of the European Powers, the Colossus of the great Slav race. All had come together in a common cause. The remaining signatory was China, boasting a civilization that was old before Rome became a city.

In the previous summer China had been guilty of the great offence. She had threatened the persons of the diplomatic representatives of the World's great states and for close on two months had laid siege to the Legations. North of the Yellow River the country had been ravaged by a horde of fanatics committing indescribable atrocities. The civilized world had not been so deeply shocked since the days of the Indian Mutiny and the massacre at Cawnpore.

Throughout the Chinese Empire the closing years of the century had been years of ' distress and commotion. In some districts risings were anti-dynastic ; in others, anti-foreign ; in

17

others especially directed against the missionaries.' [1] Owing to the lease to Germany of Tsingtao in 1898, ostensibly by way of reparation for the murder of two German missionaries in November 1897, but in fact in pursuance of her defined policy, these feelings came to a head in the Province of Shantung. The medium of their expression was a secret society of which the Chinese name was I Ho Ch'uan,[2] meaning ' Fists of Righteous Harmony,' from which the term ' Boxers ' was in due course derived. The movement could have been controlled, but a reactionary Manchu, Yu Hsien, was appointed governor of the Province in 1899. This society was now allowed to develop on anti-foreign lines.[3] At the end of the year, in response to strong diplomatic pressure, Yu Hsien was replaced by Yuan Shih-k'ai. Yuan, whose soldierly common sense was not impressed by a cult whose members practised incantations and passed through a ritual which they believed rendered them invulnerable, suppressed their activities with a heavy hand. In consequence the movement spread northward through the province of Chihli. The garrison of the city of Tientsin, the gateway of the Capital, threw in its lot with the Boxers and in June 1900 besieged the foreign settlements.[4] In Peking the Empress Dowager, despite the earnest advice of the Grand Councillor Jung Lu, took no serious step to oppose the Boxers and ultimately assumed a position of virtual leadership. Tung Fu-hsiang, fierce antiforeign leader of savage troops from the far-away western pro-

[1] *Far Eastern International Relations*, by Morse and MacNair, p. 455. See for German policy, pp. 424 et seq.

[2] In a short appendix (App. I) an attempt is made to assist the reader in the pronunciation of Chinese names.

[3] For the latest considered view of the nature and genesis of the Boxer movement, see *Twilight in the Forbidden City*, by Reginald F. Johnston, K.C.M.G., pp. 44 et seq.

[4] The foreign settlements were saved by the gallantry of a young Englishman, the late James Watts, C.M.G., who was a member of the Tientsin Volunteer Corps. The siege had began on Sunday afternoon, June 17, and by the following Tuesday anxiety was felt as regards the supply of ammunition. James Watts volunteered to ride with dispatches to Taku at the mouth of the river, a distance of more than thirty miles, through country infested by Boxers and Government troops. Accompanied by two Cossacks, after many hairbreadth escapes he got through, making one of the great rides of history. Relief measures were pressed on by the allied commanders and James Watts had the satisfaction of arriving back in Tientsin on the following Sunday morning at the head of the relieving column, before it was too late.

vince of Kansu, who had been summoned to Peking more than a year before to resist foreign aggression, as it was said, offered to drive the foreigners into the sea. Yu Hsien, now governor of Shansi Province, gave vent to his hatred and became responsible for one of the ghastly tragedies in history. 'Sending for a full list of the missionaries in Taiyuanfu, which was his Provincial Capital, and saying that he intended to send them to Tientsin under guard, he had them all conducted to the Yamen. On their arrival in the Yamen the gates were closed.'

In the hearts of those men, women and children the clangour of those closing gates may well have sounded the knell of approaching doom.

'The Yamen was surrounded by soldiers, and the Governor called in Boxers with swords, who slaughtered all of them. The Governor subsequently exposed their heads on the walls of Taiyuanfu. The total number thus killed was thirty-three including seven from Shouyang Hsien. On the next day ten Roman Catholic priests were put to death, but the circumstances are not known.'[1] The fate of isolated missionaries and their families, Chinese Christians and all Chinese known to be associated with foreigners was no less shocking.

Since then the world has seen many terrible things in China. There have been no ordinary horrors of Civil War, Communist excesses, fierce revenges upon them, foreign men and women undergoing all manner of suffering and death in bandit hands.[2] But it is not only in China that death and torture have descended on political adversaries and persons innocent of offence. There are other countries in which the twentieth century has seen the cheapening of human life. The events of 1900 are recalled in order that the terms of the Protocol may be properly understood, and as evidence of the backward state of China and the ignorance of her ruling classes.

The beginning of modern China is set by different writers at different dates and based on different events. But the last year of the nineteenth century is perhaps as truly the turning-point as any event of earlier or later years. The Boxer outbreak and its consequences shook the whole nation. The Protocol set the

---

[1] British Blue Book, No. 5 of 1901.
[2] See *Chinese Destinies*, by Agnes Smedley.

course on which the ship of state must in large measure for a time at least proceed.

The demands of the Allies were formulated in a joint note dated December 22, 1900. They were conceded a week later by Imperial Decree issued from Hsianfu, an ancient capital of China, whither the Empress Dowager and the Court had fled. The detailed terms were negotiated during the succeeding months.

Prince Ch'un, brother of the Emperor, was dispatched to convey to the Emperor of Germany the regrets of the Emperor of China for the murder of the Minister, Baron von Ketteler, on his way to the Tsungli Yamen on June 20, 1900, the date on which the siege of the Legations began. Na Tung, vice-president of the Board of Revenue, was dispatched to convey to the Emperor of Japan the regrets of his Majesty the Emperor of China for the death of Mr. Sugiyama, Chancellor of the Japanese Legation, who, nine days earlier, had been killed by Tung Fu-hsiang's soldiers. In addition, in the case of Baron von Ketteler a memorial arch was built across the Hatamen Street. Expiatory monuments were also erected in the foreign cemeteries which had been desecrated.

As regards individual punishment, Prince Tsai Hsun, a prince of the blood, who the Empress Dowager had hoped might escape with degradation, was invited ' as a favour, to commit suicide.' Others who had been sentenced to ' decapitation with reprieve ' were called upon to commit suicide. The notorious Yu Hsien, degraded and banished by Imperial Decree to Sinkiang, was ordered to be decapitated. In all between 140 and 150 punishments, ranging from execution to banishment or degradation, were inflicted. Those offenders who had since died received the old punishment of posthumous degradation. The suspension of official examinations for five years was ordered in forty-five cities where foreigners were massacred or submitted to cruel treatment. By this means a rebuke was administered to the reactionary spirit of the *literali*. In China, as is no doubt sufficiently known, the door into official life was through the medium of examination in the classical books. All but the final tests were held in provincial cities. Loss of opportunity for five years would at least bring home to youth the sins of their fathers. Finally, the honour of five courageous officials, who had opposed the Empress Dowager and been executed, was restored to them in death by Imperial Decree. Thus were the moral claims of the situation met so far as was judged practicable.

Precautions against a recurrence of such a danger to the Legations was secured by construction of a glacis round the Legation Quarter, provision for Legation Guards, destruction of the forts at Taku, and reservation of the right of the Powers to occupy certain points on the railway between Peking and Shanhaikuan for the maintenance of open communication between the capital and the sea.

The material aspects of reparation were met by provision for an indemnity of four hundred and fifty million Haikwan taels, constituting a gold debt equivalent to £67,500,000. Interest was to be paid at the rate of 4 per cent per annum and the whole sum was to be amortized in thirty-nine years.

Besides covering these matters opportunity was taken to clear up a number of points which obstructive tactics on the part of the Chinese authorities in the past had made difficult of settlement. One of these was the improvement of the beds of the Huangpu River serving Shanghai and of the Haiho serving Tientsin. These matters were to be undertaken with Chinese co-operation and provision was made for the establishment of conservancy commissions. Another was the constitution of a Ministry of Foreign Affairs. In ancient times China by reason of her exclusiveness had no need for an organ regulating foreign intercourse. But after the establishment of the Legations in Peking in the years following the Treaty of Tientsin in 1858, an office of inadequate standing and organization called the Tsung-li Yamen was formed, purporting to give effect to one of the provisions of that treaty. A ministry of foreign affairs was now to be established, with precedence over the six other ministries, in place of this unsatisfactory office. Finally, the Audience question at last was settled in a manner consistent with the dignity of great states. The country which we call China has been known by many names. But the name which has persisted through the ages, the every-day name of their country to the people, is the ' Middle Kingdom.' Originally a geographical expression when China was a country of small kingdoms, more than two thousand years ago it began to achieve another significance in harmony with the traditional title of the Emperor of China as the ' Son of Heaven ' and the idea of the

Altar of Heaven as the ' Centre of the Universe.' In modern times this attitude, which regarded the rest of mankind as ' outer barbarians ' and vassal states,[1] was the cause of much friction and contributed to more than one war. The Chinese had yet to learn that the world contained other peoples with pride of race.

The spirit reflected itself nowhere more than in the matter of the reception by the Emperor of foreign envoys. In the early days, with what appears to have been the solitary exception of Lord Macartney in 1793, no one was admitted to Audience who would not perform the Kotow.[2] To British representatives this was unthinkable. Even after diplomatic intercourse was established the years passed with but occasional contact of the foreign representatives with the Throne, and that in circumstances which subtly implied the inferiority of foreign nations despite the provision for recognition of equality contained in the Treaty of Tientsin.

To this state of affairs an end was now made. An annex to the Protocol laid down the Court ceremonial as regards foreign representatives which was to be ' in no case different from that which results from perfect equality of the Countries concerned and China, and without any loss of prestige on one side or the other.'

Thus, in brief, was China purged of her great offence and readmitted to the Family of Nations.

[1] Appendix II contains short extracts from a letter from the Emperor Ch-ien Lung to King George III which was conveyed by the hand of Lord Macartney.

[2] Kotow, strictly romanized as K'o t'ou, but commonly pronounced erroneously as Kowtow (' ow ' as in ' how ') means literally ' knocking the head.' When admitted to Imperial Audience it was incumbent on the person thus honoured to kneel and knock the head on the floor nine times. As early as 1873 one of the Censors had unsuccessfully memorialized the Throne suggesting that this ceremonial be dispensed with in the case of the foreign envoys. His argument was based on the loss of dignity in engaging in dispute with men of inferior race. In support he quoted Mencius as having asked, ' why should the Superior Man engage in altercation with birds and beasts ? ' See *China Under the Empress Dowager*, J. O. P. Bland and E. Backhouse, p. 111, for this memorial, the terms of which throw an instructive light on the attitude towards foreigners even at that comparatively late date.

Chapter 2

The Anglo-Japanese Alliance

January 30, 1902

The Anglo-Japanese Alliance was the logical consequence of Russian policy in Asia. Since the sixteenth century the eastward march of Russia had been relentless. By the closing years of the nineteenth century she threatened Great Britain in India, China in Manchuria and Japan through Manchuria and Corea.

Towards the end of the seventeenth century she had reached the Amur River and established settlements. It was not long before she came into conflict with the Chinese. After some years of intermittent warfare a Treaty was concluded at Nerchinsk, on August 29, 1689, the year in which Peter the Great ascended the throne of the Empire of Muscovy. Thus Russia was the first European power to enter into treaty relations with China.

For a hundred and fifty years Russia's advance at the expense of China in North-east Asia was stayed. She began to move on again after Count Muravieff had been appointed governor of Eastern Siberia in 1847. This marked the beginning of the modern phase. Despite Chinese protests expedition followed on expedition to the regions to the south in preparation for the opportunity. Opportunity soon came. Russia became engaged in the Crimean War. The Black Sea was blockaded by the fleets of England and France, and Black Sea ports were prevented from provisioning the coast settlements on the Sea of Okhotsk and the Straits of Tartary. In order to facilitate communication between them and the Russian inland posts, in 1854 Russia seized the Amur. In her justification first appeared in a political connection the phrase 'Necessity knows no Law.'

But the mouth of the Amur could not be made to satisfy the Russian ambition for an ice-free port giving an outlet to the Pacific, and Count Muravieff, now Muravieff-Amurski, looked farther south. In 1860, taking advantage of the alarmed condition of China resulting from the British and French assertion of their rights under the Treaty of Tientsin, and approaching her in the guise of a needed friend, Russia negotiated a further treaty which established a new definition of the boundary between Siberia and Manchuria. This gave her what became known as the Maritime Province including a harbour which she christened Vladivostock, ' Lord of the East,' a name reflecting her imperialist designs. But Russian aspirations were not satisfied. ' It was soon realized that Vladivostock was icebound for several months in each year, and that Russia's ambition was only partially achieved. The following years were therefore spent in strengthening her position so as to be prepared for eventualities. The military posts along the Amur and the garrison towns on the great Siberian caravan route were largely increased, and full advantage taken of the right of the Russian subject to trade and settle in Manchuria and China. Careful surveys were made by Russian experts, and the possibilities of the country studied at the instance of the Russian Government, who were only just beginning to realize something of the immense possibilities of China. Thus the hand of Russia had long been laid on Manchuria, and she was only waiting for the psychological moment to arrive when she might take those regions for her own.' [1]

The next spur to Russian advance was a challenge from the Chinese side. In the early eighties, C. W. Kinder, a young and able English engineer in the service of the recently established Kaiping Coal Mining Company, succeeded where others had failed in making headway against the superstitions, fears and dislike of innovation which had made impossible hitherto the introduction of railways into China. By 1888, under the protection of the great Viceroy Li Hung-chang, who had for adviser an able and far-seeing German, the late Gustav Detring, then Commissioner of Customs in Tientsin, a railway had been completed connecting the Kaiping Coalfield with Tientsin, a distance of eighty miles. Li Hung-chang wished to continue the line to Peking, but the influence of the reactionaries was too strong. He had to be content at the moment with construction at the other end towards Shanhaikuan, then the chief Chinese military camp in North China on the south-western border of Manchuria where the great wall meets the sea. In 1890 a project was conceived of continuing this railway in a north-easterly direction by way of Mukden, Kirin and other important places

---

[1] *Railway Enterprise in China*, by the present author, p. 40. Written in 1907 these observations seem in no need of qualification.

right across Manchuria. A flying survey was made which alarmed Russia, stirring her to diplomatic obstruction in Peking and further railway development in North-east Asia. In 1875 the scheme of a great railway across Siberia had been mooted but had not assumed definite shape. Plans were now hurried on. In 1891 the late Czar, then the Czarewitch, accompanied by Prince Uktomsky, most insistent of Russian Empire builders in those days, made a tour in the East. Narrowly escaping assassination in Japan, in October 1891 the heir to the throne of all the Russias visited Vladivostock and the new railway, on which construction had already begun at both ends, was formally inaugurated.

The Chinese moved too, but they moved slowly. Again Fate played into the hands of Russia. In 1894 war broke out between Japan and China. At first the sweeping victory of Japan threatened the Russian plans. Her peace terms were, in brief, the independence of Corea, the cession of the Island of Formosa and of that portion of southern Manchuria known as the Liaotung Peninsula, and the payment of an indemnity. But Russia turned the humiliation of China into an opportunity to augment her own prestige. On the publication of the peace terms embodied in the Treaty of Shimonoseki, she entered a protest, supported by France and Germany, against the cession of any territory on the mainland, and Japan was deprived of one of the chief fruits of her victory in return for an increased payment of indemnity.

For a time Russian schemes were safe. The death of the Czar and the Coronation of his son, the Czar Nicholas, provided the opportunity to advance them. China was asked to send an Imperial Prince to be present at the ceremonies. But Imperial Princes did not travel abroad in those days. It had been a stirring event in China when the Seventh Prince, who was the seventh son of the Emperor Tao Kuang and uncle of the Emperor Kuang Hsu, had made a tour of the northern ports of China and Corea in the year 1887. No member of the Imperial House had ventured so far afield since. China proposed that she should be represented by Li Hung-chang. And so Li Hung-chang undertook a world tour, the consequences of which were to become historic. England and Germany sought to stir his imagination by displays of industrial progress. Russian statesmanship, more subtle, converted him to a belief in community of interests, the Russian Foreign Minister, Prince Lobanov, concluding with him a secret treaty.

The terms of this instrument only became known in after years when it was discovered in the Archives of the Soviet Foreign Office in Moscow. More to the point even than had been conjectured, their main feature was a defensive alliance directed against Japan. By article I the High Contracting Parties engaged ' to support each other reciprocally, by all land and sea forces, at any aggression directed by Japan against Russian territory in Eastern Asia, China, or Korea.' [1] ' In order to facilitate access for the Russian land forces to points under menace ' [2] Russia was given the right to construct a railway which in effect continued the Trans-Siberian line across Manchuria to Vladivostock and largely superseded the long circuitous route following the boundary between Siberia and Manchuria. This was the Chinese Eastern Railway, the object of which was thinly disguised in the form of a concession to the Russo-Chinese Bank.

The work on the new enterprise had hardly begun when circumstances occurred which resulted in the concession to the Russians of the right to drive a branch line southward through the heart of Manchuria.

The occupation of Kiaochao by Germany in 1898 has already been recorded. On the happening of this event Russia took possession of Port Arthur. Subsequently on March 27, 1898, she secured a lease for twenty-five years of the Liaotung Peninsula, which, as we have seen, Japan had won by right of conquest and of which by the diplomatic representations of Russia, France and Germany she had been deprived. The Lease contained also the grant of the right of railway construction southward, which has just been mentioned, and which resulted in a branch line from Harbin with termini at Port Arthur and Talienwan. [3]

It would not have been characteristic of Russia to lose time in exploiting this valuable strategic and commercial right. By the time of the Boxer outbreak, barely two years later, the line

[1] *Japan Speaks*, by K. K. Kawakami, p. 7.
[2] *Russia and the Soviet Union in the Far East*, by Yakhontov, p. 365, quoted by Prince A. Lobanov-Rostovsky in *Russia and Asia*, p. 223.
[3] Talienwan was renamed Dalny by Russia. Under Japan it is known as Dairen.

was through, with the exception of bridges, a distance of 980 versts, or 646 miles.

Meanwhile Russia had not been idle in Peking. Devoting her attention to blocking Chinese advance from the south-west, attack was directed against the engineer-in-chief of the Imperial Chinese Railway Administration, C. W. Kinder, whose earlier success in promoting railway development has been referred to. The Russian objection was based on the desire to exclude any foreign influence other than their own from Manchuria. They alleged a promise from China to employ Russian capital and Russian engineers for the extension of the Chinese line beyond the Great Wall, and urged that the employment of a British engineer constituted a violation of the understanding. Sir Claude MacDonald, the British Minister to China, pointed out to the Russian Minister, M. Pavloff, that it looked as though it were desired to get rid of Mr. Kinder because he was an Englishman. M. Pavloff replied characteristically that there was no wish to get rid of Mr. Kinder because he was an Englishman, but because he was not a Russian. At the same time he stated frankly that ' the Russian Government intended that the provinces of China, bordering on the Russian frontier, must not come under the influence of any nation except Russia.' [1]

Nevertheless Mr. Kinder remained engineer-in-chief. The line was nearing Newchwang on the Liao River and was pointing northward to Hsinmintun when the Boxer troubles broke out.

The chaos in North China during the summer of 1900 seemed to offer Russia a further opportunity. Russian military engineers arrived from Port Arthur and began tacitly to assume charge of the line between Tangku and Tientsin, subsequently endeavouring to extend their control in both directions. To this proceeding, as soon as its significance was properly appreciated, objection was taken. The railway was a Chinese Government Railway constructed mainly with British capital and subject to certain conditions for British management for the protection of Bondholders. It was not until the beginning of the following year that the Russians decided that the time was not ripe for any designs they might have against North China. They retired, therefore, into Manchuria, taking with them two-fifths of the rolling-stock on the entire railway, and practically clearing out

[1] China Blue Book, No. 1 of 1898, p. 5.

the bridge works at Shanhaikuan, some of the materials from which were, according to current reports, shipped to Port Arthur.[1]

It is not surprising that to Great Britain and Japan, the two countries whose interests were involved all along the border-line between northern and southern Asia, an alliance should seem a wise measure. The principle of the Treaty left no room to doubt either its inspiration or design. It provided that if either party in defence of its interests ' should become involved in war with another Power, the other High Contracting Party would maintain a strict neutrality, and use its efforts to prevent other Powers from joining in hostilities against its ally.'

Chapter 3

The Mackay Treaty

September 5, 1902

In addition to the provisions which have been referred to in the first chapter, the Protocol recorded agreement by the Chinese Government ' to negotiate the amendments deemed necessary by the foreign governments to the treaties of Commerce and Navigation and the other subjects concerning commercial relations with the object of facilitating them.' Such needed amendments covered a wide field. From the days when the Great Wall was built to protect the northern marches, the policy of China had been one of exclusion. Concessions to the ideas of foreign powers and their desire to establish relations had been grudging and as restricted as the circumstances of the times permitted. Nor when we recall the predatory policy of Russia in the north need we be surprised at Chinese suspicions of the aims which inspired the policies of what are called the Maritime Powers.

[1] Blue Book, No. 7 of 1901, p. 101.

In another connection we shall refer later to the long and for the most part peaceful assault on the outworks of Chinese exclusiveness at Canton. Now we may come direct to the early treaties the conditions of which regulated foreign intercourse with China, imposing limitations on foreign effort that were a constant cause of friction and loss of legitimate opportunity for development of the commerce of China as well as that of foreign nations.

The main foundations on which has been built up the position of foreigners in China are briefly diplomatic and consular representation, religious toleration, rights of residence and trade at certain ports on the China coast or up China's rivers, extraterritoriality and a fixed tariff. Reference has already been made to the diplomatic difficulty, which will be referred to again in greater detail, and something will be said of missionary effort in a later chapter. Similarly the right of residence can be more conveniently referred to when we discuss the Treaty ports. Here we may limit ourselves, so far as any sort of detail is concerned, to the questions which in a sense have loomed largest and are least easy to comprehend without explanation. These are extra-territoriality and the tariff.

Extra-territorial jurisdiction in China, so far as British subjects are concerned, is the exercise of jurisdiction by the British Crown over British subjects in China to the exclusion of Chinese jurisdiction. More simply, if an Englishman in China commits a crime, breaks a contract, commits a civil wrong technically called a tort, or otherwise by his actions brings himself within reach of the law, he can only be brought before a British Court and his case, whether criminal or civil, can only be disposed of in accordance with the principles of English Law. In other words, an Englishman's person and property in China have the same judicial protection which they enjoy in England.

Mutatis mutandis these descriptions apply to similar rights enjoyed by other Powers. An American writer defines Extraterritoriality generally as ' an exemption from the operation of local law, granted either by usage or by treaty on account of the differences in law, custom and social habits of civilized nations from those of uncivilized nations.' [1] But this definition is not quite satisfactory, since the need, as in the case of China, may

[1] Moore's *International Law*, Vol. II, p. 953.

result from a conflict of civilizations giving rise to fundamental differences of legal conception.

Where China came in contact with her neighbours by land on the north the principle was recognized as early as the Treaty of Nerchinsk between Russia and China, signed in 1689, which has already been referred to in connection with Russian aggression. But in the south, where the maritime nations established contact, the adoption of the principle was of slower growth. This was due to the sincere desire, especially of the British and the Americans, to limit their demands to facilities for trade without interference with Chinese institutions or encroachment upon Chinese Sovereignty.

The Treaty of Nanking, concluded in 1842 between Great Britain and China, made no specific mention of extra-territoriality, but provided for the appointment of Consular Officers to reside at the five ports now to be opened, ' to be the medium of communication between the Chinese authorities and the said merchants, and to see that the just duties and other dues of the Chinese Government . . . are duly discharged by Her Britannic Majesty's subjects.' General Regulations for the British trade at the five open ports were drafted in July 1843, and under No. 13 provision was to be made for the punishment of English and Chinese criminals according to the laws of their respective countries and at the hands of their respective officials.

In the following year the principle of extra-territoriality was laid down more clearly in the Treaty between the United States and China in terms which were subsequently adopted in the Treaty of Tientsin, concluded between Great Britain and China in 1858, and Treaties from time to time concluded between China and other Powers.

In the Chefoo Convention of 1877 between Great Britain and China and in the Supplementary Treaty between the United States and China, signed at Peking, November 17, 1880, the application of the principle was somewhat amplified, Article IV of the latter Treaty being as follows :

> ' When controversies arise in the Chinese Empire between Citizens of the United States and subjects of His Imperial Majesty's which need to be examined and decided by the public officers of the two nations, it is agreed between the Governments of the United States and China that such cases

30

shall be tried by the proper official of the nationality of the defendant. The properly authorized official of the plaintiff's nationality shall be freely permitted to attend the trial, and shall be treated with the courtesy due to his position. He shall be granted all proper facilities for watching the proceedings in the interests of justice. . . . If he so desires, he shall have the right to examine and to cross-examine witnesses. If he is dissatisfied with the proceedings he shall be permitted to protest against them in detail. The law administered will be the law of the nationality of the officer trying the case.'

Such was the framework on which has been built up a foreign judicial system in China which includes His Britannic Majesty's Supreme Court in all the panoply of scarlet and ermine supported by an English Bar, British Consular Courts, the United States Court for China, French and other tribunals. It is these Courts which function when any of their respective nationals are accused of crime, are defendants in civil proceedings, seek dissolution of the bond of marriage, subject in English Law to certain exceptions due to domicil, and finally die.

Passing to the Tariff system, this dates back to the Treaty of Tientsin in 1858. Nearly twenty years had elapsed since the Nanking Treaties, and the hampering effects of uncertain taxation on the import and export of goods and during transit had been experienced. An Import and Export Tariff, therefore, amounting to 5 per cent on the value, was made the subject of Treaty. Additional taxation under what was known as 'The Transit Pass System' was also defined. In China, during the Taiping Rebellion, what may be referred to by way of illustration as the toll-gate principle was developed to an altogether remarkable extent. Barriers, as they were called in foreign parlance, existed along the trade routes at most points where effective control could be established. At these barriers taxes were collected on all goods passing inwards and outwards. This tax was called Likin, which means literally the 'Contribution of a thousandth,' that is to say the nominal amount of one-tenth of one per cent of the value. But as Selden wrote in the seventeenth century of Equity as larger or narrower according to each Chancellor's Conscience, so in China the amount of this levy varied with each official's conscience in the matter of his duty towards himself. According to the ideas that prevailed in those days, this was rather a matter of inconvenience than of offence.[1] It was only in order that foreign trade should escape these uncertain levies that serious attention was drawn to this state of affairs. The difficulty was met by a provision that foreigners should be at liberty to compound for all internal transit dues by a single payment of $2\frac{1}{2}$ per cent on the value in consideration of which a pass was issued freeing the goods to their destination.

Unfortunately this tax was not approved of by provincial officials, since it not only decreased the provincial revenues but deprived the tax collector in part of the opportunity to make provision for the future. In consequence it became the cause of much friction and abuse. In later years, through the development of an old form of nominal taxation called the ' Consumption Tax,' the purpose of the transit pass was defeated. Foreign trade interests, therefore, were entitled to call for redress of grievance.

To deal with these problems was by no means the whole task. There were a number of other questions all calling for adjustment.

Great Britain lost no time in approaching this further task, with the result that a treaty was negotiated by Sir James Mackay (afterwards Lord Inchcape), on broad liberal lines which might well have formed the foundation of modern China. Provision was made for a revised system of taxation which would have given China an effective import and export duty of $12\frac{1}{2}$ per cent including transit dues, subject to the abolition of likin. The Consumption Tax was to be limited to articles of Chinese origin not intended for export. Help was to be given to China in the improvement of her judicial system, and extra-territorial jurisdiction was to be abolished as soon as conditions would justify it. Other provisions dealt with the missionary problem, trade marks, inland water navigation and other questions. The treaty is known as the Mackay Treaty. Similar treaties were negotiated in 1903 and 1905 by the United States and Japan. Unfortunately the vision and authority were lacking in China to secure administrative reform such as would have made these treaties operative. They remained a dead letter until resuscitated twenty years later at the Washington Conference.

[1] *The Trade and Administration of the Chinese Empire*, by H. B. Morse, p. 82 and p. 106 et seq.

Chapter 4

The Russo-Japanese War

1904–05

It is not too much to say that contemporary observers in 1900 believed that Manchuria was lost to China. At the close of the century the break-up of China was freely prophesied.[1] To redress the adverse balance of power established by Germany and Russia in the north, France had insisted on a lease of the port of Kwangchouwan in the south. Great Britain, at the secret hint of China, had secured a lease of Weihaiwei. She was even unable to avoid a departure from her cherished principles and entered into an agreement with Germany defining their respective spheres of influence. The American Note of Secretary Hay, proclaiming the principle of the Open Door, was useful but did not promise to be entirely effective. Certainly no one supposed it would dispel Russia's dreams of Far Eastern Empire.

The years which followed only strengthened this conviction. Harbin became a great railway city, a point for the accumulation of troops and supplies. The fortification of Port Arthur proceeded apace and would soon present to an attacking army a ring of modern fortresses. The commercial port of Talienwan, or Dalny as it was now called, was laid out on spacious lines, worthy of the imagination which had planned the Nevsky Prospect. Construction of the harbour and railway connections was pressed on. By 1903 people could travel by train under conditions of almost European luxury from Port Arthur to St. Petersburg, there to join the famous Nord Express. The picture was completed by the Czar's appointment of Admiral Alexieff as his Viceroy in the Far East.

During these years Japan sought in vain by negotiation to stem the steadily rising Russian tide. Despite her humiliation and hate, such in those days was the awe of Russia that it seems probable that she would have been content with security. Certainly her attitude for the time being was primarily defensive. For fifty years the menace of Russia had been recognized. As long ago as 1861 when Russia established herself in the Maritime

[1] *The Break-up of China*, by Lord Charles Beresford.

33

Province and founded Vladivostock, she took the island of Tsushima which belonged to Japan and was a stepping-stone between Japan and Corea. She was only dislodged by the threat of a British squadron. In the following year she seized the island of Saghalien. Japan, whose title, if doubtful, was certainly much stronger than that of Russia, and who certainly regarded it as her territory, after fruitless negotiations failed to recover it and had no power to enforce her claims. Later developments have already been referred to, except that no mention has been made of Corea, which the terms of Article I of the Li–Lobanov secret Treaty of 1896, already quoted, showed clearly also came within the Russian purview. A footing had indeed already been established.

But at no stage of her history could Japan afford to be indifferent to the fate of Corea. Ever since events in modern times compelled her to look outwards and have a foreign policy, consciously or unconsciously Corea was the key. There were constant bickerings with China in regard to respective rights in that distressful country, so pathetically named the 'Land of the Morning Calm,' but these had been disposed of by the recognition of Corea's independence under the Treaty of Shimonoseki.

That independence, however, was to prove merely nominal. A palace revolution in Seoul, the Corean Capital, early in 1896 gave Russia a chance to intervene. Ultimately an arrangement was reached between Russia and Japan which recognized the independence of Corea but at the same time included terms which have been interpreted as establishing a Condominium.[1]

But agreements were only fresh starting-points to Russia. After a time she began to exploit this one to her own advantage, and although her attitude was subsequently moderated as she found her commitments increasing in Manchuria, there could be no certainty that she was not merely pursuing her traditional policy of *reculer pour mieux sauter*. Japan looked forward with apprehension to a time when Corea might cease to be independent of Russia, and the menace to her existence would be brought to shores washed by the water of the Tsushima Straits, which would then be her last defence. In 1903 Prince Ito went to St. Petersburg expressly to negotiate for a guarantee of the indepen-

[1] *Russia and Asia*, by Prince A. Lobanov-Rostovsky, p. 229.

dence of Corea, but this the Russians would not give. And so war became inevitable.

By the beginning of 1904 it seemed only a matter of a few weeks and the question of chief interest was whether it would begin by a declaration or the outbreak of hostilities. Except that on February 6, 1904, she broke off diplomatic relations, Japan preferred the advantages of the latter course. And so it came about that on an icy night in February 1904, while a ball was in progress in Port Arthur, the Japanese Navy made two gallant dashes into the harbour, and torpedoed half a dozen Russian cruisers. Two of these were sunk partially blocking the entrance. A few days later Japanese troops effected a landing on the narrow neck of the Liaotung Peninsula twenty-five miles above Port Arthur and the famous siege began.

This is not the place to write in detail of the heroism of the Japanese soldiers in their assaults upon 203-metre Hill or the seemingly impregnable fortresses, of the strategy of Nogi or of the naval prowess of Togo. From the standpoint of Japan, however great the future of her arms, it is hard to imagine a war which will hold a greater place in her history or on which future generations will look back with keener pride. It was a supreme test. She met an enemy of unknown calibre and supposedly illimitable resources. Borodino, Sebastopol and many Asiatic campaigns had set their hall-mark on the soldiers of this brilliant and much-enduring race.

The war was fought by the ' Land of the Rising Sun ' for self-preservation, revenge and empire. At sea there was skill and dash worthy of the lessons her sailors had learnt in the British Navy. There was a battle with plenty of sea room which might have added an outstanding page to naval history if the dice had not been so heavily loaded against a gallant enemy. The land campaign contained most of the elements which go to make great warfare. The soldiers of Japan were brilliant in self-sacrificing siege and trench operations and sweeping manœuvre over vast open spaces with unprecedentedly long battle fronts. And in the end was victory and a foremost place amongst the Great Powers.[1]

[1] It is generally agreed that the surrender of Port Arthur was premature. But General Stoessel, the Russian Commander, considered it inevitable and apparently thought that surrender in January instead of

But yet it was only half victory. Russia may suffer a reverse or a series of reverses, but the land spirit is never conquered. With her vast resources in men and territory, she is never quite beaten and was not beaten then. Unlike Japan, who has only the sea behind her, she can make withdrawals of unlimited extent and reorganize. Russia remained a great Asiatic Empire. She need not even have made peace. The winter of 1905 and spring of 1906 had restored her resources and she was ready for a great campaign of open warfare in Manchuria, under Linevitch, who had superseded Kuropatkin. She might have done much to redress the balance. But the Czar Nicholas lacked the greatness of some of his predecessors while the country was threatened with revolution.

The war was brought to an end by the Treaty of Portsmouth which was signed in September 1905. The course of negotiation reflected the economic stress of Japan. Although she secured recognition of her ' paramount political, military and economic interests ' in Corea and transfer of the Russian rights under the lease of the Liaotung Peninsula, she only recovered half of the Island of Saghalien and the railway up to a point about half-way between Mukden and Harbin. Russia paid no indemnity, and she still controlled the line to the north and the Chinese Eastern railway which involved Russian political domination of the rich Amur regions of north Manchuria.

a few months later could not affect the land campaign in view of the severity of the long Manchurian winter. In this he proved to be wrong. He was subsequently court-martialled and held guilty on various grave charges. According to the late Dr. Morrison, correspondent of *The Times*, the garrison contained 20,000 troops and stores and ammunition for several months. The Japanese were also fortunate in the battle of the Straits of Tsushima, or the Yellow Sea, as they prefer to call it. Admiral Rodjestvensky, who was in command, strongly impressed on the Government at St. Petersburg the futility of sending the Baltic fleet to fight so far from its base. But his objections were overruled. Compelled to sail round the Cape he could only coal at sea off Cape Town and Singapore. By the time he arrived in Far Eastern waters his ships were in no state to manœuvre or maintain high speeds. His only hope was to slip through the Japanese scouts and reach Vladivostock where he could refit. Owing to thick weather he almost succeeded in doing so. Only a lagging transport or hospital ship sighted by a Japanese torpedo boat enabled the battle fleet to establish contact. See *Rasplata* (*The Reckoning*), by Commander Wladimir Semenoff, Imperial Russian Navy. Translation by L. A. B. (Vice-Admiral Prince Louis of Battenberg).

These arrangements were, of course, subject to the consent of China with whom a convention was negotiated by Japan at Peking in December 1905. The interpretation of the extent to which Japan was recognized as taking over Russian rights, and the limitation of Chinese activity in the ' Three Eastern Provinces,' [1] was to form matter of violent dispute. But in substance she succeeded to the Russian position in south Manchuria. In addition China granted to Japan the right to construct a railway from Mukden to Antung, on the north bank of the Yalu River, designed to connect with the Corean railway system. Japan also acquired the right to participate in the construction of a second branch further north between Kwangchengtze and Kirin.

Thus she achieved safety and opportunity. The future would depend partly on the wise use she made of them and partly on the spirit of the Chinese. China had cause to be grateful to Japan for saving her from Russia. But it would be no gain if there was merely substituted a more exacting master.

Chapter 5

A Page of Earlier History

In contrast to Japan at this time China was a different world. The thought and standards of her rulers were those of a long-past age. It was the Empress Dowager's third Regency. For nearly half a century she had dominated China either seated on the Dragon Throne or as the power behind it.

Born in 1835, her span of life extended from the early treaty days and the Taiping Rebellion, which seriously threatened the Dynasty. Externally it was a period of strong anti-foreignism and of shock arousing the ' divine wrath ' at the pretensions of the

[1] Manchuria is known to the Chinese as the ' Three Eastern Provinces,' i.e. the three provinces east of the Barrier or Great Wall.

' outer barbarians ' and ' puny hobgoblins,' [1] rather than of grave alarm. Internally its characteristics were maintenance of the old traditions so long as they did not conflict with the Empress Dowager's continued power, insensible decay through the growing influence of eunuchs and obstinate failure to recognize the needs of changing times.

The girl who without experience and knowledge of the outside world was to be called upon to gauge the stress of epochmaking events through the haze of intrigue and ignorance in the Forbidden City, who was destined to be compared by serious writers to Elizabeth of England, Catherine the Great, Catherine de Medici and even Jezebel, was a daughter of the Yehonala clan, one of the oldest and most powerful of the noble Manchu houses, but not of Imperial blood.[2] According to the Historians of the Times her ' education followed the usual classical course, but the exceptional alertness and activity of her mind, combined with her inordinate ambition and love of power, enabled her to rise superior to its usually petrifying influences and to turn her studies to practical account in the world of living men. At the age of sixteen she had mastered the Five Classics in Chinese and Manchu, and had studied to good purpose the historical records of the twenty-four Dynasties. She had, beyond doubt, that love of knowledge which is the beginning of wisdom, and the secret of power, and moreover, the chroniclers aver, a definite presentiment of the greatness of her destiny.' [3]

In 1850 the Emperor Tao Kuang died and his son Hsien Feng, a youth of nineteen, reigned in his stead. Rather more than two years later, when the twenty-seven months of Imperial mourning were accomplished, Yehonala, as she was then and afterwards known up to the time when she became Empress Dowager and received the honorific name of Tzu Hsi, was one of a small band of noble Manchu maidens called upon to make their

---

[1] The term ' outer barbarian ' as a description of foreigners in the early days has become traditional. For the delicious phrase ' puny hobgoblins ' we are indebted to the scholarly translations of state papers contained in *China under the Empress Dowager*, by J. O. P. Bland and E. Backhouse. The English equivalents of reign and other names have been adopted from the same source.

[2] The Imperial House consisted of the direct descendants of Nurhachi, who founded the Dynasty which took the name of Ta Ch'ing, ' Creat Purity.'

China under the Empress Dowager, p. 8.

lives in the mysterious and often tragic environment of the Forbidden City. Another was a certain Sokota, destined, as Empress Dowager under the name of Tzu An, to be Joint Regent with her in years to come. While still the Heir Apparent, Hsien Feng had married an older sister of Sokota, but she was already dead. In the fullness of time Sokota, reputed lovely and of gentle disposition, found favour in her Lord's eyes and was promoted to become Empress Consort. Yehonala, a delicate silken figure, added to her personal charm an intellectual ascendancy. She was also fortunate enough in 1856 to provide an heir.

In 1861 Hsien Feng died at Jehol, a hundred and fifty miles north of the Capital, whither he had retired before the British and French advance on Peking in 1860 to enforce the terms of the Treaty of Tientsin signed two years before. The inevitableness of his death had been obvious for some time and a conspiracy had been on foot to eliminate Yehonala, already the object of envy and suspicious fear amongst the enemies and rivals of the Yehonala clan, and to secure the appointment of the chief conspirators as Regents.

The conspiracy was a formidable one. It was led by the heads of two of the Manchu princely houses, Princes Yi [1] and Cheng, and a certain Su Shun, an Imperial clansman and Prince Cheng's foster-brother, a man who had risen rapidly in the Emperor's favour and held important office. In the course of his official service he had accumulated a vast fortune, said to have been computable in millions of sterling.

The plans of these three men, skilfully laid and backed by unlimited financial resources, rapidly came to fruition. The Emperor was persuaded that Yehonala was on improper terms with her kinsman Jung Lu, who had been a playmate of her childhood and to whom, it has been said, she was betrothed in infancy. In consequence she was denied all access to the Emperor, who caused her to be deprived of the custody of her son, the Heir to the Throne. At the same time the Palace folk were largely won over to the side of the conspirators and Yehonala

[1] The Prince of Yi, Ts'ai Yuan, whose name was given to the conspiracy, was one of the reactionary advisers of the Emperor in 1860. It was an unpremeditated but just revenge which resulted in his Palace in Peking being chosen for the British Legation. See *Narrative of Events in China*, by Henry Brougham Loch (Lord Loch), p. 172.

became practically isolated with her personal attendants. On the Emperor's death, the customary valedictory decree was issued, which was found to have appointed the three chief actors in the conspiracy to be the Regents and to have ignored entirely the claims of the Emperor's brothers. An early decree of the new reign bestowed on the Empress Consort the rank of Empress Dowager and the honorific title of Tzu An, ' Motherly and Peaceful,' which as Empress Consort was her right. For form's sake the same decree conferred like rank on Yehonala with the honorific title of Tzu Hsi, ' Motherly and Auspicious.' The latter also became by virtue of her motherhood the Empress Mother. At the same time Tzu An, as the late Emperor's senior consort, became Empress of the Eastern Palace while Tzu Hsi became Empress of the Western Palace.

But Tzu Hsi, as she must now be called, was not deceived. She had early realized the serious nature of the conspiracy as regards herself, and at twenty-five she was not disposed to regard her life's work accomplished by the provision of an heir. In secret communication with Prince Kung, the most able and influential of the Emperor's brothers in Peking, and Jung Lu, who held a command as an officer of the Imperial Guard, counter-plans were worked out.

Etiquette required that when the Emperor's body was removed to the Capital, it must be accompanied by the Regents and be received in the Forbidden City by the new Emperor and the Empress Dowagers. This necessitated the Empress Dowagers with the boy Emperor going on ahead to Peking. According to the Historians of the Times, there was to have been an ambush on the road and Tzu Hsi murdered. But Jung Lu ensured her safety on the journey and she arrived in Peking, with her son and Tzu An, three days before the Imperial remains.

For the details of the nemesis which overtook the conspirators as well as of the picturesque and tragic happenings in the course of Tzu Hsi's long life, and the wealth of illumination thrown on life in the Forbidden City, methods of Government and the statecraft of Tzu Hsi, the reader must be referred once and for all to the great story of her life and times which has already been referred to. Suffice it to say here that the conspiracy was ruthlessly broken up. The principal actors were executed, their properties confiscated, and the princely titles of their houses annulled. The immense accumulation of Su Shun's treasure found its way into the vaults of the Forbidden City.

The usurping Regents had selected a name for the reign by which the Emperor would go down in history. A new name was now selected, T'ung Chih, meaning 'All pervading Tranquillity.' In a long decree in the Emperor's name the course of events was narrated and the Empress Dowagers were appointed Joint Regents. Such a course was without precedent. Moreover it was unlawful, since under the House Law of the Dynasty no woman might hold the supreme power. But such was Tzu Hsi's personality, swiftness of judgment and courage to apply the principle of absolutism with remorseless severity, that backed by the powerful support of Jung Lu the departure from precedent could not be seriously opposed.

The Regency lasted twelve years. It is not possible to chronicle the events of that period, but some must be referred to in view of their consequences.

Historically the crushing of the Taiping Rebellion in 1864 was the most important event. Incidentally it strengthened the confidence in Tzu Hsi. It was remembered that ten years before, while yet a girl of less than twenty, her study of state affairs had led to a belief in the ability of Tseng Kuo-fan, who on her initiative had been put in supreme command of the Imperial forces. In the hour of victory and self-glorification it was not necessary to reflect that Tseng's undoubted ability and worth might have failed to save the Dynasty but for the organizing ability and soldierly qualities of 'Chinese Gordon.' [1] The only serious blot on the period was the pitiful murder of French nuns in Tientsin in 1870 for which she could not be held responsible.

In palace politics two occurrences must be noted which had far-reaching consequences. At first the government was conducted with great discretion in the name of the Emperor with Prince Kung as Prince Adviser. Unfortunately, as the years went by, the latter showed a tendency to presume on his position which offended the pride of Tzu Hsi, whose masterful disposition had by now established her as the supreme power without any serious resistance on the part of her senior colleague. In 1865 Prince Kung was degraded, and although he was largely restored

[1] *China under the Empress Dowager*, p. 66.

to favour a little later on, the issue of this trial of strength in favour of the Western Empress encouraged the autocratic vein in Tzu Hsi's nature.

A still more serious matter in the moulding of her character occurred in 1869 when she was thirty-four years old. At that time the influence of the eunuchs was increasing and they were growing aggressive. Prince Kung therefore seized a favourable opportunity to have the chief eunuch and several of his immediate supporters decapitated. This was secured by means of an edict reluctantly issued on her own authority by the Eastern Empress, Tzu An.

Whatever his crimes of corruption and arrogance as the years passed, and they were many, An Te-hai, as the chief eunuch was called, had been Tzu Hsi's faithful servant in 1861, and without his co-operation secret communication with Prince Kung and Jung Lu could scarcely have been maintained. When she heard the news her rage, which was at times ungovernable, is said to have been terrible to witness. At the moment she confined herself to upbraiding her colleague and Prince Kung. But she neither forgave nor forgot. Driven back on her own resources, and more than ever standing alone, her character became the more self-reliant.

In 1873 the Emperor reached his majority, attaining the age of seventeen. From amongst the eligible Manchu maidens a wife was found for him, called Alute. The Regency then terminated in a valedictory decree.

But it was a grievous experience for Tzu Hsi to lay down the reins of power. Her regrets were intensified by the Emperor's attitude. As a child he had found his happiness with Tzu An rather than in the company of his own imperious and brilliant mother. When he ascended the throne he and his young wife went their own way, even denying her any part in their counsels on affairs of state.

Tzu Hsi might have realized that such an attitude was reasonably to be expected of her son since it merely indicated the inheritance of some of her own qualities. But embittered by his boyhood's preference for Tzu An and impatient of his shortcomings she seems to have become unnaturally hostile. Unfortunately T'ung Chih, with but little share of her ability, did not see this, and being feeble of constitution and of dissolute habits he was in fact already doomed. It was only necessary to allow him to run his course unrestrained. Had he been wiser he would have realized the value of her support and sympathy. Possibly his span of brief authority would not have ended by his premature death in 1875, which was to open to the Empress Dowagers, which really meant Tzu Hsi, another long spell of power.

When T'ung Chih died, the Empress Consort Alute was enceinte. If she lived to have a son, hers would be the place formerly held by Tzu Hsi as the Empress Mother. Failing a son of Alute the adoption of an heir to the late Emperor would be called for who must be of a lower generation. There was such a candidate, but his position was technically weakened by the fact that his grandfather had only been adopted by the Emperor Tao Kuang into the Imperial line. In the same generation as T'ung Chih, and therefore technically not eligible since he could not perform the rites of ancestor worship to the late Emperor's shades, was a son of Prince Kung who was sixth son of the Emperor Tao Kuang. But apart from this difficulty he was seventeen years of age and he and his father between them would have secured gently or forcibly the elimination of the Western Empress. Another candidate was the infant son of Prince Ch'un, seventh son of the Emperor Tao Kuang, whose mother was one of Tzu Hsi's younger sisters. He, of course, was still less eligible, both as being the son of Prince Kung's younger brother, and because the hope of his providing an heir who might be adopted to the deceased Emperor must be postponed for several years. Nevertheless love of power and the gratification of her revenge on Prince Kung for the execution of her favourite carried the day. Such was the forceful character of Tzu Hsi that, backed by Jung Lu whose guards held the Palace Gates, she forced the election of the young child through the Grand Council, and the ill-fated Kuang Hsu, as he became known, was placed upon the throne. Tzu Hsi again became Joint Regent with Tzu An, and the real ruler of the Empire.

But these irregular proceedings did not escape public notice.

It would be misleading to say that the First Regency commanded the approval of the people in the sense usually understood by these words. In those days in China there was no press and the people had no voice. The news of the day as regards important events was contained in Memorials and Edicts published in the Government Gazette and disseminated throughout the provinces by the viceroys. News and rumour circulated through the tea houses where current events were discussed. The only medium for the expression of opinion was the Court of Censors, which exercised some of the functions of the censors of ancient Rome.

When the Emperor Hsien Feng died and the usurping regency of Princes Yi and Cheng and Su Shun was proclaimed, its irregularity on many grounds was earnestly proclaimed. Subsequently the Censors, as well as the great Viceroys, all technically members of the Court of Censors, approved the Joint Regency. Without in any sense, therefore, resting on the consent of the masses, the ' stupid people ' as they used to be referred to in the language of Imperial Edicts, it may be taken that the Regency was acquiesced in by the country at large.

Now the position was very different. In 1861 Tzu Hsi was fighting for her life. In 1875 she was contending for the governance of four hundred million souls. In the place of sympathy for the young Empress Mother there was nothing but criticism and hostility for the mature woman whose craving for power took precedence of the welfare of the State and human obligations.

The stream of criticism was intensified by news of the death of Alute, with her unborn child, a few weeks later. The story from the Palace was that she had committed suicide as a protest at the wrong which had been done her. The general belief was that she owed her death to Tzu Hsi.

The protest was renewed four years later on the occasion of the funeral of the Emperor Hsien Feng, when a courageous censor selected the honourable method of suicide to emphasize the wrong which had been done to the Imperial Shades. This solemn sacrifice, with its strong appeal to the sense of the fitness of things, seriously shook Tzu Hsi. But she held on determinedly. There was nothing else she could do. In an impressive Edict she renewed her assurances that in the fullness of time an heir should be provided to perform the ancestral duties before the shrine of the Emperor T'ung Chih. As will be seen this obligation was not finally discharged for nearly thirty years.

Chapter 6

The Empress Dowager and the Emperor Kuang Hsu

In 1881 the Eastern Empress, Tzu An, was taken suddenly with a mysterious illness and shortly died. Her share in the rule of the country had been unimportant. She had yielded to the strong leadership of her colleague and rarely asserted herself in government councils. It was perhaps inevitable that foul play should be suspected. Notoriously the two Empresses were on bad terms, while Tzu Hsi's nephew the Emperor Kuang Hsu had found happiness, much in the way her own son the late Emperor T'ung Chih had done, in the palace of the Eastern Empress.

In 1887 the Emperor Kuang Hsu came of age and was provided with a wife, who was a niece of the Empress Dowager, thus further strengthening the position of the Yehonala clan.

With these events the Empress Dowager should have resigned the Regency. But she remained in power, allegedly at the instance of the Grand Council, for two years more. She then retired to the Summer Palace [1] which was in course of rebuilding at vast expense largely from funds which had been provided for the Navy. There she might have stayed, with leisure for literature and art, enjoying painting in which this amazing woman was highly skilled, while still keeping a hand on the pulse of politics, but for the war between China and Japan which produced important consequences. Amongst the more remote, as has been seen, was the Boxer outbreak. A nearer consequence was the movement of 1898, which became known as ' The Hundred Days' Reform.'

Chinese pride was shaken to its foundation by the country's defeat by a people who had borrowed the chief elements in their culture from China and had been regarded for centuries as a tribute race. When the first shock had subsided the causes of

---

[1] The former Summer Palace, the famous Yuan Ming Yuan, was destroyed by Lord Elgin in 1860. Such an act was peculiarly abhorrent to the son of the man who had saved the sculptures from the Parthenon. But it was necessary to bring home to the Emperor the gravity of breaches of treaty and violation of flags of truce. Contrary to common belief the loss to the world of art was not great. See *Narrative of Events in China*, by Henry Brougham Loch (Lord Loch), p. 167 et seq.

China's defeat began to emerge and a feeling grew towards westernization following the example so successfully set by Japan. In June 1898 the Emperor issued two Imperial Edicts, of which the first instructed the Viceroys to look for men of ' good reputation in everyday life, with a knowledge of modern things ' for employment in the public service. The second emphasized the urgent need of Reform.

In response to the first of these Edicts a Cantonese of the name of K'ang Yu-wei was introduced to the Emperor's notice by one of the Imperial tutors. K'ang was not alone in the field of reform, having associated with him a certain Liang Ch'i-ch'ao, who in after years was destined to become a great moral force in Chinese affairs, and others including his own brother. A strong ascendancy was soon established over the mind of Kuang Hsu. Far-reaching plans were discussed and no sooner decided upon than orders were issued that they be put into execution.

' Reform Decrees followed each other in rapid succession. The celebrated classical essay system, skill in which represented the hall-mark of scholarship, the basis of the country's intellectual life and the path to office, was abolished. Schools and colleges for the dissemination of modern learning were to be established in all provincial capitals, prefectural and district cities. The Board of War was ordered to look into and report on several proposals for army reform. The foundation of naval colleges was decreed with a view to reorganization of the fleet. A bureau was to be opened at Shanghai for translating western scientific and literary works and text-books for schools and colleges. Exhortations were delivered to officials to address themselves conscientiously to the questions of reform, and several sinecures were designed for immediate abolition. In a word, there were to be engrafted on the most conservative of polities changes such as, in their aggregate, the world had never witnessed, and with the inauguration of which must cease many of the emoluments of the occupants of high places.' [1]

It was unfortunate that Prince Kung had died early in the year. With one foot in each camp, it is probable that neither would his nephew, the Emperor, have gone so far or so fast, nor the Empress Dowager, his sister-in-law, have yielded so readily to the reactionaries. As things turned out it became clear to the

[1] *The Passing of the Manchus*, by the present author, p. 15.

Reformers that the forces of reaction would prove too strong for them unless without delay they could be stemmed. In a mad moment the idea occurred to secure the person of the Empress Dowager.

At that time the faithful Jung Lu was Viceroy of Chihli, with his seat at Tientsin, but eighty miles away. One of his subordinates was Yuan Shih-k'ai, who had sworn with him years before the oath of ' blood brotherhood.' This factor may have been unknown or overlooked. On all other grounds Yuan seemed to the Emperor and his advisers the best instrument that was to hand. He was sounded, it was said, with satisfactory results, and in secret audience entrusted with the desperate task of removing Jung Lu. With this preliminary accomplished, troops were to be brought to Peking and the Summer Palace was to be surrounded. Yuan then left for Tientsin. Probably what happened next will never be truly known. According to Yuan Shih-k'ai, the news had leaked out and on arrival at Tientsin he was faced with the facts by Jung Lu. The Emperor, on the other hand, believed to the day of his death that he had been betrayed. Jung Lu came to Peking and in this the third great crisis in her life brought the Empress Dowager back to power.

In relation to the times the zeal of the inexperienced Emperor and of the theorists who advised him had exceeded all reasonable bounds. But the price they paid was not the price of error of judgment and failure to appreciate the fundamental need of moving slowly. It was the price of the Empress Dowager's revenge. On a lovely September morning following audience, which customarily took place at dawn, Kuang Hsu was seized and removed to an island in a lake in the Forbidden City which, for most of ten years, was to be his prison. As an independent ruler he had issued his last decree. The Edict which was now issued in his name, recited the difficulties of the times, recalling the Empress Dowager's past services to the State and announcing that she had at length condescended to comply with the Emperor's repeated request to resume the task of government.

No doubt the Emperor owed his life to Tzu Hsi's fear of Chinese opinion. But no such sentiment deterred her in the case of the reformers. The blow fell so suddenly that several of them were arrested and executed. But some escaped, including K'ang Yu-wei and Liang Ch'i-ch'ao. Both these men were staunch monarchists and even when the Revolution came years later they remained true to their old allegiance. Both hated the Empress Dowager and could think no good of her, but neither believed that China could be governed otherwise than by an Emperor. All their reforming activities were directed towards progress under the Manchus and the establishment of constitutional monarchy.

The *coup d'état* restored the spells of reaction, only broken by the Boxer disturbances which by a curious paradox seemed to give the Dynasty a new lease of life. Probably also they prolonged Kuang Hsu's life. Early in 1900 a son of Prince Tuan, a boy of fifteen, had been adopted as heir to T'ung Chih and as Kuang Hsu's successor. But he did not promise well and Tzu Hsi availed herself of the fact that his father had been proscribed as a notorious Boxer leader, to cancel this solemn act. At the time the abdication of Kuang Hsu was certainly contemplated, and this would no doubt have been followed by his early death.[1]

When Tzu Hsi returned to Peking on January 6, 1902, she had rather more than six years still to live. With remarkable energy she set herself to the task, doubtless with strong mental reservations, of reconstructing her world on which she now looked with partially opened eyes.

Diplomatically the new rules of Audience were turned by her to good account. A Memorial to the brave German Minister now spanned Hatamen Street. A bullet-marked corner of the British Legation bore the legend ' Lest We Forget.' Yet men and women of the Legations, principally women, did seem to forget. Of course, relations had to be renewed and the Empress Dowager was a museum piece of extraordinary virtuosity. Still it was a little shocking that admiration and adulation could be poured at her feet so soon.

In the years which followed Tzu Hsi by the irony of circumstance found herself faced with the need of introducing those same reforms which a few years since had cost the Emperor his Throne. Allowed by the wisdom or unwisdom of the Powers to continue to act as Regent and her fears for her future thus allayed, it does not seem to have occurred to her to have admitted

[1] *China under the Empress Dowager*, by J. O. P. Bland and E. Backhouse, p. 303.

the Emperor to play a part in the realization of his former ambitions for the country's good. Obsessed with arrogance and pride of power, any achievement had to be for her honour and glory alone.

Actuated by the new ideas which Fate had forced upon her, ' she addressed herself, in the first instance, to laying the foundations of a new social structure. Formerly it had been forbidden for Manchus and Chinese to intermarry. Now, not only was the restriction removed, but it was pointed out that the social differences that had rendered it desirable had largely ceased to be, and only good could now result from a fusion of two races. In short Manchus and Chinese were urged to intermarry, the only exception being that of the Emperor's wives, who would still be selected from amongst the daughters of the great Manchu houses. In the same decree Tzu Hsi deprecated the Chinese practice of binding their women's feet, and urged its abolition.' [1]

Army reform had already received attention. Attempts at administrative, intellectual, moral, and political reforms now followed each other in rapid sequence.

By 1904 the Empress Dowager had decided that the classical essay system, which Kuang Hsu had sought to abolish in 1898 and she had subsequently restored to its honoured place, must go. Henceforward graduation in the modern colleges would be the passport to official life.

The question of the wisdom of virtually ruling out of the nation's life the humanizing influence of its ancient literature and the moral value of Confucian principle, the loss of which was to be realized in after years, does not appear to have been considered.

Another reform cutting deep into the life of the people was the abolition of the growth, import, and consumption of opium, which by the time of the Revolution had been almost completely achieved. It remained for modern China to revive the cultivation, which in later years reached unprecedented proportions.

In the political field decrees were issued remodelling the Administration of the Central Government. At the same time reference was made to the creation of a deliberative assembly in Peking to be called the Tzu Cheng Yuan, a species of Senate, which was to provide a training ground for the Parliament. The

[1] *The Passing of the Manchus*, p. 3.

establishment of Provincial Assemblies was also decreed, but as in the case of the Tzu Cheng Yuan, they were to be nothing more than a medium for the expression of public opinion and debating schools for future legislators.

Meantime Commissioners had been sent abroad for the purpose of studying the constitutions of foreign countries. They now submitted a framework of principles which would in course of time control the relationship of Sovereign and subject.

But just as the murder of a reformer in 1904, beaten to death in Peking under peculiarly atrocious conditions by Tzu Hsi's order, showed no real change of heart in the woman who in 1900 would gladly have meted out death to every foreigner in China, so an edict which was now issued accepting these proposals showed the limited sense in which they were intended to be applied. ' The important point,' ran a significant passage, ' is that there should be no departure from the many Imperial Decrees already issued, and that the supreme authority should continue to be vested in the Sovereign, whilst the people should have the right to deliberate on public questions. In founding a system of Constitutional Government, inaugurating a Parliament, and arranging the methods of election, this guiding principle must always be kept in view, that the authority of the Throne still retains its full effect and cannot be encroached upon in the smallest degree.' [1]

How far on the foundations which were thus laid would have been constructed the fabric of a modern state under the Empress Dowager cannot be determined, for she was near the end of her long life.

Early in November the Emperor fell sick and there were rumours of the illness of Tzu Hsi. On November 14 Kuang Hsu, in the picturesque language of the Edicts, became a ' guest on High,' and on the following day the Empress Dowager ' mounted the Dragon ' and followed him. This was in accordance with expectation if not with plan. It had always been supposed that the Emperor would be made to predecease her in order that she could regulate the succession. But the general belief that prevailed at the time of their deaths would appear to have been erroneous.

The Emperor is thought to have died a natural death. Before

[1] *The Passing of the Manchus*, p. 40.

he passed away the succession was settled in favour of the infant son of Prince Ch'un, the Emperor's brother. Yuan Shih-k'ai and Kuang Hsu himself had both expressed a view in favour of an adult, but the Empress Dowager, masterful to the end, brushed their objections aside. Prince Ch'un's wife was a daughter of Jung Lu. Tzu Hsi had given a promise to Jung Lu that in reward for his faithful service his grandson should one day sit on the Dragon Throne.

A long Regency again promised. Though nearing seventy-four it did not seem to occur to Tzu Hsi that some years of life did not still remain. But it was destined otherwise.

What were her thoughts as, in anticipation of her journey to the ' Yellow Springs,' [1] she gave directions for her Valedictory Decree ? Did she reflect only on great historic events, the future of her country and half a century's memories of unbroken power ? Or did she spare a moment for the hapless Kuang Hsu, whose life she could have made but whose possibilities of achievement and happiness she destroyed ? Did she remember the flight in 1900 and her denial of the wish of Kuang Hsu to stay in his capital and face the wrath of the Foreign Powers ? Did she see again that well in the Forbidden City into which, at her command, was thrown the gentle Pearl Concubine, whose only offence was to support the Emperor's plea ? Did she recall Alute, the girl-widow of her son the Emperor T'ung Chih, and their unborn child, and other shadows from the long vista of her past ?

It does not seem so. Confident in her destiny while scarcely more than a child she was no victim of remorse now. She died, as she had lived, conscious of her real moral strength and superior to sentiment and qualm.

[1] ' The Yellow Springs ' also known as ' The Nine Springs ' are the Chinese equivalent for Hades.

Chapter 7

The Prince Regent

1908–11

The new Emperor, P'u Yi, was a child of between two and three years old. As the son of Prince Ch'un he was the late Emperor's nephew. Kuang Hsu, it will be recalled, was a son of the Prince Ch'un of the generation earlier, who himself was the seventh son of the Emperor Tao Kuang and known as the Seventh Prince, to whom reference has been made. The new Emperor was therefore a great-grandson of Tao Kuang who was the last Emperor of the Ta Ch'ing Dynasty to leave his mark on history. P'u Yi was not, however, the senior great-grandson, and the choice should have fallen on the adult Prince P'u Lun. Thus ' for her oath's sake,' as we have already seen, Tzu Hsi committed her last breach of law.

When Kuang Hsu's end was near, a decree was issued appointing Prince Ch'un Regent. Associated with him in decisions of vital importance was Kuang Hsu's widow, Tzu Hsi's niece the Empress Lung Yu. Unfortunately for the Dynasty Prince Ch'un was a well-meaning but weak man while Lung Yu was an obstinate and rather stupid woman.

Their lot was not a happy one. In the first place they had to face the problem of Yuan Shih-k'ai. Kuang Hsu, in his last hours it is said, had drawn up a rough holograph will. ' We were the second son of Prince Ch'un,' it ran, ' when the Empress Dowager selected Us for the Throne. She has always hated Us, but for Our misery of the past ten years Yuan Shih-k'ai is responsible, and one other ' (the second name is said to have been illegible). ' When the time comes I desire that Yuan be summarily beheaded.' [1]

' Yuan at this time was a member of the Grand Council and the most influential Chinese in the Empire. Up to 1907 he had been Viceroy of Chihli, with the control of China's new army. But it would almost appear as though he was thought to be becoming too powerful : at any rate the Empress Dowager saw

[1] *China under the Empress Dowager*, by J. O. P. Bland and E. Backhouse, p. 460.

fit to call him to higher things. Apart from this the change had been a wise one. Yuan Shih-k'ai had always stood for progress on sound and moderate lines, and his elevation to the Grand Council had brought to the Councils of the nation a great accession of strength. His reputation also stood high with foreigners, and especially with the diplomatic representatives of the foreign Powers.' [1]

But it was humanly impossible for Prince Ch'un and scarcely less difficult perhaps for the widow of Kuang Hsu, though she had had little affection for him and was Tzu Hsi's niece, to set the needs of state before personal feelings. They dared not carry out the dead Emperor's last request, but at least Yuan could be stripped of power and office. Even that was masked by an ironic pretext. A Rescript was issued in which it was said that he had been seized with a disease of the feet which made it difficult for him to move about and thus rendered him unfit to perform his duties. As a mark of compassion he was allowed to vacate his posts and retire to his native place for the purpose of treating his complaint.

This step caused no surprise in China. It was commonly believed that Yuan had betrayed the Emperor. But the Court policy had left an enemy who would only cease to be a potential danger as he drew his latest breath.

For a time affairs moved on in their accustomed way. Prince Ch'un was a supporter of Constitutional Government and was prepared to assist in its realization. Unfortunately he was overwhelmed by the forces which had been let loose. Under a despotic form of government China had in fact developed many of the features of democracy. From force of circumstance it was an inarticulate democracy. But the Chinese as a people have great dialectical gifts. It was not long before the Provincial Assemblies and the Senate, or the Tzu Cheng Yuan, as it was called, were not content with the right of mere debate which had been assigned to them. Towards the end of 1910 delegates from many provinces met in Shanghai, subsequently going to Peking and presenting a Memorial. Demand was made for the opening of Parliament and the formation of a Cabinet, with the result

---

[1] *The Passing of the Manchus*, by the present author, p. 42. See also pp. 43–66 of the same work for a detailed account of this period and translations of the more important Decrees.

that the probationary period was reduced to three years. But neither Assemblies nor Senate were satisfied. The Grand Council, the most venerable organ of government, first collectively and later on individually, was impeached. The Grand Councillors, who had no mind to be made responsible for their actions to the Tzu Cheng Yuan, resigned. Their resignations were not accepted, but the Senate had made one of its points. In an Edict of December 25, 1910, the Throne conceded the immediate formation of a Cabinet, and ordered its constitution to be framed forthwith. The campaign for the earlier opening of Parliament was attended with less successful results. The Government stood firm on the position it had taken up and Parliament as a legislative organ was not to come into being till the fifth year of Hsuan T'ung (1913).[1] Public Opinion, or what passed for Public Opinion, was strong, but as yet the arm of authority was stronger still.

The ease of mind of the Prince Regent had not been increased by an attempt which was made on his life in the previous year. The leader in this enterprise was Wang Ching-wei. Cantonese by birth, he was the son of scholarly parents and was brought up in a highly cultural atmosphere until he lost first his mother and a year later his father while still under fifteen. By his efforts as a private tutor he succeeded in continuing his studies, taking the first of the classical degrees in 1902 when he was nineteen. But he had developed independent lines of thought and decided that there were no prospects of a career of usefulness under the old order. Meanwhile he had to live. History, however, is largely made up of ironic accidents. A year later he was selected by the Provincial Government as a promising student for study abroad and was sent to Japan. In about 1905 he met Sun Yat-sen. If not associated in the formation of the T'ung Men Hui, which was the first serious revolutionary society, Wang Ching-wei soon became a prominent member. Thereafter, proscribed and his scholarship withdrawn, he supported himself by journalism. In 1909, against Dr. Sun's wishes, and in association with other young revolutionaries, including three young girls, one of whom,

---

[1] Hsuan T'ung (' Proclaiming Succession ') was the reign name selected for P'u Yi in allusion to the fact that he was adopted into the line of succession and became heir to T'ung Chih. At the same time he was to perform the ancestral rites to Kuang Hsu.

the daughter of a rich Penang merchant, subsequently became his wife, a plot was devised to assassinate the Prince Regent. For this purpose a party of them went to Peking. But the plot failed and Wang Ching-wei and another young man were arrested.

However detestable assassination, the courage and daring of these young intellectuals testified to their deep sincerity. In the ordinary course they would have been executed. But Fate was reserving Wang Ching-wei for greater things. It is said to the credit of the Prince Regent that he favoured clemency, in consequence of which the sentence was reduced to imprisonment for life. A more romantic story is that by a strange piece of good fortune a certain General Wu Lu-chen, a secret sympathizer with Revolution, of whom we shall hear again, was in a position to exercise influence. Both stories are partially true. Perhaps neither influence by itself would have prevailed. However this may be, Wang Ching-wei and his companion, Huang Fu-seng, lived to be released by the Revolution two years later.[1]

Meanwhile a further danger became acute. Of recent years there had grown up much antagonism between the Provinces and the Government in Peking. The pressure from without had resulted in the development of what was called the ' Rights Recovery ' movement, with its cry of ' China for the Chinese.' It was loudly proclaimed without much truth that the Peking Bureaucracy had sold, and was daily selling, the birthright of the people to foreigners, who were enabled to acquire their interests, irrespective of the merits of their schemes, by illegitimately smoothing their path with the officials with whom they had to deal.

In the matter of railways, around which the ultimate battle was destined to be waged, the Central Government succumbed comparatively early. In 1906 the Hankow-Canton trunk, which had formerly been proposed as the subject of American finance, was, on the urgent advice of the Viceroy of Hukuang,[2] Chang Chih-tung, handed over to the Provinces concerned. Similarly with the important trunk that was to open up the Province of

---

[1] For authority for these statements see respectively *Twilight in the Forbidden City*, by Sir Reginald Johnston, p. 82, and biographical sketch by T'ang Leang-Li, p. xiv prefacing *China's Problems and Their Solution*, by Wang Ching-wei.

[2] Hukuang, literally ' Broad Lakes,' is the administrative area comprising Hunan and Hupeh, two provinces in Central China.

Szechuen and bring that distant region into commercial relations with the outside world on a scale commensurate with its potentialities. The sanction of many other provincial schemes followed.

The inconveniences of provincial railway systems have often been demonstrated and in 1911 a serious effort was made by the Central Government to resume control. The consequences were not encouraging. Meetings of protest and riots occurred in the aggrieved provinces and serious apprehension was felt as to the outcome. In the distant western Province of Szechuen a revolt broke out, which apparently had revolution behind it.[1] Meanwhile quite unconnected with these events, in fact merely taking advantage of them, a revolutionary plot was formed for a rising in Canton in May 1911. The leader was a certain Hwang Hsing. The rising was stamped out with merciless severity, but Hwang Hsing escaped to Hongkong and under the protection of the British flag lived to achieve fame as a revolutionary leader.

At the time the significance of this forlorn hope was insufficiently appreciated. It has been claimed recently by Wang Ching-wei, that ' no other single event throughout the three or four decades of the Chinese National Revolutionary Movement can vie in glory and in poignancy with the insurrection that took place at Canton, on the 29th day of the 3rd Moon in the 3rd year of Hsuan Tung (April 27, 1911), and which resulted in the death of its participants, seventy-two in all—the flower of China's youth and the most noble examples of Revolutionary China's spirit of self-sacrifice.' [2]

It has often been said that if Tzu Hsi had lived this chaotic and dangerous state of affairs would never have developed. And that is no doubt true at least in part. She was recognized as a strong and able ruler. Yuan Shih-k'ai would have continued to be virtual head of the Government. He was supported by numerous progressive and experienced men, such as T'ang Shao-yi and the late Liang T'un-yen, the first-fruits of education in foreign countries. In face of such a combination of strength and talent the Provincial Assemblies and Tzu Cheng Yuan would surely have been less aggressive. China was not ripe either for

---

[1] *Chinese Testament*, p. 85 et seq. From internal evidence there is reason to believe the *Autobiography of Tan Shih-hua, as told to S. Tretiakov* reflects much of the mental make-up of the Revolution.
[2] *China's Problems and Their Solution*, by Wang Ching-wei, p. 7.

Parliamentary Government or for Revolution. The people had no sense of any need for change. The country at large was still content to be carried on under a despotism, the claims of which were limited by custom and reason. They had no other conception of government. Outside the Princes of the Imperial House, class distinctions had their root in a democratic system, only recently abolished, based on an intellectual ideal. At that time neither the decencies of life nor the self-respect of mankind had been seriously outraged.

On the other hand, the opportunity for self-expression which had been provided brought men together and gave shape and force to Public Opinion. It was to prove a dangerous, if unavoidable, experiment. ' He who rides a tiger,' says the Chinese Proverb, ' is afraid to dismount.' The Manchu efforts in the direction of representative government were to be important factors in sealing the Fate of the Dynasty. Education and acquaintance, mostly slight and doctrinaire, with western ideals of government had been at work. Although the masses were untouched with the new ideas, sections of men and women, some of them of the higher classes, had drunk at the well of political theory. They could not foresee that they would plunge their country into a condition in which its existence would be still more precarious, while the people would suffer horrors not experienced since the days of the Taiping Rebellion. Had they been able to look into the future no doubt they would have still gone on. Although for many years it was to be nothing more than the substitution of a series of rapacious oligarchies for the old Imperial sway, the fate of the toiling millions was not, any more than it had ever been, a serious factor. The individual does not sacrifice his convictions for the good of his fellow-man, and in China, as elsewhere, it has always been the few who have moulded events to their own ends.

But apart from this aspect of Revolution, a point had been reached in world history where government of the type of which the Empress Dowager's rule was the great exemplar had become an intolerable anachronism.

PART II

THE FORGING OF NATIONALIST CHINA—(1911–31)

Chapter 8

The Revolution

1911–12

Although the T'ung Men Hui had been founded in 1905, widespread organization of revolutionary activity was always difficult. Police work in China is efficient and not unduly hampered by humanitarian scruple. Small groups of men worked far from their base, maintaining such contacts as were practicable and assuming risk and responsibility as opportunity offered. But such groups were more numerous, their subterranean activities were more extensive, and their contacts were maintained more effectively than many have supposed.

The premature explosion of a bomb on the afternoon of October 9, 1911, in the Russian Concession at Hankow, fired the train which led to revolution. In the incredibly short space of forty-eight hours a successful rising took place at Wuchang. The Viceroy fled. Three-fourths of the Government troops threw in their lot with the revolutionary cause. Colonel Li Yuan-hung, second in command, a man of liberal sentiment but no revolutionary, was forced to accept the command of the revolutionary forces. The members of the Hupeh Provincial Assembly, sitting at Wuchang, went over in a body and their President took office in the administration which assumed control. Twenty-four hours later Hanyang, on the opposite bank of the Yangtze, with its great arsenal, and Hankow, the third treaty port in China, were in revolutionary hands.

Consternation reigned in Peking. In the Forbidden City there was moral collapse. It was as though a beam of mental clarity had shown the rebirth of racial strife and the impossibility of five million Manchus continuing to dominate the four hundred millions of the Chinese race.

Autumn manœuvres, involving the modern units of the Army, were taking place in the country a hundred to a hundred and fifty miles east of the Capital. Everything suggested preparation and a well-chosen moment.

The troops were rushed to entrain at Lanchow, the nearest point on the Peking–Mukden railway, which made connection near Peking with the Peking–Hankow railway. By an Imperial Edict, issued only five days after the outbreak, Yuan Shih-k'ai was recalled and appointed Viceroy of Hukuang and ordered ' to direct the suppression and pacification of the rebels.'

But Yuan did not respond immediately to the Decree that concealed so slightly the alarm of the Manchu Court. To gain time he somewhat cynically indicated the need of further rest. Whether for his own ends or in order that he might better serve the Country or the Dynasty, he had no intention of being hurried into a position where he could not dominate the situation.

In Peking there was difference of opinion as to the meaning of Yuan's attitude. The younger Princes wished to fight without him. The older members of the Imperial clan, who thought of him as a man at heart of the old school with a slowly moving mind towards change, did not believe that he would set outraged feeling before his old loyalties. The latter view prevailed. A further Edict issued on the 27th of October appointed Yuan Shih-k'ai High Commissioner. All available forces were placed under his command, independently of the General Staff and Ministry of War. No greater gesture could have been made to counter opportunism.

By about the end of the month, Yuan had arrived at Headquarters in the field. In the neighbourhood of the ' Three Cities,' the Imperialist forces now controlled the country north of the river with the exception of the Chinese city at Hankow, and Hanyang. Some cities along the Yangtze, Changsha the capital of Hunan, and surprisingly Hsianfu the ancient capital of China, had declared themselves for the revolutionary cause. But the country at large had not risen and a vigorous campaign could have saved the fortunes of the Manchu House. At the worst they might have returned to Manchuria, the country of their origin, and have abandoned their ancestor's great conquest. China would have made no complaint then. It would have appealed to the Chinese sense of compromise and neither morally nor at law could objection have been taken to such a course.

Early in November Yuan Shih-k'ai was appointed Premier and after a further display of diffidence he accepted the post, arriving in Peking towards the middle of November. As he alighted from the train, it was noticed that he was wearing the ' Yellow Riding Jacket,' a high Manchu honour bestowed upon him by the Empress Dowager. A picturesque reflection in the stream of time, it was taken by some as an indication of his loyalty. By now the situation at the ' Three Cities ' was well in hand. The revolutionary forces had been driven out of Hankow, two-thirds of which had been destroyed by fire. The recovery of Hanyang was imminent. A few days later it was to fall, thus re-establishing Imperial domination north of the Great River.

Meanwhile a certain General Chang Chao-tseng, who had been on autumn manœuvres and with his troops had shown signs of disaffection, had been left at Lanchow. Already in secret co-operation with that General Wu Lu-chen whose efforts were said to have saved the life of Wang Ching-wei two years previously, and who was in command at Shihchiachuang to the south of Peking, and a certain General Lan Tien-wei, commanding at Mukden, a plan was devised to march on Peking and compel a Manchu surrender. By way of preliminary, Memorials embodying various demands were addressed to the Throne, while in support of an immediate constitution the Tzu Cheng Yuan brought to bear the full force of a body which a few months before had been fairly, if somewhat sketchily, representative.

This movement, apparently quite independent of the revolutionary outbreak at Hankow and indicative of dangerously widespread possibilities, came as a severe shock to the Prince Regent and his advisers. It resulted very shortly in a complete renunciation of Manchu privileges and the acceptance of nine articles of constitutional government which had been prepared by the Tzu Cheng Yuan.

To the generals this was disappointing. They held republican views and had undoubtedly hoped for a refusal of the demand for an immediate constitution, in order to justify more drastic measures. These were still being threatened when the combination was broken up owing to the miscarriage of a letter which disclosed the leading part played by Wu Lu-chen, who was thereupon disposed of by loyal officers under his own command.

On November 14 Yuan had an Imperial audience and then proceeded to the difficult task of forming a cabinet. The honour of being a minister of state was one which men were not desirous of having thrust upon them in such uncertain times. But Yuan's determination overcame hesitancy, and a cabinet of strongly liberal tendencies was formed. Amongst the ministers was Liang Ch'i-ch'ao, the colleague of K'ang Yu-wei, who had narrowly escaped the wrath of the Empress Dowager in 1898. No doubt it was thought that this well-known name would help to convince the revolutionaries of Imperial good faith. But in fact it only emphasized the cleavage in ideas. Liang Ch'i-ch'ao, as K'ang Yu-wei had been, was a professed monarchist on constitutional lines.

Yuan's next step was to bind the Throne by a bond more solemn than the issue of an Imperial Edict. It was arranged that the Imperial promises should be fortified by a solemn oath. ' The time chosen was the morning of the 26th of November. Snow had fallen during the night, and the Forbidden City wore an unfamiliar aspect as the Imperial party, accompanied by the Premier and the members of the Cabinet, made their way to the Sacred Hall of Ancestors, there with frequent prostration and elaborate ceremonial to perform the most solemn of Manchu rites, to abjure for ever the ancient principle of autocracy, to descend to a social compact of which the Imperial Dead had never dreamed and they themselves had failed so lamentably to foresee.' [1]

Yuan Shih-k'ai was now in a position to make a formal approach to the revolutionaries for a peaceful adjustment of the situation. Informally his emissaries had already been at work while he was still at Hankow. He was not disposed to press military advantages if it could be avoided. Li Yuan-hung had sent back a written refusal of Yuan's proposal of a limited or constitutional monarchy under the Manchus, in which he recalled the Manchu failure, the slaughter of reformers and the successes the Revolution had already achieved in the direction of emancipation.

With the fall of Hanyang, and Nanking still strongly held by

---

[1] *The Passing of the Manchus*, by the author, p. 191.

the Imperialists, Li Yuan-hung and the revolutionary army in Wuchang had become less hopeful. A message was now sent accepting Yuan's terms and, through the medium of the British Consul-General at Hankow, an armistice was arranged on December 3. But in the few days which had elapsed the situation had again changed. During November the Provinces south of the Yangtze had adhered to the revolutionary cause. Shanghai had declared itself the headquarters of the Republican Armies. On December 2 Nanking, the old capital of China, had fallen to the Revolutionaries by assault. On December 3 a written Republican constitution was published. Republicanism had become a force once more.

Charge of the situation was assumed by the Shanghai group. In the City Hall of the International Settlement a meeting took place between representatives of both sides. It was called a peace conference, but nothing that could be called a conference, in the shape of negotiation, took place. The Revolutionaries insisted on a Republican form of government. They would not listen to the idea of Constitutional Monarchy. There was talk of a national convention. This presented difficulty since much time must be occupied if a representative body was to be assembled, which would have been prejudicial to the revolutionary cause. Something spectacular required to be devised to satisfy its sentiment and to establish solidarity amongst its adherents.

The opportunity was not lacking. With the fall of Nanking, full of historic Chinese associations whose crudities had been mellowed by time, a splendid scene became available for the next act of the drama. The arrival in China of Sun Yat-sen on Christmas Eve provided the principal actor. The advent of the New Year made the moment one of happy augury.

Sun Yat-sen was the embodiment of the spirit of revolution. As a young man he had been engaged in revolutionary activities in Canton. He had fled to Hongkong where he studied medicine under Dr. Cantlie, who became subsequently a well-known specialist in tropical disease in London. In 1898 he was kidnapped in England and made prisoner in the Chinese Legation. But for a chance message reaching Dr. Cantlie, resulting in interference by the British Government, Dr. Sun would never have been heard of again and the course of history would have been changed.

Little that is reliable is known of Dr. Sun's activities in the intervening years. A mysterious and legendary figure, as we know he formed in 1905 amongst Chinese students in Japan the T'ung Men Hui, the first serious revolutionary society. He was also credited with organizing resources amongst overseas Chinese, and with keeping alive the flickering flame which had been lit in Peking in 1898.

When the Revolution broke out it seems that no one was in touch with him, thus evidencing its sporadic nature. Some revolutionary association in Canton, his native place, sent a cable to Dr. Cantlie's house in London offering Sun Yat-sen the position of first president. His whereabouts, however, were also unknown to Dr. Cantlie and some time elapsed before Dr. Sun next visited him. It was in response to this telegram that he had arrived in China, though guided by the course of events he had come to Shanghai.

On the 29th of December, with few dissentients, Sun Yat-sen was elected Provisional President. On New Year's Day he arrived at Nanking. ' Shortly before midnight the booming of guns announced that the oath had been taken, binding him to the restoration of peace, the establishment of a Government based on the will of the people, and the dethronement of the Manchu ruler. These things accomplished, he solemnly undertook to resign office in order that the people of United China might elect their President.' [1]

Thus the new year began with a clear-cut issue. In Peking, the northern capital, was a form of constitutional government, in Nanking, the southern capital, a nominal republicanism.

The inner thoughts of Yuan Shih-k'ai have never been revealed. Only facts can speak. It seemed to some that, playing for his own hand, he allowed a position to develop when armed conflict would meet with condemnation in the forum of world opinion. To others it appeared as merely an error of judgment as regards his own powers to compel compromise and in estimating the moral force of the revolution working on the discontent in the country.

Superficially the facts are against Yuan. After the fall of Hanyang the recovery of Imperial control in the three great cities in the heart of the country could have been effected. Nanking

[1] *The Passing of the Manchus*, by the author, p. 279.

might have been reinforced. By prompt action the tide might have been stayed. Nevertheless it does not appear to have been a deliberate betrayal. In a sense Yuan Shih-k'ai was not a big enough man for that, and he was too cautious. His intention was to rule China under the Manchus. This would have been a far easier task, as no one knew better than he did. And it was the best hope for China, as is now admitted.[1] But opportunist, his policy had all the drifting weakness of opportunism. He left too much to talk and the element which the Chinese call ' li ' or Reason. And there was no room for Reason left.

The impasse was ended by a telegram signed by the Viceroy of Wuchang and forty-six generals of the modern army, inspired, many believed, by Yuan Shih-k'ai, whose subordinates they had mostly been. The Empress Dowager, on behalf of the boy Emperor, was urged to complete the Manchu surrender. An understanding was quickly reached. There was to be no unseemly violence against sacrosanct personages. The young Emperor was to be allotted the Summer palace and a handsome annuity, and with his entourage would be treated with respect. He and the nobles would retain their titles, and Manchus, Mongols, Mohammedans and Tibetans would be the equals of Chinese in the new order.

The issue of an Edict of Abdication and a Valedictory Decree completed the tale.

' From the preference of the people's hearts,' said the Decree of Abdication, ' the will of Heaven can be discerned.'

' In ancient times,' began the Valedictory Decree, ' the ruler of a country emphasized the important duty of protecting the lives of his people, and as their shepherd could not have the heart to cause them pain.'

Thus passed from the rulership of China, if not technically from the Dragon Throne, the Ta Ch'ing House, or the Dynasty of Great Purity, but not yet out of History its last reigning Prince.

[1] *Twilight in the Forbidden City*, by Sir Reginald Johnston, p. 131 et seq., quoting at p. 133, E. G. Cheng's *Modern China*.

Chapter 9

Dictatorship of Yuan Shih-k'ai

The sonorous echoes of the Imperial Decrees had scarcely died away when it became clear that uniformity of idea had still to be achieved. In Peking, the capital of the great Khan, which reflected also the greatness of the famous Ming Emperor Yung Lo and for close on five hundred years had enshrined the mysteries of the Forbidden City, sat the last statesman of the old order. With more than a quarter of a century's experience of the art of government in troublous times, Yuan Shih-k'ai looked south to the ancient capital of the famous dynasty of Han, which was now the seat of the shadow Republican Government of untried men. Sun Yat-sen, more understanding than his followers of the conflict of the Spirit which had yet to come and of the material weakness of the revolutionaries to impose their impracticable ideals, looked northward with far-seeing, troubled eyes. He was wise enough to see that government of the country could only be carried on through the medium of Yuan Shih-k'ai. At the least there must be a period of transition when the strong experienced hand and personal prestige alone could hold the country together. But his mind was full of foreboding, doubtful of Yuan's willingness to give Republicanism a trial.

By the terms of the Provisional Constitution it was provided that, pending the election of a more fully representative body to be called the National Assembly, affairs of state should be placed in the hands of a National Council. The National Council was to be composed of five representatives from each of the eighteen provinces of China proper, Outer and Inner Mongolia and Tibet, with one member for Kokonor.[1]

[1] Inner Mongolia was divided in 1928 into four administrative areas, Jehol, Chahar, Suiyuan and Ninghsia, the latter including part of Kansu. Eastern Tibet has also been divided into Tsinghai (Ch'inghai) and Sikang (Hsik'ang). China's former suzerainty over Tibet came to an end in 1911 when the Tibetans declared their independence. China has since replied by incorporating portions of Eastern Tibet with the western ends of the Provinces of Kansu and Szechuen and creating the above administrative areas. It is to be assumed that when the appropriate moment arrives the *de facto* independence of Western Tibet will be recognized by Treaty between China and Great Britain. As exercising

On February 15 the National Council elected Yuan Shih-k'ai President. To persuade the members had been no easy task. The Republicans resented the idea that the new order should rest upon an Imperial Decree. But the moderation and spirit of conciliation of Sun Yat-sen prevailed. The election took place in the afternoon. The morning was occupied by Dr. Sun in ' paying a ceremonial visit to the tomb of the first Emperor of the Mings, the last purely Chinese Dynasty (A.D. 1368–1644), who had delivered the country from the Mongol domination, and for a few years had had their capital at Nanking. There he performed an impressive ceremony in which was symbolically offered back to their old rulers the country which the Manchus had wrested from them.

' It was a curious proceeding, this representative of republican institutions discharging rites at the shrine of one of an Imperial race, but it was calculated from the purely Chinese national point of view to make a powerful appeal.' [1]

Delegates were next sent to Peking to persuade Yuan Shih-k'ai of the need of a visit to Nanking to take the oath of office and to remove the seat of government to the southern capital. When their representations failed the Nanking leaders agreed to the oath being administered in Peking, and on March 10 Yuan was sworn in as Provisional President.

Yuan's first task was to form a cabinet. This he succeeded in doing to the satisfaction of the National Council which continued to function at Nanking pending the calling into existence of the National Assembly. Wisely including a number of men of republican sentiment, he appointed Sung Chiao-jen, one of the outstanding figures of the Revolution, minister of Agriculture and Forestry. Ts'ai Yuan-p'ei, the leader of the Nanking delegation, was appointed Minister of Education. A member of the famous Hanlin Academy who subsequently studied abroad, he had passed through the old Chinese literary mill and was no hasty convert to the merit of modern things. A young man, C. T. Wang,[2] destined to become a successful foreign minister,

spiritual leadership in the Buddhist world, the integrity and independence of the country of which Lhasa is the capital should be maintained. Politically Tibet has importance as a buffer state.

[1] *The Passing of the Manchus*, by the author, p. 322.

[2] In modern times many Chinese have adopted initials for their personal names. Others prefer to adhere to the Chinese form. In this

deputised for the minister of Industry and Commerce who was unable to come to Peking. Another young man, Wang Ch'ung-hui, until recently Chinese member of the Court of Arbitration at The Hague, was minister of Justice. Besides these many others, mostly of a liberal stamp if not actually of the Revolution, received office. General Tuan Ch'i-j'ui, who had held the command at Hankow and headed the Memorial of the forty-six generals, became Minister of War. The two chief revolutionary soldiers, Hsu Shao-cheng and Huang Hsing, became respectively Chief of Staff and Commander-in-Chief of the southern armies. T'ang Shao-yi, who had been educated in America and had occupied high official position under the Manchus, became Premier.

Meanwhile steps had been taken to call into being a more representative National Council. The body hurriedly convened at Nanking necessarily failed to fulfil the elective conditions of the Constitution.

The new National Council met at Peking on April 29. It was addressed in terms of moderation and sound sense by Yuan, who emphasized the country's primary needs : the restoration of order, the improvement of the economic condition of the people, reconstruction work on practical lines.

The detractors of Yuan Shih-k'ai say he was not sincere. In the ideal sense that possibly is true. Although a republican president he was not prepared to be a president subject to checks and balances. His nature could not endure either dictation or control. On the other hand the opportunity was great for a man with a sense of opportunity and appreciation of the needs of the people. He understood the fundamental requirements of a country based on agriculture. He thought he could rule the country through extension of the existing institutions. China for centuries had been a democracy under a theoretical, in a sense a theocratic, absolutism. No doubt Yuan's ideas were limited to a slow progress towards representative institutions under a benevolent despotism.

The revolutionaries on the other hand required a full-fledged republic, rather on the French than the American model. But

work the form is adopted by which the person designated is best known. In the same way place-names settled by Custom or by the Postal Authorities are preferred to the correct romanized form.

that was impossible as even Doctor Sun knew. Insistence must end in civil war or dictatorship.

It was not long before the cleavage became manifest. The chief business before the National Council was to frame an electoral law under which the National Assembly would be called into being. But the members were too anxious to participate in the government and to assert their rights as legislators. In the process they inevitably became absorbed in matters of form, which were not vital while dividing the members into several groups, producing disunion and inefficiency. This state of affairs reflected itself in the Cabinet. There were several resignations and great difficulty was experienced in getting men to take up the vacant posts. If Yuan Shih-k'ai showed little sympathy for republican sentiment, he on his side received little support from the republican legislators.

Meanwhile the country was deeply stirred by the murder in Peking of General Chang Cheng-wu, who had been prominent in Wu-ch'ang. For some reason he had come to Peking, or had unwisely allowed himself to be enticed there. Suspected of being connected with some conspiracy, he was taken out, after a dinner in his honour, and summarily shot. Such a dramatic outrage in Peking could not have been staged without the knowledge of the President. In the National Council feeling rose to fever heat. Resolutions were passed in condemnation of the Chief Executive in the strongest terms. But Yuan Shih-k'ai vouchsafed neither denial nor explanation.

The hopes of the Republican Party were now set on the National Assembly. The elections, after many delays, took place early in 1913. They resulted in a great republican majority led by Sung Chiao-jen. But Sung did not live to lead the fight for parliamentary authority. When getting into the train at Shanghai which was to carry him north, he was shot. No Chinese believed that this fine character was not removed at the instigation of Yuan.

Nevertheless, the sight of the National Assembly at last in being, despite the tragedy of the leader who had done so much towards its accomplishment, filled the men of the Revolution with hope. The body was as nearly representative of the nation as was then practicable. The members of the

Kuomintang,[1] the great republican organization, were in a large majority. At last there must be an end to absolutism. More than twenty years of self-sacrifice of the workers for the new ideas would now have their justification.

The power of the National Assembly to assert itself was to be put to an immediate test. The Revolution had entirely disorganized finance. Provincial revenues had ceased. Broadly speaking Peking could only rely on the current revenue of the railways and the sale in advance of railway freight. But with abdication and the republican recognition of Yuan Shih-k'ai there was in theory such a political merger of conflicting ideals that there was no occasion for continued foreign abstention from giving such assistance as might be practicable. Substantial temporary assistance was obtained from various foreign sources. For a time monthly advances had been made by an international group which had been formed previously for railway and more extended financial purposes, such as currency reform. A million pounds came from a Belgian group in the spring of 1912, while a loan floated in the autumn by a member of the London Stock exchange, which became known as the ' Crisp Loan,' provided a further five million pounds which tided over the winter. But what Yuan Shih-k'ai required was the command of a great sum in order to consolidate the position. For the provision of this money he was committed to the international group of British, French, German, Japanese and Russian bankers which became known as the Consortium, America standing out. Negotiations had reached the last stage when the National Assembly met in Peking.

Decisions as to the making of Public Loans was one of the duties of the legislative body under the terms of the Provisional Constitution. But Yuan Shih-k'ai hurried on the completion of the documents, basing his action on the consent already given by the former National Council. The agreement was signed on April 25, 1913, under a hail of protests and threats of repudiation at the earliest opportunity, and the Reorganization Loan for £25,000,000, which in those distant days was a large sum of money, was in due course floated.

---

[1] The ' Kuomintang ' or ' National Party ' organization emerged at the time of the Revolution. It was designed to unify, and substantially succeeded in absorbing, the various revolutionary societies which were already in existence.

This financial operation had far-reaching effects on Chinese domestic politics and international relations. The policy of the Governments of the banking institutions concerned has often been severely criticized. But without reflecting on the sober judgment of those who have come after, one may observe that to most of those foreigners of experience and knowledge living close to the Revolution support of Yuan Shih-k'ai seemed to offer the only hope of avoiding chaos. Had it been possible to look into the future probably the contending forces would have been left to put their differences to the arbitrament of battle. But the mind of mankind had not been hardened either by the carnage of the Great War or the excesses in China of the post-revolutionary period. Western diplomacy had its knowledge of revolution elsewhere and thought something might be done to save China from its worst features.

Of the proceeds of the loan much was well accounted for. Nearly half repaid advances and certain old indebtedness. £2,000,000 was spent in the Reorganization of the Salt Gabelle by Sir Richard Dane who became Associate Inspector, with vast financial benefit to China. The balance was supposed to be spent in further reorganization, but there was no machinery of control to ensure this. No doubt its chief use was to strengthen Yuan's position.

Disheartened by what it regarded as the stultification of the republican ideal, the National Assembly turned its attention to the preparation of the permanent constitution, in which it saw its only hope.

Meanwhile, south of the Yangtze, the conviction that Yuan Shih-k'ai aimed at dictatorship and the suppression of republican sentiment crystallized. In July a rising took place which became known as the Second Revolution. But it was badly organized and insufficiently equipped. It was not long before the northern troops, trained on western lines, established their superiority.

But, although Yuan Shih-k'ai had no difficulty in maintaining his position, he was embarrassed by the fact that the Government had not yet been recognized by the Powers, with the exception of the United States. It was therefore desirable that his position as Provisional President should be converted as speedily as possible into the substantive post. It was not difficult to persuade the National Assembly, awed by the severe measures against the rising on the Yangtze, and subjected to other influences, to expedite the completion of that part of the constitution which provided for the election of the President, and to turn it into law. Yuan Shih-k'ai was formally elected ' Great President,' taking the oath of office on October 10, 1913. Thereupon the Republic of China secured the recognition of the European Powers.

In theory the position was now altogether better; in fact the Republican party was on the brink of further disaster. Members of the National Assembly, who belonged to the Kuomintang, were suddenly charged with having been working in conjunction with the leaders of the July rising. The Kuomintang was proscribed. Members of the party in the National Assembly were required to leave Peking forthwith lest worse befall. The result was to reduce the number of the Assembly below that necessary to form a quorum, so that it became impossible to carry on business. Gradually the Assembly faded away with the uncompleted Constitution upon its hands.

From this time onwards Yuan Shih-k'ai exercised an unfettered dictatorship. A believer, however, in appearances, he had a new instrument prepared in the following year by a certain Dr. Goodnow, an American Professor of law who had been recommended to the President as his legal adviser. This instrument was called the Constitutional Pact. It introduced a presidential system based on, or rather an extension of, that prevailing in the United States. At the same time the system of government in the Provinces was patched up, following in the main the old lines. The study of Confucius was enjoined on the nation as the foundation of China's culture and great past. Worship at the temple of Heaven was also restored, reviving old precedents. Sun Yat-sen's forebodings had been realized. There was not much left of the republican ideal.

Chapter 10

The Great War, Japan's Twenty-one Demands and closing days of Yuan Shih-k'ai

The Presidential election law in the new constitution enlarged the terms of the Presidency to ten years, with eligibility for re-election. The Constitutional Pact, whose only sanction was the will of Yuan Shih-k'ai, provided machinery which could be invoked to secure a semblance of constitutional government. Unconsciously anticipating something of certain modern types of government in Europe, Yuan Shih-k'ai no doubt thought that the country would settle down under a scarcely disguised dictatorship. It might have been so. Such a condition would have reproduced the political atmosphere to which the people were accustomed. Unfortunately events were destined to occur which effectually prevented any such desirable consummation.

The first of these was the Great War in which it was difficult for China to avoid being entangled. Germany was established at Tsingtao where she had a naval base. At first Yuan hoped to negotiate with the German Minister for retrocession of the leased territory to China. Japan, on the other hand, who had revenged herself on Russia ten years before, was determined to seize the chance of revenge on Germany for her share of the interference in 1895 to deprive Japan of the fruits of victory in the Sino-Japanese War. Sentiment apart it was also a great political opportunity. She approached Great Britain, who had a couple of British battalions in Tientsin, and it was arranged that a joint expedition should be launched against Tsingtao.

Tsingtao fell early in November 1914. The task accomplished, the British contingent was shipped to England, leaving the Japanese in possession, and in a strong position to negotiate with China as to the future of the leased territory and the German rights in Shantung. But Japan had broader ideas on the subject of negotiation. Although she had neither cause for offence against China nor any outstanding questions calling for settlement other than those arising from the military operations in Shantung, she presented to China, in January 1915, what became known as the Twenty-one Demands. They were called the Twenty-one

Demands because, presented under five groups, they fell into twenty-one paragraphs. Their nature and the surrenders which the Chinese were compelled to make under stress of an ultimatum after over three months' negotiation will now be briefly indicated.

The first group concerned the Province of Shantung. By a short treaty China agreed to assent to all arrangements that should be come to between Japan and Germany relating to the disposition of the rights of Germany in the Province of Shantung, to accept Japanese finance, if agreed by Germany, in the construction of the railway which was projected from Chefoo to connect with the Tsingtao–Tsinanfu railway, and to open further suitable places to foreign trade and residence. In return Japan undertook that when Kiaochao Bay should be at her free disposal she would return it to China on condition that it be opened as a commercial port and that Japan should have a concession under her exclusive jurisdiction. In addition notes were exchanged covering declarations by the Chinese Government against alienation to any foreign power of any territory in Shantung or islands along its coast.

A treaty and note also covered the demands contained in the second group, which required extension of all Japan's leases and rights in Manchuria to ninety-nine years, right of residence and leasing by Japanese subjects throughout south Manchuria and the opening of suitable places in Inner Mongolia to foreign trade and residence.

The third group of demands reflected a far from loyal attitude towards the position of her ally Great Britain in the Yangtze Valley, since it sought by means of an exchange of notes to secure the control of the main source of iron and coal supply in Central China.

The fourth demand was for an undertaking by China not to cede or lease to a third power any harbour or bay or island along the coast of China. Fifthly and lastly China was required to consult Japan with reference to her needs of foreign capital for railways, mine and harbour works in the Province of Fukien, while certain provisions regarding police, arms and advisory functions would have gone far to put China in the position of Japanese protectorate.

The demands included in this last group were subsequently described by Japan as *desiderata* which it was suggested would be helpful to China. It was further claimed that the only point partially ceded by China was in relation to the Province of Fukien. With its littoral washed by the waters of the Formosa Channel, the island of Formosa being already a Japanese possession as a result of the Sino-Japanese War, the development and future of that province was naturally of concern to Japan. China now declared that her government had ' given no permission to foreign nations to construct on the coast of Fukien Province dock-yards, coaling stations for military use, naval bases, or to set up other military establishments ; nor does it entertain an intention of borrowing foreign capital for the purpose of setting up the above-mentioned establishments.'

The main features[1] of the Twenty-one Demands have been thus referred to because of the light they shed on later clashes between Japan and China. They reflected something more than a cynical opportunism. Rather they constituted a declaration of policy coupled with an attempt to fortify that policy by concessions from China as far-reaching as could be obtained. From the Japanese standpoint the moment was supreme. Europe was in the crucible of the greatest war in history, involving consequences in the reorientation of forces that could not be foreseen. Even her puissant ally Great Britain might cease to be a factor in Far Eastern affairs. In China the Manchu dynasty had been swept away and republicanism scarcely dared raise its head. Yuan Shih-k'ai, a sinister figure in Japanese eyes, was extending his sway over an increasing area of the country. It is not surprising that to Japan, with her fixity of purpose, the logic of events brought the conviction that the hour had struck.

On the Chinese side the wisest course was pursued. A declaration of freedom from responsibility for any interference with other foreign interests was sufficient in the circumstances to clear China and to maintain the international position unprejudiced at a period of preoccupations elsewhere. Time was on her side and some day might bring relief. Unhappily for Yuan Shih-k'ai his long-sightedness was interpreted as surrender and did nothing to soften the bitterness in the hearts of the Chinese people. In the national consciousness his position was not improved, and it was with little sympathy that he entered upon the final act of his career.

[1] For details of the events which are here briefly chronicled see *The Fight for the Republic of China*, by B. L. Putnam Weale, p. 109 et seq.

For some time past the family of Yuan Shih-k'ai and his friends had been urging him to ascend the Dragon Throne. There can be no doubt that Yuan's caution was against the step which was to prove so disastrous. But in the end his ambition was stirred and he was persuaded at any rate to play a passive rôle. In the absence of right of conquest a new and strange technique was devised. A symposium was issued in which were discussed between a Chinese scholar and a haphazard stranger the merits of Monarchy and Republic, and their advantages and disadvantages, as applied to the present state of affairs in China. The conclusion, of course, was that the only hope of salvation to China was a reversion to a monarchical regime.

This curious effusion was followed shortly by a Memorandum by Dr. Goodnow which sought to show, by historical analogy, the grave difficulty of making a change from a Monarchy to a Republic in a country where the people were not prepared by long experience of self-government for the responsibility of directing the machinery of state through the medium of their elected representatives.

At this point Liang Ch'i-ch'ao, the famous scholar who, it will be remembered, had been associated with K'ang Yu-wei as one of the reformers of 1898 and had been included in Yuan's first Cabinet as Minister of Justice, felt it incumbent upon him to make a contribution to the discussion. It is said that Yuan, or Yuan's friends, had sought his assistance when the movement was first set on foot. Liang had hitherto been a pronounced Monarchist. He had even risked his reputation and personal safety by advocating the retention of the Manchus when the Revolution was at the height of its apparent success. It was supposed that he must necessarily still entertain monarchical leanings, and that his standing in the country would be a valuable asset. Instead, he came out on the other side.

The document produced by Liang Ch'i-ch'ao is one of great illumination. Its foundation was a distinction between government and forms of government. Opposed to changes of form of government, and believing that good government was independent of the form of government, he had formerly urged, he admitted, the retention of the Manchus so as to avoid too great an upheaval. But that upheaval having taken place, it would be unwise in his judgment to make another change. Denying the applicability of Dr. Goodnow's historical analogies to China, he made a good case for a reasonable constitutionalism under a President enjoying wide powers. He did not advocate curtailment of Yuan's share in the country's government. On the contrary, he considered he would be serving his country more usefully as an active President than as a constitutional Monarch.

The effect of this document throughout the country was to consolidate the forces against Yuan Shih-k'ai. Nevertheless the monarchists persisted in their designs. The Legislature, which was functioning under the recently framed constitutional Pact, caused a referendum to be made to the Provinces. Organized from Peking a result favourable to Yuan's pretensions was a foregone conclusion. Although the moral sense of the Western Powers could not sympathize with a course involving betrayal of the Republic, they were not likely to intervene. Japan was discouraging and offered what was described as friendly advice. But matters had gone too far for Yuan to retire from the position without loss of dignity. Possibly he thought too that any opposition from Japan would swing popular favour in his direction. On December 12, 1915, therefore, still under the influence of unwise counsels and shut in his Palace far away from small events which could have helped his mind to form an independent opinion as to the realities, he agreed that the Monarchy should be proclaimed.

But he had underestimated the strength of the feeling of the country that was arrayed against him. Towards the end of December the far-away south-western Province of Yunnan revolted. Within a few weeks its lead was followed by the other provinces south of the Yangtze. After that the end came swiftly. Despite some military successes of the northern troops it was deemed advisable that the enthronement should be postponed. On March 22, 1916, the monarchical scheme was abandoned by Presidential Decree. A month later Yuan agreed that all authority should be vested in the Cabinet. General Tuan Ch'i-jui became Premier and proposed to convene the National Assembly. Meanwhile a new Republic had been proclaimed by the southern provinces under the ægis of the Kuomintang. General Li Yuan-hung, who had been elected Vice-President when Yuan Shih-k'ai became President, was designated as the Chief Executive. What would have been the ultimate solution of this crisis had Yuan lived can only afford matter for speculation. It was solved suddenly and unexpectedly by his death, from natural causes, on June 6, 1916.

Such were the closing days of Yuan Shih-k'ai. The glamour torn away, deserted by friends, he died, in the common phrase, ' eating bitterness.' Despite the severity of the Judgments which have been passed upon him,[1] a more just posterity will not judge so harshly. That there were dark deeds in his public life and in his private life cannot be denied. He was but typical of his generation in China, even after allowance is made for the fact that he was a little in advance of it. Brought up in the ruthless school of the Empress Dowager, he had not got far enough away from the old standards to realize the fierce antagonism which his methods must arouse in his opponents, inspired by a more liberal civilization. The spiritual food of those in revolt against the old order had been the ' Social Contract ' and ' the Rights of Man,' the idealism of Abraham Lincoln and the liberty and equality before the law secured by the English Constitution. They could not understand, as he understood, that for the mass of the people a government which secured the opportunity to till the fields and to go about the affairs of life in safety was enough. In China mankind at large lives, and has always lived, on the brink of economic disaster. In Yuan's time, except for the periodic scourge of famine, they kept on the right side. The masses had no complaint to make of him. He made out of the people no fortune that could be mentioned in the same breath as the vast accumulations of wealth in the hands of many who have succeeded him in the task of trying to govern the country. He had many qualities which in a ruler of China were admirable. But they necessarily clashed with republican ideals, which to him were empty words. If Yuan Shih-k'ai failed in his loyalties to the Manchus and to the people of China, and was impatient of the talk of parliament, on the other hand he saved the country from foreign intervention. Moreover subsequent events have justified the policy which he pursued towards Japan and the principle of government for which he stood.

[1] *The Fight for the Republic of China*, by B. L. Putnam Weale, p. 109 et seq., and *Twilight in the Forbidden City*, by Sir Reginald Johnston, p. 36.

Chapter 11

The Mantle of Yuan Shih-k'ai

The death of Yuan Shih-k'ai did not put an end to dictatorship. On the contrary the struggle for supreme power has never ceased. It is only in its quality that it has changed. For rather more than ten years the struggle lay between military chiefs of the old regime. In 1926 a new struggle began. On the one side were the reorganized forces of the Revolution, represented by General Chiang Kai-shek and the Kuomintang; on the other were, in the first years, the old military parties in the north of China and later on the left wing of the Kuomintang, the South Western provinces and still the disruptive forces of Communism.

Yuan Shih-k'ai was succeeded by the Vice-President, General Li Yuan-hung, who had been persuaded by Yuan to remove to the capital in December 1913. Although General Li had strongly disapproved the Yangtze rising in the summer of that year and his loyalty was not in question, at the Presidential Election in October votes had been cast for him. There was always danger that if he remained at Wuchang he might become the leader in a new struggle for republican ideals. He was assigned as residence the 'Ocean Terrace' which had been the small island home in the Forbidden City of the ill-fated Emperor Kuang Hsu. There, aloof from politics, he waited on the workings of Fate.

President Li Yuan-hung was determined to be loyal to the Republic. Parliament was reassembled and the task of completing the Constitution was proceeded with. General Tuan Ch'i-jui continued in office as Premier with a new cabinet composed of men from the north and south. The arrest of the prime movers in the monarchist plot was ordered, but without any untoward consequences since time had been allowed in which they might remove themselves from Chinese jurisdiction. The key-note to President Li's policy was union by conciliation under constitutional forms.

The northern militarist party, known as the Peiyang Party, watched the President's republican sentiment with ill-concealed hostility. It foresaw the chief power passing gradually into the hands of the radical party in the south, which it would not allow. It could only be a matter of time before a clash occurred.

The occasion was the declaration of war against Germany. The advantages to China of such a course were obvious, and on March 11, 1917, diplomatic relations with Germany were broken off at the instance of the United States as a protest against the unrestricted submarine campaign. But Parliament refused to debate the declaration of war until the Cabinet had been re-organized, which was tantamount to a demand for the dismissal of the Premier, General Tuan Ch'i-jui. The latter, continuing to insist on a declaration of war, was summarily dismissed. Nevertheless the Parliament was doomed. President Li, in dire need of support against the militarist backing of Tuan Ch'i-jui, adopted the desperate step of calling for the mediation of a certain General Chang Hsun, an old-time soldier, who had held Nanking for a time against the Revolutionaries and had been one of the few loyal supporters of the Manchu House. His army, composed of the old type of Chinese brave, marched on Peking. Unfortunately, he found himself sufficiently in agreement with his more modern brother commanders to join them in insisting on the dissolution of Parliament. With Peking under grave threat on every side, Parliament was dissolved on June 12 by Presidential Mandate.

By the end of June General Chang Hsun had established himself in a commanding position at Peking. He then proceeded to give rein to his old loyalties.

On July 1 he endeavoured to bring about a Manchu restoration. The President became a prisoner in his palace and in the name of the boy Emperor the restoration of the Dynasty was announced.

To this movement the modern army chiefs had promised their support.[1] But when they observed Chang Hsun's attempt to take the front place, they decided against the restoration and marched on Peking. Chang Hsun collapsed and sought sanctuary in the Legation quarter. The *status quo* was quickly restored, with the exception of President Li Yuan-hung, who had escaped to Tientsin and refused to resume office.

The Vice-President, General Feng Kuo-chang, became Presi-

[1] *China, Japan and Corea*, by J. O. P. Bland, p. 60.

dent, and General Tuan Ch'i-jui returned to Peking as Premier. On August 14, 1917, war was declared against Germany.

The logic of events was not lost upon Sun Yat-sen and the leaders of the revolutionary party. They realized that they must reorganize and build anew. In concentration of all their forces at Canton, the historic home of revolution, lay the only hope. Numerous members of Parliament, refusing to accept dissolution, went first to Shanghai and thence to Canton as the Parliament in being. Formal declaration was made of what was claimed to be the true republican government of China. Thus was established a defined cleavage between North and South. But, as has been already indicated, the South was not to make its weight felt for some years.

Neither space permits, nor interest demands, anything in the nature of a detailed account of the chaos, political rivalries and civil wars which China suffered in the ten years immediately following the death of Yuan Shih-k'ai. But an indication of the forces and the salient features is necessary to satisfy the historical requirements of this phase and to enable us to understand the Nationalist phase which followed.

It will be recalled that in 1907 Yuan Shih-k'ai had been appointed a Grand Councillor in Peking, owing, partly at any rate, to fear of his growing power as Viceroy of Chihli which was largely based on control of the modern army. During his subsequent presidency, his adherents became known as the Peiyang party, so called from the name given to North China at large. By the time of his death the military element in the party had become the dominating factor. But the party was not homogeneous. The army was about equally divided between two cliques. It had been officered in the main from the provinces of Chihli and Anhui, with the result that a tendency had manifested itself to divide on provincial lines.

When in November 1911 Yuan Shih-k'ai left the front at Hankow and came to Tientsin, the command was left in the hands of General Feng Kuo-chang with General Tuan Ch'i-jui as his chief of staff. Of these men the former, a Chihli man, was the head of the Chihli section, while Tuan Ch'i-jui, who came from Anhui, was the acknowledged leader of the Anhui party. Notoriously these men were far from being on cordial terms, and one was now President, the other Premier. Friction was inevitable, but General Tuan Ch'i-jui was in the stronger position. Organizing an electoral body consisting of nominees of the military governors he eliminated his rival at the next presidential election. This took place in the following year, when in October 1918 Hsu Shih-chang was elected president by what became known as the Tuchuns' parliament, ' tuchun ' being a new name for a military governor. General Feng Kuo-chang died shortly afterwards, but the Chihli party did not become extinct.

Roughly the forces of China, apart from Canton, were as follows.

In the first place there was the Anhui party which now became the Anfu party, by reason of certain accession from the Province of Fukien. Happily also the first characters in the names of Anhui and Fukien have the meanings of ' peace ' and ' happiness,' while by a coincidence the party found suitable accommodation for its headquarters in the ' Anfu Hutung,' or ' Lane of Peace and Happiness,' in Peking. The party became known familiarly as the Anfu Club.

Secondly there was the Chihli party, the leadership of which, on the death of Feng Kuo-chang, fell into the hands of General Ts'ao K'un, at that time Tuchun or military governor of Chihli Province. His chief supporter was General Wu Pei-fu, at this time commanding a Division.

Manchuria represented a third party, called the Fengtien party, Fengtien being the Chinese name of Mukden and of the chief of the three provinces in Manchuria, of which Mukden is the capital. It had been controlled for many years by General Chang Tso-lin, whose character and meteoric rise is briefly sketched in Dr. Dugald Christie's *Thirty Years in Moukden.*

' As a lad he had served under General Tso at Ping-yang in the Chino-Japanese War. When the Russians dominated the land he had headed a band of banditti and conducted a systematic guerrilla warfare. Later on the Government, recognizing his military powers, had invited him to return to the service of the Emperor and bring his men with him. His natural gifts found a place for him, and he was now practically Commander-in-Chief. To a man of his training, absolute power naturally seemed the only right method of government. It was not to be expected that he should sympathize with the idea that every peasant and workman had the right to say how the country should be governed. His soldiers worshipped him, for he treated them well, justly, and generously ; but they feared him too, knowing that he had the power of life and death, and would never hesitate to use it.'[1]

General Chang shortly became military Governor, or Tuchun, at Mukden.

This description of General Chang's position and estimate of his character, as he was at the age of thirty-six when the Revolution broke out in 1911 and he enabled the Viceroy to carry out a policy of neutrality until the issue had been decided inside the Great Wall, explains largely why Manchuria was the best-governed and the only reasonably prosperous part of China during the period of his military governorship. This lasted from this time until June 3, 1928, the date of his death. The other part of the explanation lay in the economic benefit of the south Manchurian railway, owned and operated by Japan, and the steadying influence of the organization within the Japanese railway zone.

The struggle between these three groups, the consequences of defections by such famous and uncertain quantities as General Feng Yu-hsiang, once known as ' the Christian General,' and the support or vacillations of less important stars in the military firmament, was destined in the main to dominate the situation north of the Yangtze for rather more than ten years.

The first phase of the struggle began in 1920. Although the Anfu party was in power under the premiership of General Tuan Ch'i-jui, the position was not over-secure. It was therefore planned to dislodge the Chihli leader, Ts'ao K'un, from the military governorship of Chihli Province. But the forces that were to be roused against the Anfuites proved too strong for them. Wu Pei-fu came up from Honan to the support of his chief. Feng Yu-hsiang, the then Christian General, served in support of General Wu. Chang Tso-lin allied himself with the Chihli party, and although his troops were not in time to participate seriously in the fighting, the political rearrangements were made by him and Ts'ao K'un in consultation. Friendly sentiments between the leaders were enhanced by the marriage of one of Ts'ao K'un's sons with a daughter of Chang Tso-lin.

[1] *Thirty Years in Moukden*, by Dr. Dugald Christie, p. 263.

This combination of forces in the north of China sustained the machinery of government in Peking for some two years. Meanwhile the Canton Government established under the leadership of Dr. Sun Yat-sen in 1917 shortly gave way to a Committee of seven. Dr. Sun was a member of this Committee, which essayed to assume the functions of government over seven provinces in the south and west of China. It proved to be short-lived and is only of interest in that it was the origin of the idea of what became known as the South-Western Federation. Originally loosely knit by sentiment against the northern militarists and by not much else, it subsequently transferred its antagonism to the Nationalist Government which, springing from Canton, became established ten years later in Nanking. As is current knowledge, these separatist tendencies have recently manifested themselves strongly, producing important consequences to which the necessary reference will in due course be made.

The characteristic of the following years at Canton was the constant struggle of Sun Yat-sen to maintain himself as the head of the Republican party. The glamour which surrounded the man who had spent his life inspiring revolution and organizing its resources, quickly faded on close contact with a man without experience in government or aptitude for administration. Dr. Sun was compelled to flee on various occasions and to take long periods of sanctuary in Hongkong, Shanghai and elsewhere.

Chapter 12

The Treaty of Versailles (1919) and the Washington Conference (1921)

The declaration of war against Germany gave China a great opportunity. Although the idea had been discussed of sending Chinese troops either to Mesopotamia or to strengthen the Russian front, in the event their services were not used. China's effort was limited to the enrolment of Chinese labour corps to work in France on the lines of communication in the service and pay of France and Great Britain. Economically, therefore, China was called upon for no sacrifice either in men or treasure. On the contrary she made great economic gains. The payment of the German share of the Boxer Indemnity and the service of German loans immediately fell into abeyance. In order to help China in her difficulties of reconstruction, the Allies agreed to suspend payment of the instalments of the Boxer Indemnity, falling due severally to them, for the period of the War. The magnificent results of the reorganization of the Salt Administration under Sir Richard Dane were now coming to hand. The price of silver rose without any ill-effect on the export trade, which reached unprecedented volume owing to the demands of war for raw material. A government with appreciation of its duty to the country could have reduced the national debt to a negligible figure. Instead the national debt was increased by a series of loans from Japanese financiers, known as the ' Nishihara loans.' At the same time the condition of the country steadily deteriorated.

Meanwhile the cleavage between North and South continued. On the so-called election of Hsu Shih-chang the South threatened a punitive expedition, which it was not in a position to implement with any effectiveness. President Hsu propounded a policy of unification of the country by pacific means, but it did not pass beyond the phase of earnest hope. In consequence China was represented at the Treaty making at Versailles by emissaries from the governments of both Peking and Canton, although the northern delegates alone could be recognized. The draft treaty included clauses settling the question of Shantung in the way desired by Japan, but demonstrations by students in China, a new form of

85

manifestation of popular opinion, compelled the Cabinet in Peking to instruct its representatives to withhold signature. China therefore did not become a party to the Treaty and the Shantung question was left outstanding.

In the following winter, in consequence of earnest representations by the Powers that a serious attempt should now be made to settle the differences between North and South China, a peace conference was convened in Shanghai. A friendly gathering, it soon agreed to differ. For a time, however, it remained in being without seriously conferring, trying to effect some sort of a bargain behind the scenes. In due course it faded away, and the Washington Conference, which opened on November 12, 1921, found complete disunion still continuing.

The primary object of the Washington Conference was the limitation of armament. Of subordinated but inter-related importance was the discussion of Pacific and Far Eastern problems, with a view to the elimination, or at least the reduction, of points of possible conflict.

President Harding's proposal had met with a warm response. Japan alone showed reluctance. She foresaw that her policy on the mainland of Asia must be questioned. She feared the substitution of some other instrument for the Anglo-Japanese Alliance.

Outside the contracting parties, no one liked the Anglo-Japanese Alliance. When England emerged from her policy of ' Splendid Isolation ' to join hands with the rising Asiatic Power, the Chanceries of the Continent and America were pained and shocked. China in those days was inarticulate. It has been claimed since that she resented the alliance, notwithstanding that it provided a check to Russian aggression. Certainly we know that the policy of Li Hung-chang, who died less than three months before the alliance was entered into, was to support Russia. But he probably stood alone. To Englishmen who understood these matters, it appeared in the circumstances of the times to be a wise departure from traditional policy. The Japanese nation was filled with gratified pride.

In his book *China at the Conference*, Professor Willoughby says :

' That Japan used her Alliance with Great Britain as an occasion for herself coming into the war and thus bringing its military operations into the Far East and upon the soil of China is, of course, well known.' . . .

and again :

'It is scarcely open to doubt that the existence of her alliance with Great Britain gave to Japan a reasonable assurance that she would not be effectively interfered with in the pursuance of the aggressive policies embodied in her Twenty-one Demands upon China, just as it had been that same alliance which had given her the courage in 1904 to bring her controversies with Russia to the issue of war.' . . .

He concludes therefore :

'Reduced then to its simplest and baldest terms, the chief political problem which the Conference was called to solve was to find means of placing a restraint upon the imperialistic ambitions of Japan.'

If these are American views at all widely held, they will come as a surprise perhaps to some readers. An English writer may be forgiven for pointing out that the Alliance possibly brought Japan in on the side of the Allies instead of on the side of the Central Powers, thus saving America three years of war. In August 1914 few people in the East, except the English and the French, believed that the war could result otherwise than in German victory. Japan might pardonably have thought that her weight on the side of the Central Powers would have dispelled any doubt which might be entertained. An English writer may also be permitted perhaps to observe that, at the time of the Twenty-one Demands, England in the field was entrenched on the Aisne, while at home she was busy training 'the first hundred thousand.'

The main aim of the Conference was achieved by establishing the 5–5–3 ratio between the British, American and Japanese fleets, and an undertaking between the Pacific Powers to maintain the *status quo* as regards the fortification of islands in the Pacific.

What Professor Willoughby has called the chief political problem was solved by two further treaties. Of these one between Great Britain, France, Japan and the United States provided that 'any controversy between any of the High Contracting Parties arising out of any Pacific question and involving their rights . . . in relation to their insular possessions and insular dominions in the region of the Pacific Ocean,' should be referred, failing diplomacy, to a joint conference for consideration and adjustment. Any threat to any party's rights ' by the aggressive action of any other Power,' was to be dealt with by full and frank communications between the High Contracting Parties ' in order to arrive at an understanding as to the most efficient measures to be taken, jointly or separately, to meet the exigencies of the particular situation.' A declaration accompanying the Treaty made clear that Mandated Islands in the Pacific Ocean were within the scope of the Treaty. A supplementary treaty laid down that the term ' insular possessions and insular dominions,' in its application to Japan, should include only ' Karafuto (or the Southern portion of the island of Sakhalin), Formosa and the Pescadores, and the islands under the mandate of Japan.'

The other treaty, which became known as the Nine-Power Treaty, was concluded by the above four powers, China, and four other European powers with Far Eastern interests, namely Belgium, Italy, the Netherlands and Portugal. The principle of the Treaty was laid down in Article I. The remaining articles were directed to ensuring its observance. Article I was as follows :

' The Contracting Powers, other than China, agree :

(1) To respect the sovereignty, the independence, and the territorial and administrative integrity of China ;

(2) To provide the fullest and most unembarrassed opportunity to China to develop and maintain for herself an effective and stable government ;

(3) To use their influence for the purpose of effectually establishing and maintaining the principle of equal opportunity for the commerce and industry of all nations throughout the territory of China ;

(4) To refrain from taking advantage of conditions in China in order to seek special rights or privileges which would abridge the rights of subjects or citizens of friendly States and from countenancing action inimical to the security of such States.'

The procedure to be observed in the event of any developments intended to be guarded against in the Treaty was laid down in Article VII, which should also be quoted.

' The Contracting Powers agree that, whenever a situation arises which in the opinion of any one of them involves the application of the stipulations of the present Treaty, and renders desirable discussion of such application, there shall be full and frank communication between the Contracting Powers concerned.'

The remaining questions discussed were the peculiar concern of China.

The Conference had provided the opportunity to China to arraign the rest of the world on a charge of eighty years of interference with the old-established order. That the consequent disharmony and encroachments on China's sovereignty were not the outcome of foreign imperialistic design but were compelled by circumstances, history has already determined.

Acute difference of view in the matter of personal responsibility, the absence of law in China suitable to the adjustment of many of the most important of human relationships, the methods of administration of justice, the state of prisons and punishments, had combined to make extra-territoriality inevitable.

The uncertainty of Chinese official exactions had necessitated a tariff treaty on *ad valorem* principles. This required readjustment in the matter of values, but need not have waited for the Conference, since the Chinese had the right under the Treaty to apply to the signatories for its revision.

The inadequacy of postal communications in earlier days had necessitated the establishment of foreign post offices. We have seen that the attack on the Legations in 1900 and the horrors perpetrated on defenceless men, women and children in the interior had resulted in the inclusion in the protocol of certain protective clauses for the future. China's backwardness had also resulted in some radio and telegraphic installations, all of which in theory constituted ground for criticism.

But China, with her militarist duumvirate in the North, and in the South the precarious control by Sun Yat-sen of the smouldering fires in revolutionary Canton, reflecting something of the causes which had produced her present state, could only fear lest reason be found to take further charge of her affairs.

In the event she achieved a notable success.   Her able band of delegates, youthful and inexperienced compared to the elder statesmen of Europe—for their ages ranged from thirty-six to forty-five and their political education with one exception had only begun with the Revolution—presented their country's case with dignity and distinction.   Helped by the liberal sentiment of Great Britain and America, a series of understandings were reached which opened to China the greatest opportunity.   The Nine-Power Treaty provided a charter under which she could work out her own salvation.   A tariff treaty provided for immediate revision, pending a wider scale of adjustment by means of a tariff commission.   A resolution provided for a commission to investigate the question of extra-territorial jurisdiction.   It was decided at the Conference itself that foreign post offices should be removed within a year.   Other matters were taken into account and resolutions passed, which at least produced a re-orientation of view in many important particulars.   Finally, although outside the scope of the Conference, China challenged Japan's policy in Shantung and negotiated, with the friendly assistance of Mr. Balfour, a treaty under which Japan agreed to evacuation, and for all practical purposes abandoned her claims.

It only remained for China's leaders to lay aside their personal ambitions for wealth and power.

Chapter 13

"Coup d'état" of the Christian General, Feng Yu-hsiang
November 5, 1924

The years following the Washington Conference were to show that so far from composing their differences the leaders in the North remained intent as ever on enforcing their personal ideas, although the conflict of principle between Peking and Canton smouldered the more menacingly by reason of the introduction of new factors only slowly appreciated.

But in 1922 the South hardly counted. Although what were called ' punitive expeditions ' were threatened against the northern militarists, they did not materialize so as to cause serious alarm. There was no commercial marine to transport southern troops, and with the exception of comparatively short lines radiating from Shanghai there were no railways. The maritime province of Kiangsu, with the rich revenue possibilities of Shanghai, was held by a military governor associated with one of the northern parties. The maritime province of Fukien was also controlled by one of the northern group. In like manner the riverine provinces of Chekiang, Kiangsi and Hupeh were broadly on the northern side, since they shared the antagonism to the Kuomintang. The Yangtze, therefore, and Nanking and Hankow, the southern termini of the two northern trunk railways, were in northern control, even had there been suitable lines of communication from the South by which they could have been reached. Finally, had there been any real menace from the South, at that time a northern confederacy could have been formed and troops concentrated rapidly at almost any point, while the southern armies would have been solely dependent on their powers of marching. Ultimately it was destined that the South would assert itself by these means, but as yet its resources were not organized.

As one looks back and recalls the high hopes that were formed in turn of Chang Tso-lin and Wu Pei-fu, and even of the Christian General in the early days of his emergence, one wonders if they were entirely visionary. The story might well have been different if Chang Tso-lin had been big enough in 1920 to treat Wu Pei-fu as something more than a subordinate commander. Wu Pei-fu was perhaps the only honest and loyal military leader. He would have been an admirable instrument in the hands of a wise chief. The people believed in him. He had no desire to play a political part. He was satisfied to be a soldier supporting the right cause. In the circumstances Ts'ao K'un would have had to be content with retention of the Chihli Governorship. Tuan Ch'i-jui could have been kept permanently in retirement or admitted to office as seemed expedient. Military opposition everywhere could have been suppressed, while a liberal and conciliatory policy towards Canton might have been formulated. The arrogance of Chang Tso-lin lost China this opportunity.

The Washington Conference had hardly dispersed when Chang Tso-lin decided that the moment had come to carry out a project he had entertained for some time, namely the suppression of Wu Pei-fu. The result was a second campaign in which General Wu again showed himself the most competent of all Chinese commanders. The Manchurian War Lord, to adopt a phrase which came into use at that time, retired precipitately to Mukden, where he declared the independence of Manchuria. In this campaign General Wu again received valuable support from General Feng Yu-hsiang, still a professing Christian.

In Peking one of the earliest consequences was the resignation of President Hsu Shih-chang. His place was reluctantly taken by the former President, Li Yuan-hung. Once again this patriotic and well-meaning man essayed the task of re-establishing the constitution. He summoned the Parliament, which twice during the past ten years had been so summarily displaced, and did his best to form a liberal cabinet. But his liberal effort was brought to nought by the machinations of General Ts'ao K'un.

The Chihli War Lord, embarrassed possibly by his family tie to Chang Tso-lin, had not participated actively in the campaign. But he was determined to gather the fruits. With the always reliable support of General Wu and with the Christian General seemingly under General Wu's influence, Ts'ao K'un disposed of the strongest military combination in China. The time seemed ripe to achieve his ambition to become the chief executive. The constitutional action of President Li Yuan-hung in re-convening Parliament assisted his plan. In little over a year the President's position had become untenable and for the second time he had resigned. The Parliamentarians, bribed it has been stated by reliable authority at a cost of fifteen million Chinese dollars, then about two and half million sterling, elected Ts'ao K'un to the vacant post. But his tenure too was to be short-lived. He assumed office on October 10, 1923, and fell on October 23, 1924, in highly dramatic circumstances.

The two years which had elapsed since Chang Tso-lin had been driven back into Manchuria had been occupied in strengthening his army. He had incorporated large numbers of white Russians, who had found their way into China after the Koltchak debacle. Furthermore he had greatly improved his material as a result of the reorganization of the arsenal at Mukden by ' One-arm ' Sutton.[1] General Wu Pei-fu had been engaged in the task of unification of the country by force, and his military supremacy was acknowledged except in the extreme south and one of the Yangtze Provinces, Chekiang, whose military governor supported Chang Tso-lin.

In the summer of 1924, Chang launched a campaign designed to re-establish his control of Peking. Wu Pei-fu decided to hold the line of the Great Wall. He himself moved north to Shanhaikuan, where the Great Wall meets the sea, and sent Feng Yu-hsiang to hold the pass at Jehol. But no sooner was battle joined at Shanhaikuan and other places than Feng returned to Peking secretly, covering the distance, 136 miles, by forced marches, and executed a *coup d'état.*

The President, Ts'ao K'un, was imprisoned. He was not released until April 1926. His brother Ts'ao Jui was less fortunate, being cruelly handled and executed. The Court of the boy-Emperor, Hsuan Tung, was suppressed. The Emperor himself was transferred from the Forbidden City to his father's palace in the northern part of Peking, where for the time being he became virtually a State prisoner. He was saved from a dangerous situation by his English tutor, Mr. R. F. Johnston, who contrived a plan for his escape to the safe haven of the Japanese Legation. Subsequently the Emperor removed to Tientsin where he lived in the Japanese Concession for eight years, until a turn in Fortune's wheel opened the way to a

[1] Captain F. A. Sutton, M.C., served in the War in the Royal Engineers and lost an arm. His adventures in Manchuria are told in his book, *One-arm Sutton.*

semblance of power in the land of his race. The terms of favourable treatment to the Manchu House were cancelled, and General Feng, in the name of the State, assumed charge of the priceless collection of Chinese Art in the Imperial Palace.[1]

General Wu Pei-fu was compelled to fall back on Tangku, at the mouth of the Haiho, whence he took ship with the remnants of his troops to West China by sea and the Yangtze. At a meeting which took place shortly afterwards at Tientsin between Feng Yu-hsiang, Chang Tso-lin and Tuan Ch'i Jui, the latter was appointed chief executive.

Disappointed in his share of power General Feng retired ostensibly to the western hills in the neighbourhood of Peking. Chang Tso-lin, establishing himself along the railway lines, controlled the coastal belt from Mukden to Shanghai.

Chapter 14

Turning-point in History (January 26, 1923) and the Death of Sun Yat-sen (March 12, 1925)

While these struggles for power were continuing between the great satraps of the North, events took place in the South which were destined to have more far-reaching consequences than anything that had happened since the Edict of Abdication.

In 1921 the parliamentary fragment which purported to function at Canton had elected Sun Yat-sen to the office of President. This was resented by some of his former supporters, who in the following year forced him to flee from Canton. Taking refuge on a gunboat in the West River, for the Navy always seemed to remain loyal, he committed the blunder of destroying a large part of Canton by bombardment, fire even being opened without

[1] For a detailed account of this episode see *Twilight in the Forbidden City*, by Sir Reginald Johnston, p. 376 et seq.

warning the inhabitants of the densely populated city. At the same time fierce warfare raged for the mastery between the men who rose to power in the various provinces.

The authority of Sun Yat-sen had ceased to be. The Kuomintang, the organ on which he relied for chief support, was disorganized and exercised no real power. It was not the only revolutionary society nor, as we have seen, the oldest. Yet such are the strange turns in the wheel of Fate, that the time was not far distant when it was to absorb or eliminate all rivals save Communism and establish itself, as it had striven to do in 1912, as the force of Nationalist Revolution.

The foundations for this development now began almost unwittingly to be laid. Dr. Sun had realized that without help from outside there could be no end to the anarchy in the south-west, which was more terrible than anything experienced in the north of China. He had sought vaguely for support from England, the United States and France, but these powers were too fully concerned with their post-war problems apart from any distaste for meddling in Cantonese politics. Meanwhile, he was approached by Russia with offers of financial assistance, advice and co-operation. A turning-point in history had been reached.

In 1922 a mission was sent by the Soviet Government to China under the chairmanship of a Commissar of the name of Joffe. Expelled from Canton, Sun Yat-sen went to Shanghai where discussions between the Soviet Envoy and himself took place. It appears that from the outset Dr. Sun made it clear that Communism was far away from his thoughts, and for the time being the Russian Delegation appeared to acquiesce. To establish an understanding, and at the same time to avoid suspicion of Communist influence, a joint Declaration was made by Dr. Sun and Mr. Joffe on January 26, 1923, in the sense that while it was recognized that conditions rendered China unsuited to Communism, Russia would help in the task of reconstruction.[1] At the same time supporters of Sun Yat-sen from Kwangsi and Yunnan invaded Kwang-tung and took Canton, shortly restoring Dr. Sun's authority.

[1] When on May 31, 1924, the Chinese Government in Peking accorded recognition of the Soviet Government, the need of protection against Russian aggression was recognized. The point was covered by a reciprocal pledge ' not to engage in propaganda directed against the political and social systems of either contracting party.'

In the following autumn a Russian called Michael Borodin was sent to Canton in pursuance of arrangements made with Joffe. He was accompanied by a number of military officers and had command of funds for the establishment of a Military Academy at Whampoa, some fifteen miles down the West River from Canton, where a rival port to Hongkong was projected. At the same time the reorganization of the Kuomintang was taken in hand. Members were requested to re-register, and it was arranged that Communists might become members subject to their undertaking to adopt the Kuomintang's principles. As a result many of the old members dropped out, many Communists became members and, under the reorganizing ability of Borodin, the society shortly became a vital force.

According to the best Chinese authority, Communism in China, as a political movement, owes its origin to the agitation amongst the Peking University students which arose in 1919 as a reaction to the Treaty of Versailles. Two years later the Chinese Communist party was formed in Shanghai. A representative of the party was sent to ' the Congress of the Far Eastern Proletarians which was convened at Moscow under the auspices of the Comintern. It was there that the affiliation of the Communist party with the Kuomintang was for the first time contemplated. Moscow was favourably inclined to the proposal, its object being to exploit the national-revolutionary movement under Dr. Sun Yat-sen for the purpose of Communist propaganda in the interior.' [1]

It is clear now that the declaration by Joffe, and what Dr. Sun always regarded as ' a gentleman's agreement ' with Borodin not to push Communist doctrines, was a cloak under which Soviet designs were intended to be worked out.

Thus by the irony of Fate the successes in North China of the more conservative elements in the country, coupled with the lack of interest on the part of the leading Western Powers, had the effect of throwing Dr. Sun into the arms of the Communists. But Sun Yat-sen died before he realized the deception.

In the autumn of 1923 the regime in Peking, in the establishment of which Feng Yu-hsiang had played so prominent a part, invited Dr. Sun to come North and discuss the situation with a

[1] *Suppressing Communist-Banditry in China*, edited by T'ang Leang-li, pp. 8 and 9.

view to securing some sort of unity. Nor were the circumstances in some ways unfavourable. Chang Tso-lin as we have seen was in a strong position and had formerly been in loose alliance with Sun Yat-sen. C. T. Wang, who has already been mentioned as one of the younger leaders of the Revolution, and during 1924 had negotiated in Peking the Treaty which recognized Soviet Russia, was Minister of Foreign Affairs. The Christian General was supposed also to have strong Nationalist leanings. Sun Yat-sen proceeded therefore to the North. But before anything could be achieved he fell sick and in the early part of 1925 he died in Peking.

Dr. Sun was destined to a greatness in death which had been denied to him in life. The leaders of the Kuomintang, many of whom had despised and betrayed him, were keenly alive to the need of an inspiration and a policy on which to build the future.

Dr. Sun had been a prolific writer and speaker. His Russian advisers had insisted that he must, for propaganda purposes, develop his theories more publicly, and in 1924 he had been lecturing freely in Canton. His death made the opportunity for something like a canonization of Sun Yat-sen, and the adoption of his work as a political faith. The day before he died he put his signature to a political testament since famous as ' Dr. Sun's Will.' This brief document, said to have been drafted by Wang Ching-wei, was adopted as the foundation of the reorganized party.

' For forty years,' it runs, ' I have devoted myself to the cause of the people's revolution with but one end in view, the elevation of China to a position of freedom and equality among the nations. My experiences during these forty years have firmly convinced me that to attain this goal we must bring about a thorough awakening of our own people and ally ourselves in a common struggle with those peoples of the world who treat us on the basis of equality.

' The work of the Revolution is not yet done. Let all our comrades follow my *Plans for National Reconstruction, Fundamentals of National Reconstruction, Three Principles of the People*, and the *Manifesto* issued by the First National Convention of our Party, and strive on earnestly for their consummation. Above all, our recent declarations in favour of the convocation of a National Convention and the abolition of the unequal treaties should be carried into effect with the least possible delay.

'This is my heartfelt charge to you.' [1]

But this amounted to nothing more than an exhortation. The real guidance was to be sought from his published works.

The writings and recorded lectures of Sun Yat-sen constitute a substantial volume of political thought and economic theory. For our present purpose the main features which have influenced Chinese political development fall into three themes, which may be defined as, firstly, the aims of Revolution in the widest sense, secondly, the methods of achieving Revolution, and thirdly, the theory of government.

Dr. Sun's ideas on the aims of Revolution as thus defined, are set forth in his best-known work *San Min Chu I*, or *The Three Principles of the People*. These principles are Nationalism, Democracy and the People's Livelihood. When he developed these ideas, several years prior to 1911, Nationalism meant nothing more than assertion of the Chinese Nation and expulsion of the Manchus. With the Abdication Edicts, therefore, the first step was achieved. But later on Dr. Sun modified his views. He came to interpret the foreign loans made to Yuan Shih-k'ai and the loans subsequently made by the Japanese to the Anfu party as activities of so-called Imperialist powers designed to keep China in a condition of servitude. Russian influence appeared to complete his conversion to a strongly anti-foreign sentiment, despite the fact, paradoxical as it may sound, that he never ceased to advocate the view that China should be developed by foreign capital, while he owed his professional education to a British Colony and subsequently his life to England. In consequence of this frame of mind the principle of Nationalism was extended to embrace the elimination of foreign influences as the first aim of the Revolution.

Democracy, as the second aim, stands on its normal definition and calls for no comment. But it is otherwise with the third principle, which has aroused considerable argument as to its meaning. Dr. Sun defined it vaguely as ' the livelihood of the people, the existence of society, the welfare of the life of the masses.' The point of interest is whether Dr. Sun was aiming at Communism, and if not what is the precise distinction that

[1] Sun Yat-sen, *San Min Chu I*, translated by Frank W. Price, p. vii.

he has in mind. It is not possible to follow the matter in any detail, but it is probably true to say that, although in lectures during 1924 he used terms which made his principle and Communism appear indistinguishable, he was never a believer in the principles of Communism as they are, broadly speaking, understood. It is common ground amongst the great majority of students of the Chinese social fabric that Communism is alien to the sentiment of the Chinese people.[1] Dr. Sun himself had criticized the Marxian doctrine and had shown apprehension of Communism. A student of his country's sentiment, he must have realized its inapplicability. No doubt he was seeking something in the nature of a formula of compromise between his principle and the principles of his Russian allies.

Turning now to the second theme, the ' Method of achieving Revolution,' this can best be given by quoting a summary contained in a series of able papers by Mr. Tsui Shu-chin, published in the *Chinese Social and Political Science Review.*

' In his *Outline of National Reconstruction,* written in April 1924, Dr. Sun proposed to divide the procedure of the Chinese Revolution into three different stages. In each of these stages, certain tasks would have to be accomplished. The first stage was to be called " the period of military operations," during which " the area of operations shall be subject to martial law." The military authorities would have two functions to perform during the first stage, namely, " to suppress reactionary and counter-revolutionary forces and to propagate the principle of reconstruction so that the people may be enlightened and the country unified." As soon as order should have been restored in a province, the second stage, or " the period of political tutelage," would begin in that particular province. During this period officers who have passed the civil service examination would be sent out to train the people in the rights and duties of citizenship. During the same period, all the preliminary steps necessary to pave the way for the actual application of the Principle of livelihood would be taken. When all the districts within any province should have become fully self-governing, the final stage or " the period of constitutional Government " would commence in that province, and when a majority of the provinces should have reached the period of constitu-

[1] *China's Problems and their Solution,* by Wang Ching-wei, p. 39.

tional government, then a constitution for the whole nation would be adopted and promulgated. In this last stage the San Min Chu I would be put into practice in its entirety.'[1]

The necessity of three stages, the establishment of power, a transitional period and the achievement of the ultimate aim, is obvious and common to all revolutions. The interesting point is in what way the second stage, ' the period of tutelage,' of Dr. Sun Yat-sen differs from the Soviet idea of the Proletarian Dictatorship. It appears to be this. While Dr. Sun had it in mind that the medium of government during the ' period of tutelage ' would be the Kuomintang and that the Kuomintang would be composed of all elements in the nation, the Soviet idea was dictatorship by a class, namely the Proletariat.

At a later stage we shall see how far Dr. Sun's ideal has been attained. Similarly it is advisable to wait until we reach the point of a nationalist government in being before describing Dr. Sun's third theme, the ' Theory of Government.'

Chapter 15

The Shanghai Incident

May 30, 1925

Opportunity for testing the organization of the Kuomintang in one direction and uniting its members in a campaign of hate and passion was furnished by the Shanghai incident of May 30, 1925. The year had been prolific of strikes which were being exploited to advance Bolshevik ideas. Early in May a Chinese worker had been killed in an attack on a Japanese mill. The students then took charge. It may sound strange to western

[1] *The Chinese Social and Political Science Review*, Vol. XVIII, No. 2, p. 179.

readers to find students as leaders of strikes and other forms of agitation. But so it was and, though in less virulent form, still is in China. Relaxation of old restraints, text-book distortions of history, gross misrepresentations of present-day conditions and of the meaning of contemporary events, combined to produce a class which under the guise of a vitalizing patriotism of youth rapidly became an organ of violence and terrorism.

According to an account in the *China Year Book of 1926*, determined on bringing the facts to the notice of the public by means of hand-bills and lectures, a section took advantage of the occasion to spread extreme political propaganda, attacking England, America, France and Japan as alleged Imperial Powers. The more violent aspect of the demonstration took place on May 30 in the district of the Louza police station in the International Settlement. Some arrests were made. Other students crowded into the charge-room and refused to leave. All peaceful means having been exhausted they had to be forcibly ejected. A crowd at once assembled which was reinforced by loafers from neighbouring streets and alleyways and soon became a riotous mob, which pressed steadily forward shouting ' Kill the Foreigners.' As they were about to enter the station, some constables were ordered by the British Inspector to open fire, with the result that four students were killed and a number were wounded. A foreign missionary testified that it seemed to him that the British Inspector had no option.

A brilliant summary of the forces behind the incident by George E. Sokolsky,[1] which appeared in the *China Year Book of 1926*, may with advantage be quoted.

' The Communists, through the influence of Comrade Borodin, had convinced the Kuomintang during the 1924 Party Congress to determine to concentrate the Anti-foreign Movement on Great Britain, on the assumption that as Great Britain is the most powerful of the foreign Powers in China, if Britain falls the entire structure of foreign rights and privileges in China would also fall.

' Therefore, when the Communist Party of China sent

---

[1] *China Year Book*, 1928, p. 1326. Mr. Sokolsky is an American citizen of Russian race, whose wife was a Chinese lady. He enjoyed exceptional opportunities of observation and was remarkably qualified to assess the results. He is the author of a brilliant book, *The Tinderbox of Asia*.

Li Lih-san, a Moscow-trained labour leader, to Shanghai to organize an anti-foreign movement, there was no resistance. British and American returned students, who should have known better, bankers and merchants whose interests were being sacrificed, not only did not resist but assisted this movement. Money poured into the coffers of the Strike Committee from every part of the country. The strike fund was enormous. Chang Tso-lin, Ts'ao K'un, Tuan Ch'i-jui, the most reactionary and anti-Communist officials in the country, contributed. Marshal Feng Yu-hsiang, the redoubtable " Christian " General, actually delivered an address declaring war on Great Britain, which the British had sense enough to ignore. From May to October, every child in the land sang songs of hate against Great Britain. There was a concentration—a mass concentration—of enmity towards a Great Power which had never done a single thing in China worse than any other Power. It will take a generation to overcome the effects of the propaganda against Great Britain during 1925-6. It was the most perfect and complete attempt of one nation to destroy the influence of another without warfare in the whole of human history.' [1]

Such was the outcome of necessary use of force in discharge of the duty to maintain order. It is in strange contrast to the attitude towards the bombardment of Canton by Sun Yat-sen in 1922, no memory of which remains save in the hearts of the families of the defenceless victims.

A diplomatic commission which sat in Shanghai inclined to a somewhat defeatist line. It was saved by the grasp of the situation and determination of the British Consul-General, Sir Sidney Barton, who was later to be better but not more deservingly known to fame as British Minister in Abyssinia.

Of the ' Shanghai Incident,' however much it is to be deplored, Justice requires two further notes. The first is that although there is a preponderant British voice in foreign Municipal affairs in Shanghai, the Council is international and the then Chairman was an American. Secondly, the justification of the police action

---

[1] *China Year Book*, 1926, pp. 948, 954 and 952. This publication under the able Editorship of Mr. H. G. W. Woodhead, C.B.E., is much more than the ordinary book of reference. It contains very valuable historical data enabling contemporary events to be appreciated in their true perspective. The author takes this opportunity to make special acknowledgement of indebtedness to numerous issues of this work.

was subsequently upheld after an exhaustive judicial inquiry by an International Commission of Judges designated by the American, British and Japanese representatives in Peking, at the request of the diplomatic representatives of the American, Belgian, British, Danish, French, Italian, Japanese, Netherlands, Norwegian, Portuguese, Spanish and Swedish Governments. Independent opinions were given by the several members of the Commission.

The American member, Judge E. Ginley Johnson of Manila, stated his conclusion in the matter of the firing as follows :

' After reading and re-reading the evidence several times, including the exhibits, I am fully persuaded that with a much larger force of policemen on duty at the scene of the disturbances before 3.15 p.m. the necessity for the firing might have been avoided. I am equally persuaded that due to the absence of a larger number of policemen at 3.30 p.m. it was impossible.'

The report of the British member, Sir Henry Gollan, Chief Justice of Hongkong, on this issue was as follows :

' After full and careful consideration of all the evidence adduced by the witnesses, of their demeanour, and of the inherent probabilities of the respective stories told by them, I am clearly of opinion that the evidence given by the police witnesses, and supported by the large body of independent testimony, is substantially correct, and that Inspector Everson was justified in coming to the conclusion that, if the crowd had not been fired upon, the lives of the police under his command would have been sacrificed, and the crowd could have gained possession of the Louza Police Station with results that might have been most serious in view of the quantities of arms and ammunition stored there.

' And it is also to be remembered that a mob had in December 1905 seized and destroyed the Louza Police Station, in the face of strenuous opposition offered by a body of unarmed police.'

The Japanese member, Mr. K. Suga, stated :

' Inspector Everson's order to fire was justifiable, inasmuch as it may be considered to have been necessary in order to protect Louza Station and thereby avert serious danger to life and property.'

But from the point of view of the Kuomintang the opportunity was everything. Reason counted for nothing. Hongkong also was soon paralysed by strike and mass withdrawals of labour. The small foreign community at Canton was threatened to be overwhelmed by mob violence. Subsequently the little foreign settlements at Shameen, ' Face of Sand ' as the narrow strip of land on which they stand is known, were attacked and had to be defended by British and French Marines, resulting in fighting and loss of life. There was also much trouble elsewhere.

Thus Russia carried on her campaign for the destruction of the British Empire which had been decreed by the Third International. The grim picture of hate stood out in all its starkness. Englishmen paused in their daily task to wonder at this strange phenomenon. Were they really those predatory beings to whom compassion was such a stranger ? Surely not. Between China and Great Britain, who had not only ' done no worse thing ' than any other nation in China but for nearly a hundred years had been China's most understanding friend as well as perhaps the closest in cultural sympathy, seeds of terrible discord had been sown. Borodin had been in China barely eighteen months. It was little more than two years since Joffe had joined Sun Yat-sen in a declaration, which was understood to protect China from a dangerous political theory. But the bare pretence had been torn aside. The Communist designs of Russia were advanced to a point which caused unspeakable sufferings to hundreds of thousands of harmless people and created a situation from which China has taken ten years only partially to recover. ' We did not make May the thirtieth,' said Borodin in a speech at Canton, ' it was made for us.' [1]

[1] *The House of Exile*, by Nora Waln, p. 212.

Chapter 16

The Tariff Commission and the Commission on Extraterritoriality

1925-6

Such was the background of national sentiment against which the two commissions, constituted in pursuance of the decisions reached at the Washington Conference, sat in Peking. The pseudo-governmental position was scarcely less discouraging. In the North a new orientation of forces had taken place. Feng had allied himself secretly with General Sun Ch'uan-fang who controlled the Province of Chekiang. He had also made a pact with a certain General Kuo Sung-ling, Chang Tso-lin's chief of staff. Kuo Sung-ling was to revolt and march on Mukden simultaneously with an attack by General Sun on the Fengtien advanced positions on the Tientsin–Pukow railway and an attack by Feng himself on Chang Tso-lin's henchman at Tientsin.

The combination of events was sufficient to send General Chang back to Manchuria. Sun Ch'uan-fang's campaign resulted in his establishment in control of five provinces based on the Yangtze, including Kiangsu and consequently Shanghai. Feng made a successful advance on Tientsin which was taken from the Mukden Commander. But Kuo Sung-ling's revolt failed owing to the combination of an enveloping movement of cavalry and the moral effect on his supporters of the strict neutralization of the South Manchurian Railway which was equivalent to general Japanese support of Chang Tso-lin. Feng's position at Tientsin became untenable and he withdrew to Peking. In the spring of 1926 he decided to visit Moscow. His troops were then withdrawn from Peking in a north-westerly direction, into Mongolia, a *rapprochement* having by now taken place between the Fengtien War-lord and General Wu Pei-fu, who sank their differences in a common desire for revenge on Feng Yu-hsiang.

Meanwhile the Tariff Commission had opened at Peking on October 26, 1925. The Commission to report on Extra-territorial Jurisdiction was convened for December 12, 1925, but owing to nearly three weeks' interference with communications by the military operations it could not meet until January 1926.

The work of these Commissions had been delayed for over three years owing to a dispute between the French and Chinese Governments over what was known as the ' Gold Franc question.' The Protocol of 1901 had defined the relative values of the currencies in which payment of the Boxer Indemnity was to be made, but the Chinese proposed to pay the French share in francs of current value. Until the French interpretation of the Protocol was admitted, the French Government refused ratification of the Washington Treaties.

It is probable that had the Washington arrangements been implemented without undue delay not unsatisfactory results would have been achieved. As it was, when the Tariff Commission at last assembled it did so in an entirely different atmosphere to that which had prevailed at Washington. The situation contained two elements which, though not new, had developed out of all expectation during the intervening period. The first of these was the national movement, which owing to the Shanghai incident had attained such proportions amongst the students and other exponents of so-called public opinion, as not only to encourage China's representatives to make excessive demands but also to make it difficult for them to act in a spirit of moderation. In addition to this the Civil Government had lost all authority.

The Nine-Power Customs Tariff Treaty concluded at the Washington Conference, to give effect to which the Commission had been convened, opened with the words ' with a view to increasing the revenues of the Chinese Government,' and then proceeded to lay down how this was to be done. In the first place, the existing tariff was to be revised to an effective 5 per cent. Secondly steps were to be taken to provide for surtaxes over and above the revised 5 per cent import duty, the surtaxes in mind being those contemplated by the Mackay and other treaties made in 1902 and 1903 which have been already analysed.[1] But since these taxes were dependent on the abolition of likin, the Conference was to ' consider the interim provisions to be applied prior to the abolition of likin.'

Such a modest programme was almost laughable under the

[1] *Ante*, p. 31 et seq.

then conditions of the country. 'At the opening meeting,' to quote one observer, 'the Chinese bluntly asked for Tariff Autonomy within three years; for a surtax of 5 per cent on ordinary goods and 20 per cent and 30 per cent on luxuries; for collection of the surtaxes to begin within three months; and on their part offered no more than to abolish likin simultaneously with the attainment of tariff autonomy. These proposals went much beyond the Washington promises, to give effect to which the Conference had been convened, but the foreign delegations, being quite unprepared to act in concert, listened to them without comment.' It was speedily recognized that they would have to be accepted as the basis of discussion if a break-up of the Conference was to be avoided.

In the discussions which ensued on the question of Tariff Autonomy the Chinese Delegates maintained that it should be unconditional. The Foreign Delegates, on the other hand, felt that it should be made dependent upon the fulfilment by the Chinese of the obligations undertaken by them, the chief of which was the abolition of likin. A formula which was ultimately evolved provided for a declaration by the 'Government that likin should be abolished simultaneously with the enforcement of the Chinese National Tariff Law on January 1, 1929.'

From the Tariff Autonomy formula the Conference turned to the task of devising interim surcharges which would produce enough money to compensate the provinces for the loss of likin and other dues, to consolidate China's unsecured debts and to provide the Chinese Government with a sum for administrative expenses. But while various proposals were being discussed, political developments, giving rise in some cases to apprehensions for personal safety, eventuated in the retirement of the Chief Executive, Marshal Tuan Ch'i-jui, and the withdrawal from Peking of a majority of the Chinese representatives on the Conference. Without a government and with a Chinese Delegation reduced to impotence, no formal agreement could be reached. Nevertheless before the dissolution of the Conference an attempt was made to secure unanimity on the subject of the immediate imposition of the surtaxes proposed at Washington. But Japan was not willing to give her consent to any tariff increases which did not distinguish between the qualities of goods, fearing that her China market in cheap goods might be affected.

In December 1926, therefore, the British proposed to the signatories of the Washington Treaty the immediate grant of these surtaxes. In February 1927 they began to be levied by the Chinese authorities on their own initiative and British subjects were advised to pay them. Other treaty powers were non-committal but made no objections. Although the Tariff Conference had faded away without noticeable achievement Tariff Autonomy was only a matter of time. It was in fact established by various Treaties during 1928 and the new Tariff came into force as from February 1, 1929. But this is to anticipate by implication events which by that time had made it inevitable.

In the field of Extra-territorial Jurisdiction, the foreign members of the Commission, although actuated by sympathy for Chinese aspirations and representing powers anxious to be rid of a system which provoked hostility, could find no basis on which China could look forward to the restoration of her sovereignty within any definable distance of time. The Commission's Report recorded, *inter alia*, an absence of many important branches of law, that personnel was inadequate in training and experience, that the Administration of Justice was not independent, and that with few exceptions prisons fell far below western standards.

The conclusions of the Commission were not lacking in confirmation by current events and contemporary authority. At the time the Commission began its deliberations the President, Ts'ao K'un, had been held a prisoner without trial for over a year. While it was sitting some peculiarly horrible outrages in defiance of all law were perpetrated.[1]

As regards contemporary authority, T'ang Shao-yi, one of China's Elder Statesmen,[2] writing on the eve of the sitting of

---

[1] *Extraterritoriality in China : the Case against Abolition*, by H. G. W. Woodhead, C.B.E. This brochure, published by the Tientsin Press Limited, brought the matter down to 1929, when conditions from this point of view were considerably worse than when the commission sat.

[2] Mr. T'ang was one of the early students educated abroad and has been referred to in Chapter VII. He served under Yuan Shih-k'ai in Corea and Tientsin and held high office in Peking under the Manchus. He was Yuan's representative at the Shanghai Conference in 1911, when he surrendered to Republican sentiment. Subsequently he became Premier in Yuan's first Cabinet. Of later years he had been a man occupying a unique position to whom men of all parties paid respect if they did not defer to his views.

the Commission, expressed himself in the *North Daily News* in no uncertain terms.

' The sanctity of the law courts is an elementary condition to the development of good government. In China unfortunately a system has come into existence of certain individuals regarding themselves as superior to the courts. They not only cannot be subjected to judicial procedure, but they interfere with the operations of justice. They write letters to the judges making suggestions as to decisions. They insist upon the appointment of their henchmen as judges and order such judges to obey their dictates. They even hold courts of their own on the subterfuge that they are enforcing a martial law and throw men into prison without due process of law. . . .

' The judiciary has to be reorganized. Trained experienced judges have to be appointed. As suggested, the judges have to be made absolutely independent and the body of the law must be respected by all officials of the government. . . .

' It is important here to reiterate the point of view that in rewriting our codes, in remodelling our courts, in improving our prisons, our point of view should not be to satisfy any commissions appointed under the Washington Treaties, but to benefit the Chinese people. It is absurd, for instance, for the Ministry of Justice to ignore the Chinese people and their needs and then to rush mandates and telegraphic messages about the country ordering sudden and not well-planned improvements to impress these commissioners. What we need is a thoroughly considered plan which will give the Chinese people a judicial system and a law which shall protect them and their property. That cannot be done in a day and therefore no attempt should be made to accomplish it in a day. We can request the Washington Conference Commission to wait until we have satisfied ourselves that any criticism will be unjustified. As a matter of fact, no system can be suitable for the Chinese people which is not good enough for the foreigners living in China.'

A year later Dr. Hu Shih, Professor of Philosophy in the Chinese Government University at Peking and one of the foremost thinkers of China, addressed the ' Central Chinese Union of students in Great Britain ' on the subject of conditions in their country. The occasion was the annual dinner which took place in London in October 1926. Mr. Hu's speech, from which what follows is a short extract, was a fine example of intellectual independence.

' On this solemn occasion, the eve of the fifteenth anniversary of the Chinese Revolution, our thoughts naturally turn to the history of the last fifteen years ; and, in the face of the chaotic conditions now prevailing in our country, two questions inevitably arise in our minds ; has the Revolution of 1911 been a failure ; and, if so, wherein lies the cause of its failure ? We cannot better commemorate this historical anniversary than by answering these two questions squarely and honestly. There is no denying that the Revolution has been a failure in practically all its constructive phases. We have overthrown the Manchu Dynasty, but we have failed to establish a true republic. We have eliminated the old parasitic nobility, but we have not been able to produce great modern leaders to take their place. We have broken away from the old political order, but we have not succeeded in establishing a new one, nor have we been able to check and control the evil forces which have been set loose by the Revolution. In short, fifteen years have passed since the Revolution, and we have so far failed to make China a great modern state worthy of her potentialities.'

This impressive description of the ills of the China of barely ten years ago, clearly reflects the thought of a deeply penetrating mind disdaining to embark upon a defence of conditions which it recognizes are indefensible. Dr. Hu's explanation of these ills is inspired by the same profound sense of the seeker after truth.

' My answer is a simple one : The Chinese Revolution has failed to achieve its purpose because there never was a real revolution. There was a downfall of a dynasty, and there was a superficial change in the form of government, but there was no fundamental change in the ideas and thoughts of the people, which, and which alone, can be called a revolution. As a great nation with a glorious past, China has been too self-conceited to come to a real understanding of the modern world and its new civilization. We have never sincerely and whole-heartedly been willing to recognize the merits and spirit of civilization, and consequently have never earnestly prepared our young men to undertake this great task.'

Turning to a more material aspect of the situation, the resources of the country were being squandered and so-called government carried on in callous disregard of the sufferings of the people. In ten years the railways underwent the gravest deterioration. Not content with using trains and even detached locomotives to convey themselves from place to place, troops would use them as billets on the main lines or elsewhere. Locomotives were neglected, wagon floors used for firewood, rails removed and bridges destroyed. Indirect losses were still more serious. The Government Railways of China up to that time had cost only $629,000,000, say sixty to seventy million sterling, to build. The loss of commerce in one period of sixteen months in the year 1924–5 was estimated by Mr. J. E. Baker, an American statistician formerly attached to the Ministry of Communications, to have amounted to a sum sufficient to build another system of railways as big as the existing system. The debt remaining unpaid on the Government railways was then less than $370,000,000, say forty millions sterling. The loss of commerce in North China during these sixteen months was sufficient to have paid off this debt twice over with still enough to have completed the Canton–Hankow line.

This period was also notable for the immense increase of the growing of opium. At the time of the Revolution it had been practically eliminated. It was now grown not merely by acquiescence on the part of the authorities but even at the instigation of provincial governments owing to its revenue value.

The condition of the people had become indescribable. Dr. W. W. Yen, who in May 1926 had reluctantly felt himself impelled to accept the premiership of the ' Regency Cabinet ' which was formed when Tuan Ch'i-jui ceased to be Chief Executive, circularized the country by telegram analysing abuses and indicating the need of putting an end to the civil wars which had lasted for ' upwards of fifteen years, the blood of fighters staining the countryside, the crowds of people fleeing along the roads, the condition of the people pitiful, crying aloud for a way to be found to put an end to strife and save their lives.' Dr. Yen, who has since become well-known at Geneva, spoke with the authority of two civilizations. He is at once a graduate of the University of Virginia and has the degree of ' Chin Shih,' the highest degree, short of Fellowship, of the famous Hanlin

Academy obtainable in the Chinese Classical Examinations of former days.

The War Lords had reduced their country to the lowest ebb of judicial, legislative and administrative competence.

Chapter 17

Russian Ascendancy in Canton

In the South no more than in the North could be descried the signs of approaching dawn. The mortal sickness followed by the death of Sun Yat-sen had removed the last restraint on Borodin. There was no longer any pretence. In March 1925, the month in which Sun Yat-sen died, Canton's nearest considerable neighbour, the important Treaty Port of Swatow, fell to ' Bolshevism, Communism and anti-British propaganda in South China. A rag-tag-and-bobtail army from Canton salted with a small force of Russian-trained and Russian-officered cadets marched overland, drove out the mediæval baron then in occupation and Swatow forthwith became " Red," red flags, red emblems, hammer and sickle, all complete. From March until June, when the torch was lighted in Shanghai, the insidious work of secretly poisoning the Chinese mind went on actively. Labour organizations were formed, workers' and employees' guilds were persuaded to model themselves along Soviet lines and a host of other Soviet-Russian ideas were imported second-hand from Canton.' [1]

Space precludes any account of attacks on British persons and property, including assaults on the British Consul at Swatow,

[1] Memorandum No. 12 of the Tientsin British Committee of Information dated from Swatow August 28th, 1926, by Mr. John Robinson of the old-established firm of Bradley and Co. and the Rev. A. Guthrie Gamble of the English Presbyterian Mission.

on Christian missions of every nationality and creed, on western schools whose teachings necessarily were opposed to Bolshevism ; of the detail of strikes, boycotts and monstrous taxation ; of the Russian propaganda through the medium of the primary text-books in Chinese schools. But the efficacy of the methods employed can be gauged by the speed and extent to which Sovietization and Communism spread throughout the southern provinces.

These events but reflected the Russian ascendancy at Canton. The Chinese stage was held by men destined soon to be the nominal rulers and ten years later to approach real rulership of China.

Of those surrounding Sun Yat-sen the closest had been two Cantonese, Hu Han-min and Wang Ching-wei.

The former represented the more conservative or perhaps one should say the less violent or far-sweeping element in the Kuomintang. Like all members of the revolutionary society he and his followers, constituting the so-called right wing, were strong for political change. But he believed the welfare of the country would result without any violent social and economic upheaval. He was therefore anti-Communist. While studying in Japan he had become associated with Sun Yat-sen and was one of the founders of the T'ung Men Hui. From the time of the Revolution the two men had been in closest association. At the time of Dr. Sun's death Hu Han-min was about forty-one years of age. He held the position of Governor of Canton and Minister of Foreign Affairs.

Of Wang Ching-wei we have already heard. He was about the same age as Hu Han-min. But when the Revolution suffered set-backs at the hands of Yuan Shih-k'ai he decided that the opportunity was a good one to study in Europe. So he married one of the young revolutionaries who had joined him in the attempt on the life of the Prince Regent and went to France.[1] He was away from China about five years. He then returned to Canton. As we have seen, he accompanied Sun Yat-sen to Peking and was with him when he was taken ill and died. At this time he held the office of Chairman of the Kuomintang Central Executive Committee. He represented the radical element in the Kuomintang and was leader of the left wing.

[1] *Ante*, p. 54.

Although working closely with Borodin, it does not appear that he was ever a member of the Communist party or accepted the principle of Communism. He was a believer in social and economic revolution, but he was faithful to Sun Yat-sen's principles, of the spiritual value of which as a binding force he was fully aware. That he went far in the direction of Communism for political purposes cannot be denied, and there is evidence that at a later stage of his career when virtual oligarchy was established, the Communist and the extreme radical element in the party regarded him as the betrayer of the Revolution.

It may be noted here that these two men always remained, without any particular effort on their part and whether in office or out of office, the acknowledged leaders of the two broad lines of thought. Nationalist Governments were hardly ever without one of them, but in all these latter years they failed to combine in an attempt to secure their leader's ideal of unity in the Kuomintang in which was to reside sovereignty until the time came for it to be vested in the people.

By position in the party and in the Government Wang Ching-wei, who was Sun Yat-sen's favourite disciple, was his natural successor. But he forewent his claim, and on the advice of Borodin a government by committee somewhat on the Russian model was instituted.

The Government at Canton at the time of Sun Yat-sen's death also included a certain Liao Chung-kai as Finance Minister. In August 1925 Liao was assassinated. He was a strong Communist and his assassin was an anti-Communist. At this stage Chiang Kai-shek,[1] who was without position in the Government but was President of the Whampoa Military Academy, first appears prominently upon the scene.

A native of Chekiang Province, Chiang was born in 1886, receiving a military education at the Paotingfu military school and later on in Japan. In Japan he had become a member of the T'ung Men Hui. In 1911 he joined the Revolution and served in the campaign round about Nanking. When in 1917

[1] General Chiang's name provides an interesting illustration of the difficulty in the matter of Chinese names. In his native place it is pronounced Tsiang Chia-tsa. In the Cantonese dialect it is Chiang Kai-shek. In Mandarin it is pronounced Chiang Chieh-shih. The Cantonese variety by which he is best known is retained throughout this book.

Sun Yat-sen was established in Canton as Generalissimo, Chiang became his Chief of Staff. After the *entente* between Russia and Dr. Sun in 1923, General Chiang went to Russia to study the military system. On his return he became President of the Whampoa Military Academy, which was situated a few miles down the river from Canton. In this position he asserted a strong ascendancy over the minds of his students, an ascendancy destined soon to be extended throughout the Nationalist political field.

When Liao Chung-kai was assassinated the Whampoa cadets under Chiang Kai-shek, supported by the strike pickets which were controlled by Borodin, took charge in Canton. Hu Han-min, the leader of the right wing of the Kuomintang, was suspected of complicity and exiled to Moscow, ostensibly to study agrarian questions. Prominent anti-Communists fled from Canton. General Chiang, who was supposed to be a Communist in sentiment from his Russian associations, assumed the leadership of the Kuomintang, though still associated in the Government was Wang Ching-wei, the leader of the left wing.

T. V. Soong now made his first entrance into politics, becoming Finance Minister. Mr. Soong, whose father had been educated in America and was a close friend of Sun Yat-sen,[1] was born in 1891 in Shanghai. He received his early education at St. John's College, a missionary foundation under the presidency of the Rev. F. L. Hawks Pott. From Shanghai he went to Harvard and studied economics. After a period of training in a New York bank he returned to China. In 1924 he was appointed president of the Central Bank of Canton. One of his sisters was Sun Yat-sen's second wife. Another sister was married to Dr. H. H. Kung, a descendant of Confucius educated at Yale, who later on was to play a prominent rôle. A third gifted sister was destined to marry Chiang Kai-shek.

The position ultimately achieved by Chiang Kai-shek, the authority resulting to T. V. Soong by his financial measures, and the position of H. H. Kung in the party, earned for this brilliant family group in later years the name of the Soong Dynasty. In other days it might have become more than a derisive appellation. It is of interest that they profess the Christian faith.

[1] *Sun Yat-sen*, by Lyon Sherman, pp. 38, 76 and 178. This critical biography is strongly recommended to students of the growth of the revolutionary movement.

In the new regime Borodin was appointed High Political Adviser and exercised almost dictatorial powers. Although the anti-Communists embarked on civil war, the rising was easily quelled by the new army of Chiang Kai-shek, assisted by the general staff work of a Russian officer, General Galen. The peak of Russian influence was now reached. Canton approached perilously near the Soviet model.

Close observers were gravely alarmed. The hope built on the individualist spirit of the Chinese people and the institution of the family in China, which is necessarily opposed to the spirit of Communism, had been disappointed. Vast stretches of country between Canton and the Yangtze owned allegiance to the new idea. Under the exactions of the militarists since the Revolution the farmers and the country people had been reduced to the lowest state of poverty and despair. Nothing in the Manchu regime had approached the monstrous demands of their new masters. They were ready to grasp with eager hands the promises of anyone who seemed to speak with the voice of confidence and hope. Perhaps never was a more fertile soil for a sowing ; perhaps never was a more rapid and abundant harvest. But the people were to learn that life could hold still greater tragedy. ' The Communists,' wrote Wang Ching-wei in after years, ' have perpetrated in the bandit areas cruel outrages of which their comrades in Europe, America, Japan, or Russia, are utterly incapable.' [1]

In 1924 Sun Yat-sen had designed that the Kuomintang should absorb the Communist party. The Communist party had now gone near to absorbing the Kuomintang.

China was saved by the spirit of China working through one of China's sons. The Man of Destiny was Chiang Kai-shek. Borodin miscalculated the man, the Chinese characteristic to use a foreign instrument only so long as it serves its purpose, and Chinese pride of race.

In February 1926 Borodin went north to see Feng Yu-hsiang. For this there were many reasons. It was necessary to come to an understanding as to Feng's co-operation with the Nationalist

[1] *China's Problems and their Solution*, by Wang Ching-wei, p. 37. This book should be read if it is desired to appreciate the gravity of the Communist menace. The atrocities beggar description. See also *Chinese Destinies*, by Agnes Smedley.

advance northward, which although not definitely determined upon must inevitably take place soon. Russian policy also required an alternative base for Communism to meet the contingency of Chiang's defection. Finally Feng was toying with the idea of a visit to Moscow and this required to be encouraged. At this time, it will be recalled, acute differences of opinion between the northern militarists had caused Feng's withdrawal to the north-west of Peking.

It is not known when Chiang Kai-shek first realized that the political issue had become one between Communism and Nationalism. But with Russian control of a hundred thousand strikers, the chiefs of the Kuomintang were not strong enough to challenge the position. Borodin's departure for the North provided an opportunity for the Nationalists to make their stroke.

In March several arrests were made. A number of the Russian advisers were deported. The strike pickets, on which the Russians relied, were disarmed, and Hu Han-min, the leader of the right, was recalled from Moscow. At the same time it was made impossible for the leader of the left, Wang Ching-wei, to remain in Canton and he went abroad.

On May 4 news reached Canton that a force dispatched by Wu Pei-fu had taken Changsha, the capital of Hunan, and that General T'ang Sheng-chi, a supporter of the Kuomintang, had been driven south. Although Changsha is roughly 400 miles north of Canton, the occupation of the neighbouring province of Hunan by northern militarists blocking the northern march was a matter of vital concern. Marshal Wu, established in Central China, had been slowly recovering from the blow sustained as a result of Feng Yu-hsiang's treachery in 1924. He appreciated better than most the trend and force of developments in Canton. Unless he were to be given further time to organize anti-Kuomintang forces in Central China the expedition against the North could not longer be delayed.

A day or two later Borodin returned to Canton. He had formerly urged the delay of military operations, having a preference for preparing the ground still further by the process of honeycombing the defence. But in the altered circumstances he was compelled to acquiesce. Nevertheless Borodin managed to go far towards restoring his ascendancy. It has been publicly stated that he promised material help with supplies from Vladivostok on condition that Chiang Kai-shek's anti-Communist colleagues should be deprived of office. It would appear that General Chiang's military needs overpowered his sense of loyalty and he agreed. Hu Han-min again became an exile, taking refuge under the British flag at Hongkong.

Chapter 18

The Nationalist Advance to the Yangtze

1926

The expedition started in July. Like the Taipings three-quarters of a century before they marched north with songs on their lips. But the Hammer and the Sickle, not the Cross, were their inspiration. Their songs were not the songs of Christianity as the Taiping leader, the self-styled Heavenly Prince, crudely conceived it, but songs of the Third International and anti-Christian hate. Opposition faded before these troops with Russian staffs in the higher commands. By September, before the outside world had realized the march of events, Hankow and Hanyang, and a little later Wuchang, the scene of the beginning of the Revolution, were in Nationalist hands. About the same time Nanchang, the provincial capital of Kiangsi, and Kiukiang on the Yangtze, about two hundred miles below the Han cities, military headquarters of Sun Ch'uan-fang, who a year before had taken Shanghai and controlled five Provinces, had also fallen. But events of the first importance were to happen at Hankow before Chiang Kai-shek became engaged in the final struggle to drive the forces of the North across the Great River.

When Chiang Kai-shek made what was to prove but a temporary submission to the will of Borodin, Hu Han-min's place as Minister of Foreign Affairs in Canton was taken by one Eugene Ch'en.

Mr. Ch'en was born in 1878 in Trinidad, and he was therefore by birth a British subject. By profession he was a solicitor, having become qualified in London. After a period of practice in Trinidad he had come to China in 1912 and first came into notice for his writings, which caused his imprisonment by Yuan Shih-k'ai in 1916. He would have been shot doubtless but for the intervention of British friends and the influence of the British Minister. After that Eugene Ch'en went south to Canton, joined Sun Yat-sen's party in 1917, and was successively a member of a Cantonese Mission which went to America in 1918, personal assistant to the late C. C. Wu the representative of Canton at the Washington Conference in 1922, and thereafter adviser to the Canton Government until 1924, when he was appointed a member of the Central Executive Committee. Proceeding north with Sun Yat-sen on his last political mission, after Sun's death he stayed in Peking as Editor of a Chinese newspaper. In 1926 he was kidnapped by Mukden troops and again narrowly escaped execution. His present appointment was his first government post.[1]

Towards the end of the year with Madame Sun Yat-sen and others he had established at Wuchang what was claimed to be the Nationalist Government of China. It became known as the Wuhan Government from a combination of the names of the 'Three Cities,' Wuchang, Hanyang and Hankow. Although like Sun Yat-sen, Eugene Ch'en owed his life to the British, he showed as little gratitude. Without affection for the Empire from which he derived his infant nurture, unappreciative of the country whose institutions had given him education and professional status, he became the most active assistant to Borodin in his steps to destroy the British position in China.

As ever, Borodin's policy was to provoke the British in such a way that Chinese blood might be spilt and the whole of China inflamed. An attack was therefore planned against the British Concession at Hankow. By way of preliminary, mass meetings on a huge scale were organized at which Borodin and others made speeches denouncing the so-called 'unequal Treaties.'

At this stage the British Minister paid Hankow a visit. In the

[1] See the 'Who's Who' section of the *China Year Book* which is or should be available in every public library. This section is a mine of information concerning Chinese personalities.

autumn there had been a change in British diplomatic representation in China. The new Minister, Mr. (afterwards Sir Miles) Lampson, arrived in December. Landing at Shanghai, before proceeding to Peking he visited Hankow where he had an interview with Eugene Ch'en. If there were characteristics that stood out in the make-up of the new minister they were frankness and sincerity. A real sense of friendliness and good faith emanated from a presence which typified many of the English virtues. It cannot be doubted that he made clear the disinterested aims of the Government which he represented. What occurred after that was an acid test of the political honesty of Mr. Ch'en and the group which assumed to rule China from Wuchang.

But political honesty was not amongst their ideals. Borodin had reassumed the dictatorial power he had formerly exercised at Canton. The more moderate elements in the Kuomintang were treated as anti-Communist, as in fact they were, and driven out. The residue was bitterly anti-British, anti-Christian and Communist.

At another demonstration, which took place on December 20, and at which Borodin, Madame Sun and others spoke, a deliberate effort was made to work up anti-British feeling. Borodin stated that the revolution was only half through, and that the remaining and most important half was the overthrow of the British, and their alleged ally, Chang Tso-lin, together with the element amongst the Chinese who saw no sense in a bitterly anti-foreign attitude and in a phrase of the day were unjustly labelled ' running dogs of the Imperialists.' ' I have come,' he said, ' to give my assistance towards the accomplishment of this purpose.' Sun Fo, the son of Sun Yat-sen by his first marriage and a graduate of California and Columbia Universities, after sneering at the visit of the new British Minister coming to Hankow ' with sweet words, while his heart is sour,' urged ' a complete boycott of everything British.' [1]

Under the constant incitement of Borodin and other Communist agitators a tense and dangerous situation developed. The British Community appealed for more effective protection, but their request passed unheeded. Thus the opportunity was lost of sending such reinforcements as could have commanded the

[1] *China Year Book*, 1928, p. 1353, quoting the *North China Daily News*.

situation and would at least have removed all risk of massacre. Matters came to a head on January 3, 1927, when a large demonstration assembled on the boundary of the British Concession. The little strip of land, in area some eighty-four acres, with its magnificent bund along the banks of the Yangtze, an object lesson of what British administration and capacity can achieve, was to be overrun by a Communist mob. In harbour were three or four river gunboats and a destroyer. Marines, no doubt, would be landed and they and the volunteers would be compelled to fire on the mob. Thus would Borodin's plan be accomplished.

But Fate had ordained otherwise. On December 18, 1926, the British Government had sent a note to the Great Powers, outlining a new policy in China based on wide concession to Chinese aspirations. Moreover there was danger to the women and children in Hankow and to many foreigners in isolated places in the interior. But it was chiefly the consideration of policy that prevailed. When, therefore, on January 3, 1927, these troubles arose, no shot was fired. The British Concession was partly overrun by the mob. Acting under orders Englishmen with arms in their hands suffered indignities unparalleled in the history of our race. The Nationalist Government was requested to take over charge.

On January 27 a statement of ' Measures for Treaty Modification ' was communicated to the Chinese Authorities in Peking and to Eugene Ch'en at Hankow.

When communicating these proposals to Mr. Ch'en at Hankow the Councillor of the British Legation, Mr. O. St. C. O'Malley, prefaced them with the following paragraph :

' When a satisfactory settlement has been reached in respect to the British concessions at Hankow and Kiukiang, and when assurances have been given by the Nationalist Government that they will not countenance any alteration except by negotiation of the status of the British concessions and international settlements, His Majesty's Government will be prepared to concede at once and on the lines indicated in the enclosure hereto a part of what is desired of them by the Chinese Nationalist party. So liberal and generous a step cannot in their view be regarded otherwise than as an earnest of the fair and conciliatory spirit with which they are animated.'

The full proposals are set out in Appendix 3. Paragraph 6 which dealt with concessions was as follows :

> ' His Majesty's Government are prepared to discuss and enter into arrangements, according to the particular circumstances at each port concerned, for the modification of the municipal administrations of British concessions so as to bring them into line with the administrations of the special Chinese administrations set up in former concessions at Hankow or for their amalgamation with neighbouring concessions or former concessions now under Chinese control or for the transfer of police control of the concession areas to the Chinese authorities.'

Regulations accordingly were negotiated and on February 19, 1927, they were signed by Mr. O'Malley and Mr. Ch'en, establishing the British Concession as a Special Administrative District under a Chinese Administrator assisted by a Municipal Council with a Chinese majority.

Unfortunately the British gesture was not recognized either as the fine fruit of long and earnest deliberation or as a proof of moral strength. It was interpreted by the Chinese as a policy of surrender and a great triumph for the Wuhan Government. The flame spread from the Yangtze throughout the country and British subjects in the interior had to be called in to the Treaty Ports.

As one looked on the first result of the liberal policy of Great Britain it seemed almost that the Chinese were still a race, as Sir Harry Parkes once said, ' which yields everything to force and nothing to reason.'

Chapter 19

Chiang Kai-shek and Michael Borodin

1927

Nationalist arms having been established in the Province of Kiangsi, the elimination of Northern forces from Shanghai and Nanking was the next military objective. The issue was decided in February 1927 in the neighbourhood of Hangchow. Sun Ch'uan-fang's troops, demoralized by Communist propaganda, suffered defeat and he was compelled to evacuate Shanghai. Towards the end of March Nanking fell to Nationalist arms. But Chiang Kai-shek's victory was disfigured by what was known as the ' Nanking Outrage ' on March 24. The section of the victorious Nationalist troops which entered Nanking was definitely Communist. Whether inspired by Russian intrigue with the object of embarrassing Chiang Kai-shek, or by their commander's jealousy of the Generalissimo, these troops systematically looted Nanking, killing and committing various degrees of assault on foreign men and women. Ultimately the foreigners in Nanking were rescued under a protective barrage by H.M.S. *Emerald* and the United States Destroyers *Noa* and *Preston*.

The shocking details of the Nanking outrage cannot here be given, but the following extracts from a statement prepared by American Missionaries give perhaps a sufficient indication.

' Out of our own first hand experience and observation we unequivocally affirm that those outrages were committed by armed Nationalist soldiers in uniform, who acted with the knowledge and approval of their superior officers. Those outrages consisted not only in the looting of foreign homes, consular offices, schools, hospitals and places of business, but also in the burning of foreign homes and schools, in deliberate murder ; in twice shooting and wounding a young American woman ; in shooting at and attempting to kill foreign men, women and children ; in the attempted rape of American women, and in other shocking indignities to foreign women too indecent to be published.

' It is our conviction that the firing from the naval vessels prevented the murder of many foreigners who were caught in the city. It was immediately after the shelling was begun by the American and British ships that bugles were sounded and the soldiers ceased their systematic work of destruction, thus demonstrating that they were under the control of higher military officers. These are all incontrovertible facts.

' It now seems well established, in the opinion of both Chinese and foreigners, that those responsible for these outrages are of the Communist wing of the Nationalist Government which is dominated and directed by Russian Bolshevik advisers.' [1]

On the fall of Nanking Chiang Kai-shek, leaving the field to his subordinates, went to Shanghai, where he arrived without troops on March 26. The primary purpose of his visit was to frustrate a Communist manœuvre against the richest and most important city in China. The next and scarcely less important purpose was to consolidate his position by establishing a government in Nanking, which could only be based on the security and support of the great commercial capital of the country.

By this time foreign confidence had been restored by the arrival of battalions drawn from the Brigade of Guards, English county regiments, the United States Marine Corps and other foreign troops. Under their protection missionaries and other foreigners from the interior sought refuge in Shanghai. The stark realities of conditions were at last beginning to be appreciated. An important group of American missionaries added a further statement to that already issued by some of their colleagues. This second statement admitted that in the month of February a cablegram had been sent to the American Government and public urging conciliation and the prompt negotiation of new treaties on a basis of equality. ' In but little more than a month,' it continued, ' we had to depend on foreign force to save our lives. We have favoured the return of concessions to China, but to-day a foreign settlement is our only place of refuge. We have assured our people abroad that the Nationalist movement was not anti-Christian nor anti-foreign, but now we are driven

[1] See *China Year Book*, 1928, pp. 723–36, for copies of sworn statements, Mr. Austen Chamberlain's not very convincing statement in the House of Commons May 9, 1927, and the futile notes of the Wuhan Government. The failure of the Nanking Government when subsequently established to cashier General Chang Chien, who was immediately responsible, left an unhappy impression of its sincerity.

from our homes and dispossessed of our property. We who remained in Nanking on March 24 were not personally depending on extra-territorial privileges nor any other form of foreign protection, but were putting our trust in the assurances of the Nationalists. The events show that our faith was not justified.'

The Shanghai Defence Force made possible the salvation of Shanghai. Within the cordon which it established round the International Settlement and the French Concession much of the portable wealth of the richest part of China was stored. Here were the head offices of the great banks whose vaults contained accumulations of gold bars, silver bullion and dollars.

Chiang Kai-shek had yet to establish himself in foreign eyes. But the big Chinese Bankers and businessmen, better able to interpret ' the writing on the wall,' decided to support him as the white hope against the red ruin of Communism. Hu Hanmin, already known to us as the leader of the Right Wing of the Kuomintang and twice victim of the Russian Communist designs, with many of his supporters, was in Shanghai. They rallied to Chiang. The chief intellectual leaders also gave him their support. The students for once played a useful part, holding a great meeting when they declared themselves anti-Communist. Amongst the masses, the clan spirit of the big element of men from Ningpo, General Chiang's birthplace, swung feeling in his favour. Even Wang Ching-wei, who owed his exile to Chiang Kai-shek and had arrived from Paris by the Siberian railway *en route* to Wuchang, is said to have attended conferences at which critical decisions ignoring the Wuhan Government were made. Nor was he the only member of the Left Wing of the Kuomintang with the perspicacity to distinguish between the consequences for China from extreme radical views, for which they stood, and Russian Communism under the leadership of Michael Borodin.

It was a fight against time. The Communist agents had long been preparing for the demonstration which was to take place when the hour struck in Shanghai. But somehow or other the personality of Chiang Kai-shek and the common fear drew diverse elements into temporary union. Certain secret societies and the forces of the underworld, who had no more use for Communism than the legitimate vested interests, lent themselves to a ruthless campaign of extermination of Communists, including no doubt many innocent people, in Greater Shanghai.[1] As soon as a form of government had been established in Nanking, the slaughter of Communists over the ever-widening area controlled by that part of the Nationalist armies which served under Chiang Kai-shek continued. It was called the campaign for the purification of the party.

Meanwhile, earlier in the year, the differences of outlook between Chiang Kai-shek and Michael Borodin had resulted in a split in the Kuomintang over the question of capital. Borodin wanted it in Wuchang where the Communist element could control the Government. Chiang Kai-shek at that time insisted on Nanchang, the capital city of Kiangsi, where was situated the military headquarters. The issue was forced by General Chiang calling a meeting of the General Executive Committee of the Kuomintang at Nanchang for March 1. The Communist members from Hankow refused to attend and themselves called a meeting at Hankow, the purpose of which was summarized in the following terms :

' This session shall determine whether the individual is to belong to the party or the party to the individual. It is a question whether the minority is to submit to the majority or the majority to the minority. It will decide whether the military force is to rule the party or the party is to rule its military force. It will also decide whether we will have a system of individual dictatorship or a system of democratic centralization. In short, the question involves not only the fate of our party but also the destiny of the country.' [2]

The meeting, which met in the middle of March, constituted a direct challenge to Chiang Kai-shek. Strengthened by his successes over the northern troops and by the support of Shanghai he accepted it, insisting on an immediate break with Communists. For the moment the Kuomintang, in the form in which it had been reorganized by Sun Yat-sen, lay in fragments. Two so-

---

[1] In recent years Shanghai and its environs outside the International Settlement and the French Concession had been established as a Municipality called Greater Shanghai. Under the able and enlightened administration of the late V. K. Ting a sound administrative start was made with the scheme and some remarkable results have been achieved. Dr. Ting was a graduate of Glasgow University.

[2] *The Kuomintang and the Future of the Chinese Revolution*, by T. C. Woo, p. 227.

called governments struggled for the right to collect the broken pieces and to make of them again an organ of Revolution.

On which side would the scale come down? The Wuhan Government, now in substance Communist, had achieved a success over the British at Hankow. It had been recognized at least to the extent of negotiation with a diplomatic representative of His Majesty's Government. Its forces were making a demonstration northward along the Peking–Hankow railway. It had the support of General T'ang Sheng-chi, whose expulsion from Changsha by the troops of Wu Pei-fu in the previous year had been the signal for the Canton decision to embark on the northern expedition. Communication had been opened with Feng Yu-hsiang, who a few months before had returned from Moscow and had almost imperceptibly moved his troops down from the north-west to a strategic position south of the Yellow River. The ' Christian General ' had gone further and declared himself on the side of the Nationalists. This had been before the split in the ranks of the Kuomintang, and Borodin had reason to suppose that his support would be given to the Communist-inspired Left Wing. As was shortly to be revealed, the Soviet Government held Marshal [1] Feng's acknowledgement of indebtedness in a sum in excess of six million gold roubles for war material already supplied, and his indent during the previous year, on the occasion of his visit to Moscow, for a further four and half million gold roubles' worth of war material.[2]

The situation of the Government at Nanking seemed much more precarious despite the financial backing of the Shanghai Bankers. Although the troops of the northern militarists had been driven over the Yangtze, they were still on the north bank opposite Nanking and Chinkiang preparing to recover the lost ground. The seat of government was frequently under shell-fire.

The difficulty seemed insoluble. Yet a solution had to be found before the next phase of the revolutionary struggle, the march on Peking, could be undertaken. It came in an entirely unexpected way through action by the Government in Peking which thereby hastened its own downfall.

[1] The rank of Marshal was held by most of the Northern leaders, though it was sometimes difficult to determine the authority which had made the promotion.

[2] See Appendix 4 for these documents.

Chang Tso-lin had long known or at least suspected that the Soviet Embassy was being used as a basis for Communist activity. Negotiations were therefore set on foot with the Diplomatic Body, which did not include the representative of the Soviet Government still unrecognized by the majority of the Treaty Powers, to secure authority for Chinese police to enter the Diplomatic Quarter and to raid the Soviet Embassy. The raid took place on April 6, 1927, with astonishing results.

Li Ta-chao, the head of the Chinese Communist party, and several other Russian and Chinese Communists, were found on the premises. Masses of documents were brought to light which proved the full extent of the Soviet aims in China.

The substance of one of the documents proving the relations between Marshal Feng and Moscow has already been referred to. Other documents showed the contempt of the Russians in Canton for their Chinese colleagues. ' Chinese Generals and officers,' said one report, ' are not only completely ignorant as regards the art of war but also most unbalanced in all other respects. Even their common routine work can yield desirable results only with Russian advisers. The popularity of Russian advisers is so great that their enormous political, military and moral influence on any general or officer in the ranks of the National Revolutionary Army is beyond doubt.' Again an instruction from Moscow to the Soviet Military Attaché in Peking gave orders to exploit the success against the British at Hankow as an illustration of the weakness of the Foreign Powers. The same instruction urged the creation of incidents to involve the Foreign Powers. As it was inadvisable to fall foul of Japan, and the application of this policy to all other powers might arouse suspicion, the British were to be made the target whenever opportunity offered. Finally it said that instructions had been sent to Borodin to keep the Communistic programme in the background for the time being and to direct all action as action by the Kuomintang. The historical value of this document is great for the light it throws on the course of events since the institution of the Borodin regime.[1] Another document records Communist success in Shanghai and steps taken to deal with all opposition. ' The campaign of the Red Terror,' it reports, ' has been success-

[1] See Appendix 5 where the fragment of this document, which suffered by fire, is set out.

fully carried out in Shanghai. More than 10 strike-breakers, provokers, and people who opposed the workers at the factories, were killed. This campaign had a sobering effect on the above-mentioned people. Many were forced to flee or change their tactics.'

The cumulative effect of the evidence was to show that China was gradually being drawn into the grip of Russian Communism. Nevertheless the Left Wing of the Kuomintang took no immediate steps. But they were seriously alarmed. Their alarm was accentuated a little later by another event. It had been agreed that Borodin should produce for the information of his colleagues all suggestions received from Moscow. About this time he received an instruction which he suppressed. In view of what are said to have been the terms of the instruction he could not well do otherwise, since it involved the complete elimination of the Kuomintang, the establishment at Hankow of a purely Communist Government and the organization of a Communist Army.

On this matter coming to the notice of the Kuomintang members at Wuhan they communicated for help and advice with Feng Yu-hsiang who after consultation with Chiang Kai-shek, rendered possible by the circumstances related in the next chapter, telegraphed on June 20 that the Russians must go. A day or two later Borodin and his assistants left by the only way open to them, overland through the north-west territory controlled by Marshal Feng.

Thus ended the formal Russian connection with the Nationalist party, and for the second time in the century Russian design was frustrated. It had come perilously near success. The Slav temperament may ' dream dreams and see visions,' but political Russia has always had a grip on realities. Borodin created something like order from what was largely ' without form and void.' His work rendered possible the Nationalist success, but he left behind a legacy of trouble and suffering for the people of China far outweighing the value of his service to the Nationalist cause.

Chapter 20

The Nationalist Advance on Peking

1928

While these important political events were taking place the northern advance of the Nationalists had not been stayed. It remained their ambition to end the 1927 campaign in Peking. Hitherto Chang Tso-lin, rapidly approaching the zenith of his power, had not taken the Nationalist military effort seriously. So-called 'punitive expeditions' had been launched from the South before and had faded away. But the political success of Wuhan and the military successes of General Chiang in the provinces of Chekiang and Kiangsu could no longer be ignored. While Sun Ch'uan-fang and Chang Tsung-ch'ang, the military governor of Shantung who had come to the support of the northern position, were left to deal with Chiang Kai-shek either by encompassing the destruction of his forces or at least containing them, Marshal Chang dispatched a force in March down the Peking–Hankow railway to eliminate the Nationalist combination at Wuhan. The advance was met in April about 100 miles north of Hankow, in the neighbourhood of Chengchow, by the grass-sandal-shod and barefoot troops of T'ang Sheng-chi, supported on their left by the troops of Marshal Feng Yu-hsiang, who had been appointed second-in-command of the Nationalist Armies. The northerners after strenuous fighting were defeated and fell back on Peking. Their position was further imperilled on June 5, when Marshal Yen Hsi-shan, Governor of Shansi, declared himself as a supporter of the Kuomintang.

As it happens he was one of its early members. But the tide of the Revolution had swept him into the governorship of a province and he decided as a young man of thirty-six to stay there. Shansi became known as the 'Model Province.' It developed and became prosperous. If, as has been stated, the Governor acquired a fortune of eighty million Chinese dollars in less than twenty years, the Chinese under his rule made no complaint. They saw the armies of rival militarists in their marches and counter-marches ravaging their neighbours and heard echoes of the struggles of war-lords in every other province

in China. The blessings of strong rule stood out in bright contrast to the miseries throughout the rest of the country. The
possibilities of China under peaceful conditions, even in a province of no great wealth and far from the seaboard, were clearly
demonstrated.

Whether from deep-rooted principle aroused to life after lying
dormant for many years, or from a desire to play a part in the
establishment of the new order which seemed imminent, Yen
Hsi-shan called upon Marshal Chang Tso-lin to subscribe to
' The Three Principles ' of Sun Yat-sen. At the same time he
moved his troops to Shihchiachuang on the Peking–Hankow
railway roughly 150 miles south-west of Peking. In consequence
the Nationalist troops were prevented from exploiting their
victory. In any case this might have presented difficulty at least
so far as General T'ang was concerned. Wuchang was threatened
from the rear by troops moving to the support of the Communist
element in the Wuhan Government, and although suspected
of Communist leanings he could not risk being absent from
headquarters in such a crisis.

Marshal Chang did not accept the invitation to embrace ' The
Three Principles.' His reply was to declare himself Dictator
and assume the chief control. A war ensued which was known
as the Shansi-Fengtien War. There was a good deal of fighting
and movement of troops over a wide area and it was one of
the few interesting campaigns from a military point of view.
The result was indecisive, but it prevented Chang Tso-lin from
reinforcing the northern troops threatening Nanking, a threat
which might have become important if seriously pressed. Thus
history seemed to repeat itself. The loss of Nanking to the
Revolutionaries through lack of Imperial support in 1911 had
been a turning-point. Perhaps in 1927 an opportunity too was
lost by the northern side. So far from being annihilated or
contained by the available northern forces, Chiang Kai-shek drove
northward in late May and shortly occupied Hsuchoufu.

The capture of Hsuchoufu put the lateral communications
between the two Nationalist expeditions under their control, a
fact of which Feng Yu-hsiang took advantage to go to Hsuchoufu
for a conference with Chiang Kai-shek on June 20. It seems
to have been the first time the two men met. The result was
encouraging. Apart from his professions of Christianity soon

to be discarded, Feng Yu-hsiang seemed to have found at last his spiritual home. An agreement was made for co-operation. It was at this point that Marshal Feng telegraphed to Hankow supporting the Kuomintang view that all Communists must be eliminated from the Government.

As the Wuhan–Feng Yu-hsiang forces had been prevented from advancing on Peking, so Chiang Kai-shek's further advance was stayed by not dissimilar causes. The Japanese Government professing not unreasonably to be alarmed lest there be a repetition at Tsinanfu, the capital of Shantung, of the outrage at Nanking, had thrown troops into Shantung to guard the Tsingtao–Tsinanfu railway and Tsinanfu, where foreign residence had long been permitted and where there were said to be some 4,000 Japanese. Critics averred that the Japanese were alarmed by the rapidity of the Nationalist advance and aimed to save Chang Tso-lin from annihilation.[1] General Chiang was also threatened in his rear by a concentration of the notorious Ch'eng Chien's Communist troops, the perpetrators of the outrage at Nanking, co-operating with a militarist from Kwangsi who now came into prominence called Chang Fa-kwei and his so-called ' Ironsides.' In the circumstances Chiang Kai-shek had no alternative but to fall back on Nanking whither he was followed by the northern troops who reoccupied Pukow and the north bank opposite Chinkiang. Once more Marshal Sun made an abortive attempt to recover Shanghai.

The necessary introduction of the forces occupying the stage at this critical period, coupled with this brief account of their military activities, may at first sight seem confusing. A glance at the map of China, however, should make the position clear. The situation may be visualized by picturing a gigantic letter A made by the Peking–Pukow and Peking–Hankow railways. At the apex is Peking. At the base of the left stroke are Wuchang, Hankow and Hanyang and at the base of the right stroke is Nanking. The cross stroke is made by the Lunghai railway which thereby creates two nodal points at Hsuchoufu, beyond which Chiang Kai-shek had been able to advance but from which he had now fallen back, and Chengchow on the Peking–Hankow railway which was now Feng Yu-hsiang's headquarters.

[1] The liberal government of Baron Shidehara had been superseded recently by a chauvinistic government led by General Baron Tanaka

With cessation of major military operations so far as the Nationalists were concerned we have time to turn to the political situation.

On the departure of Borodin the members of the Left Wing of the Kuomintang, led by Wang Ching-wei, were prepared to make peace with Nanking, but they demanded the retirement of Chiang Kai-shek. Feng Yu-hsiang urged conference between Wuhan and Nanking, but Wuhan stood firm for General Chiang's resignation on the ground that he had broken the rules of the party and had not submitted to the orders of the Military Council. It was made a point of discipline. On August 12 Chiang Kai-shek resigned, issuing a long manifesto in which he explained the course of events and concluded in terms which made it practicable for him to return and for the party to recall him when his services should be required. By the end of the year he had been invited to resume office and was in command of the Nationalist Armies as Generalissimo. In the meantime he had embraced Christianity and married Miss Mei-ling Soong. Important decisions were made at this time at a plenary session of the Kuomintang. In particular it was laid down that the Commander-in-Chief might be appointed concurrently Chairman of the Military Council, a device to harmonize the theory of subjection to the Military Council with complete independence of command, which regularized Chiang Kai-shek's position.

In March 1928 the outstanding matter of the Nanking Outrage was settled diplomatically. All was now set for the advance on Peking for which some preparation had already been made. While politicians were busy with the adjustment of their differences, Marshal Feng had performed useful service occupying the attention of the northern troops on the Pukow railway. Pushing across from Chengchow on the Peking–Hankow railway, where his position was covered by the operations of Yen Hsi-shan farther north, on December 17 he captured Hsuchoufu in the Nationalist cause. There he remained until Chiang Kai-shek was in a position to arrange to take over the position in the spring of 1928. The apparent intentions of the Christian General had been deceptive on more than one occasion in the past and Nanking could not risk a threat from forces under a commander who until recently had been strongly entrenched in the northern arena and was also in Moscow's debt in the sum of ten million gold roubles for the supply of arms. Apart from this his troops were needed elsewhere.

The Nationalist offensive opened at the beginning of April 1928. The plan of campaign involved a movement on Peking from three directions. Marshal Feng was to attack along the Peking–Hankow railway. Marshal Yen was to advance from the north-west. General Chiang, amongst whose chief commanders were Li Tsung-jen and Pai Chung-hsi of the south-western province of Kwangsi, who were to be heard of more than once again, would move up the Tientsin–Pukow railway.

Everywhere the military operation was successful, although Chiang Kai-shek's advance was checked at Tsinanfu once more, owing to Japanese occupation. An unfortunate conflict arose which resulted in Japanese and Chinese casualties. The Chinese troops were forced to retire, but certain units were ultimately allowed to pass in order that General Chiang might reach Peking.

At the beginning of June Chang Tso-lin, recognizing the inevitableness of defeat, withdrew his troops to Mukden. He himself left Peking on June 3. But he was only destined to reach the Manchurian capital, where for fifteen years he had exercised despotic sway, a dying man. As his train approached the city a bomb exploded causing the old Marshal mortal injuries. Whether this was attributable to a Nationalist conspiracy, a Communist revenge, a Japanese political design or some other cause, has never been determined.[1] But it was a momentous happening. With the death of Chang Tso-lin the last strong man of the old regime, a man who gifted with more vision might perhaps a few years before have gone far in the direction of the unification of China, who had he lived would have influenced the course of history in Manchuria, passed for ever from the scene.

A few days later Marshal Yen occupied Peking ahead of the other two commanders, and North China became a huge armed camp. The foreign garrisons at Tientsin had already been reinforced. All foreigners in the interior had been called in, just as foreigners in central and southern China had been concentrated in Shanghai and Hongkong. The greatest uncertainty of

---

[1] Suspicions in Japan are said to have been in part responsible for the downfall of the Tanaka ministry. See *The Problem of the Far East*, by Sobei Mogi and H. Vere Redman, p. 302.

outlook prevailed. But the commercial capital of North China, with its traditions of its siege by the Boxers in 1900 and inured to threats of being overwhelmed in surging tides of civil war, remained calm. Loyal and liberal at heart the British element in the community was determined to resist by every means within its power anything in the nature of the humiliating surrender which had taken place at Hankow.

Fortunately the worst does not often happen. The Nationalist occupation of North China was accomplished without untoward incident.

In July a memorial service was held for Sun Yat-sen at Pi Yun Ssu, the 'Temple of Azure Cloud,' a Buddhist Temple in the Western Hills, where his remains lay pending burial in Nanking. In the same way as Sun Yat-sen had made his formal communication to the Shades of the first Ming Emperor of the release of China from the alien domination, so his Shades were placated by the news that the first stage of Revolution had been accomplished. The second stage, the period of 'Political Tutelage,' was now at hand, when education of the people in their political duties would be embarked upon.

The impressive ceremonial accorded deeply with the sentiment of an ancestor-worshipping people. But the hollow nature of the pretence that all would now be well must have been borne in upon Chiang Kai-shek as he stood at the salute in the moment of profound silence in the course of a nation's tribute. An account of major events aiming to secure broad historical perspective and necessarily shorn of much detail, can but reflect faintly the atmosphere of sordid intrigue and bitter jealousy and the ramifications on the surface and beneath the surface of Chinese politics. At this great moment in his country's destinies the Man of the Hour stood virtually alone. He saw on every side the evidences of militarism, which on slight provocation would be turned against him. Wherever he looked upon the political horizon, were there any of whom he could say with certainty, 'in this one and that I can place my trust'? There was his *fidus Achates* in the political world, Chang Chin-chiang, a sort of Colonel House perhaps, a civilian ten years his senior. Friend and supporter of Sun Yat-sen, Chang Chin-chiang had seen in Chiang Kai-shek a coming man and for years had supported him to the extent of his private fortune. Presumably his brothers-in-law, T. V. Soong and H. H. Kung, were amongst the number. There were a few intellectuals who at least would not betray him. But where were the chosen disciples of the dead leader ? Where was his only son ? Where were the other acknowledged chiefs of the Kuomintang ? Most of them were either in opposition or travelling in foreign lands.

If the politicians in China are sometimes charged with selfishness and self-seeking, if they are thought to be not consistently big enough for great gestures of loyalty and the sacrifice of self, surely they have only themselves to blame. To many of them, no doubt, the dominating personality and the methods of Chiang Kai-shek were distasteful. He was something new in public life, and indeed a contradiction of the slow-moving punctilious racial temperament, a man who thought rapidly, who wasted no time in philosophic doubt but went straight for achievement and risked failure. A man, not too patient of opposition, like most soldiers impatient of civilian control. And withal an astute politician. But still the needs of the Country called.

At the end of the ceremony of Pi Yun Ssu a military conference took place in that vale of peace where the beautiful temple is set in the rugged grandeur of the Western Hills. Appropriately enough it talked of disbandment. And such was the personality of Chiang Kai-shek that general agreement was obtained. Unhappily it was to be ' more honoured in the breach than the observance.'

Chapter 21

The Machine of Government

The victory of the Nationalist forces, implying theoretical union of the Country, called for the reorganization of the Government at Nanking on broad coalitionist lines. Hu Han-min and Sun Fo cabled from Paris expressing the view that the time had now arrived when Sun Yat-sen's Five-Power System of Government should be adopted. In due course this was agreed to. The machine of Government was brought into being by means of an instrument promulgated by the Kuomintang generally known as the Organic Law of 1928, an introductory note to which summarized the position claimed to have been reached and the objects which it was sought to attain. This note was as follows :

> 'The Kuomintang of China, in order to establish the Republic of China on the basis of the Three Principles of the People and the Constitution of Five Powers, which form the underlying principle of the Revolution, having conquered all opposition by military force and having now brought the Revolution from the military stage to the educative stage, deem it necessary to construct a framework for the Constitution of Five Powers with a view to developing the ability of the people to exercise political power, so that constitutional Government may soon come into existence and political power be restored to the people. In virtue therefore of the responsibilities hitherto entrusted to the Party for the guidance and supervision of the Government, it hereby ordains and promulgates the following Organic Law of the National Government.'

The principle of the Constitution devised by Sun Yat-sen which was thus enacted was the division of the functions of government into five powers each independent of the others, with effective powers of ultimate sovereignty vested in the people. But electioneering and parliamentary experiments in the past had not been successful. The people had to travel far before the suffrage could be intelligently exercised. 'The Master of the Revolution,' Sun Yat-sen had written in terms of vague idealism, ' is a new-born child. The Kuomintang who has brought it into the world must nourish and educate it during its

137

minority. Like a child at school China must learn Democracy and she needs a far-sighted revolutionary government as a child needs good instructors.'[1]

Sun Yat-sen's inspiration seems to have been derived from the theory of Constitutional Government developed by French writers of the eighteenth century, who based themselves on their conception of the English Constitution. This they supposed to consist of three powers, namely the Legislative, the Judicial and the Executive, which were separate and independent of each other. On this theory largely is based in France the ' Droit Administratif,' which operates, at the discretion of an administrative tribunal, to withdraw official acts from review by the ordinary courts. But although under English Law the independence of judges is assured, there is no recognition of the separation of the judicial and executive powers as these writers inferred. ' The Common Law Courts have constantly hampered the action of the executive, and by issuing the writ of Habeas Corpus as well as by other means, do in fact exert a strict supervision over the proceedings of the Crown and its servants.'[2]

Under the Manchus officials were of course above the law as administered by the ordinary Courts. But it is matter for surprise that Sun Yat-sen, whose life had been spent brooding over the wrongs perpetrated by autocracy, should have perpetuated a system so dangerous to the persons and property of private citizens. Unfortunately it has proved a far greater abuse than ever it did in Manchu times.

To the Legislative, Judicial and Executive powers, Sun Yat-sen added two further powers borrowed from the Manchu regime. One of these was an Examination Board or Yuan, as these departments of governments were called, whose function was to control the qualifying tests of candidates for government office. The other was the Control Yuan, which in principle exercised the power of impeachment formerly vested in the Censorate, and also had extensive rights of audit.

Under the Executive Yuan came the various ministries, from

---

[1] *Les Cinq Pouvoirs*, by Tch'en Hiong-fei, Docteur en droit, quoting from *The Theories of Sun Yat-sen*, p. 178. Dr. Tch'en's monograph, published in France by the Librairie du Recueil Sirey, 22 Rue Soufflot, Paris Ve, will be found of interest by those wishing to make a more detailed study.

[2] *The Law of the Constitution*, by A. V. Dicey, K.C., p. 327.

one of which, the Ministry of the Interior, Provincial and Local Governments were to derive authority.

Dr. Sun illustrated the ultimate operation of his government machine by the following diagram :

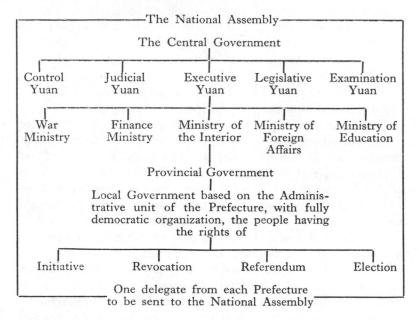

If this be studied it will be noticed that between the National Assembly and the Five Yuan is an organ called the Central Government. In the Organic Law of 1928 this was called the National Government, in which were concentrated all the powers of government, supreme command of the forces, power to declare war, the treaty-making power, and powers of amnesty, pardon, reduction of punishments and restoration of civil rights.

The National Government was to consist of a president and twelve to sixteen members, including the presidents and the vice-presidents of the Five Yuan. It was to exercise its powers through the medium of a State Council. And since the State Council was to be composed of the members of the National Government, it became in fact the National Government. A particular attribute of the State Council besides the powers already enumerated was to determine any differences arising between the various Yuan.

At first sight the State Council might appear to correspond to a Cabinet and no doubt it has some of its features. In practice, however, the functions of the Executive Yuan have approximated more nearly to those of a Cabinet, since it is in direct control of the Executive Departments of State. It remains to add that the President of the Council of State acts as the Chief Executive until such time as a President of the Republic of China is elected. The President of the Executive Yuan is substantially the Premier.

We now have to see how the Kuomintang discharges the trust reposed in it during the period of political tutelage.

In the first place for the National Assembly is substituted the Congress of the Kuomintang. In addition we have to insert between the Congress of the Kuomintang and the National Government, that is to say the State Council, two committees of the Kuomintang. These are the Central Executive and the Central Supervisory Committees which are combined for government purposes under the name of the Central Political Council.

This Council has wide and important powers. It discusses and determines such things as programmes of reconstruction, constitutional questions, questions of policy, and military affairs. It appoints all high officials from members of the Council of State, ambassadors and the presidents and vice-presidents of the Five Yuan, down to members and presidents of provincial governments and mayors of special municipalities.

' It is consequently from this political council, which may be called perhaps a court of peers of the Kuomintang party, that the National Government derives its being. Representative organ of the party, it is the point of departure for the working of all government services.' [1]

In brief the Kuomintang in determining its functions sought to retain control and to reserve to itself dictatorial powers.

In his final words summarizing the virtues of the constitution which he had devised and commending it to the Nation, Sun Yat-sen expressed himself in these words :

' After the separation of the five powers in the Constitution, the most important element is local government. There direct democracy, which is true democracy, must apply. That involves four rights in the people, that is to say, the

[1] *Les Cinq Pouvoirs*, above, p. 100.

right of election, the right of revocation, the right of initiative and the right of referendum. The five powers constitute a great machine of government of which the four civic rights are like a starting apparatus which controls it. The people, who have the right of election or voting, can remove an official whom they have elected. By the right of initiative they can initiate laws based on public opinion. They can also annul any law voted by the Legislative Assembly if they find it inconvenient, and if a good law proposed to the Legislative Assembly is not passed, the people can approve its adoption : this is the referendum.'

Such in brief outline was Sun Yat-sen's machine of Government and such the authority which brought it into being. It remains in principle the same to-day although modified in some directions and expanded in others, resulting in a machine the operation of which is too complicated to describe in any reasonable space.

' The wit of man,' wrote Mr. Lionel Curtis, a sympathetic observer, ' has seldom devised a more effective mechanism for fomenting intrigue, hampering decisions and obscuring responsibility.' [1] Reflecting in its detail of checks and balances the distrust of its framers for their fellow politicians, it is difficult not to agree. Moreover governments, like laws, depend for their success on being within the understanding of the people and at least in sight of former experience. But the Five-Power theory of government satisfied neither of these requirements. It is true that the system of civil service examinations, carried a stage further in theory so as to include inquiry into the qualifications of politicians aspiring to high office, was familiar. Again the long and honourable history of the Censorate in China, with its records of courageous men denouncing officials in high places and not failing to draw even the Emperor's attention to his own shortcomings, was well known and appreciated amongst the people. But the separation and even the definition of Legislative, Judicial and Executive functions was outside the realm of thought of the ' stupid people ' now to be endowed with the ' rights of man.' They had their simple code of right and wrong. In Manchu times it was known perhaps in general that in the early years of the Dynasty a code had been enacted, which was not too difficult because, like all early essays in legislation by

[1] *The Capital Question of China*, by Lionel Curtis, p. 185.

societies retaining some of the more primitive elements, it has an almost exclusively criminal basis. The Emperor from time to time issued Edicts the effect of which would be expounded by the village scholar or talked about in the tea-houses. The people were also conscious of certain elementary rights and obligations sanctioned by Custom. But save for these their horizon was bounded by the local official. In the Manchu hierarchy individuals wielded authority and power, mankind in the mass obeyed. So it has been going backward through the ages to the dawn of Chinese history. Government was an extension of the family. China, even so short a time ago as thirty years, was in fact the one untouched instance of the patriarchal system still extant. Although a broad democracy existed under the officials through guilds and village councils in relation to community affairs, based on the co-operative spirit in the non-political things of life and the advantage and cheapness to the Government of allowing the less important local affairs to be thus dealt with, the real ruler nearest to the people was the policeman under the district Magistrate, ' the father and mother of the people.'

But Sun Yat-sen would have none of this. ' Mencius,' he wrote, ' has said " there are two divisions of people : those who work with their intelligence and govern and those who work with their hands and are governed." Formerly our people were like children and allowed themselves to be ruled by others. To-day they are grown up and are awakened. The class difference between rulers and governed has been abolished. In Europe also they have driven out the Kings and liberty has been won by the people. Our constitution of five powers is consecrated to the same destruction of class distinctions and envisages a system of true democracy.'

And so the last vestiges of the old system were swept away. It was the evidence of the Revolution. Yuan Shih-k'ai began by retaining and ruling in general through the old channels which were understood by the people. But the militarists who followed him and the revolutionary theorists, without experience of the art of government and without appreciation of the important element in political affairs of the Spirit of the People, between them broke up the institutions which had stood the test of centuries of time. They shut their eyes to essential facts. In those days they refused to recognize that more than 80 per cent of the population were agriculturalists and more than 95 per cent wholly illiterate. How could such a population be brought to appreciation of the elaborate machine of government in which they were to be the ultimate repository of sovereignty and power? As one surveys the scene it is difficult not to accept the dictum of M. Taine that ' to replace old forms in which lived a great nation by different forms, both suitable and lasting, is a prodigious enterprise probably beyond the human spirit.'[1]

Chapter 22

First Years of the National Government at Nanking

1928–30

The first National Government, as distinguished from former Nationalist Governments, was formed at Nanking on October 10, 1928. It was a ministry of ' All the Talents ' except for the absence of Wang Ching-wei. Chiang Kai-shek became Chairman of the State Council and the Head of the Government. The key-men Hu Han-min, Sun Fo, Marshal Feng Yu-hsiang, General Yen Hsi-shan, T. V. Soong, and H. H. Kung held high office. Wang Ch'ung-hui became President of the Judicial Yuan. C. T. Wang was appointed Minister of Foreign Affairs.

At the risk of some reiteration it is of interest to recall that in the development of all but one of these men foreign Universities and Colleges had played no unimportant part. Tokyo Military Staff College could claim two of the soldiers, Chiang Kai-shek

[1] *Les Origines de la France contemporaine,* Titre III, p. 169, quoted in *Les Cinq Pouvoirs,* above, p. 183.

and Yen Hsi-shan, and Tokyo Law College Hu Han-min. Sun Fo was a graduate of Columbia and T. V. Soong of Harvard. Yale claimed H. H. Kung and C. T. Wang. Wang Ch'ung-hui was almost international. Graduating at Yale he then studied in Germany and England, making the first translation of the German Civil Code into English and becoming a member of the English Bar.

Unfortunately but inevitably the appearance of unity proved illusory. A broad appreciation of the situation shows important elements in the country looking to Wang Ching-wei for leadership and constituting an opposition only waiting its opportunity to assail Nanking. At Wuhan the radical group, constituting the remnants of the former Wuhan Government, continued in effect to control affairs in central China under the guise of the Wuhan Branch Political Council. Li Tsung-jen, the Kwangsi leader, who had been prominent in the northern advance during the previous year, was now its chairman. It was therefore controlled by a military combination based on Kwangsi, one of the more powerful provinces of the south-western Federation, known as the Kwangsi clique. North of the Yangtze were the three military groups represented by the 'Young Marshal,' Chang Hsueh-liang, in control of Manchuria; the 'Christian General,' Feng Yu-hsiang, whose forces known as the North-western Army occupied the Province of Shensi; and Yen Hsi-shan, Governor of the 'model' Province of Shansi. Finally the Province of Kiangsi was the stronghold of Communism.

China was on the eve of one of the most critical and complicated periods since the Revolution. Beneath the surface was deep hostility towards Chiang Kai-shek, bred of envy of his success, resentment of his policy of unification, and fear of the consequences of centralization to individual and regional interests. The resolutions of the Disarmament Conference which sat in Nanking in January, reducing the men under arms to sixty-five divisions, each of 11,000 men, seemed to some of his opponents designed to strengthen his position. The main features of the conditions prevailing in China since the death of Yuan Shih-k'ai rapidly reproduced themselves. There were times when the Writ of Nanking scarcely ran beyond its walls.

Early in 1929 the scarcely fledged Government was called upon to fight the first of a series of major campaigns which were to decide its fate.[1] On the eve of a National Congress of the Kuomintang, convened for March 15, 1929, which it had been hoped would result in the consolidation of the forces of the Revolution and prepare the way for reconstruction, the Wuhan group showed the cleavage. The Chairman of the Province of Hunan, who had commanded an army in the advance to the Yangtze in 1926 and retained his old loyalties, constituted a threat to the undisputed control of central China by the Kwangsi clique. In February 1929, therefore, the Wuhan Branch Political Council issued an order for his dismissal and Kwangsi forces marched into Hunan. Nanking promptly accepted the challenge. Instructions were issued to Wuhan to rescind the order and for the retirement of the Kwangsi forces to their garrison towns. When these were not complied with the National Congress decreed a punitive expedition by resolution passed on March 27. Chiang Kai-shek with characteristic dispatch moved off three days later. In a brief inglorious campaign the Kwangsi militarists suffered defeat and Nanking's control was re-established at Wuhan and in the Province of Hunan.

Meanwhile trouble was brewing with Feng Yu-hsiang, who planned to control Shantung on the retirement of the Japanese which was expected when the outstanding diplomatic incident had been adjusted.

This embarrassing issue was disposed of by an agreement dated March 28, 1929, under which there was a joint declaration in terms which are pathetic in the light of subsequent events. While looking at the matter ' as most unfortunate and even tragic in view of the traditional friendship between Japan and China,' the two governments declared themselves ' ready to dismiss entirely from their minds all discordant feelings attending the incident in the expectation that their future relationship may thereby be greatly improved.' Japan then undertook to withdraw her troops from Shantung, and China guaranteed protection to Japanese subjects. The damages suffered by each party were to be assessed by a joint commission making investigations on the spot. But by arrangement the Japanese did not retire until

[1] Neither militarily nor politically can anything but the briefest sketch be given of outstanding movements of these two eventful years. To those seeking detailed information reference should be made to the *China Year Books*, 1929–30 and 1931. Reference may also be made to *China in Revolution*, by H. F. McNair.

May, which gave Nanking time to make the necessary disposi-
tions to thwart the obvious and dangerous design of Marshal
Feng to establish himself on the flank and astride of the Tientsin–
Pukow railway, and thus to control communication between
Nanking and Peiping.[1]

This proceeding angered the Marshal who had possibly been
led to expect a more complacent attitude. In May he denounced
General Chiang and addressed a warning to the Legations calling
upon Foreign Powers to observe strict neutrality. At the same
time he announced his appointment as Commander-in-Chief of
the Revolutionary army for the protection of the Party and the
relief of the Nation. But the early defeat and extinction of
Chiang Kai-shek which he promised had to be postponed owing
to the defection of two of his more important commanders.[2] In
May Feng Yu-hsiang was expelled from the Kuomintang.

Nevertheless he and others might have purged their offences
by seizing the unrivalled opportunity which now presented itself
for the assertion of a truly national spirit and the subordination
of personal rivalries. On June 1, 1929, the state funeral of Sun
Yat-sen took place with sombre stirring pageant at Nanking. In
a vast mausoleum, constructed at fabulous cost on the slope of
Purple Mountain, within sight of the tombs of the first Ming
Emperors, the remains of the man who had been deified as the
personification of Revolution and the wise philosopher of those
reconstructive principles which were to cure the ills of China and
secure the status of the Chinese race, was laid finally to rest in
the presence of his son by his first marriage, Sun Fo, Madame
Sun Yat-sen, the available Kuomintang leaders and the Foreign
Diplomatic Body.

This ceremony was followed a few days later by a Plenary
Session of the Central Executive Committee, which essayed to
keep faith with the dead leader by determining that the period
of Political Tutelage should be limited to six years, coming to

[1] Immediately after the capture of Peking by the Nationalists in 1928
its name, which means ' Northern Capital,' was changed to Peiping,
meaning ' Northern Peace.' The same course had been pursued when
the Mings drove out the last of the Mongol or Yuan Dynasty in the
fourteenth century when the same name was given to the former Capital
City. Henceforward the name will be used appropriate to the period
to which reference is being made.

[2] One of these was General Han Fu-Chu, of recent years a notably
successful administrator of the Province of Shantung.

an end in 1935. At the same time it recognized the task of government to educate the people in local self-government, without which the establishment of the democracy planned by Sun Yat-sen would be impracticable.

A little later in a further attempt to settle the military problem of the North, Chiang Kai-shek summoned Yen Hsi-shan and Chang Hsueh-liang to a conference in Peiping. Neither of these militarists showed any enthusiasm for the meeting, but they could not refuse without arousing misunderstanding and suspicion. General Chiang's courage and directness in making this attempt to find a solution was ill-rewarded. The young Marshal had his hands full with his policy of eliminating Russian influence from the Chinese Eastern Railway which brought China to the verge of war. For the moment he was not a serious factor. The position in regard to Yen Hsi-shan was somewhat more complicated. Feng's abortive revolt in May had been planned to synchronize with the establishment of an independent government in Canton. This was to have been brought about by Kwangsi, whose forces had been by no means annihilated. But the attack on Canton failed and for the time being there was something like a stalemate. Yen Hsi-shan suggested as a solution of the situation that Feng should go abroad, he himself promising to accompany him. Feng had then gone into ostensible retirement and taken up residence at Taiyuanfu, the capital of the Province of Shansi. To the departure of Yen Hsi-shan, who was apparently the only stabilizing factor in North China, Chiang Kai-shek could not agree, and as Yen would not be moved from his promise to accompany Feng if the latter went abroad a complete deadlock ensued. The only effect of the conference which Chiang had undertaken at so much personal risk was to convince him of the hostility of the Northern militarists and of the inevitableness of a combination of Yen and Feng against Nanking.

The first overt act was a premature movement in the autumn. The much-talked-of tour abroad, never sincerely contemplated, had not materialized. A number of subordinate commanders of the North-Western Army called upon their chief and Yen Hsi-shan to devise means for dealing with the National Government, which they attacked in no unmeasured terms. But it would seem that the understanding with Wang Ching-wei and his supporters, now called the Reorganizationists, were not sufficiently advanced for the leaders to commit themselves and they advised abstention from interference in questions which should be settled by the people. Thereupon the North-Western Army moved on its own initiative under the leadership of Sung Cheh-yuan, Chairman of the Shensi Provincial Government, who has recently come into prominence as the Chairman of the Hopei [1] and Chahar Political Council resulting from the so-called autonomy movement in North China which is hereafter dealt with. Occupying the Province of Honan, they aimed to move down the Peking–Hankow railway and attack Wuhan, but a further successful campaign, in which Chiang again participated personally, drove the forces of the North-Western Army back into Shensi.

Simultaneously with this movement against Nanking, General Chang Fa-kwei, a strong supporter of Wang Ching-wei, denounced the Generalissimo and took the field. He has been heard of previously as the leader of troops in former campaigns whose exploits earned the name of ' Ironsides.' Dismissed for complicity in the Communist rising at Canton in the winter of 1927, he had been reinstated by Chiang Kai-shek and subsequently given a command at Ichang on the Yangtze above Hankow. He now marched across China to support Wang Ching-wei in what was to prove an abortive attempt to establish an independent government in Canton. In December another adherent of Wang Ching-wei, General T'ang Sheng-chih who played a part as the governor of Hunan in 1926, and who now held a command in Honan, came out and, alleging corruption of Nanking and demanding the recognition of Wang Ching-wei as head of the party, sought unsuccessfully to help by creating a military diversion. These events dispelled the last hope of unity so far as securing the co-operation of Wang Ching-wei was concerned. The challenge to established authority could no longer be ignored. By resolution of the Third Plenary Session of the Central Executive Committee passed March 1, 1930, Wang Ching-wei was expelled from the party.

But this was merely to set the seal on recognition of the fact

[1] The notification from Nanking which changed the name of Peking also changed the name of the former metropolitan province, Chihli to Hopei, which means North of the River (Yellow River). Chahar is now the eastern end of what was formerly Inner Mongolia, which was divided in 1928 for administrative purposes into Jehol, Chahar, Suiyuan and Ninghsia, the latter including part of the former province of Kansu.

that the die had been cast. As early as February Yen Hsi-shan had sent a telegram to Chiang Kai-shek recording the view that unification of the country by force of arms was impracticable and inviting the Generalissimo to retire and go abroad with him. The latter replied, not without perhaps a touch of irony, urging Yen to abandon the idea of retirement and requesting his ' continued co-operation ' in the work of reconstruction. Although further telegraphic discussion followed no competent observer supposed that hostilities would not ensue.

The isolation of Nanking now seemed almost complete. The prospects in Chinese estimation of the success of the Yen-Feng combination supported by other malcontents may be gauged from the course pursued by Yen Hsi-shan. No supporter of lost causes, he clearly thought the hour had struck. Abandoning the policy of caution which with one exception he had maintained for twenty years, he assumed in April the office of Commander-in-Chief, with Feng Yu-hsiang and Li Tsung-jen as Deputy Commanders-in-Chief operating from Shensi and Kwangsi respectively. Thereupon the State Council dismissed Yen from all his offices and ordered his arrest.

Hostilities broke out in May on the usual fronts as dictated by the railways. Tsinanfu was occupied by the Shansi Army. Feng Yu-hsiang began operations in Honan with a view to attacks on Wuhan to the South, and eastward on the flank of the Nationalist forces operating northward. South of the Yangtze Kwangsi forces occupied Changsha. Thus a further civil war was initiated which was destined to last for six months and involve 150,000 casualties, representing the most serious fighting that had taken place during all these troublous times.

Political events in the North kept pace with the military campaign. Early in April Yen Hsi-shan assumed charge in Peiping and ejected the Branch Political Council which had been established by Nanking. In June the Tientsin Customs were seized. Towards the end of July the Reorganizationist leaders with Wang Ching-wei at their head arrived in the North, called a Plenary Session of the Kuomintang and declared the establishment of a Government at Peiping with Yen Hsi-shan as Chairman of the State Council and Wang Ching-wei, Feng Yu-hsiang, Li Tsung-jen, Chang Hsueh-liang and others as members.

But the military situation now developed in favour of the

Nanking Armies. Although in the early stage of the campaign Chiang Kai-shek had been embarrassed by the operations of the Kwangsi troops in his rear and had to be content to remain virtually on the defensive north of the Yangtze until he had disposed of this menace, he had latterly embarked on a vigorous offensive. Shortly after the pseudo-government had declared itself in Peiping he inflicted a severe defeat on the Shansi troops, and it became clear that Nanking would emerge victorious unless Chang Hsueh-liang should come to the support of the Yen-Feng combination. Even then the record of the Fengtien troops was not such as to suggest that they would necessarily turn the scale. Meanwhile the Young Marshal who had not thus far accepted the office of State-Councillor to which he had been appointed in the new Reorganizationist Government at Peiping was in receipt of overtures from both sides. The trouble with Soviet Russia which had threatened war in the previous year had now been adjusted and he was free to participate. He elected to support Nanking and with his armies came inside the Great Wall.

Thereupon the Reorganizationists rapidly faded away. The Tientsin Customs returned to its allegiance.[1] Wang Ching-wei retired to Canton where he proposed once more to establish a government independent of Nanking. General Yen retired to the fastnesses of Shansi, whither Feng also retired for philosophic meditation and the practice, it was said, of calligraphy. Chang Hsueh-liang became deputy-Commander-in-Chief of the National Armies with a bailiwick politically which extended to the Yellow River.

---

[1] The seizure had been effected by B. Lenox-Simpson who started life in the Customs Service and subsequently became well known as a publicist under the name of B. L. Putnam-Weale. Mr. Simpson functioned as Commissioner of Customs for the Reorganizationist regime until he was shot in the Commissioner's residence in Tientsin, receiving wounds from which he subsequently died. This occurred on the eve of the debacle.

Chapter 23
The year 1931

The year 1931 was the twentieth year of the Republic of China. When the historian of the future looks back on events in East Asia he will perhaps regard it as one of those turning-points in history which, escaping notice at the time, stand out in retrospect with startling clearness. It was charged with fate for the West, China and Japan.

The liberal Far Eastern policy of Great Britain, developed anew in 1926 in relation to Chinese aspirations, was mistaken for a policy of scuttle. The apparent success of terrorist methods at Hankow in 1927, the weakness of the Treaty Powers in the face of the Nanking outrage, the real success of the anti-Christian and anti-foreign drive throughout the country had encouraged the politicians of ' Young China ' to go from strength to strength in prosecuting their demands. The Kuomintang lay like a great octopus over the country, tentacles in the form of branch offices known as Tang Pu promoting strikes and disturbances wherever its demands were not complied with. The Chanceries of Europe and America were seriously perturbed.

Some of the lesser Powers, unable to resist the pressure of events, agreed to the abrogation of their treaty rights. An ill-judged surrender of extra-territoriality, which would have produced not less disadvantage to China than to their own nationals, was on the eve of completion by America and Great Britain. China for her part began to suffer the penalty of an unwise policy in Manchuria and years of disintegrating weakness. Japan embarked on a policy dictated in the main by her militarists which may yet result in disaster to herself, even world catastrophe.

We have seen how Chiang Kai-shek's successful march on Peking in 1928 and the establishment of government at Nanking on the model laid down by Sun Yat-sen did no more than reflect a theoretical union. But it is difficult to conceive the degree of hostility which tore men asunder. In the summer of 1930 one very near to Wang Ching-wei, a certain T'sen Tson-ming, published a brochure under the title *La Chine qui Lutte*. Leaving aside the merely personal attacks on Chiang Kai-shek, there still remain observations which are illuminating. It is true they come from the pen of a partisan. On the other hand the writer was a man who received his education in Paris and presumably must be credited with a reasonable sense of responsibility and be free from a desire to publish in a foreign language statements calculated to be prejudicial to the foreign estimate of his country. He begins his preface as follows :

'Struggling China is democratic China fighting against China under dictatorship, against China under Military rule. The root of militarism unhappily has not been able to be wiped out. People suffer, for liberty of speech, the press and meetings no longer exist in our country. Our revolutionary forefathers have given their blood for the Republic, but they have obtained no result.'

Again in the body of the work :

'To a superficial observer, the establishment of the National Government at Nanking in October 1928, its recognition by the Great Powers, the participation of Manchuria in the Government of Nanking, and the successful campaign of Chiang Kai-shek against the military clique in Kwangsi, prompted the hope of the inauguration of a new era in disturbed China. The Government proposed a series of reforms which were to be instituted in all departments. There were national conferences on education, economic reconstruction, financial recovery and the reorganization and distribution of troops. A commission was established for the budget and a national commission for the suppression of opium. . . .

'Close study of the situation, however, shows these things as quite otherwise and deceptive. . . .

'Corruption and nepotism are so unbridled at Nanking that the Oligarchy which reigns there has become the laughing-stock of all well-informed politicians, both in China and abroad. Certainly the Capital has been removed from Peking ; but the spirit prevalent in the new Capital is the same, the corrupt mandarinate having been transferred to Nanking, with the exception of individuals too seriously compromised.'

In October 1930 Chiang Kai-shek himself bore testimony in a similar sense. Addressing a meeting of the Kuomintang at the party headquarters on his return from his successful campaign against the Yen-Feng combination and the Reorganizationists, he allowed his audience to rest under no illusion.

' It is highly deplorable that in almost all the places which I have visited of late, party members have left extremely unfavourable impressions in the minds of the people. Not only is it impossible to find a single party headquarters which administers to and works for the welfare of the people, but all are stigmatized for the most reprehensible practices, such as corruption, bribery and scrambling for power.

' The Manchus were overthrown because they constituted a special caste. But now, we who staged the Revolution for the overthrow of the Manchus have ourselves come to be regarded by the people as a privileged caste. They are now cherishing towards us the same hatred and repugnance with which they looked upon the Manchus.

' The danger of such a situation can hardly be over-estimated. Unless we quickly correct our faults, the Party will meet with rapid downfall, and we shall thereby be guilty of betraying the trust confided to us by our late Leader.' [1]

Looking at the situation from another angle we see how little current events reflected the ideal of democracy even in the hearts of the leaders. In the early part of 1931 Chiang Kai-shek was strongly of opinion that with appearances favouring unity for the second time steps should be taken to formulate a constitution. Hu Han-min strongly opposed the idea as premature. In order to remove the latter's opposition General Chiang resorted to the uncon-stitutional course of arresting the veteran colleague of Sun Yat-sen, and for a time Mr. Hu was under a measure of restraint as regards his personal freedom.

Thus was the foundation laid for estrangement if not enmity which could scarcely fail to be at least partly accountable for the continued differences between Canton and Nanking. It is true that Hu Han-min was a man of fine patriotic sense and when Canton espoused his cause it was despite his cabled protests that on May 27, 1931, a rival Nationalist Government was established.

Headed by T'ang Shao-yi, the elder statesman who had served under the Manchus and once been Yuan Shih-k'ai's Premier, and Wang Ching-wei, Canton demanded Chiang's retirement. But Nanking and the solid business elements in Shanghai still

[1] *China Year Book*, 1932, p. 512.

stood firm behind the Generalissimo. Representatives were sent to Canton to secure cohesion in the ranks of the party and a united government for China in Nanking. But all was of no avail. Meanwhile these dissensions encouraged increased activity of the Communists, against whom it became necessary in the middle of the year for Chiang Kai-shek to take the field.

On July 21 the Canton Government issued orders for an expedition to enforce the retirement of General Chiang and in August Nanking had no alternative but to mobilize against the South. Yet another civil war had been launched in which few parts of the country could or would have avoided being involved. Ostensibly the exponents of the civil ideal of government were fighting the principle of military dictatorship. In fact the enemies of Chiang Kai-shek refused all overtures to co-operate with him and desired to rule the country. Certainly Chiang Kai-shek exercised virtually dictatorial powers to enforce the aims of government. But reconstructive ideas were being worked upon with the assistance of experts of the League of Nations. On the whole the National Government was moving slowly in the right direction. That it had not made further progress is not surprising. The surprising thing was that it had succeeded in surmounting its difficulties to the point of maintaining the semblance of a government at all.

In addition to the course of events and Chinese opinion evidencing the tragic condition of the country, foreign opinion, unemotional and deeply reasoned, is also available. Ever since the Shanghai incident of May 30, 1925, the task of municipal government in the International Settlement had become increasingly difficult. One never heard of such difficulty in the French Concession because the oligarchic form of government was so firmly and unchangeably established that no Chinese ever thought of challenging it. It was only where Anglo-Saxon views of representation were in the ascendancy that Chinese ratepayers considered they had a grievance. As demands became stronger and reasonable concession proved ineffectual, towards the end of 1929 the statesmanlike decision was taken by the leaders of thought in Shanghai to secure an independent survey of the situation. Accordingly Mr. Justice Feetham, of the Bench of South Africa, who had served with distinction on Arbitration Commissions, notably on the Commission to determine the boundary of Ulster, was invited to undertake the task. With the consent of the Government of the Union of South Africa Mr. Feetham accepted the invitation.

The terms of reference primarily called for consideration of conditions in Shanghai and advice as to steps which could be taken to create municipal conditions in the International Settlement which should be just to Chinese aspirations and practicable in relation to the requirement of security. But clearly it was not possible for Mr. Feetham to confine his studies to purely local circumstances. He could not come to a correct conclusion without considering the conditions of China at large and the jurisdictional and political ideas which dictated action. His report, therefore, contains a valuable contribution to contemporary knowledge.

One of the fundamental questions which was present to Mr. Feetham's mind throughout his investigations was the existence or otherwise of the ' Rule of Law,' by which is meant security of person and property and liberty of thought, speech and action subject to the obligations imposed by Law.

As regards the International Settlement at Shanghai he reached the conclusion that ' speaking generally, the authority of law is upheld, and private rights are respected, and that the Settlement is governed by an executive authority (the Council of the Settlement) vested with powers which are limited and defined by its constitution, and subject, in respect of the exercise of those powers, to the control of Courts of law which are independent of itself.'

But when addressing himself to the wider problem he says :

' If the question is asked whether the rule of law, in the sense above indicated, prevails in China generally, it is clear that the answer must be :—Not as yet. One reason for the answer is that there are large areas in which the National Government is not at present in a position to make its authority effective ; and another reason is that as the Government, in the present disturbed state of the country, has to rely very largely on military power, its military commanders often dominate the situation, and not only set up military Courts, which claim a wide jurisdiction, but also intimidate or otherwise interfere with the ordinary civil Courts. But there are more fundamental reasons of a constitutional and historical character. The constitutional reasons may be briefly indicated by saying that, as things stand to-day, the powers vested in the National Government are not the limited powers of a constitutional government, but the unlimited powers of an autocratic government, and that Chinese Government authorities generally are not subject, in the exercise of their powers, to the control of independent Courts of law.'

At another point Mr. Feetham refers to the matter of taxation.

' It is in regard to matters of taxation that the gravest abuses seem to occur. Innumerable complaints are made as to the levying of illegal taxes, that is, taxes which are levied without legal authority, or in excess of the amounts legally authorized, or which are collected for long periods in advance, or which include sums by way of ' squeeze ' for the benefit of the tax collectors. The natural question to ask would seem to be : If taxes are illegal, why do people pay them ? But it does not, in fact, seem to occur to any one concerned with such complaints to ask that question, for the idea that payment of a tax can be avoided, merely because there is no legal authority for levying the amount demanded, involves an unfamiliar, and as yet unfounded, assumption that there is some effective means of compelling Government authorities and officials to keep within the law. The answer to such a question would, however, appear to be, that people pay taxes which they regard as illegal either through fear or under duress ; that is, they pay either because they are afraid to refuse owing to their belief that, if they do not pay the tax demanded, the official or authority concerned will be in a position to make them suffer, directly or indirectly, some more serious loss than the payment of the tax involves ; or under duress, in order to obtain release of the goods on which the tax is to be levied : and further, that people do not rely on the protection of the Courts against such acts of official oppression, because the idea that it is the function of the Courts to protect private individuals against illegal demands made by civil or military authorities has not as yet taken root, and present circumstances do not admit of such a function being successfully performed.' [1]

These conditions notwithstanding, China's statesmen, not unnaturally wishing to achieve in their own lifetime, were not

[1] Report of the Hon. Mr. Justice Feetham, C.M.G., to the Shanghai Municipal Council, pp. 358 and 363.

content to hasten slowly and to see foundations well and truly laid even if clamant ' Young China ' would have allowed them to do so. They negotiated, or rather they made their demands, in utter disregard to the realities of the situation. And the Foreign Powers allowed themselves to be carried with the stream.

Few events in diplomatic history can surely be so remarkable as the list of China's achievements by the simple procedure of unilateral denunciation. The semblance of central government at Nanking hung upon a single slender thread, the life of Chiang Kai-shek. History was rapidly repeating itself, creating a position similar to that under Yuan Shih-k'ai. While the strong hand exerted control there was no one strong enough to oppose it. But once it was removed the question of succession to power would again open an unending vista of civil war which was even now about to break forth anew. In the event of a dissolution of the present oligarchy at Nanking ambitious militarists would never have submitted themselves to the authority of the civilian element in the political party. Nor was the civilian element above reproach. As we have seen, far from it. Yet the representatives of Great Britain and the United States of America were negotiating the surrender of their nationals' only safeguard and the chief bulwark of China's economic fabric.

Against the policy of the British Government which had passed from liberalism to defeatism by reason of the issue, on a check in negotiations, of a Chinese Government Mandate abolishing extra-territorial jurisdiction unilaterally as from January, 1932, the views of the British communities, neither illiberal nor lacking in capacity to estimate the actualities of the situation, were of no avail. Even the tragic disappearance of John Thorburn was productive of nothing more than a pause in the negotiations. Admittedly in certain aspects it was not the best of cases, any more than was the case of Don Pacifico. But it was conclusive of the absence of the ' Rule of Law.'

John Hay Thorburn, a British youth, aged nineteen, educated in Shanghai, was a victim in part at least of the economic conditions of the age. Depressed by failure to make a satisfactory start in life he decided to leave Shanghai in search of opportunity. Setting off on the morning of June 1, 1931, by train to a place a few miles from Shanghai called Henli, the headquarters of the Shanghai Rowing Club, he left the train there and began walking in the direction of Soochow following the railway. What happened after that is not fully known. It is probable that he came into conflict with railway guards and wounded two of them, since he was known to be carrying a revolver, and two Chinese railway guards that night or next day were wounded. It is possible that when arrested his attitude was provocative. It is certain that he was maltreated. Admittedly he was shot by the regimental commander at Soochow, before whom he was brought, who entered an obviously unconvincing plea of self-defence. Thereafter Thorburn's body was made away with in order to conceal the crime.

In a densely populated country like China, with a police system notoriously effective in certain directions, it cannot be doubted that the responsible officials of the Government were aware or could have become aware of the details of what had taken place. By means of independent British inquiry part of the story was pieced together by about the middle of June, but the Chinese officials charged with inquiry professed inability to trace Thorburn, and His Majesty's Minister was so informed in July. It was only after some weeks of pressure that the murder was admitted, a report by the Acting Minister of Foreign Affairs being addressed to the British Minister on October 20, 1931, four months afterwards.

Allowing for the folly of Thorburn's action in leaving Shanghai in the way he did and the possibility of his having committed some subsequent offence, nothing can justify either the brutal murder of a young Englishman by a responsible officer when he was under arrest and disarmed or the Chinese Government's failure for several months to recognize its obligation. For political considerations it preferred to evade by every means within its power the performance of an obvious and simple duty. It would be difficult to find more striking proof of the absence of the Rule of Law or of the spirit which is required for the exercise of jurisdiction over members of a race brought up to look to the Law for the protection of its property and the guardianship of its liberties.[1]

How far the British and American policies were destined to be modified by this event it would be unfair perhaps to conjecture. The evidences were that its implications would be ignored.

[1] For documents in the case see *China Year Book*, 1932, p. 268.

But while British and Americans in China waited anxiously, events occurred in Manchuria which were destined to have far-reaching consequences. On the night of September 18, 1931, a slight explosion occurred on the South Manchurian railway in the neighbourhood of Mukden, though by whose agency could not be determined. The Japanese, claiming that Chinese had destroyed the track and attacked a Japanese railway post, elected to treat it as the culminating act in a long course of alleged obstruction to what the Japanese regarded as their legitimate rights in Manchuria. By morning Mukden, the capital of the ' Three Eastern Provinces,' was under Japanese military control. From this beginning developed the Japanese military and political campaign which has since changed and continues to work towards the further change of the political and economic position of North-East Asia. In December the Nanking Government cancelled its mandate abolishing extra-territorial jurisdiction.

PART III

THE FOREIGN CONTRIBUTION TO THE ECONOMIC FABRIC OF CHINA AND IN THE CULTURAL FIELD

Chapter 24

Early Western Contacts

In the foregoing pages the attempt has been made to recall the essential features of thirty-one years of vital history. We have seen the despotism of an Oriental Court yielding to not less harsh forms of human tyranny. Incidentally there has been brief reference to the cultural aspect of Chinese life, and to earlier events when it seemed necessary to understanding of the modern phases. But the picture remains incomplete. Nothing has been said of the foreign contribution either to the economic fabric of China or in the cultural field.

To fail to make such a reference would be a serious omission. Though at first sight it might seem to be a digression such is far from being the case. It would be impossible to understand the course of developments which have created the present position in the Far East in its relations with the West without a reference to its origins. That is particularly the case when one approaches one of the greatest of present-day problems, that of the Treaty Ports. Again, much of what has been done in the economic and cultural field and most of its fruition belongs to the Twentieth Century, and it is difficult to appreciate these things without some knowledge of their small beginnings. Before, therefore, we embark on a survey of the last five momentous years and try to analyse the forces of the present critical times some light must be shed on these important factors.

Unfortunately so much has been written in criticism of the effect of the influence of the West on the East that anything suggestive of a contrary view must seem to partake of the nature of special pleading. Nothing could be farther from the design of this book, which aims at a just perspective. Apart from that the question may be asked, why on behalf of ' the men from afar ' should an *apologia pro vita sua* be called for ? What was the alternative to relations between East and West in a world growing rapidly smaller ? Intrepid exploration had brought the nations of Western Europe round the Cape to India, Malaya and the South Seas in one direction, and to the American Pacific seaboard in another. Russia had penetrated by land to the Manchurian borders. Were the maritime nations to stop at the Straits of Malacca, in the phrase of Gibbon ' the Pillars of an Oriental Hercules ' ? Would it have been possible to persuade the ' Czar of all the Russias ' to forego his dreams of Eastern Empire, in order to leave the Far East in slumberous isolation ? How in the last resort could it have remained possible in an age of steam and electricity producing steamships, railways, the electric cable and wireless ?

East and West had to meet and strive to harmonize their outlook. The manner of their meeting was the accident of evolution. As the primordial civilizations one after another became stationary and with the exception of Chinese Civilization faded or were destroyed, and the Roman Empire was submerged by barbarism, the spirit of science and invention died. Centuries later progressive scientific and inventive genius was reborn in the West and forced the approach from that side. In order to understand the resulting conflict with China it is necessary to look far back into Chinese history.

Many theories have been advanced as regards the origin of the Chinese race. By some they are supposed to have come from a region farther north which modern discovery suggests as possibly the cradle of the human race. They settled along the banks of the Yellow River, which, if they came from the North, would be the first great water-way to be met on the migration southward.

Along the Yellow River they established a civilization which flowered in what is now the Province of Shantung. Centuries before Christ the written language achieved a literary wealth scarcely less than the language showed in K'ang Hsi's time or to-day. In 552 B.C. Confucius was born under the shadow of the Sacred Mountain.

As the centuries passed the Chinese, who had begun to honour men according to their occupations, placed the *literati* or lettered class from whom were drawn the officials first, the husbandman second, the artizan third and the trader last. Although amongst the officials there were military officials and China has been the scene of many devastating rebellions,[1] the profession of arms seems to have had no recognized status. As a race they early developed a love for the arts of peace. The fruits of such a development rendered the Chinese an easy prey to the nomad tribes inhabiting the grazing and desert country to the north. From the earliest times China had her Wardens of the Marches, and finally in the second century before the Christian era she constructed as a defence the Great Wall. The term ' outer barbarian ' therefore has an historic significance and in those days had a just application. Its extension to include all men outside the Chinese race was the result partly of ignorance and partly of pride.

The geographical features of the country made for isolation. Impenetrable jungle and vast mountain ranges protected the southern and western borders of the lands which were to become the Empire of China. Only by the far north-western trade route and by the sea could there be communication with the outside world.

In primitive times such intercourse was necessarily slight, but by no means so slight as many have supposed. Religion, as elsewhere, played its part. Buddhism came from India and early established itself. In the seventh century the Nestorian Christians appeared and exercised substantial influence for two or three centuries but left few traces. Trade brought about intercourse between Europe and China. The great trade route, the ' Silk Road,' wended its way across what the maps now show as Sinkiang or the New Dominion to the cities of Samarcand and Bokhara and thence to the Mediterranean shores. ' The caravans,' says Gibbon, ' traversed the whole latitude of Asia in two hundred and forty-three days from the Chinese ocean to the sea-coast of Syria.' There were times when ' a pound of silk was sold at Rome for twelve ounces of gold.'

[1] See *The Chinese and their Rebellions*, by Thomas Taylor Meadows, *Hills of Blue*, by A. E. Grantham, and the famous *San Kuo, or Romance of the Three Kingdoms*, translated by C. H. Brewitt-Taylor.

In the intervening centuries isolated travellers and missions from Europe found their way to the Court of Cathay. But religious thought and examples of western culture were without effect on the civilization of China. It was already old, characteristic and satisfying to the people's needs. To Europe on the other hand, China was just a distant land of mystery and marvel which except for her silk could add nothing in the early days of the Christian era to the glories of Rome. In later centuries Europe was too concerned with her own development and at different times with her own defence against the fierce nomad horsemen from North-east Asia to be influenced by occasional travellers' tales.

And so the civilizations of the Far East and of the West, for Japan as will be seen was even more isolated, grew up for all practical purposes independently. Mr. H. A. L. Fisher puts it even more strongly. ' The two chief civilizations of the planet,' he says, ' grew up in mutual ignorance.' [1] It is to the last three centuries that we have to look for marked influences.

Chronologically European maritime contacts with the Far East followed the course of Empire. Portugal led the way. After a series of misadventures up the China coast, she succeeded in 1557 in effecting a settlement at Macao, which was to prove ' a monument of Portuguese tenacity and of Chinese toleration.' [2] Meanwhile Spain had completed her conquest of the Philippines and passing on to China about 1575 for a time had a monopoly of trade at Amoy. The Dutch followed at the turn of the century. A few years later in 1622, having first unsuccessfully attacked Macao with a fleet of fifteen vessels, they sailed away northward and established themselves in the Pescadores, ultimately securing for some years the mastery of part of Formosa.

Writing of this earlier period Abbé Raynall records that ' when Europeans first appeared upon the coast of China they were admitted into all the ports. But their extreme familiarity with the women, their haughtiness with the men, and repeated acts of insult and indiscretion, soon deprived them of that privilege.' In consequence from the middle of the eighteenth century onward they were only allowed to put in at Canton.

Of the nations coming later, France did little, her energies

[1] *A History of Europe*, by the Rt. Hon. H. A. L. Fisher, Vol. I, p. 23.
[2] *The Englishman in China*, by Alexander Michie, Vol. I, p. 287.

being concentrated on India. It was not until 1728 that she established a factory at Canton. The United States sent her first ship in 1784.

As regards Great Britain the first attempt to open up a trade between England and China was made in 1596 when Queen Elizabeth dispatched an expedition of three ships, bearing a letter written in Latin, to the Emperor of China by the hands of two merchants, Richard Allen and Thomas Bromfield, asking that ' they may have full and free liberty of egress and regress, and of dealing in trade of merchandise,' promising on her part not only to ' perform all the offices of a well-willing Prince ' but to ' grant unto all and every of your subjects (if it shall seem good unto your Highness) full and entire liberty unto any of the parts of Our dominions to resort, there to abide and traffic and then return.'

' What happened to this interesting document,' writes Mr. Lanning, ' was never discovered, for the expedition came to an unknown end, but its spirit was the spirit which filled all the early efforts of England to become acquainted with China, and we may boldly add, after three centuries of experience, is still the spirit in which we would see all our intercourse carried on, a spirit of good will, fair dealing, and equal opportunities on all sides.' [1]

The East India Company was formed on the last day of the sixteenth century, but exactly a hundred years elapsed before the Company began to establish itself firmly in the China trade. This was in 1699 when the Court of Directors in London established for the Empire of China what was called a Presidency similar to the Presidencies which had been established for the management of the Company's affairs in India. This body consisted of a President and a Council of five and in it was vested the fullest powers. Its first President even received a commission from William III ' appointing him King's Minister or Consul for the English nation. This is the first occasion on which England was represented in China by any kind of agent appointed by the Crown.' [2] Although it does not appear that diplomatic

---

[1] *History of Shanghai*, by G. Lanning, p. 88.
[2] *The English in China*, by James Bromley Eames, p. 52. This book covers within a reasonable compass the period 1600–1843, and is well documented.

functions were ever exercised, thenceforth the Company's senior officer was regarded as the head of the British Merchants in China until 1833 when its reign in the East was terminated.

The first idea of the Court of Directors was to establish its headquarters farther north than Canton in order to be nearer to Japan, with which country it was especially desired to open up trade relations. In the event, however, Canton proved the more convenient port and in 1704 the Company's headquarters were established there.

The prospects for trade should have been particularly favourable. China was ruled by the enlightened Emperor K'ang Hsi, whose ' decree published in 1692 permitting the exercise of the Christian religion is indicative,' as Mr. Eames points out, ' of a spirit of toleration towards foreigners.'

Unfortunately there were many difficulties. The chief of these were the impositions of local officials and the establishment in 1702 of a Chinese monopoly. At first a single broker was appointed, known as the ' Emperor's Merchant,' through whom all buying and selling was to be conducted. In course of time the number of these brokers or merchants was increased, varying from two to fourteen, the members then being known as the *co-hong*. Although every effort was made to secure freedom of trade, the China trade never escaped from this incubus until the system was abolished by the Treaty of Nanking in 1842.

Echoes of friction at Canton and at other ports possibly reached Peking, for even the liberal-minded K'ang Hsi reflected in the year 1717 that there was ' cause for apprehension lest, in centuries or millenniums to come, China may be endangered by collision with the various nations of the west, who come hither from beyond the seas.'

As the years passed and trade reached substantial proportions, exactions increased and protests multiplied. An ' effort in 1754 to obtain some redress ended in greater control than ever over foreign trade, and it was but three years later when an Imperial edict (1757) made Canton the one legal trading port, or " staple," for foreigners, who were thus delivered to the spoilers without hope of redress.' [1]

These were not the only troubles. About 1736 communication with the local officials began to be accompanied by such

[1] *History of Shanghai*, p. 93.

166

difficulties and humiliations as to make the history of the trade at Canton for the next hundred years far from agreeable reading ' to the patriotic Englishman. It is mainly a record of acquiescence in humiliations of every kind, put, it is true, on all foreigners alike, but not the less such as must have lowered the dignity of the British nation in the eyes of the Chinese.' [1] But at least it stands out that this phase of the approach of the West to China carried in it no hint of Imperial design.

Apart from these troubles life itself had its unpleasant aspects. In the early days foreigners were not allowed to reside permanently at Canton. When the season was at an end they were compelled to leave for Macao, the only accessible place, where the off season was spent. When in later days continuous residence was allowed it was limited to the restricted area on the river front at Canton on which were built the famous factories. Under conditions which excluded foreign women and only permitted movement outside the allotted area three times monthly, the pioneers enjoyed a status scarcely comparable to that of *peregrini* in ancient Rome. But such was their spirit and good fellowship that they made for themselves a life which most looked back on with pleasure and left with regret.[2]

[1] *The English in China*, p. 72.
[2] See *The Fan Kwae (Foreign Devils) at Canton* and *Bits of Old China*, by W. C. Hunter, and *Memoirs of William Hickey*.

Chapter 25

Fifty years of Foreign Effort to establish Self-respecting Relationship

1793–1842

Such a manner of maintaining commercial relations between East and West could not persist indefinitely. It was inevitable that European pride should revolt against the indignities to which European merchants were called upon to submit. Efforts were made particularly by Great Britain to ameliorate the situation.

The first mission aiming to establish relationship between Great Britain and China on a self-respecting basis was no more fortunate than Elizabeth's trade mission at the end of the sixteenth century. Advised by the East India Company that an appeal must be made to Peking if relations were to be improved, the British Government in 1787 dispatched Colonel Cathcart as a special envoy to China. His untimely death in the Straits of Sunda on the outward voyage prevented the mission from proceeding.

Lord Macartney's Mission, to which there has already been brief reference, followed in 1793. Bearing a vast assortment of presents, from a chariot and field guns to mathematical instruments and Wedgwood China, it was characterized by every circumstance of distinction calculated to gratify the Imperial Court. The Emperor Ch'ien Lung was then in his eighty-third year. Partly perhaps from curiosity and partly from liberal sentiment, he was prepared to dispense with the kotow rather than that the Mission should not be received. For nearly two months it was sumptuously entertained at Peking and at the Emperor's hunting seat at Jehol. But diplomatically and from the point of view of improved trade relations there were no results. Lord Macartney had aimed to reach understandings in the matter of diplomatic intercourse involving a British Resident at Peking, improved conditions of residence at Canton, reduction of fees and duties on trade and shipping and permission to reside and trade at Ningpo and Tientsin or some other northern port. The matter of the Christian religion was also in his mind. The liberal attitude of K'ang Hsi had been departed from and restrictions had been imposed by his son, Yung Cheng, on its propagation. Lord Macartney hoped to have these removed. But not only was no agreement reached in these matters, but he failed to secure any encouragement in regard to any one of them. The requests were said ' to militate against the laws and usages of the Empire and at the same time were wholly useless to the end professed.' The Emperor could not therefore acquiesce in them, while the request in regard to the Christian religion was described as ' utterly unreasonable.' Realizing the hopelessness of his task Lord Macartney returned to England bearing a condescending dispatch, an extract of which is contained in the second appendix.

In the following year the Dutch, whose earlier missions in the seventeenth century had been merely occasions for their humiliation, seized the opportunity to send a mission of congratulation to the Emperor Ch'icn Lung on reaching the sixtieth year of his reign. Disregarding the lessons of the past they again adopted an attitude of humility, and were rewarded with nothing but contempt and degradation. The Emperor's ' hauteur,' says Wells Williams, ' was a befitting foil to their servility, at once exhibiting both his pride and their ignorance of their true position and rights. They were brought to the Capital, like malefactors, treated when there like beggars, and then sent back to Canton like mountebanks. Van Braam's account of this Embassy is one of the most humiliating records of ill-requited obsequiousness before insolent government lacqueys which any European was ever called upon to pen.' [1]

Lord Amherst's mission twenty-three years later fared still less fortunately. On arrival at Tungchow, about twelve miles distant from Peking, he was informed that the Emperor Chia Ch'ing was impatiently awaiting his arrival, and that no delay could be permitted for rest and preparation for the audience. Protesting, they were rushed to Jehol where they were met with the further difficulty of the kotow, with which the Emperor Chia Ch'ing was not prepared to dispense as his more liberal father

---

[1] *The Middle Kingdom*, by S. Wells Williams, Vol. II, p. 439. Dr. Wells Williams was the first foreigner to write comprehensively on China. His great work is still authoritative. An American citizen coming to China to work in the Mission field, in later years his country called for his services as Chinese secretary to the Legation and at times as Chargé d'Affaires.

had done. As the King's representative Lord Amherst could not agree and the mission was hustled away under circumstances of grave humiliation and insult. A portrait of King George III in his robes of state, destined as a present to the Emperor, was brought back to Canton to honour the walls of the Company's hospitable mess. ' It was the last attempt of the kind,' says Wells Williams, ' and three alternatives only remained : the resort to force to compel them to enter into some equitable arrangement, entire submission to whatever they ordered, or the withdrawal of all trade until they proposed its resumption.' [1]

The next landmark is the year 1834 when the East India Company's monopoly came to an end and it became necessary to replace the chief of the Company's staff as the representative of British trade. ' Free Trade,' as Mr. Lanning points out, ' had won its victory over western monopoly but not as yet over the eastern.'

The British Government decided to appoint a diplomatic officer as Superintendent of Trade and Lord Napier was nominated to the post.

Nearly twenty years had passed since the rebuff to Lord Amherst and it does not seem to have been anticipated that there would be any difficulty. Instructed to observe all possible moderation, the British Superintendent was to enjoin on British subjects the duty of conforming to the laws and usages of the Chinese Empire. After announcing his arrival by letter to the Viceroy, as a step to establishing direct communications with the Imperial Court at Peking, his residence was to be taken up at Canton.

Lord Napier reached his destination on the morning of July 25, 1834. Two days later, with characteristic disdain, the Viceroy expressed his views to the Hong Merchants.

> ' As to the object of the said Barbarian Eye's [2] coming to Canton it is for commercial business. The Celestial Empire appoints officers—civil ones to rule the people, military ones to intimidate the wicked. The petty affairs of commerce are to be directed by the merchants themselves. The officers have nothing to hear on the subject.'

---

[1] *The Middle Kingdom*, by S. Wells Williams, Vol. II, p. 459.
[2] ' Barbarian Eye ' was a contemptuous term applied by Chinese officials to a foreign overseer or controller.

When a dispatch was addressed to the Victory by Lord Napier explaining that in addition to being charged with duties in relation to British trade in China, he was invested ' with political and judicial powers to be exercised according to circumstances,' the Viceroy refused to receive it. The secretary who carried it to the city gate was exposed to indignity for three hours, in the first place because the dispatch was not a petition and secondly for the reason that he had come in person instead of communicating through the Hong Merchants. ' Old scenes, equally insulting and ridiculous,' said the *Chinese Repository*, ' played with more or less success a hundred times before, were re-enacted.'

As Lord Napier still remained, Chinese soldiers intruded threateningly on the restricted area where foreigners had their being. A guard of marines was sent for. Then trade was stopped and the alternative offered, ' obey and remain : disobey and depart.' At the same time the factories were blockaded, supplies were cut off, regulations which had fallen into partial desuetude were revived with all their original severity, and edicts were directed at the King's representative couched in terms of arrogance and contumely.

In the autumn, after seventy-seven days of unremitting strain, Lord Napier left Canton for Macao, a seriously sick man. His last dispatch to the British Government made clear that the use of force was the only alternative to humiliation and exactions. But the British Government would not concede this point of view. The Duke of Wellington, who was then Prime Minister, soldier though he was and leader of ' the stern unbending Torics,' wrote that ' it is not by force and violence that His Majesty intends to establish a commercial intercourse between his subjects and China, but by the other conciliatory measures so strongly inculcated in all the instructions which you have received.'

By the time this dispatch reached Canton Lord Napier was dead. Five years only were to pass before the truth of all he had written was demonstrated.

Captain Elliott had been superintendent of British Trade for nearly three years when Lin Tse-hsu in the early part of 1839 was appointed Imperial Commissioner at Canton. Outranking the Viceroy he was invested with powers never before given to a Chinese subject.

Commissioner Lin had formerly been Viceroy of Hukuang.

At this time he was fifty-four years of age and enjoyed a reputation for integrity and honesty of purpose. He was a man of inflexible determination and marked ability. Dr. Robert Morrison, the translator of the Bible and compiler of a famous dictionary, who came to Canton in 1807, is said to have described one of his reports as the best state paper he had ever read. On the other hand Commissioner Lin was prejudiced and narrow and violently anti-foreign. According to the *Chinese Repository* he was one of ' a war party determined to catch, cage and behead foreigners whose skins were to be given to the soldiers to lie on.' Mr. Morse wrote that his policy was ' to crush the English.'

The contraband trade in opium was made the spear-head of his attack. Here China had a legitimate grievance. But it was not against the British any more than other foreigners, and it was mainly against the Chinese Authorities of Canton.[1]

China had known and used opium for more than a thousand years before British merchants first had a hand in the trade. This was in 1773 and the trade was in private hands. When eight years later ' Warren Hastings, in his official capacity as Governor of Bengal, did send a cargo of opium to China, it is on record that the Directors protested on the ground that, opium being contraband in China, it was beneath the dignity of the Company to engage in what was but a smuggling trade.'[2]

This protest was disregarded by the men on the spot for various reasons. In the first place the fact that duty was payable on import of opium showed that at least for some purposes import was allowed. The further fact that there was a growing trade in the hands of other foreign merchants indicated that the Imperial Edict of fifty years before had fallen into desuetude. There was also a balance of trade calling for redress by means of the import of some commodity into China instead of the Carolus dollars and other silver which had to be shipped to China to pay for the export of tea and silk.

In 1799 an Imperial Edict formally forbade the import in any ship. In 1800 the sale of opium was interdicted. From that time onward neither the Co-hong merchants nor the East India

[1] See Lord Palmerston's dispatch of February 20, 1840, addressed to the Minister of the Emperor of China.
[2] *History of Shanghai*, by G. Lanning, p. 175.

Company's agents at Canton dealt in the drug, while at no time did the East India Company or the British Government give any countenance to the trade. It became altogether contraband. But as large numbers of the highest in the land smoked it, evasion of the opium law was as simple as smuggling of French brandy into England in the days of an inefficient preventive service or evasion of the liquor laws in modern times in certain of the United States.

No doubt there was sincere anxiety in high government circles in Peking as to the moral effect of the drug on the nation. There was still greater alarm as regards the economic aspect. It was demonstrable beyond all doubt that the increase in the import of opium had reversed the balance of trade and was establishing an increasing drain on silver. A drastic cleansing of the official hierarchy was called for in conjunction with improvement in the efficiency of the preventive service. Co-operation of foreign governments should also have been called for. Apart from such steps nothing more was practicable in contemplation of law except confiscation of smuggled opium found within Chinese jurisdiction.

But such modest measures, however effective in the long run, did not commend themselves to Commissioner Lin. He was determined on a far more drastic course. With nothing short of the surrender and destruction of all opium that could by any means be brought within the influence of the British Superintendent and merchants of Canton would he be satisfied. Orders were issued for wholesale surrender regardless of jurisdiction or legal principle. When these orders were not complied with he surrounded the factories with troops, cut off supplies and threatened foreign lives. Contemporary evidence of unimpeachable character is available to show that men went in fear of death.

Captain Elliott, who was absent at Macao, immediately returned to Canton to share the fate of his countrymen if he could not ameliorate it. When the gravity of the situation only increased he ordered all British owners of opium on British ships to surrender it. Traders of other nations under such duress followed the British lead. Opium amounting to upwards of 20,000 cases representing a cost of $11,000,000 was surrendered and destroyed.

The apologists of Commissioner Lin's action have failed to

justify it by any principle of law, and authoritative Chinese writers have been found to characterize it as harsh and unjust.

The destruction of the opium did not conclude the matter. Demands upon foreigners became increasingly burdensome. Lord Napier's forecast which had been received so unsympathetically by the Duke of Wellington was more than justified. The British were compelled to withdraw from Canton. War was the only alternative to abandonment of intercourse with China which could only be carried on in circumstances of insufferable ignominy.

An expedition was fitted out in India the objects of which were stated by Lord John Russell, in answer to a question in the House of Commons, in the following terms :

> ' In the first place they were to obtain reparation for the insults and injuries offered to Her Majesty's Superintendent and Her Majesty's subjects by the Chinese Government ; and, in the second place, they were to obtain for the merchants trading with China an indemnification for the loss of their property incurred by threats of violence offered by persons under the direction of the Chinese Government ; and, in the last place, they were to obtain security that the persons and property of those trading with China should in future be protected from insult and injury.[1]

War still might have been avoided had not the Chinese Authorities continued to refuse all reasonable negotiation and intercourse.

It was not a very serious war as may be gauged by the modest strength of the British naval and military forces, sixteen warships under sail with four light draft steamers and 4,000 officers and men. Hostilities covered a period of two years and eight months, much of which was taken up by abortive negotiations. The Treaty of Nanking was signed on August 29, 1842, embodying terms the more important of which have been referred to in relation to the Mackay Treaty. Others will be mentioned as called for in later chapters.

By hostile critics of Great Britain and many British critics of the Government's policy this war has been called ' The Opium War.' Rarely has a war been more unjustly labelled. It was fought to secure recognition by China of the equality of the members of the Family of Nations. Opium was an incident and

[1] Hansard : *Parliamentary Debates*, Vol. 52, p. 1223.

not a cause. As John Quincey Adams, once President of the United States and son of Washington's successor, said at the time, ' in the so-called Opium War England has the righteous cause.' Three-quarters of a century later Mr. Morse, an American writer who has already been referred to, expressed a similar view. ' The real cause of the war,' he wrote, ' was that the Chinese refused to treat on terms of equality, either diplomatically or commercially, with foreigners, and the latter insisted on the right to be so treated.' [1]

Chapter 26
Macao and Hongkong

The inspiration of navigators in the fifteenth century was the discovery of a sea route to the Indies. The caravan routes had proved the existence of eastern countries of fabulous wealth. But Western Europe had no share in it. The Genoese and other Mediterranean peoples absorbed the trade. When the Cape was first rounded in 1487 by the Portuguese, Bartholomew Diaz, the existence of a way by sea to India seemed certain. Ten years later Vasco da Gama proved it.

A Knight of the Order of Christ, whose ship enjoyed the picturesque privilege of carrying on its sails a great red cross, he had been commissioned by the King of Portugal to round the Cape and to go up the East Coast of Africa in search of ' Prester John and the King of Calicut.' If Vasco da Gama failed to discover Prester John, at least he reached India and established the first European Settlement at Goa. Half a century later the chain of Portuguese trading posts had reached Macao. Thence-

[1] *Trade and Administration in the Chinese Empire*, by H. B. Morse, p. 25. See also *The International Relations of the Chinese Empire*, by the same writer, p. 539. See also *The Chinese, their History and their Culture*, by Professor K. S. Latourette of Yale and *The Case for Manchoukuo*, by G. Bronson Rea, another American writer.

forward ' for three hundred years,' as Alexander Michie wrote, ' it was for foreigners the gate of the Chinese Empire, and all influences, good and bad, which came from without were infiltrated through that narrow opening, which also served as the medium through which China was revealed to the Western world. It was in Macao that the first lighthouse was erected, a symbol of the illuminating mission of foreigners in China. It was there also that the first printing-press was set up, employing movable type instead of the stereotype wooden blocks used by the Chinese. From that press was issued Morrison's famous Dictionary, and for a long series of years the *Chinese Repository*, a perfect storehouse of authentic information concerning the Chinese empire, conducted chiefly by English and American missionaries. The first foreign hospital in China was opened at Macao, and there vaccination was first practised. It was from Macao that the father of China missions, Matteo Ricci, started on his adventurous journey through the interior of the country in the sixteenth century, ultimately reaching the capital, where he established an influence over the Imperial Court scarcely less than miraculous, thus laying the foundation-stone of the Catholic propaganda in China.

' Of those associated with its history, the most brilliant, or at least the best known, was St. Francis Xavier, the apostle of the Indies,' whose name with that of Ricci ' casts a halo over the first century of the existence of Macao.'

' Another of the earlier residents of world-wide fame was the poet Camöens, who in a grotto formed of granite blocks tumbled together by nature, almost washed by the sea, sat and wrote the Portuguese epic " The Lusiad " celebrating the adventures of the great navigator Vasco da Gama.' [1]

During these years, as we have seen, Macao played an important part in the China trade, and massive houses, with deep verandahs and spacious and cool interiors, attest to this day ' the

[1] *The Englishman in China*, by Alexander Michie, Vol. I, p. 296. No excuse is needed for extended quotation from this brilliant writer, who as no one before or since has reflected the spirit of his country's intercourse with China during the Victorian Age. Familiar with the Far East as resident and traveller for many years, he made the overland journey through Siberia to Europe as early as 1864. Subsequently he made an important contribution to the Missionary Problem. He also founded and edited from 1887-91 in Tientsin a weekly paper called *The Chinese Times*, which for literary ability and erudition is entitled to rank with the famous *Chinese Repository*.

luxurious life led by the Company's agents and the private merchants during the off season in the days before the treaty.'

But although the Portuguese Settlement at Macao, which later
in the nineteenth century in days when its glory had already
faded was to attain the status of a colony, had met to some extent
British requirements in China waters, the advantages of a harbour
in which to careen their ships and of a place from which to control
and develop trade became increasingly evident. The decrees of
Commissioner Lin virtually compelling the British to retire from
Canton and denying them sanctuary at Macao, in which the
Governor of Macao with scant regard for Peninsular memories
and the traditions of Lusitanian chivalry acquiesced, made it a
matter of necessity. For British ships and refugees the island
of Hongkong, which formed the southern side of an extensive
land-locked harbour affording splendid anchorage, offered in the
circumstances the only resort. By the Treaty of Nanking it was
ceded to Great Britain.

At that time Hongkong was a rocky, little-cultivated island, the
home of a few poor fishermen and the resort of pirates. Lying
at the mouth of the West River, its insalubrious nature belied its
name of 'fragrant streams.' It gave no promise of a brilliant
future. Serious doubts even were entertained as to the advantage
of its retention.

In twenty years the island underwent a complete transforma-
tion. Pick and mine succeeded in creating room for the city of
Victoria. Subsequent reclamation schemes added substantially
to its area. Upon the steep slopes of the Peak houses arose,
tier upon tier, gradually accommodating a big population of
Europeans. As time went on vast numbers of Chinese were
attracted by the orderliness and safety of government under the
British Flag. The value of its situation as a point of entry to
South China and of commercial relations with Indo-China, the
Philippines and Malaya, was at length recognized.

Established as a Crown Colony it has survived the limitations
and difficulties which beset that form of government. Save
perhaps in the matter of domestic slavery,[1] the problems of

[1] The reference here is to the notorious ' mui tsai ' system, which is
still part of the social system of China. With no serious attempt to
eradicate it on the mainland the difficulty of Hongkong in dealing with
the problem is greatly increased.

control of a vast Chinese population and of bringing an alien race within ' the moral pale of English law ' have not proved beyond its powers, despite deep-rooted custom fighting to preserve its cherished institutions.

Industrially Hongkong has established a position all its own. One of the largest sugar refineries in the world deals with the raw materials of the Far Eastern sugar-growing countries and has a substantial export trade. The Colony led the way in the engineering and shipbuilding trades and has graving docks capable of accommodating modern battleships.

Commercially as a free port, intermediary between the Far East and the rest of the earth, as port of entry and port of transshipment, the prosperity of Hongkong increased until it reached a position which placed it for a time at least head of the world's great shipping ports.[1]

Since the Revolution, especially in latter years, it has become less prosperous though scarcely less important. Strikes, generated by Russian influence designed to undermine the foundations of the British Empire, and cutting at the roots of British trade in the Far East, have played their part, as we have already seen, and only now is Hongkong slowly recovering. The development of Canton and the harbour of Whampoa will also have some influence in attracting a portion of the direct trade with South China, although beyond this it would appear that it cannot seriously compete. Japanese competition, especially in the sugar market on the mainland, has already had its effects.

Even so Hongkong must continue to play a leading rôle as the basis of British influence in the Far East. For it is not only in commercial matters that Hongkong has its importance. Strategically it has a value which was recognized in its early days, but under present conditions of fortification and projectiles is a matter of debate except for the protection of mine-fields. In the years preceding the establishment of the Colony it became obvious that the acquisition of territory on the adjacent mainland was essential to its existence. Not only did the cramped conditions of life on the island promise to form an obstacle to its development, but from a strategic point of view, with the mainland in hostile hands, the island was untenable. As Wingrove Cooke, the correspondent of *The Times*, put it, ' if any other powers

[1] *International Relations of the Chinese Empire*, Vol. II, p. 396.

should take Kowloon—and what is to prevent them?—the harbour of Hongkong is lost to us.'

Wingrove Cooke was not the only man who saw the necessity that had arisen. Harry Parkes, later on Sir Harry Parkes, was also acutely conscious of it, and very shortly after the Canton Provisional Government was established in 1858,[1] he took the opportunity, which his position as one of the Commissioners gave him, to arrange with the Governor of Canton a perpetual lease of an area of four square miles in the Kowloon Peninsula. The lease was subsequently confirmed by the Chinese Government in the Peking Convention of 1860. In 1898 a further area of mainland was brought under British jurisdiction by the grant of a lease for ninety-nine years.

Turning to the arts of peace, Hongkong has shed her light through the medium of education, whether by means of missionary or government schools. Early in the history of the Colony a College of Medicine was founded for Chinese of which Dr., afterwards Sir James, Cantlie, the teacher and friend of Sun Yat-sen to whom the latter owed his life, was Dean from 1889 to 1896. It was this college that gave Sun Yat-sen his training. Hongkong also has her University which includes the medical School and occupies a leading place amongst far-eastern universities on European lines.

' Hongkong,' once said an anonymous French writer, summing up an account of the Colony in the years before the war, ' is, before everything, a place of affairs. It is this aspect in the main which interests the great majority of those who pass by. But it is also the fruit of one of the most magnificent victories which have ever rewarded the energy and perseverance of man against an ungrateful nature, which only presented one advantage, a beautiful harbour outside the mouth of the Canton River at the foot of a barren and burnt-up mountain.

It might pardonably be added that it represents an achievement of the Pax Britannica which strives to give security and opportunity without distinction of nationality or race.

[1] As part of war measures which again were called for in 1858, it became necessary to establish a provisional government at Canton, under which the Viceroy was induced to function.

Chapter 27
The First Treaty Ports

The corner-stone of the Treaty of Nanking was the opening of five ports to foreign residence and trade, with the privilege of Consular representation or, as regarded from the Chinese standpoint, under Consular control. When in discharge of their obligations the Chinese set apart areas for foreign residence removed from their own cities and people, they laid the foundation for the creation of foreign settlements which had many features in common with the settlements established in foreign countries in the Middle Ages by the Hanseatic League.

The first port named in the Treaty was of course Canton, where foreign trade and residence were to be relieved, in theory at least, of the limitations to which they had been subjected. The other new treaty ports, starting from the south, were Amoy, a Portuguese corruption of Haimen, ' gate of the sea,' Foochow, Ningpo and Shanghai.

The latter ports were selected as a result of former contacts, and some traditional reputation for trade. Far away in the hinterland of Foochow, their nearest port, were the famous Bohea Hills, productive of the finest tea perhaps the world has ever known. Amoy had been a well-known mart in ancient times. A thousand years before ' Arabs had a stronghold there, while Amoy traders were found in all parts of the Malayan Archipelago and India and in the early days, even as far off as Persia.[1] It was one of the places in the sixteenth century where the Portuguese settled and traded until their lawlessness provoked a massacre. The same fate overtook them at Ningpo where their unbridled rapacity again brought vengeance and destruction upon a growing colony.'[2]

With both these places British trading contacts were also made. At Amoy there was once a post for the tea trade. On the island of Chusan, opposite and some forty miles distant from Ningpo, the East India Company for a time had a factory. Pleasant

[1] *The China Coast*, by Ivon A. Donnelly, p. 57.
[2] *Ibidem*, p. 48.

Consular and Customs post in years to come, Ningpo's chief
title to fame lies in its having been the Consulate of the late
Professor Giles which saw the compilation of his great dictionary.
Amoy and Pagoda Anchorage at Foochow may have inspired
some of the stories in his wife's volumes of *China Coast Tales*.
But for a time at least all three, but more particularly Foochow,
were to have their day.

In the half-century between 1840 and 1890 sailing ships reached
the pinnacle of their development.

' Ships were built such as the world had never known
before and will never know again. They were the fine
flower of the slow growth of maritime progress through the
ages : the triumphant climax to which the patient work of
generations of shipbuilders had been steadily leading up
since the days of the first skin-covered coracle and dug-out
canoe.

' It was a splendid culmination to the long story of sail :
and it was also to prove a splendid finale. Even before she
had attained the full height of her glorious heyday, the
influences were already at work which were destined, within
so amazingly short a space of time, to sweep the clipper ship
for ever from the face of the waters. Within less than a
century—nay, within less than three-quarters of a century—
from the building of the first of that proud and beautiful
sisterhood, the last of them was to give up the unequal
struggle with the irresistible invasion of her realm by the
once-despised " steam kettles " past which she had been
wont to surge so disdainfully in the first days of their coming ;
and all those wonderful fleets which in their day made lovely
all the harbours of the world were to vanish as completely
as ice-floes in the Gulf Stream, or as one of their own fore-
topsails snatched out of the bolt-ropes by the rough breath
of the Westerlies.' [1]

The opening of the first five ports in China synchronized with
the beginning of this splendid epoch and it was in the romantic
setting of the China Seas that the clipper ships achieved their
highest fame. As the tea trade developed ships were built sur-
passing in speed and sheer beauty anything that ever sailed the

[1] *Sail, the Romance of the Clipper Ships*, pictured by J. Spurling,
storied by Basil Lubbock and Edited by F. A. Hook, F.R.G.S., Introduction by C. Fox-Smith, p. vii.

seas. And of the vessels best known to fame, the *Cutty Sark* at least, now lying in Falmouth Harbour, still lives in the memory of the China Coast.

' Except in 1872, the *Cutty Sark* was never in company with another racing tea ship. But in that year she and her great rival, *Thermopylæ*, loaded together at Shanghai, and sailed within a few hours of each other. The two ships were constantly in company down the China sea, and owing to *Cutty Sark* having her way blocked by several water-spouts, she was led by *Thermopylæ* through Anjer Straits, the latter being 1½ miles ahead off Anjer, and when last seen outside Java Head was 3 miles W. by S. of Willis's clipper. However, Captain Moodie sent the *Cutty Sark* flying across the S.E. trades with three consecutive runs of 340, 327 and 320 miles, and he always contended that he was over 400 miles ahead of *Thermopylæ* when the *Cutty Sark* lost her rudder off the Cape coast.

' Captain Kemball, of *Thermopylæ*, was one of those secretive navigators who would never allow anyone aboard to know the ship's position, and as he refused to compare his log-book with that of the *Cutty Sark* after the two ships had arrived in London, one cannot say for certain which was leading when the *Cutty Sark* lost her rudder, though the generally credited belief in London at the time was that *Thermopylæ* was 600 miles astern.' [1]

The story of the *Cutty Sark* has brought us at last to Shanghai, where the story is a very different one from that of the other ports. From the earliest days to the present times the record has been one of almost continuous growth. Situated on the banks of the Whangpoo above the point where it joins the Yangtze, with a population estimated at a quarter of a million, Shanghai already had considerable trade and even substantial junk-borne foreign trade. Although it may seem strange that a settlement for trade should be chosen say on the banks of the Medway instead of at London, to suggest an analogy, there were reasons which made it sound. One of such reasons was the net-work of waterways facilitating distribution throughout the Province of Kiangsu, which, with a density of population equal to that of Belgium, must have been a potent element in the develop-

[1] *Ibidem*, p. 100.

ment of Shanghai before it was opened to foreign trade. Another was its situation in the heart of the rich alluvial country comprised in the Yangtze Delta, which formed in the course of ages, leaving the site of Shanghai despite its name far removed from the sea. A not unimportant reason for the choice, though perhaps an unconscious one, was the modest status of Shanghai as only a district city and so removed from the oppressive weight of high Chinese officialdom which had been such a fruitful cause of trouble at Canton.

On the opening of Foochow, which was the seat of the Viceroy of the Province of Fukien, obstructive tactics were employed. But at Shanghai no difficulty was experienced in giving effect to the Treaty. The conciliatory policy of the British Government coupled with the reasonableness of the then Chinese Superintendent of Customs in the Province of Kiangsu, commonly called the Customs Taotai, and the absence of hostility on the part of the people, made the important task of the first Consul, Captain G. Balfour, a less difficult one than might have been supposed. Not unsatisfactory premises were found to house the British Consulate until the Government could be persuaded to incur financial liability or commitments even to the extent of buying land and erecting buildings suitable for Consular residence and offices. The method of collection and payment of customs duties was easily arranged and an early attempt to introduce the monopoly system of Canton was defeated. Nor did the provision of accommodation for foreigners give rise to any friction. For many reasons the most satisfactory way of dealing with this requirement would have been by the sale or lease in perpetuity of an area to the British Government for lease to their nationals and approved foreigners, and this was at first proposed. The Chinese authorities, however, preferred to indicate a place where foreigners might settle making their own arrangements with the Chinese owners. An area of about 140 acres with adequate water frontage was marked out accordingly. The next question was that of control, it would hardly be called local government, of the affairs of the infant settlement. The formation of a ' Committee for Roads and Jetties ' was the modest origin of a Municipal Council that now disposes of a Budget in the neighbourhood of twenty-five million Chinese dollars of Ordinary Revenue, to which has to be added some ten million Chinese dollars [1] from so-called extraordinary sources, which however are in their nature constant. Regulations suitable to a young community, some of which nevertheless still survive in the Land Regulations to-day, were prepared and in due course promulgated by the Chinese authorities.

In 1846, with a record of three years of sound accomplishment, Captain Balfour elected to abandon the consular career for which he had been seconded and to return to his soldier's life. His successor was Rutherford Alcock.

The central figure of Alexander Michie's great book, *The Englishman in China*, Rutherford Alcock was born in 1809. He started life as a surgeon, and as a young man saw service in the Peninsula, first in a British Portuguese force in the dynastic struggle to seat the rightful sovereign on the throne of Portugal, and later in the Spanish Foreign Legion in defence of Queen Christina of Spain. In the years that followed his return to England his experience and ability were opening up possibilities of great promise in his profession when in 1844, at the age of thirty-five, he had to abandon surgery through an affection of the hands resulting from some mysterious fever, a legacy, it was supposed, from Peninsular campaigns. His prospects in life seemed over when the opportunity presented itself which was to lead him successively to the legations at Peking and Tokio. He was chosen one of the five consuls needed for the new treaty ports in China. After a few months' service in Amoy and a year and a half at Foochow he was transferred to Shanghai where in the course of eight years he was once and for all to establish his reputation.

The happy relations subsisting from the earliest times with the country people of the neighbourhood led to the authorization of free movement by foreigners in the neighbourhood of Shanghai

[1] To those unacquainted with China the use of the term Chinese dollars is confusing. On the other hand an inaccurate impression would be produced by reducing it to sterling. When the writer came to China thirty-five years ago, thirty-five million local dollars, roughly the present revenue of the International Settlement, would have purchased three and a half million golden sovereigns. To-day it can only buy two million pound notes. But the local value as the measure of municipal revenue, though not so great now as then, is by no means represented by such a great discrepancy. It has to be remembered that the Chinese dollar is the unit of the country and except in relation to imported goods and commitments in foreign currencies it is not primarily affected by foreign exchanges. It is the rise of the standard of living which has reduced in some directions the purchasing power of the local dollar.

within a radius of thirty miles. But in 1849 those happy relations
were disturbed by an attack on three English missionaries within
the radius, not by any of the inhabitants but by some discharged
junk-men from the government grain-junks cast adrift and left
to fend for themselves much in the manner of disbanded soldiers
to which Chinese and foreigners have in recent years become so
unhappily accustomed. Representations failed to obtain redress.
The situation which then arose is thus stated by Mr. Michie :

' An absolutely unprovoked murderous outrage had been
perpetrated on three Englishmen ; the Chinese authorities
refused redress with insolence and evasion ; acquiescence
in the denial of justice would have been as fatal to future
good relations at Shanghai as it had been in the previous
decade in Canton. What was the official charged with the
protection of his countrymen to do ? He had no instructions
except to conciliate the Chinese ; there was no telegraph to
England ; communication even with the chief superintendent
of trade at Hongkong, 850 miles off, was dependent on
chance sailing vessels. Delay was equivalent to surrender.
Now or never was the peremptory alternative presented to
the consul, who, taking his official life in his hands, had to
decide and act on his own personal responsibility.
' Fortunately for the Consul and for the peaceful development of British trade, one of Palmerston's specific instructions had been obeyed in Shanghai. There was a British
ship of war in port, the 10-gun brig *Childers*, and, what was
of still more importance, a real British man on board of her,
Commander Pitman, who shared to the full the Consul's
responsibility for what was done.
' The measures adopted by Consul Alcock—when negotiation was exhausted—were to announce to the Chinese
authorities that, until satisfaction had been obtained, no
duties should be paid on cargo imported or exported in
British ships ; furthermore, that the great junk fleet of 1,400
sail, laden and ready for sea with the tribute rice for Peking,
should not be allowed to leave the port. The *Childers*,
moored in the stream below the junk anchorage, was in a
position to make this a most effective blockade. The rage
of the Taotai rose to fever heat, and it was then he threatened,
and no doubt attempted to inflame the populace and the
whole vagabond class. At the same time Vice-Consul
Robertson, with Parkes for interpreter, was dispatched to

Nanking on board her Majesty's ship *Espiegle* to lay the whole case before the viceroy of Kiangnan. The matter was there promptly attended to, full redress was ordered, and the culprits punished exactly three weeks after the assault. The embargo on the rice-junks was removed, and affairs resumed their normal course.' [1]

In the following year, 1854, was fought the famous ' Battle of Muddy Flat.' On March 19, 1853, Nanking had fallen before the Taiping rebels practically without a struggle, the Tartar garrison of 20,000 being put ruthlessly to the sword. The consequent panic was taken advantage of by the Triad Society, the most famous of China's secret societies, to seize the Chinese city of Shanghai, which they succeeded in occupying for some eighteen months. But it was the Imperial troops gathered to expel them who proved the menace to the Foreign Settlement. Not only did it become unsafe to proceed beyond the Settlement limits, but the soldiery became so aggressive, despite all official protests, that it was necessary to retaliate in self-defence.

After the necessary plans had been duly concerted, a demand was sent to the Chinese general for the withdrawal of all his soldiers from the vicinity of the Settlement, failing which his position would be attacked by all the available foreign forces. When this ultimatum was not complied with marines and blue-jackets from British and American ships with sailors from the merchant ships in port and about two hundred of the residents as infantry volunteers, delivered an attack on the Chinese position. It may have been ' a hazardous, if not a reckless, undertaking,' as one of the volunteers writing ' forty years on ' described it. But to compare great events with lesser so was Plassey. Both necessarily involved unavoidable risk which gallantry, determination and good fortune overcame. Thenceforward the Imperial troops were never lacking in respectful behaviour towards foreigners. Subsequently several foreigners served with them against the rebels, while a British officer, ' Chinese Gordon,' was destined ten years later to lead them to victory.

The threat to the Settlement from the Imperial troops was not the only dangerous consequence of the Taiping Rebellion. Another was the great inrush of Chinese seeking protection and raising new problems of taxation and control. If Chinese were

[1] *The Englishman in China*, by Alexander Michie, pp. 130–2.

to live in the Settlement clearly they must contribute to its support. The question of taxation became acute in 1862. Chinese in the area had now been taxed for some years when the Chinese authorities claimed the right of taxation also. By then, as we have seen, there was a British Minister in Peking and Sir Frederick Bruce upheld the Chinese view. Criticizing the policy which from mixed motives of gain and humanitarian sentiment had led to the sacrifice of the comfort and security of the Foreign Settlement by admitting Chinese to live in the area, he pointed out that by the acts of foreigners themselves it was no longer a foreign settlement but a Chinese city. When to meet the difficulty a proposal came from Shanghai that it be made a free city with a joint consular and municipal government under a joint protectorate of the Treaty Powers, he asserted vigorously the objections in principle, incidentally showing once more how far removed was British policy in China from Imperial design.[1]

However, the point had really been settled by a Proclamation issued by the Taotai in 1855 making new land regulations, adopted by the foreign residents, in the previous year, binding on Chinese and making them liable to contribute to ' any general assessment.'

The control of a considerable Chinese population also made advisable if it did not necessitate the establishment of some sort of tribunal in the settlement to deal with Chinese offenders. The need was met in 1864 by the establishment of a mixed Court presided over by a deputy of the Shanghai Magistrate, with Consular assessors in certain cases.

Meanwhile the French and American Settlements had been steadily growing and local sentiment favoured the amalgamation of the three areas. To that end Land Regulations were prepared in 1866. But before they became effective in 1869 the national sentiment of the French caused their withdrawal from the scheme, leaving British and Americans to form what was for many years known as the British-American Settlement until it was gradually transformed into the microcosm we know to-day. Shanghai had now emerged from the chrysalis stage. Its foundations had been laid. Henceforth there were to exist side by side three municipal organs : the Chinese city, which in modern times was to be included in the great Chinese municipal scheme of Greater Shanghai, the International Settlement and the French Concession.

[1] See Bluebook, China, No. 3, of 1864.

Chapter 28
Modern Shanghai

Shanghai steadily grew. An able line of British Consuls which included Wade and Parkes, both destined to follow Rutherford Alcock to Peking, maintained proconsular tradition. From time to time advantage was taken of the international relations that existed in Victorian times to revise the Land Regulations of the International Settlement, the last revision taking place in 1899. Similarly, while negotiation with the Chinese Authorities was not too difficult, steps were taken to enlarge the areas of the International Settlement and the French Concession. Keeping pace with these aspects of its growth Shanghai's public men exercised the usual civic functions with liberality and forethought. The community experienced, of course, the set-backs that must inevitably be associated with the process of harmonizing western principles and methods of municipal administration with the long-established customs of the East. Nevertheless writing at the end of 1900 of the Shanghai Municipal Council, as the Council of the International Settlement, then often called the ' Model Settlement,' was and still is known, Alexander Michie claimed that it had established ' as fine a record of public service as any such body has ever done.'

But Michie wrote of the comparatively easy days of Shanghai, of those pleasant times in China which inspired Bland's *House-Boat Days in China*, and Sowerby's *Sportman's Miscellany*. It was before the period of huge growth. The Cathedral chimes could still be heard from people's homes. He was contemplating a municipality which in 1900 disposed of a budget of less than a million and a half Chinese dollars. To-day it disposes of a revenue from all sources increased twenty-fold, reflecting a growth, with its concomitant complications and responsibilities, which has won for Shanghai a place within the ten great cities of the world. In 1900 its testing times had still to come.

In the last chapter it was written of as long ago as 1866, when foreign Shanghai was little over twenty years old, that the foundations had been laid. It was no mere figure of speech that was employed. For from those days dates the genesis of the major

188

problems of Shanghai which can be traced running like threads through the story of the past until resulting in the critical questions of the present.

In the first place, there is and always has been the problem of the control of the vast Chinese population which had called into existence a local Court. The fears voiced by Sir Frederick Bruce in 1862 have been fully realized. By 1900 the Chinese population in the International Settlement was 350,000. The need of security for business and successive waves of refugees during disturbed times have increased it till to-day it exceeds a million.

As political consciousness grew in China objection was taken to a Court in which consular officers participated, although only in an advisory capacity. But paradoxically the Revolution saved the Mixed Court for several years. Instability of the local government at the time of the Revolution and the absence in succeeding years of a central government controlling a unified China made change impossible and compelled the Consular Body to assume responsibility for its continued maintenance. For fifteen years Shanghai was the rich goal of successive militarists. It was not until 1927 that the Court was dissolved. In its stead was then established what was known as the Provisional Court. This in time yielded to the establishment of a District Court and Branch High Court under the scheme of the Chinese Judiciary under the modern laws. These courts function under agreements which give rise to many points of difficulty and fall far short of meeting the judicial and police needs of such a community. Still they function, if uneasily and not without justifiable criticism.

Another problem, the seeds of which were sown when Chinese were admitted to take up land set aside for foreign residence, has been the growth of a foreign population living outside the Settlement to serve which roads have been built, maintained and policed by the Council, and necessarily made the subject of taxation. Reference has already been made to the extensions from time to time of the boundaries of the International Settlement and the French Concession. The last extension of the French Concession was in 1914 as a result of which it stands at 2,525 acres. There has been no extension of the International Settlement since 1899 when the area was increased to 5,583 acres. But there has been settlement outside the International Settlement over an area of between 40 and 50 per cent greater than the area of the Settlement itself. These important developments, formerly acquiesced in, were to give rise in later days to questions involving the matter of Chinese Sovereignty, and to form one of the numerous and difficult problems of Shanghai under the name of ' External Roads Areas.'

A not less difficult problem has been that of Chinese representation. Unfortunately this was a field in which the leaders of Shanghai thought seem to have shown a lack of political vision. It was not till 1920 that in order to meet Chinese political consciousness, already a child of robust growth, an advisory Committee of Chinese was brought into being. Later in the same year a Chinese Ratepayers' Association was formed to voice their views. In 1926 it was proposed by the foreign ratepayers that three Chinese members should be added to the Council, which at that time consisted of nine foreigners. This was not acceptable to ' Young China ' and it was only in 1928 that the Chinese Councillors first took their seats. In 1930 the number was increased to five.

A similar complication arises from the international factor resulting from the generous policy of the British, reflected in 1863 by the amalgamation with the much less developed American area. Great Britain might have adopted a nationalist policy at Shanghai as France has done. Instead she has shared with all other nations the rights and benefits which she herself has won. She was content to impress the area with the freedom of English institutions.

After the Sino-Japanese War and Japan's entry into China as a Treaty Power in 1895, there was a gradual and important infiltration of Japanese into the Treaty Ports, more particularly at Shanghai. The importance of the Japanese element in the community was not overlooked. In recent years, the representation of the community on the Council has consisted of five British members, two American members and two Japanese members, to which are added the five Chinese members already referred to who are the nominees of the Chinese Ratepayers' Association.

This can hardly be criticized as an unfair distribution of representation. The Chinese and Japanese can combine to form a deadlock, and with the support of one American or British member could control the Council. In practice there is little danger of combination between Chinese and Japanese save in some racial crisis. But clearly political pressure by Japan in China might produce a deadlock and if there were one more Japanese Councillor it could result in a majority control.

In this delicate situation a campaign began in the press of other than British nationalities in Shanghai against the predominant position occupied by the British in the Municipal Council and its public services, having for its end the addition of one more Japanese representative on the Council at the expense of the British representation.

Notwithstanding a hint of political opportunism, the matter was considered dispassionately by the leaders of British thought in Shanghai in the light of history and existing conditions.

What then was found to be the position?

Historically the British were the founders of the Settlement. They built up the administrative machine and have always shouldered the largest share of the responsibility for its protection. To this day a great part of the arms and equipment used by the Shanghai Volunteers is loaned by the British War Office. In 1927 the British were the first to send at vast expense a defence force to guard Shanghai against an irruption of Nationalist and Communist soldiery.

As regards investments in the Settlement the *China Journal* of February 1936, put the British stake in Shanghai as computed in 1930 at £151 million as against £44 million for the Japanese and £26 million for the Americans. The average of the British contribution to the main municipal sources of revenue is at least three times that of the next highest foreign contribution.

It is only in population that the British fail to head the list of extra-territorial powers. In that respect they are out-distanced by Japan, who owing to proximity is enabled to fill junior positions in business houses with Japanese which the British fill with Chinese. There is also a poorer class of Japanese, occupied commercially or vocationally independently of big business, who contribute comparatively little to the Council's revenue but are asking for, and getting, an increasing share in its disbursements.

On review of these things could it be suggested that either

on moral or on material grounds the British should surrender the important voice in local affairs to which their achievements and interests entitle them ? Fortunately the voting strength, based on land and rental assessment franchises, of the three principal foreign national communities having seats on the Council being between 1,200 and 1,300 British, 900 Japanese and 400 American, the issue was settled in favour of the British at the polls.

This does not mean, of course, that the British fail to recognize the need of constitutional reform. When Mr. Justice Feetham was invited to Shanghai towards the end of 1929 it was expressly for the purpose of securing advice as to a possible solution of the problem, including the constitutional problem, of an area composed of round about fifty thousand foreigners of different nationalities and a million Chinese under existing political conditions in China. As the findings of the Report neither satisfied Chinese aspirations nor justified the then British policy in China, it unfortunately for the time being became a dead letter save for its moral value.

Such then are the four great problems inherited by the International Settlement from the past. For the sake of clarity we may repeat them : Jurisdiction over Chinese within the Limits of the Settlement, External Roads Areas, Municipal Representation of Chinese, and Municipal Representation of Foreigners. Of these the first three resulted from the admission of Chinese to residence, while the last resulted solely from the adoption by the British of a cosmopolitan as opposed to a purely national policy.

The French Concession has been saved from these controversies in their acute form by reason of the strict maintenance of its national status and the limitation of its municipal activities to the Concession area. Their chief problem has been that of Jurisdiction within the Concession and in that they have yielded to necessity following the British.

But these are not the only complications of Municipal Government in Shanghai.

If from the shipping standpoint and commercially, with its vast machinery for handling ships and distributing cargo and its great banks financing half the trade of China, Shanghai has become the London or the New York of the Far East, industrially Shanghai has also become the Lancashire of China, to which it adds docking, engineering, some shipbuilding [1] and many other forms of industrialism. One of the difficulties of an enlightened administration has been the introduction of modern factory legislation, engendering conflict between the economic place of women and children in the Chinese family by age-long custom and the principles of the crusade first led by the seventh Earl of Shaftesbury.

Finally there is the general political question.

It is many years now since the birth of the ' rights recovery ' movement in China, with the demands of which all must sympathize in principle. But like every other demand involving change, its gratification must depend on circumstances. There must be due regard to existing interests and provision of safeguards for the future. The answer to the demand for rendition of the International Settlement in any measurable distance of time is given concisely by Mr. Feetham.

> ' The objections to rendition as a practical policy for immediate adoption are overwhelming. Rendition to-day would not only be fatal to the " security " which, from the point of view of business interests, is the vital feature of the present Settlement regime, but would also render impossible the continuance of local self-government in any effective form.' [2]

Mr. Feetham does not rest, however, on a merely negative conclusion. He foresees a time when rendition will be possible, followed, as he suggests, ' by the grant by the Chinese Government of a Charter conferring rights of local self-government on the inhabitants of the Settlement, foreign and Chinese.' But he postulates fair conditions which must precede rendition, namely, the establishment of conditions in China removing ' any reasonable anxiety ' as to the safety of the Settlement in the event of civil war or local disturbances ; existence of the rule of law and a constitutional government which can guarantee ' a

---

[1] Vessels up to 14,000 tons dead weight have been constructed in Shanghai, including most of those which navigate the Yangtze Gorges. *The Port of Shanghai*, issued by the Whangpoo Conservancy Board (Eighth edition), p. 41. This publication should be consulted by anyone interested in the vast achievement commercially and industrially of a handful of foreigners, comparatively speaking, in Shanghai. Not least and of fundamental importance has been the work of river conservancy.

[2] Report of the Hon. Mr. Justice Feetham, C.M.G., Vol. II, p. 139.

self-governing basis and secure the inviolability of the rights under such a Charter '; political conditions permitting ' self-governing institutions to enjoy real independence,' free from the orders of the Government or the control of any political organization; and ' sufficient experience in the working of representative institutions ' to enable the Chinese community in the Settlement to assume ' the major share of responsibility ' in its administration.

' It is inevitable,' he concludes, ' that a long transition period should still intervene before these conditions can be adequately fulfilled.' [1]

Fortunately the brains of China do not all work on the lines of demand without regard to circumstances. During the past ten years a strong municipal progressive movement has taken place resulting in the creation of Greater Shanghai, establishing municipal control and encouraging development over an area of upwards of thirty square miles.

Already a great civic centre has been built up. On the foundation laid by its first mayor, the late V. K. Ting, who received his scientific education in Glasgow and wore himself out in the service of his country, being in recent years Secretary-General of the Academia Sinica, cultural objects have an honoured place. Signs of remarkable progress—a few years ago it would have been said unbelievable progress—exist on every hand. But even so, the stage is far from being reached at which the conditions suggested by Mr. Feetham could be considered reasonably satisfied. Moreover the taxable resources of the Settlement as a highly developed area so far exceed those of Greater Shanghai which as regards development is in its infancy, that as Mr. Feetham points out, ' unless some satisfactory arrangement were made as to the allocation of revenue for the protection of the Ratepayers of the Settlement, they might find that as the result of amalgamation, the greater portion of the revenue which they provided was being devoted to the administration and development of the Chinese area.'

But if the time is not yet, at least the goal is in view. Meanwhile responsible foreigners are not without a sense of stewardship. As in the past, so to-day in the International Settlement, the British civic ideal still maintains its sway.

[1] *Ibidem*, p. 140.

In terms of statesmanship and vision, which it would be unfair to Mr. Feetham not to quote, the position was thus stated by him in 1931 and, despite much progress, remains true to-day.

> ' The chain of historical circumstances which have led to a foreign community having so large a share in governing, on Chinese soil, the most important part of the town which is the chief commercial centre of China, are circumstances which no one could have anticipated, and for which the present generation has no primary responsibility. These circumstances, coupled with the energy and enterprise of the foreign and Chinese communities in the Settlement, have created an asset of immense value for the China of to-day, and of still greater potential value for the China of the future. The Foreign Powers and their subjects are, under present treaty arrangements, trustees for China of the asset thus created : they would fail in the obligations of their trust if they, as the present guardians of the Settlement, were to hand it over to China before she is ready to receive it, and in a position to safeguard and develop it for herself. For the time being, it should be sufficient to meet Chinese national aspirations that the trust is recognized, and that the governing body of the Settlement under the present constitution is seeking, with the active co-operation of its Chinese members, to discharge its responsibilities, in the interval which must elapse before rendition, in the interests not only of foreign nations and their subjects, but of China herself and her nationals, whose interests, both as present beneficiaries and as ultimate heirs, greatly predominate over all the foreign interests taken together.' [1]

Nevertheless, Shanghai has often been criticized and much play has been made with the charge of a peculiar outlook which has been called ' the Shanghai mind.' Certainly it cannot be denied that Shanghai at times has appeared to regard its peculiar problems as the main problems of China. This mental attitude, however, is not endemic. At worst it is symptomatic of a certain type of mind which is found in most communities.

Necessarily there have been mistakes. How could it be otherwise under conditions which were often those of considerable strain, although social intercourse with Chinese, making for removal of misunderstandings, might despite its difficulties have

[1] Report of the Hon. Mr. Justice Feetham, C.M.G., Vol. II, p. 134.

been more cultivated ? Again, Shanghai has its material and sordid sides, accentuated by its cosmopolitanism, and an underworld which has little to learn from Chicago.

But with some appreciation of the problems of the International Settlement, for that is the heart of Shanghai, no impartial person can criticize too severely its limitations or underrate its achievements. Not without honourable record in the cultural field, its supreme justification lies in its vast contribution to China's economic fabric. Of this Shanghai's magnificent water-front reflects at least a measure. Approaching it in the golden dusk of a summer evening it is permissible for an Englishman recalling history to gaze with a sense of pride. And a man who has given his working life to Shanghai, taking his not unsorrowful farewell as he leaves for the last time, may be forgiven if he murmurs in his heart ' cujus pars fui.'

Chapter 29

The Later Treaty Ports

The absence of any insuperable difficulty in establishing trade relations at the early Treaty Ports north of Canton, more particularly at Shanghai, showed that the problem of foreign intercourse on practicable lines was not insoluble. But at Canton the old spirit of anti-foreignism lived on. Foreigners still had their abode in the factories, where ' they were subject to much insult and many injuries, while entry into the city of Canton was barred to consul, merchant and missionary alike. The Imperial Government had made a treaty of peace, but the people of Canton remained implacably hostile.' [1] There were faults on both sides.

[1] *Far Eastern International Relations*, by H. B. Morse and H. F. MacNair, pp. 146, 147 : see also following pages. It should be noted that anti-foreignism has always been officially condoned, except in cases where redress of outrage has been insisted on. It has also been used

In those days men were not imbued with a nice sense of legal requirement where what they regarded as natural right was interfered with. Nevertheless the occasions of foreign provocation fell far short of any justification of the treatment meted out to foreigners and of the acts of violence which culminated in 1847 in the barbarous murder of six young Englishmen when on a country walk scarcely three miles from Canton. Finally by 1852, only ten years after the Treaty of Nanking, the policy of ignoring foreign representatives, the real cause of the war, had reasserted itself.

The British Treaty of Nanking concerned itself with principles. It was not the desire of Britain to humiliate China by imposing the detail of intercourse between the two peoples. The French and American treaties which followed two years later covered this weakness by containing clauses for revision after twelve years. When this period had elapsed two attempts were made to exercise this right with consequences which compelled the conclusion that ' no revision of the treaties could be obtained, unless supported and enforced by a demonstration of armed force.' [1] The Chinese were committed to what Alexander Michie called ' the settled policy of keeping foreigners at arm's length at all costs.'

In due course war ensued. Once more circumstances thrust the main responsibility upon Great Britain in Chinese eyes, although the French were her allies and the Americans had demolished forts at Canton which fired on the American flag and had exacted other redress for an earlier incident. Again the war was misnamed, becoming known in history as the ' *Arrow* War,' although its causes were as deep-seated as ever and it could not fairly be ascribed to any passing incident however serious.

Hongkong had established a register of shipping in which the lorcha *Arrow*, a Chinese craft owned by a Hongkong Chinese, was registered. Chinese Authority was aware of the existence of this registry, which certainly involved the possibility of friction. But no protest was made, the usefulness of the registry in promoting trade being recognized.

On October 8, 1856, when lying off Canton, flying the British

at times as a means of diverting the stream of public opinion and securing cohesion.

[1] *Far Eastern International Relations*, by H. B. Morse and H. F. MacNair, p. 159.

flag, her English master being temporarily absent, the lorcha *Arrow* was boarded by some sixty Chinese soldiers with their officer, allegedly in search of a notorious pirate. The British flag was hauled down and the Chinese crew of twelve were bound and thrown into the guard boats. The demand for apology and redress made by Harry Parkes, who was now the British Consul at Canton, not being complied with, the British Navy took various steps by way of reprisal. The Chinese replied by offering rewards for English heads and in December by setting fire to the factories which shortly became a mass of smoking ruins. Other outrages followed. One was the capture of a non-belligerent packet-boat on her way from Canton to Hongkong, whose ' Chinese passengers having soldiers' uniforms under their outer clothes, produced concealed weapons and captured the ship. The eleven foreigners on board were killed, including the Spanish vice-Consul at Whampoa ; the heads were cut off and the ship run ashore and burned.' [1] Another was an attempt in Hongkong early in 1857 to poison the foreign community by arsenic introduced into the bread by a Chinese baker, Chinese officials, it is generally conceded, being implicated in this barbarous act.

Still there was no war. Sir John Bowring, the British plenipotentiary residing at Hongkong, endeavoured to have his complaints communicated to the Throne. He was consistently referred to Commissioner Yeh, the chief cause of the trouble, at Canton. Imperial Edicts confirmed the latter's authority and fitness for dealing with the crisis. A deadlock ensued to which there could only be one solution.

' The two nations,' as the American writers, whose important work has already been drawn upon, summarized the position, ' drifted into war. To the Chinese it seemed absurd that a trifling irregularity in the arrest of pirates, in whose suppression Chinese and English were actually co-operating, should bring on a war. To the English it was no less absurd that satisfaction should have been peremptorily refused for a flagrant insult to the British flag. As a matter of fact, the war had been brewing since 1842 ; each year that had elapsed had made war increasingly inevitable.' [2]

---

[1] *Far Eastern International Relations*, by H. B. Morse and H. F. MacNair, p. 168.
[2] *Ibidem*, p. 169.

This time the war was carried into more northern waters and the Treaty which brought it to an end in 1858 was concluded at Tientsin.

The importance of this Treaty has already been dwelt upon. Besides providing for a British representative to the Court at Peking, it opened five more ports on the China coast and made provision for the eventual opening of the Yangtze to foreign trade. Tientsin itself, the gateway to Peking, still remained closed to foreigners. But as we have already seen, the throwing of a boom across the mouth of the Haiho, the river on which Tientsin is situated, and resistance in 1859 to Sir Frederick Bruce's coming to Peking to take up his residence as British Minister, brought about the war of 1860, which did something to convince the Government itself that in some respects at least other nations were more than its equal. By the treaty of peace concluded at Peking, Tientsin was opened to foreign trade. By subsequent treaties and understandings, and in later times on Chinese initiative, still more centres were thrown open, until there were some fifty ports and inland cities at which foreigners might reside and trade. At many of these places the number of foreigners was never more than negligible and in most of them they neither desired nor enjoyed municipal privileges. This fact in conjunction with what we have already seen of the genesis of the older Treaty Ports and the conditions under which they developed, is sufficient to enable us to realize the unbelievable inaccuracy of a statement in the House of Commons, made only just over ten years ago, that it was 'not surprising that there was agitation in China when the external Powers took forty-nine Chinese cities, giving the Chinese no share in their government.'

To the smaller ports space forbids any reference except perhaps to say that in their way each has contributed something to the sum total of foreign influences, while the circumstances of the opening of the upper reaches of the Yangtze is matter for British pride.

' One of the romances of modern shipping enterprise, with it the names of two pioneers, both British subjects, will for ever be associated. They are the late Mr. Archibald Little and the late Captain C. S. Plant. Mr. Little first made the trip from Shanghai to Chungking in 1883. The voyage took fifty-nine days, of which twenty-one were spent on the trip from Ichang to Chungking, a distance of about 462 miles. By the Chefoo convention 1876 it had been agreed that the British Government might send officers to reside at Chungking " to watch the conditions of British trade in Szechuan." But British merchants were " not to be allowed to reside at Chungking, or to open establishments or warehouses there," so long as no steamers had access to the port. When steamers had succeeded in ascending the river, further arrangements could be " taken into consideration."

'Mr. Little made an attempt to fulfil this condition in February 1888, when he appeared at Ichang with the steamer *Kuling*, of 304 tons, which had been specially constructed for the navigation of the rapids. The Chinese authorities considered the effort premature, and eventually purchased the steamer, which was handed over to the China Merchants' S.N. Co., and used by that Company for many years on the Hankow–Ichang run. But Mr. Little, like Kipling's explorer, was obsessed with the " everlasting whisper."

'Something hidden. Go and find it. Go and look behind the ranges——
Something lost behind the Ranges. Lost and waiting for you. Go!'

'He concentrated all his energies upon the opening up of the Upper Yangtze to steam navigation. And, like many other pioneers with one idea, he eventually achieved his purpose, although it was not until 1899 that the *Pioneer*, another of Mr. Little's ventures, arrived in Chungking, having taken 73 steaming hours, or seven days in all, to make the trip from Ichang, having been brought up river by Captain S. C. Plant.'[1]

The romance of the Great River and its famous gorges, the place it has in the life and hearts of the Chinese people, the ship-designing, navigational and hydrographic activities of Captain Plant and others, may be read in other places. Here we cannot digress further. Return must be made to the main stream of our story which takes us first to Hankow and then to Tientsin to complete in general terms our sketch of the Treaty Ports.

[1] Memorandum No. 14 of the Tientsin British Committee of Information embodying under the title of ' The trouble on the Upper Yangtze,' a series of articles by H. G. W. Woodhead, C.B.E., published in November, 1926, in the *Peking and Tientsin Times*. Pleasurable reference may also be made to Mrs. Hobart's novel, *River Supreme*.

With Hankow we are already acquainted, for it saw the outbreak of the Revolution in 1911 and was the victim of Communist machinations just over fifteen years later. Situated in the heart of China, with its sister cities of Wuchang and Hanyang it forms a vast hive of human beings and human industry, the greatest indeed in the country. It has often been thought of as a potential Chicago. Splendidly situated on the Yangtze, with railway connection now completed from Peiping to Canton, it should yet achieve such a destiny. Hitherto as a foreign trading centre it has been mainly an outpost of Shanghai. Nevertheless it has played no mean part in the commercial, industrial and cultural developments of central China, the small British Concession as first-comer leading the way while in later years other nationalities made their contributions. We have seen how the British Concession became what is called a ' Special Area ' under ultimate Chinese control.

The term ' Special Area ' came into being during the Great War. When in 1917 China sided with the Allies, all German and Austrian Concessions were taken over. It was intended at first that some foreign representation should continue in these areas built up by foreign enterprise and calling for municipal administration on foreign lines, and this plan was carried out at Hankow, but nothing in the way of franchise was granted in Tientsin. When in 1924 Russian Concessions were taken over by China they were also treated in the two places differently, following the local precedents.

Arrangements made for the administration of the British Concession under what became known as the Chen.-O'Malley agreement in 1927 followed in general the Hankow lines. Provision was made for the establishment of a Municipal Bureau, presided over by a Director selected and appointed by the Minister of Foreign Affairs, his appointment being confirmed by the Nationalist Government. This Director was to be Chief Executive Officer of the district, and ex-officio Chairman of the Municipal Council. The Council was to consist of seven members, namely, the Director, and six elected Councillors, of whom three were to be Chinese and three British, elected at the Annual General Meeting.

At first, however, the Nationalists showed so little desire to implement their obligations that as early as May 9, 1927, Sir

Austen Chamberlain told the House of Commons that the question of reoccupation of the former British Concession at Hankow had been most carefully considered.

> ' The logic and justice of such a step at first strongly appealed to us. . . . Had we wished now to occupy the Concession, we have ample justification. The Nationalist Government have neither observed the spirit of the Agreement signed at Hankow nor have they made any attempt to reciprocate the friendly attitude which we have displayed towards them. I need only refer to the recent occupation of the British Concession and Consulate at Chinkiang by Nationalist troops, to the events at Nanking, and to the fact that all British subjects have had to be evacuated from up-country districts and from many of the towns of the Yangtze, and that our Consulates at Chengtu, Chungking, Ichang and Changsha have had to close. . . . On full consideration, however, the Government has decided not to take this step at present, and we hope that it will not be forced upon us, the Hankow Agreement having been signed, not for the exigencies of the moment, but with a view to our whole future policy in China.' [1]

Sir Austen Chamberlain's hopes were destined to be realized at least in part owing to the ability and determined loyalty of those members of the British Community at Hankow to whom was entrusted the task of upholding the British side. In later years the Chinese official element showed a more reasonable tendency and a *modus vivendi* has been achieved. It would be unsafe to assume, however, that the Hankow precedent is one that can be safely followed. In view of recent developments in North China it was fortunate that the British Concession at Tientsin escaped a like fate.

[1] Quoted in Memorandum No. 23 of the Tientsin British Committee of Information, compiled by H. G. W. Woodhead, C.B.E., which gives an account of the difficulties which the first three British members of the Council, Messrs. Charleton, Dixon and Dupree, were called upon to face.

Chapter 30
The Treaty Port of Tientsin

Physical conditions and the lines of commercial development have divided China into three parts, of which the gateways and commercial capitals are Canton, Shanghai and Tientsin. Politically they correspond in the South to those provinces which are loosely linked together under the name of the South-Western Federation and have only lately given full allegiance to Nanking ; in central China to the Yangtze Valley directly controlled by the central government ; and in the North to those provinces north of the Yellow River which are rapidly coming under the domination of Japan.

The origins of Tientsin are lost in the mists of antiquity. But of all the Treaty Ports, with the exception of Canton, it is historically the most interesting. Situated on the marshy fringe of the North China plain, it is thought by some that from the formation and growth of the Haiho delta it may in some remote antiquity have been on or near the sea. But within historic times it more probably owes its position to the Chinese fear of pirates, which as elsewhere dictated the growth of ports up rivers rather than on the coast, and to an important confluence of waterways to which was added in the twelfth century the Grand Canal. The latter, designed by Kublai Khan to connect his capital at Peking with Hangchow south of the Yangtze, the former capital of the Sung Dynasty, was a principal means of providing uninterrupted inland water communication between Peking and Canton. This was an advantage to transport when the pirates in the China seas had the upper hand, but it has increased the conservancy problems of the rivers it crosses.

By the thirteenth century, when Tientsin was visited by Marco Polo, it had achieved a position of substantial importance. In the Ming Dynasty its outstanding position received official recognition. In the fifteenth century the great Ming Emperor Yung Lo, who had recently transferred his capital from Nanking back to Peking, realized its strategic importance and established there a garrison. The city was then renamed ' T'ien Chin Wei,' meaning ' the Guard of the Heavenly Ford,' since the embassies of tributary states were obliged at this point to cross the waterways which barred their road to the Capital of the Son of Heaven.[1]

More than two centuries later the pre-eminent position of Tientsin was testified to by the first Dutch Embassy to Peking under Peter de Goyer and Jacob de Keyzer in 1566, which accounted it 'very populous and so full of Trade that hardly, the like Commerce is to be found in any other city in all China.'

It was opened to foreign trade by the Treaty of Peking concluded in 1860, and in the following year areas were set aside for British, French and American residence, the British Area being laid out by Gordon, then a Captain in the Royal Engineers. In 1895 Germany secured a Concession, and during the Boxer troubles residential areas were acquired by most of the remaining Treaty Powers.

The size and importance of the foreign quarter which has grown up is not always realized. Whereas the British Area at Canton is approximately 75 acres and at Hankow 115 acres, at Tientsin as a result of two extensions in 1899 and 1902 respectively it is 992 acres. Again, taking the area of foreign residence at Tientsin as a whole, it is practically equal to half of the area of foreign residence at Shanghai. It will be recalled that the International Settlement at Shanghai has an area of 5,584 acres, and the French Settlement 2,483 acres, making a total of 8,067 acres. The total area of Foreign Concessions at Tientsin, including former Concessions now Special Areas under Chinese control, is 3,475 acres.

The original area for foreign residence was a narrow strip of land situated at an appreciable distance from the city lower down the river. Consisting partly of market gardens but mainly of snipe marsh, the growth of what is now a modern city was slow in its early years. Cut off from the world for the winter months by a climate of almost arctic severity, which closed the water-ways and even froze the sea, no large sums of capital were available for its making. The foreign population was a handful of men and women, mostly British, with nothing much but courage and faith. The north of China was a *terra incognita* with no great staples of tea and silk on which to base its trade. New possibilities had to be developed, and what in future years was to become a great trade based primarily on low-grade wools is one of the romances

[1] *An Outline History of Tientsin*, by O. D. Rasmussen, p. 8.

of British pioneering enterprise. Unfortunately in recent years Russian invasion in the north-west and Japanese railway advance through Manchoukuo have reduced and now even threaten the extinction of this fine wool trade by establishing control of the vast grazing country. Its place, however, as a staple industry has been largely supplied by cotton, a product increasingly developed in North China during recent years.

Long since become the second treaty port of China, Customs statistics show Tientsin's trade over a period of years as producing a revenue between one-fourth and one-fifth of that of Shanghai, which is the port of entry of half the trade in China. But these figures do not accurately represent the proportion of trade as between the two ports, since a large quantity of goods which pay import duty at Shanghai are subsequently re-exported to northern and Yangtze ports. Tientsin, on the other hand, is entirely a port of destination and entry for the country it directly serves.

Years ago the position of Tientsin made it a nodal point in the matter of railway development far in advance of any other port in China. To the north-east the Peking–Mukden railway connects with the network of railways in Manchuria (Manchoukuo). To the north-west it serves Peking and connects with the Peking–Hankow railway and the Suiyuan railway, which taps the great wool-producing country to the north-west. Southward it is connected with Nanking by the Tientsin–Pukow railway. At the same time Tientsin has not been backward in the matter of public utilities and industrial development largely inspired by foreign enterprise.

Meanwhile it has passed through stirring times. Never quite free in the early days from the threat of a populace noted throughout China for its turbulence until Li Hung-chang's great viceroyalty, in 1900 Tientsin was besieged by the Boxers and reduced almost to the last bullets reserved for women and children when James Watts [1] rode in at the head of the relieving column. During the years of Civil War since the Revolution, Tientsin has been on the lines of communication and not infrequently called upon to mobilize in defence of the foreign areas, or against defeated troops seeking refuge. Nor has the history of modern times done anything to distract from the political importance of this northern port, while commercially, with Manchuria lost to

[1] *Ante*, p. 18.

China and Tsingtao daily coming more under the domination of Japan, Tientsin is the only substantial mart in North China which remains as the medium of European and American trade.

When in the spring of 1927 Tientsin was faced for a time with the fate that overtook Hankow, economic consequences of Russian political activities to the north-west had begun to be felt. At the same time the hand of Japan was already on Manchuria and a forward policy was indicated, though its extent could not then be foreseen. The political value of maintaining the British position in Tientsin was therefore manifest not only to the British but to the Chinese. Of equal importance to trade was the maintenance of security as guaranteed by the Rule of Law on which Mr. Feetham laid such stress when discussing the problems of Shanghai. In addition to these considerations the British interest in Tientsin was no small one.

In setting itself to the task that lay before it, Tientsin had certain points in its favour. On the foundations laid by a generation of pioneers, a succeeding generation had built up a sound and progressive Municipality. From the earliest times municipal development had proceeded on liberal lines. Men without distinction of nationality were elected to the Council. As long ago as 1874 a Chinese had been invited to a seat. In 1899, on the occasion of the first extension necessitating a Council for the new area which had to be brought to a stage of development where it could equitably be treated as an extension of the original Concession, provision was made for a Chinese representative. In 1918, the time having arrived when it was advisable for the two British extensions of 1899 and 1902 to be incorporated with the original Concession, provision was made for the election of two Chinese Councillors out of nine, one of whom was an American, the American Concession having been placed under British administration. Other departments of municipal activity were conducted on similar lines, while social relations existed at least with some of the resident Chinese.

Again the Chinese Revolution had created political insecurity, with the result that Tientsin had become something in the nature of a treasure house and a political sanctuary. Apart from this, the British municipal area was already the residence of Chinese of standing, who recognized British good faith and passively supported the continued maintenance of the Municipality. In the Great War, owing to the demand for raw materials, money had flowed into Tientsin. Prosperity made for municipal progress and there was no desire to change the existing state of affairs.

Another fortunate element in the situation was the absence of the extreme fanaticism which had prevailed in Hankow. This resulted in a less unpleasant atmosphere, though under existing conditions of strong national sentiment no Chinese could admit to being satisfied with any but the maximum demands.

Lastly, the community had cause for gratitude to Sir Miles Lampson, the British Minister, who conceived the idea that the Tientsin problem could be best dealt with in Tientsin itself through the medium of a Sino-British Commission and persuaded the Chinese Government to accept this view.[1]

In the circumstances of the times it was not to be expected that a satisfactory agreement could be reached. Negotiations in fact were only successful in producing a draft agreement which reserved certain points for consideration by the two Governments.

Political events combined to delay a solution along the lines discussed. In the meantime equality of franchise was established in the British Area and representation was still further liberalized. The Council was increased to ten members of whom five were to be British, with a British Chairman. The remaining councillors might be elected without distinction of nationality. In practice they have all been Chinese and the municipal machine has worked well.

Space forbids any extended reference to the foreign cultural contribution made by Tientsin to North China, but four institutions may perhaps be mentioned. Of these two are Hospitals and two are Schools.

The Peiyang Naval College in the French Concession has maintained for many years a French School of Medicine. The Mackenzie Memorial Hospital which, as its name implies, is British, commemorates a famous medical worker of the London Mission in the China field. The same Mission is the founder and supporter of the Tientsin Anglo-Chinese College which, modelled on St. John's College, Cambridge, was established and developed under the inspiration and brilliant direction of Dr. S.

[1] The British members were Sir James Jamieson, K.C.M.G., H.B.M., Consul-General, Mr. P. C. Young, C.B.E., Chairman of the Municipal Council, and the author. Three Chinese members were appointed by the Peking Government, but they were augmented by three appointees of Chang Tso-lin and an appointee of the Tientsin Government.

Lavington Hart, himself a former fellow of John's and a Doctor of Science of London and Paris. The Anglo-Chinese College is second to no similar institution in China in the value of its work and its contribution to Anglo-Chinese understanding. Finally, the British Municipality, besides its Grammar School, boasts a modern school for the accommodation of 1,400 Chinese boys and girls. Few, if any, middle schools in the country are better housed or more finely equipped. Registered at Nanking in order to ensure the status of its alumni, it has had the honour of leading the way in the field of Chinese education in an important direction. Many observers have felt that the elimination of Chinese classical culture from modern education was a mistake. This is now generally conceded. But the Tientsin Kung Hsueh or Public School, as it is called, of the British Municipality was the first registered school to give effect in its curriculum to this humanizing idea.

Chapter 31

Chinese Government Administrations

Not the least of the contributions by the West to the East have been western methods and standards of government administration. In China these have found their most splendid illustration in the Customs Service which has long since become the corner-stone of Chinese finance, alike rescuing the country from embarrassment and contributing to progress.

There can have been few if any institutions destined to achieve so greatly which had a more fortuitous beginning. In September, 1853, when the Triad Society captured Shanghai, the Custom House established under the Treaty ceased to function. Thereupon the Consuls of the Treaty Powers devised a provisional system under which they took bonds from their nationals in respect of the duties which ordinarily would have been collected.

It seemed a simple and just way of dealing with a difficult situation. After five months, however, the system broke down. The merchants did not like it because there were traders of non-treaty powers who were avoiding all payment of duties, thus working hardship especially to Americans and British. The Chinese did not like it, presumably because they preferred cash to bonds, and the validity of the bonds had been questioned, a point which would have to be settled by the home governments before the bonds could be liquidated. The American Vice-Consul-in-Charge, one Murphy, cut the Gordian knot in February 1854 by declaring Shanghai a free port so far as American citizens were concerned.

An attempt was next made to re-establish the Custom House, which for a time essayed to function. But for reasons too complicated to discuss here, one of the chief of which was the disregard of authority by the subjects of those powers not yet in treaty relationship with China, the Shanghai Taotai found himself unable to collect duties impartially from all foreign traders. In consequence arrangements were made by the Chinese authorities for the collection of duties outside the limits of the Treaty Port, a solution of the problem which threatened dangerous consequences. If trade was not to be diverted from Shanghai insistence had to be laid on the maintenance of the provisions of the Treaty which called for the levy of duties at the Treaty Port itself, where they were collected under foreign eyes and export produce and import goods could not be made subject to irregular imposts. On the other hand a system required to be devised that would secure to China her full revenue. All traders therefore, whether or not subjects of the Treaty Powers, had to be brought under control in order to secure equality of trading rights.

In addition to these two fundamental requirements, the maintenance of foreign rights and the protection of Chinese Revenue, there was a third matter calling for adjustment, namely the liquidation of the bonds which had been collected under the Provisional System and liability for duties which had subsequently become due and payable.

At this juncture a new British Envoy, Sir John Bowring, arrived at Hongkong. About the same time a new American Commissioner, Robert M. McLane, reached Hongkong, while the first official United States Consul had been appointed to Shanghai, proving a valuable colleague to Rutherford Alcock.

It appears that neither Bowring nor McLane had any specific instructions as to how the matter of outstanding bonds and customs duties was to be dealt with, and taking a high view of the obligations of British and American merchants they assumed that these sums would be collected. With agreement between them established on this point McLane went to Shanghai to negotiate for the solution of the major problems. Bowring was not free to leave Hongkong at that time, the Crimean War having broken out and it being rumoured that a Russian fleet was in the East.

The first hint of a possible solution of the Customs problem came from Rutherford Alcock. ' I do not relinquish hope,' he wrote to Bowring, ' if the collection of duties can in any way be brought under the effective control of the Treaty Powers as to the executive of the Custom House Administration.'

This dispatch was dated May 1, 1854. On June 15, he submitted a memorandum elaborating his previous idea and suggesting ' association with the Chinese executive who shall be placed in charge of the Custom House Administration of a responsible and trustworthy Foreign Inspector of Customs.' [1]

Less than a month later a foreign inspectorate was formed by a commission of three appointees by the three Treaty Powers. These were an American, an Englishman and a Frenchman, Mr. L. Carr, Captain (afterwards Sir Thomas) Wade, British Minister in Peking, and Monsieur Smith.

Meanwhile the question of outstanding bonds and duties had not been settled. The sum which in the ordinary course should have been collected by the Chinese Government on duties during the period since the fall of Shanghai in September 1853 exceeded a million taels, equivalent to round about £250,000 sterling. Trade of other than American and British merchants accounted for not much more than 5 per cent, British merchants were accountable for two-thirds of the balance and Americans for the remaining third. [2] Although it does not appear that any undertaking was given to the Chinese Authorities, negotiations seem to have proceeded on the basis of their ultimate payment. Sir John Bowring's predecessor, however, had taken the contrary

---

[1] See *Chinese Social and Political Science Review*, Vol. xx, No. 1, April 1936, pp. 55 and 56, being the second instalment of a valuable monograph by J. K. Fairbank entitled ' Foreign Inspectorate of Customs at Shanghai,' contained in this and the preceding number.

[2] *Ibidem*, p. 60.

view of the supposed liability. The Chinese Government, he argued, had failed in their duty of protection under the Treaty, the foreign settlements having for months been an armed camp. In his opinion foreigners were released from their obligations under the Treaty, which were in their nature reciprocal. Furthermore, the Consul had no authority to act for the Chinese and the bonds therefore had no legal basis. The law officers of the Crown took the same view. The politically sound course, therefore, pursued by Rutherford Alcock and his American colleague was overborne. The bonds given by the British were cancelled by order of the British Secretary of State for Foreign Affairs. The American Department of State followed the same course.

In all the circumstances it was an unfortunate decision. It was one which the Chinese Authorities could not understand and therefore could only regard as a breach of faith. As it happened the new administration so early justified itself, while the Government became so increasingly occupied by the Taiping menace, that it created no dangerous feeling.

Of the three officers appointed to form the Foreign Inspectorate Wade alone had any knowledge of the Chinese language or any aptitude for the duties of his post. On his shoulders, therefore, fell the chief burden of organizing the new office. On his resignation a year later, his place was filled by Horatio Nelson Lay, who had an equal knowledge of Chinese and equally good powers of organization. The board of three continued, but the actual control came into the hands of its working member.

This arrangement lasted until 1858, when Lay was appointed Inspector-General of Customs. He was not destined, however, to hold the post for reasons which Mr. Morse has thus summarized.

' Under his authority Custom Houses had been opened at seven ports when, in June 1861, he was granted leave of absence and returned to England. He resumed duty as Inspector-General on May 9, 1863, and was relieved from duty on November 30 of the same year. A man of marked ability, he conceived that he was destined to be the Clive and Dupleix, the Lally and Hastings, of a renovated China ; and when he failed to induce the Imperial Government to share this view, he fell. While in England he had been commissioned to procure a fleet of gunboats for the repression of rebellion and piracy ; and the demand of Mr. Lay and his commander, Captain Sherard Osborne, that this fleet should be directly and solely under their orders, was one that could not be acceded to. The fleet was accordingly paid off, the ships sold, and Mr. Lay permitted to resign.' [1]

Horatio Lay was succeeded by Robert Hart, whose immediate problem has been thus briefly stated by Mr. Morse :

' Upon his appointment Mr. Hart found himself confronted by the difficulty that each Custom House had continued the decentralized system characteristic of Chinese administration, and that each commissioner, acting conjointly with his Chinese colleague the Superintendent, looked to the provincial authorities and considered local needs, and was disinclined to conform without question to the lead given by the centralizing office, the Inspectorate-General. The ability and tact which he has shown so uniformly, and in so many instances since, were never more marked than in Mr. Hart's first decade of office, the sixties, when he had to reconcile the Imperial Government to a form of administration which, though working in its interests, was distinctly alien ; to lead, with small powers of compulsion, subordinates of marked personality and of different nationalities to submit their judgment to his, and accept his instructions for their guidance ; and to introduce into Customs procedure the uniformity and system which are the necessary concomitants of effective administration. During that decade elementary questions were vital, and an unwise settlement could easily have undermined the foundations of the structure he was erecting.' [2]

It was not long before the value of the Administration was found to constitute a convenient agency for securing and undertaking the service of government loans. As early as the late sixties loans were from time to time made by foreign banks to meet occasional needs. But it was not until after the disastrous war with Japan that its great value was appreciated, loans aggregating upwards of fifty million sterling being raised in 1895,

[1] *Trade and Administration of the Chinese Empire*, by H. B. Morse, Commissioner of Customs and Statistical Secretary, Inspectorate-General of Customs, p. 356.
[2] *Ibidem*, p. 358.

1896 and 1898 in the European markets for purposes of indemnity payments and reconstruction purposes. A few years later in 1901 the Customs became the chief security for the Boxer Indemnity of 450 million haikwan taels, equivalent to sixty-seven and a half millions sterling. Again in 1913, for good or ill, it was used to back the salt revenue given as the first security for the Reorganization Loan.[1] To-day all the loans prior to the Boxer Indemnity charge, with the exception of a small balance of the Anglo-German loan of 1898, have been amortized. Consequently, with the jump in net revenue from approximately ten million sterling in 1928 to seventeen and a half million sterling in 1929 as a result of Tariff Autonomy, and the steady decrease in foreign loan service requirements to approximately five million sterling in 1934, substantial surplus for securing internal loans and the Government needs should be assured, assuming normal trade and the absence of illegal interference.[2]

But these and other financial operations which could be recalled have not been the beginning and end of the service of the Customs Administration to China. In addition it has originated a number of subsidiary organizations meeting the country's vital needs. One of these was the Posts which starting primarily as a department, supplementing the government service of couriers, in order to meet foreign needs, was separated from the Customs in 1896 and is now a huge and profitable organization supplying all the requirements of a modern postal service. Other departments have represented activities not usually associated with a revenue-collecting body. Such owe their existence to the personality and progressive genius of Sir Robert Hart. Before his day the China coast was unlighted. There was no hydrographical survey. Navigation presented many dangers and difficulties. To-day there is little of which Master and Pilot can fairly complain.

Again, in 1913 when the Reorganization loan was made, it was stipulated that the Salt Administration should be reorganized

---

[1] *Ante*, p. 70.

[2] *China's Customs Revenue since the Revolution* 1911, by Stanley F. Wright and John H. Cubbon, Financial Secretary Inspectorate-General of Customs, graph facing p. 438 and p. 436. In 1934 the amount remitted to the Ministry of Finance fell just short of thirty-two million dollars or rather over two million sterling, indicating internal commitments amounting to some ten million sterling.

following the Customs precedent, modified to meet more modern political ideals. The immediate success of this later experiment under Sir Richard Dane, an experienced Salt Administrator from India, was most striking. Another valuable national asset was shortly developed to its capacity.

Unfortunately the future of these three great administrative services cannot be regarded as altogether secure. Their value in time of need may easily be impaired. Naturally the Chinese Authorities wish to secure control of these important National Departments. On the other hand prudence might dictate for many reasons a different policy. History might repeat itself as happened at Shanghai in 1912, when the local government ceased to function as in 1853.

While foreign loans are outstanding a foreign Inspector-General of Customs can hardly be dispensed with. But in recent years there has been no recruitment amongst foreigners for the junior posts in the service, while the Postal Service and the Salt Administration are fully under Chinese control. This does not detract, however, from the splendid service rendered to China by foreigners in building up the institutions the achievements of which have been broadly outlined.

Without belittling the valuable work of Hart's successors, in particular that of Sir Frederick Maze, the present Inspector-General, in the difficult circumstances of the times, we may fitly conclude with a few lines written in 1907 by the faithful Morse, than whom none were better qualified to speak, of the distinguished and loyal Briton to whom China owes so great a debt.

'Sir Robert Hart, the organizer of the Service which has done this work, was born on February 20, 1835, the same year in which the Empress Dowager of China was born. After graduating (A.B. and Senior Scholar) at Queen's University, Ireland, in 1853, he was appointed Supernumerary Interpreter to the British Superintendency of Trade at Hongkong in May 1854; and in May 1859 was granted special permission to resign in order to join the newly instituted Chinese Customs Service.

'For native ability and power of organization he may be compared, in one aspect or another, with John Lawrence and Alexander Hamilton. His monument is in the Service he created, and his life-record is in the history of the foreign relations of China during a period of forty years of transition. Another will sit in his chair, another will sign as Inspector-General, but in the history of China there will be but one " I.G.".' [1]

Chapter 32

Banking and Insurance

The opening of new ports and the removal of the chief obstacles to commerce combined with the regularization of tariffs and port dues resulted in the steady growth of commercial intercourse between China and foreign countries. The Chinese are great traders. On their side nothing was required but regularity of incidence and reasonableness in amount of taxation. On the foreign side, besides the need for protection from imposition, the primary requisites were capital and protection against the perils of the sea.

The merchant adventurers of olden times financed their own ventures and took all risks. It was not till the Lombards developed the idea of bills of exchange in mediæval Europe and a few centuries later London merchants began to meet at Lloyd's Coffee House and to make bets on the outcome of commercial ventures, that the foundations of the vast fabric of modern commerce can be said to have been completely laid.

In the old Canton days the East India Company provided certain limited banking facilities in cases where purchases of China produce could not be covered by imported goods, but it does not appear that anything was available in the way of insurance of the valuable cargoes of teas and silk which formed the chief exports.

The latter deficiency was remedied by the British merchants

---

[1] *Trade and Administration of the Chinese Empire*, p. 376.

at Canton themselves, who with characteristic self-reliance and foresight banded together just over one hundred years ago to form the Union Insurance Society of Canton. In this enterprise the firm of Dent and Company, which shared with Jardine Matheson and Company the leading position amongst British traders after the days of the East India Company, was the moving spirit. It is said that the idea was conceived in the off season of 1834 in the great verandah of Dent's house at Macao, made famous by one of Chinnery's pictures now in the Chater collection at Hongkong. Next business season it was born. Dent and Company have passed on, victims of the general financial upheaval of 1864, and Jardine's in these days is the sole survivor of the " Princely Houses." But the " Union," as it is known, has gone from strength to strength. Transferring its head office to Hongkong in 1841, it grew with the Colony until, with its extensions and affiliations, its activities are world-wide and it now ranks high in the world's great insurance institutions. In 1920 it led the insurance world in the amount of its marine risks. The fore-runner in the Far East in underwriting this class of insurance, to the lasting benefit of the Chinese and the China trade, in modern times it showed that the old pioneer spirit was not dead. In 1919 it was the Union Insurance Society of Canton that led the way in the field of aviation risks and was the first company to open a special office for aviation insurance. Many of the other great insurance companies have operated in China and been rewarded in time past by finding her a profitable field.

But with the Chinese themselves, although insurance is now undertaken by Chinese companies, progress has been less rapid than in the case of modern banking where it has been quite phenomenal.

The first foreign bank to establish itself in China was the Oriental Banking Corporation, a British enterprise, which opening a branch at Shanghai in 1848 had the honour of being the pioneer in this difficult and dangerous, however profitable, field.

It is one of the functions of banks to provide the means of moving produce from one country to another. Primarily this is a simple enough affair. Its elements are even told by Chaucer in *The Shipman's Tale.* By means of bills of exchange secured on the goods, with the merchant's capital or credit as security to meet the case of depreciation in value, loss of market, failure of the consignee or as the case might be, cash is provided to the merchant which enables him to carry on his business without waiting for the return of the proceeds of his shipment. The British merchant in China, for example, would buy his tea and against it draw a bill on his London house which a bank would negotiate. With the proceeds thus made available the British merchant in China would be enabled to pay for the tea and go on to the next deal. The bank would recoup itself on maturity of the bills in London. Meanwhile it would hold the shipping documents evidencing control of the tea, and the British merchant's name as drawer of the bills as security for the due discharge of his obligations. The security and success of the Bank is the measure of the soundness of the trade and of the honesty of the merchants.

But this is not the whole matter. England was a country whose finance was based on gold. China was a silver country and there was always the delicate question of adjustment between media, one of which was fluctuating. The merchant in China in buying his tea had to estimate the next season's price in the London market. But this was always a difficult matter since he had to sell at a price expressed in English currency which would enable him to bring his capital back to China and exchange it into the number of taels or silver dollars which he had paid for the shipment after allowing for his profit. If in the meantime the value of silver had risen his profit would be decreased or turned into a loss. By making what are known as exchange contracts with banks at the time the purchase of produce is made the merchant ensures a fixed return.

The skilful exchange banker, on the other hand, ensures his own safety by balancing his sales of any particular currencies with his purchases. In these days of telegraphs and wireless and a vast number of banks of different nationalities, making possible inter-bank business, this may not prove a too difficult matter. But in those days it was otherwise, and only the big profits then possible justified the banks in taking over in effect the merchant's risk. If the China Coast has not had its Tellsons, at least it has not been without its adventurous romance.

The Oriental Banking Corporation was followed in 1854 by the Chartered Mercantile Bank of India, London and China, but it was not until the establishment of the Chartered Bank of

India, Australia and China, three years later, that foreign banking business began to expand. The next important arrival in the field was the Hongkong and Shanghai Banking Corporation, which was destined to establish a leadership in the fields of exchange and political finance which it has never lost. In the great year in the Far East, 1920, it is even said that like the Union in its turnover of business it headed the banking world.

The history and policy of this great institution reflects the vision which characterized Hongkong with its absence of alien disabilities. Established by Special Ordinance and domiciled in a British Colony, representative men of all nationalities have sat on its board and even occupied the Chair.

It was not till comparatively late in the century that banks of other nationalities entered the field. It is to British banks, therefore, that the honour belongs of having helped China not only by inspiration but also with personnel to establish her modern banking system which is now of such incomparable value to the economic fabric.

Foreign banks have also been of assistance to China in other than the commercial field. Such assistance, of course, has been matter of business and often closely associated with political aims. But if it has not been altruistic, on the other hand it has not reduced China to financial bondage, as was at one time feared might prove the case, and that useful purposes have been served cannot be denied. The small size of China's external debt and the railway system are sufficient evidence of these things. In addition there is the reflection that with the rise in the value of silver during the Great War, the suspension of Boxer Indemnity payments, which were subsequently remitted and applied in whole or in part to purposes beneficial to China, except in the case of the Central Powers whose indemnities were cancelled outright, wise finance could in a few years have made China financially free. Unfortunately, as we have seen, internal strife, absence of leadership and self-seeking disregard by those in power of the country's interest caused her to miss the opportunity.

Chapter 33

Communications and Industry

The means of communication for man and goods in early times were much the same in all countries. Various animals were broken in for draught purposes, while the invention of the wheel made possible carts and other vehicles. Man-power was responsible for the sedan chair and the carrying pole with its numerous combinations up to the point of two hundred and fifty-six bearers of a Chinese Emperor's catafalque. For messages there were courier services amongst all the ancient peoples, Assyrians and Persians, Arabs and Egyptians, and preceding them in point of time the Chinese service, which is said to have been instituted during the Chou dynasty in the twelfth century B.C. The earliest mention in Chinese literature appears to be in the time of Confucius. 'The influence of righteousness,' goes one of his sayings, 'travels faster than royal orders by stages and couriers.' [1] Perhaps its highest efficiency was reached in the day of Genghis Khan, who it was said in his Mongolian capital of Karakorum received messages from central Asia in eight days. On the seas, the lakes and inland waterways the boat, oar and sail made their appearance.

In the primitive means of transport by land China was not behindhand, while at sea the ocean-going junk ranked with the Arab dhow. But though time passed and the World moved on, China never passed beyond this early stage. Only in the North was there any semblance of highways and these, except for the Emperor's roads from the Forbidden City to the Temple of Heaven, the Summer Palace and the Hunting Parks, and the highway between Peking and Mukden, were of earth cutting deep into the soft loess of the North China plain. South of the Yangtze the canals were the roads connected with few exceptions by single wheel tracks, the ingenious Chinese wheelbarrow, nicely balanced on its central wheel, supplementing the chair as a means of human transportation.

At sea China never achieved a ship of the class of those in

[1] *The Chinese Post Office : an historical survey*, by V. W. Stapleton-Cotton, Postal Commissioner for the Hopeh Province (Proceedings of the Rotary Club at Tientsin, May 1932).

which Portuguese, Spanish and Elizabethan navigators sailed, while the stately East Indiamen and the Clipper ships were beyond their imagination and craftsmanship.

The West brought to China everything that is modern in communications from the steam engine to wireless.

There are people who say that mankind was happier before the material progress which began with the invention of the Spinning Jenny and Stephenson's great discovery. It is an arguable point of view especially from the outlook of the Far East. Since the dawn of history most eastern countries were self-contained.[1] China was independent of the outside world when commerce first began. Foreign traders could not find needs to fill which would pay the cost of silk and tea. And since communications are the handmaid of commerce, what advantage could their improvement bring ? To answer this question in a negative sense, however, is to ignore humanitarian sentiment. Humanity demanded that steps be taken to avoid the consequences of famines and floods. In regard to floods aeroplanes have become of immense value in determining the extent and seriousness of such disasters. The railway, steam coasting ships and river boats have expedited relief to stricken areas. Railways have also played the part foreseen for them of facilitating inter-provincial migration.[2] Abused by militarists they have nevertheless helped to people sparsely inhabited areas, relieving congestion in other provinces. Surplus food supplies have been carried to provinces where there was shortage and the rapid distribution of imported foodstuffs has been facilitated.

Many of the modern means of communication have resulted in the formation of departmental administrations on foreign lines, notably railway administrations and the Chinese Telegraph Administration, which has owed much to personnel drawn from foreign cable companies.

Finally, the telegraph and wireless have been of great value in disseminating information, and are being pressed into the service of education. Every town and many a village has its public station and few are without cheap receiving sets or without access

[1] For the economic effects at a certain stage of development in some countries see *Genghis Khan*, by Ralph Fox, p. 170, explaining the Mongol campaign across Asia.

[2] *Railway Enterprise in China*, by the author, p. 143.

to one. It is to this means above all others that Chiang Kai-shek's New Life Movement, backed up by spectacular aeroplane visits to distant points by the Generalissimo and his accomplished wife, has secured its hold on the imagination of large sections of the people. As a force towards unification of a country of vast distances the wireless and the aeroplane have had no equal. Nanking with its powerful station has been little behind Berlin and Rome in the political use it has made of the broadcast.

There was no delay on the part of China in adopting the aeroplane and wireless. The war had demonstrated their value. Nor had much difficulty been experienced at an earlier stage in the introduction of the telegraph and the telephone. With railways, however, it was otherwise.

The first suggestion for railways came from India, where conditions present points of similarity to conditions in China. Both are countries of great distances with extreme density of population in many parts. Initial railway construction could be undertaken at low capital cost. While there were big trade movements connected with foreign trade there was also much of the small business characteristic of countries of village communities. Contrary to experience elsewhere, in many cases railways could be made to pay on passenger traffic alone.

In 1863 a scheme of trunk lines was proposed but proved premature. Fifteen years later a short narrow-gauge line was actually constructed between Shanghai and Woosung at the mouth of the Whangpoo by a foreign syndicate. But a confusing use of terms had secured authorization of a scheme which it was never intended to sanction. China was still a land of the grossest superstition and firmly in the grasp of the necromancers. The forces of reaction overcame wiser views prepared to accept an accomplished fact. The rails were ' torn up and together with the engines and rolling-stock conveyed to the island of Formosa, where most of the materials were simply dumped on the beach and there allowed to remain until either stolen or rendered useless by continued neglect. The closing act in the drama was the erection on the site of the Shanghai station of a temple to the Queen of Heaven.' [1]

---

[1] The International Settlement has spread so as to include this temple, which, however, is outside the police jurisdiction of the International Settlement and has at times provided sanctuary.

But in the next few years much was accomplished in North China to accustom the country, officials and people alike, to the use of the ' fire cart.' We have already seen how the ability and perseverance of Mr. Kinder who died in England while these pages were being written, succeeded in establishing the first railway arising out of the transport necessities of the Kaiping coalfield.[1] The impulse to progress caused by China's defeat by Japan resulted in permission to continue the railway to the neighbourhood of Peking. At the same time activities in Manchuria challenged the attention of Europe and America. China was still little understood. Many feared a break-up. There was a general move which resulted in what Lord Salisbury called a ' battle of Concessions ' but which a writer in the *Forum* perhaps more appropriately described as ' that mad scramble for Chinese Concessions ' which characterized the closing years of the century.

There were various new factors on the scene. King Leopold of Belgium was understood to be desirous of following up in China his politico-business activities in the Congo. Monsieur Paul Doumer, Governor of French Indo-China and since President of France, urged a forward movement in China through Yunnan and wrote of ' la lutte pacifique ' with Britain in regions ' qui semblaient reservés à notre pénétration.' France's alliance with Russia and her financial association with Belgium caused alarm when a Belgian syndicate made a bid to build the Peking–Hankow railway. There were rumours that proposals were on foot to continue this railway to Canton through the same agency and that ultimately a connection was designed with the Siberian railway by way of Kalgan and Urga.

Such a grandiose scheme, which it was supposed would eventuate in Russian domination of China, was not beyond the imagination of the late Victorian era, illuminated by the Imperial flame lit anew by Cecil Rhodes. History had shown that there was little if anything absurd in conjectures which a lethargic attitude might have turned into reality. There was a European *bloc* against Great Britain in those days of her ' splendid isolation.'

Germany's seizure of Kiaochao, followed by Russia's seizure of Port Arthur, was scarcely redressed by Great Britain's occupa-

[1] *Ante*, p. 24.

tion of Weihaiwei at Chinese instigation. Fortunately the United States insisted on undertaking the finance of the Hankow–Canton railway and thus introduced a reassuring factor.

Out of the welter of intrigue and international jealousies, however, there did in fact emerge a scheme of railways completed in the following ten years which have served China well and form a good foundation for her future system.

Of the important railways the Belgian syndicate built the trunk between Peking and Hankow. But in the matter of the Hankow–Canton railway American enterprise did not live up to its aspirations. For various reasons this trunk was not completed until the present year with funds from the British Boxer Indemnity. The line from Peking to the North into Mongolia was built in later years by the Chinese themselves long after the end-of-the-century fears of Russia had passed away. An arrangement between Great Britain and Germany provided for the finance of a third trunk between Tientsin and Pukow. England built the Shanghai–Nanking railway, and the railway from Shanghai to Hangchow and Ningpo and the Canton–Kowloon line.

In later years a Belgian syndicate financed the important cross-country trunk, running west from Haichow to the Province of Kansu, known as the Lunghai [1] Railway, of which we heard so much in the days of struggle between the northern militarists and during the northern march of the Nationalists.

All these railways, though spoken of as concessions, were destined to prove of slight, if any, political value. Great Britain, faithful to her business ideals and not seeking political influence in China, had established the principle of lending the necessary money under conditions strictly limited to technical essentials and accounting. With the exception, therefore, of the Russian rights in Manchuria, the German rights in Shantung and the French rights in Yunnan, all these contracts were in effect underwriting agreements. The loans, it is true, were secured on the railways, but under conditions of railway development in a country of dense population and much business no reasonable doubt could be entertained of their paying their way as a whole

---

[1] Chinese railways ordinarily derive their names from a compound of their terminals. Lunghsi is a certain part of Kansu Province, while Haichow is a port in course of development between Shanghai and the Shantung promontory.

if not in each individual case. And this confidence has been amply justified. China has only the militarists to thank for the wreck of railway finance and her default not only on her railway loans but in her private railway debts incurred for the supply of indispensable materials.[1]

In other industrial fields the West brought modern machinery and, for good and ill, industrial revolution. Just as the disaster of the defeat of China by Japan aroused the Court to the need of reform in all directions, so the earlier wars of 1842 and 1860 convinced men like Li Hung-chang of the need of arsenals for the manufacture of modern arms, which called for the modernizing of the iron and steel industry. Coastal defence again called for modern ships and dockyards. These needs in their turn called for the modernization of the coal industry.

Note has already been made of the effort initiated in the late seventies in the Kaiping coalfield. These mines steadily developed from the days of their opening until the present time. For the last twenty-four years they have been under the management of the Kailan Mining Administration, which has been a model for joint Chinese and foreign operation. Other modern mining enterprises exist in an advanced state of development, while iron and steel works, supplying in some small measure China's needs, have been established in various parts of China.

Passing to other fields of industry, by the eighties the importation of cotton goods had given the first impulse to the revolution that was to occur in the cotton spinning and weaving industry of China which is said to date from more than two thousand years before the Christian era. The still more ancient manufac-

---

[1] China's failure to pay for essential railway materials, without which the lines could not have been carried on, has resulted in great loss to British firms and the ruin of two of them. Of these one supplied £500,000 worth of rolling-stock to the Peking–Mukden railway, without exception the most prosperous line in China. The other supplied six splendidly appointed trains with sleepers and restaurant cars complete, known as the ' blue train,' for the express service between Peking and Pukow. The head of this firm was the late Mr. J. M. Dickinson, who rendered substantial service, over a period of more than fifty years, to British interests in Tientsin. A man who appreciated the solid worth of the Chinese people, it was a harsh fate that China's default should have swallowed up his private fortune and involved his firm, one of the pioneers, in disaster. Many of the coaches of the blue train are still in service, reconditioned after misuse by the militarists, a monument in their way of British confidence and trust.

ture of silk ascribed to almost mythical times had already been made the subject of experiment in western filatures.

But it was not till the Treaty of Shimonoseki, which brought to an end the war between China and Japan, that the hand-worker was to be seriously threatened. By that treaty Japanese were allowed to import machinery and establish industrial enterprise at the places opened to foreign residence and trade. The most favoured nation clause extended the right to the nationals of all other treaty powers.

It is not possible to give an adequate impression here of the factories, Chinese and foreign, to be found to-day all over China. But despite all that has been done it remains true that in relation to the country's vast population and needs modern industrialism is in its infancy. It is also true to say that in some branches the Chinese have failed to show those powers of organization and financial direction which are essential to success in large industrial enterprises. It is in this field that foreign aid may be utilized by China to chief advantage. For unless China can increase permanently her exports, industrial development to meet the needs of the country is the only means by which her adverse trade balance can be turned in her favour. Reliance for this purpose on what are known to economists as ' invisible exports,' consisting of the monies remitted to China by Chinese living overseas, appears to many to be unsafe in these uncertain times.

Chapter 34

The Foreign Contribution in the Cultural Field

'We Europeans,' the Warden of New College has written, 'are the children of Hellas.' [1] Ours is 'the Legacy of Greece.' On that foundation in conjunction with the Christian religion and Roman law has been built what is known as European civilization.

When Lin Yu-t'ang, the brilliant author of *My Country and my People*, speaks slightingly of western civilization as it manifests itself in China, he would appear to base his ideas on what he sees in a modern city at the 'rush hour.' It would be as reasonable to judge Chinese civilization by the brutality of the Chinese policeman 'drest in a little brief authority' and the arrogance that characterized officials in Manchu times. Mr. Lin forgets or does not know the cultured foreign homes and gardens, the foreign collections of Chinese art, often small but reflecting the taste of unpretentious souls that show a nation's quality. He forgets the work of the old *Chinese Repository* and the *China Journal* of our time. He ignores the achievements of western scholars who have assumed the task of interpreting Chinese civilization to the rest of the world, the distinction of whose work is attested by Legge's *Chinese Classics*, *The Middle Kingdom* of Wells Williams, the work of Stanislas Julien, *China under the Empress Dowager*, by Bland and Backhouse, the great geological work of Richthofen, books on ceramics, pictures and the Chinese stage, together with a host of other works in many European languages by numerous writers in diverse fields.

Interpreting to China western religion and ethics, science and culture, are Morrison's translation of the Bible, which is the foundation of all scriptural exegesis in China, the translation into Chinese of many works typical of western thought, the compilation of dictionaries and translation or adaptation of many scientific and scholastic books. All these things testify eloquently to the cultural urge of individual foreigners and the sincerity with which they have set themselves to understand China and to bring her, through the medium of the Chinese language, to a better understanding of European civilization. The truth is that the

[1] *History of Europe*, by the Rt. Hon. H. A. L. Fisher, p. 1.

West brought her treasures, but the Chinese exclusive view as to what constituted civilization for long refused their acceptance.

The path trodden by the pioneers was a hard and dangerous one. For a Chinese to teach a foreigner the Chinese language was for many years a criminal offence. Morrison had to work at night since his Chinese teacher would not dare to help him by day. The few young men in the factories at Canton who learnt Chinese had to be sent to Singapore where there was already a numerous Chinese colony attracted by the security of trade under the British flag. The story of foreign medical work in China is the story of a great crusade. The work of educationalists in other fields if less spectacular was scarcely less heroic.

Fortunately in course of time there came to be Chinese who realized the importance of understanding the West and of education on western lines. Such a man was Yung Wing who, himself educated at Mission Schools, persuaded the Throne to send a number of selected young men to America. There were only seventy of them and when they returned to China prejudice at first denied them opportunity. But time and circumstances favoured them. Their work bore fruit in their own lives, for many of them rose high in the service of the State. Some are still alive, such as M. T. Liang who only recently ceased to be active on the Famine Relief Commission, and T'ang Shao-yi who comes out at times to bless a cause or heal a breach. And there were many who were not helped by the State in those and later days who even as stowaways or in the steerage found their way abroad and secured their education in circumstances that reflect favourably on western kindness and appreciation of effort. Two such men were Charles V. Soong, father of the family whose members have become so distinguished, and the late V. K. Ting.[1]

The influence of the men who studied abroad acted as a leaven, but it could only touch the fringe of so vast a body politic. It is to the missionaries, whose activities in China have sometimes been justly criticized but more often unfairly abused, that Europe owes its debt as the true torch-bearers of its civilization. As Professor K. S. Latourette of Yale says, in concluding his exhaustive *History of Christian Missions in China*, ' the historian does not cease to be impartial when he declares that the presence and labours of the missionary were most fortunate for China. Defects

[1] *Ante*, p. 194.

the missionary enterprise undoubtedly had. Sometimes it did evil. On the whole, however, it was the one great agency whose primary function was to bring China into contact with the best in the Occident and to make an expansion of the West a means to the greater welfare of the Chinese people.'

Such work has been without distinction of nationality, though necessarily some nations have contributed more than others. Leaving aside all reference to the very early Christian contacts, such as the Nestorians in the early part of the Christian era and the Jesuits at the Chinese Court during the Mongol Dynasty, this great effort flowed in three streams, that of Roman Catholicism, the Orthodox Church and Protestantism. But the contribution of the Orthodox Church has been slight compared to that of the other faiths, and mainly concerned with the interpretation of Chinese civilization to Russia. As between Roman Catholicism and Protestantism, the former was first in the field by more than two centuries and is said to be responsible for four-fifths of the number of converts which according to latest available statistics amount to somewhat less than one per cent of the population. Nevertheless, it seems probable that the greater help to modern China has been achieved in the Protestant field. Although the vast Roman Catholic organization maintains schools and seminaries throughout China and a number of hospitals, its main institutional work has been in the direction of orphanages, which apart from their humanitarian value have been mainly directed to promoting the cause of the Church. The Protestant Missionaries beginning their work in China in a more practical and broader-minded age and with a different outlook soon saw that their opportunity lay largely in attack on social abuses, such as footbinding, and the spread of medicine and education.

Footbinding is rapidly becoming a thing of the past.[1] As regards medicine it is hardly too much to say that the progress of medicine in China would have been negligible without the Protestant medical missionary. Growing from the small dispensary and the peripatetic round to the hospital and medical college, devoted men and women took their lives in their hands in their efforts to overcome prejudice. How uphill was the task right up to modern times, has been recently recorded by Dr. J.

---

[1] Evidence comes from the interior that in many places it still persists. See *My Bandit Hosts* by Tinko Pawley as told by Joy Packer.

Preston Maxwell, head of the Gynæcological Department in the Peiping Union Medical College, in a paper read before the Lester Institute in Shanghai. Dr. Maxwell, whose father was medical missionary in Formosa in 1863, tells of the innate conservatism of human nature refusing to accept anything new, the unbelief that anything good could come out of the West, the ingrained race prejudice which led to blind attempts to ruin work simply because the agents belonged to another country, and the circulation of tales about the extraction of children's eyes to make medicine, and the like ; the necessary connection of the beginnings of modern medical work with what to China was a more or less new religion since there was no one to undertake the medical work but the medical missionary ; and the interference of the new method with the gains of temples and charlatans. But these were not the only causes of the distrust which was aroused. This was also due to the inability of many Chinese to understand that anyone could work without reward or sinister motive. Of many interesting illustrations of conditions even as late as the closing years of the nineteenth century two may be quoted. The first story is told of Dr. J. Howard Montgomery (now of the Matilda Hospital, Hongkong) who succeeded Dr. Maxwell in charge of a hospital in the Province of Fukien.

' One day a man came in and Montgomery had to send over to the house for his stethoscope. Being an athlete, he used the leisure time in walking round a stone table in the court on his hands, with his legs in the air. The man was seen and went away. Shortly after, another patient arrived sent by this man. The doctor noticed that he was not satisfied with the examination and prescription, and sent one of his students to find out the reason. The student came back with a grin on his face. " The man says you have not walked round the table with your legs in the air as you did in the treatment of his friend." '

The other illustration was an experience of Dr. Maxwell himself in the year 1901.

' Itineration work when planned and carefully conducted was one of the most interesting and often thrilling experiences a man could have. On one occasion I came into a city which up to that time had been far from friendly to foreigners. Twenty-three people, mostly children, had died during three

229

to four months from rabies. The day I arrived there, five children had been bitten, and three were brought to me. In the middle of a large house court, with audience of at least a thousand in the Court and on the roofs, my assistant and I placed these children under chloroform, and burnt out the bites thoroughly with a kitchen poker. The three lived, and the other two died of rabies. And it was the end of lack of confidence in modern medicine in that city. Later on, my successor had to get over the wall and steal away at night, not because he was being molested, but because his medicines were done, and he was being besieged by patients.'

But there were terribly tragic experiences too. The same Dr. Montgomery already referred to had been driven out by the ' Three Dots Society ' and the hospital had been looted. The man who led the looters was a man who had been operated upon successfully in a difficult and vital operation. On two occasions his wife's life had been saved and she was to be shortly in need of serious operative treatment. After the destruction of the hospital, despairing of help, she hanged herself.

In spite of everything, however, the medical missionaries succeeded, and magnificent hospitals in China commemorate their deeds to-day.

While the medical men and surgeons had been thus determinedly pursuing their self-appointed task, another group under the leadership of a distinguished scholar, Dr. Timothy Richard, was devoting itself to the diffusion of Christian and general knowledge. The Reform Movement in China, which ended so disastrously in 1898 for the Emperor Kuanghsu, owed much to the important literary output of this body, while Dr. Richard's extraordinary personal influence upon some of the highest officials of that stormy epoch, and through them upon the Throne, has been insufficiently appreciated.[1]

In the matter of educational institutions it has to be remembered that before the impulse to reform given by China's defeat by Japan in the middle nineties China's system of education was limited to the classics. Very few attempts had been made to establish and maintain schools or colleges which furnished an education adapted to modern conditions. Notable among these were ' the Tung Wen Kuan in Peking, the Pei Yang University

[1] See *China and England* by the late W. E. Soothill, Professor of Chinese at Oxford, Chapter X.

in Tientsin, and Nan Yang University in Shanghai. For the founding of all these, government officials had turned to men who were or had been Christian missionaries.'[1] Before 1905, therefore, when the examinations were abolished and the government began its great effort to establish schools throughout the country, foreign education was mainly in the hands of mission schools.

Admittedly schools under the auspices of Protestant missionaries were at first established as an adjunct and aid to evangelization. Once established, however, the schools indicated their right to live by serving the wider ends which missionary work began to set for itself. As a result in the case of the education of boys they grew in number and size, ranging from the kindergarten to the college, and even in a few cases undertaking postgraduate work. But ' it is almost impossible to have any real conception to-day of the obstacles and difficulties which the pioneers in the establishment of schools for girls in China had to meet. It was necessary not only to combat custom, but also to overcome the innumerable fears, suspicions, and prejudices inspired by the fact that the teachers were foreigners. It was possible, at first, to secure only little slave girls, homeless foundlings, or the children of the poorest of the poor, who were induced by promises of food and clothing to risk the perils of entrusting the children to the foreigners. Yet through these pioneer school-girls the believers in Chinese womanhood gave to China convincing proof that her daughters were as capable and worthy of education as her sons.'[2]

A great impetus to foreign medical and educational progress came after the Boxer trouble from the fact that money became available from unexpected sources in addition to the subscriptions for the support of missions.

It would seem that all the powers, with the exception of Great Britain, overestimated the amount required to compensate their nationals for damages sustained in the Boxer troubles.[3] Or

[1] *Christian Education in China :* the Report of the China Educational Commission of 1921–2, p. 26.

[2] *Ibidem*, p. 232.

[3] The Boxer troubles were largely confined to North China where British interests predominate and presumably suffered most. Nevertheless the Russian Indemnity was more than two and a half times that of Great Britain, that of Germany was nearly double, while the French compensation exceeded the British by 40 per cent.

perhaps their computations proceeded upon a different principle. Anyhow, if there were such balances after compensation for losses sustained, with the exception of the American balance, they were retained until some time after the Great War.

The amount of the American Indemnity was approximately G$25,000,000, of which about half covered the claims. It was decided by the Government of the United States in 1908, during the second term of President Theodore Roosevelt, ' as a proof of sincere friendship for China to voluntarily release that country from its legal liability for all payments in excess of the sum which should prove to be necessary for actual indemnity to the United States and its citizens.'

With interest up to 1945 that represented a sum in the neighbourhood of fifty million gold dollars, which it was understood the Chinese Government would make available partly to the education of Chinese students in America and partly to the foundation of a school in China, the present Tsinghua University just outside Peiping.

American medical work in China was also promoted by the benefactions of the Rockefeller Foundation.[1]

Unfortunately the British proportion of the Boxer Indemnity was barely sufficient to meet losses of British merchants even when assessed on the strict principle of English Law in the matter of damages. Nevertheless Parliament decided in 1925 to remit the balance of the Boxer Indemnity together with a sum kept in suspense during the period of the War, the whole amounting with interest up to 1945 to nearly £12,000,000.

The educationalists wanted the money for education and this was the original plan. It was subsequently modified to meet the wishes of the Chinese Government to admit of assistance to railway and river conservancy. A plan has been devised whereby capital is lent to certain defined railway enterprises and con-

---

[1] The outstanding instance is the Peiping Union Medical College, which with its brilliant American, British and Chinese staff provides the specialist needs of North China and even farther afield. It also shares with the Lester Institute in Shanghai the leading position in research work in China. In establishing its benefactions in Peiping the Rockefeller Foundation took over the existing Union Medical College which was a British foundation in memory of James Lockhart who first undertook medical work in Peking in the early sixties. The Lester Institute was founded under the will of the late George Lester, an English business man who spent his life in Shanghai and died there.

servancy works at 5 per cent per annum. The income derived from these loans is applied in scholarships awarded to selected Chinese candidates proceeding to England and in assistance to various educational institutions in China. Amongst railway projects thus assisted by far the most important has been the Hankow–Canton railway the completion of which, as Mr. H. G. W. Woodhead pointed out in *Oriental Affairs* of July 1936, was in effect a present from England to China. The Huai River and the Yellow River conservancies have also been assisted.

Proceeds of remissions made by other nations are applied on somewhat similar lines.

Amongst educational establishments hitherto benefited has been Hong Kong University. But the claims of British educational enterprises in China have been somewhat overlooked.

Summarizing this brief sketch, we may say that attempts at interpretation of China to Europe and of European civilization to China, the propagation of the Christian religion, the introduction of western medicine and the spread of modern education, constitute in the main the foreign contribution to China in the cultural field. And surely the results represent no ignoble achievement? We do not need to go to China's leaders to-day for justification. The brilliant band of Chinese medical men and nurses, educationalists, bishops and pastors, economists, engineers and men and women in other walks of life, all earnestly engaged in the task of building up modern China, affords a still more convincing reply.

Finally, as thankful for opportunity but with a due sense of limitation in achievement, we reflect on the sum total of the foreign contribution to the economic fabric and in the cultural field, we should not forget either the work of the Foreign Red Cross in times of stress, the vast sums of money, mostly American, subscribed for famine and flood relief, or the labours of experts from the League of Nations. All these have also assisted in recent years in the great campaign of progress of the Chinese Government and towards the well-being of the Chinese people.

PART IV

JAPAN AND THE MAINLAND OF ASIA

Chapter 35

Old Japan

When in 1853 the ' Black Ships ' of the American Commodore Perry sailed into Yedo, now Tokio, Bay, false indeed would have been thought the prophet who foretold that in just over forty years Japan would beat her giant neighbour China to her knees and less than ten years afterwards would challenge successfully the might of one of the Great Powers. The fact is the more astounding since the task of working out her own salvation was not seriously embarked upon by Japan until 1868, thus reducing the period of her transformation by fifteen years.

What, may be asked, were the antecedents, what the mental and moral qualities of the people, what the conditions of the country which rendered possible so remarkable and fateful an achievement ?

According to a theory formerly strongly held the Japanese are of Malayan or Indonesian descent. But though these elements are generally believed to be present in the race mixed with what is possibly a Caucasian strain derived from the aboriginal Ainus who were found in possession of the country, the more recently received theory is that ' there is a strong if not a predominant Mongolian strain.' [1] If this is true the race is derived in part from a stock which, supposed to have been cradled in the regions of Lake Baikal, has produced peoples that have made great history. Apart from the Chinese, whose possible origin in these regions has been referred to, there was the Hun who overran Asia early in the Christian era and, ultimately settling along the banks of the Danube, under Attila broke the power of Rome. A few

[1] *Japan : A Short Cultural History*, by G. B. Sansom, C.M.G., now Sir George Sansom, p. 1.

centuries later the tribes which became known in history as the Turks marched westward and built their empires. Finally, in the twelfth century came the Mongols who swept Asia and Eastern Europe, shaking the foundations of Christendom.

The Japanese, however, do not take this ethnographic view of their origin. According to tradition they are descended from the Gods. The first Emperor in mythical times was claimed as the earthly grandson of the Sun Goddess, and a religion was developed known as Shinto, the ' Way of the Gods.' Although in the sixth century of the Christian era, Buddhism reached Japan from the mainland of Asia and became firmly established, it never succeeded in displacing the old religion of the people. In modern times the political value of an indigenous belief has been appreciated and it has been fostered to increase the sense of patriotism.

The elements that go to make a nation in addition to Religion, are Culture and the social and political aspects of life. Culture came from China. Prior to the fifth century of our era Japan had no writing. Chinese ideographs were then introduced from the mainland, but more than two centuries were required to assimilate the Chinese written language in relation to the Japanese spoken language. It is not till the seventh century that Japanese history has its first certain date.[1] From that time onwards, however, records exist as to how Japan, based on Chinese civilization, developed her laws and institutions and her own delicate and pleasing art as it is known to us to-day.

Socially and politically the development of the country was on lines of strong feudalism out of which grew a code of chivalry, self-sacrifice and loyalty known as Bushido, the ' Way of the Soldier.' [2]

By the twelfth century Japan had reached a level at which it was for all practical purposes to remain for several centuries. It was then, in A.D. 1155, that was established what was called the Shōgunate, giving rise to that curious species of dyarchy which with one intermission lasted until 1868, a period of roughly seven hundred years.

[1] *The Making of Modern Japan*, by J. H. Gubbins, C.M.G., p. 18.
[2] In contrast to China the soldier in Japan ranked first, the four classes, after the nobility, being the Samurai or two-sworded men, the farmers, the artisans and the merchants or tradesmen.

Up to that time the theory of government following the Chinese model at the time of the T'ang Dynasty (A.D. 618–907) was that of an absolute Monarch assisted by a Council of State. But it was inevitable that the Daimyos, as the Chiefs or Lords of the Clans were called, should struggle for a position of influence with the Mikado, and having secured the mastery should exercise the substance of power. The ' divinity that doth hedge a King ' did not protect successive Mikados from such encroachments on their authority as to reduce them to a puppet condition or even to involve them in abdication. On the other hand there was never a ' King-maker ' in the sense of a great feudal lord effecting a dynastic change. The sacrosanct character of the line sprung from the ' earthly grandson of the Sun Goddess ' kept his descendants firmly seated on the Imperial throne.

Such clan domination necessarily tended to become hereditary, at least for such time as the strength of the clan was able to maintain itself in power. The grant, therefore, by the Mikado of the title of Shōgun scarcely did more than recognize an existing relationship. Its importance is derived from the fact that it turned a usurpation of authority into a political institution.

The title of Shōgun or General was ' a contraction of the fuller appellation Sei-i-Tai-Shōgun. This may be rendered "Barbarian-quelling Generalissimo," and was the term originally applied to generals employed in fighting the Ainu aborigines in the north-eastern marches. With the assumption of this title the term itself developed a new meaning, for it was not as the general of an army that he thenceforth figured but as the virtual ruler of Japan.' [1]

So pre-eminent did the Shōgun's position become, that under the title of the Tycoon of Japan, he was mistaken in the early Treaty days for the ruler of the country. The first British Treaty was expressed to be made between ' Her Majesty the Queen of the United Kingdom of Great Britain and Ireland and His Majesty the Tycoon of Japan.' It was some years before it was discovered that there was a still higher power than that of the Shōgun, and that the title of Tycoon was merely ' adopted for the occasion in accordance with a precedent created many years before, in order to conceal the fact that the Shōgun, though ruler, was not the Sovereign.' [2]

[1] *The Making of Modern Japan*, by J. H. Gubbins, C.M.G., p. 20.
[2] *Ibidem*, p. 23.

Such a system had many elements of weakness. Based on force, the energies of the Shōgun had to be devoted to maintaining his authority over the other clans, of which there were upwards of two hundred and forty, by a policy of *divide et impera*. When this failed feudal wars took place to secure the coveted post. Again holders of an hereditary office are men of different calibre. The succession may even devolve on a child. In practice therefore, government of the country by the Shōgun found its way into the hands of the more able and ambitious members of the clan who ruled in the Shōgun's name. Finally, the theory of dyarchy found little reflection in the practice of government. The Mikado had his Court at Kyoto while the Shōguns generally ruled the country from elsewhere. Latterly the seat of Government of the Shōgunate was Yedo which was to become known in modern times as Tokio, meaning ' Eastern Capital.'

Speaking broadly the next four to five centuries of Japanese political history but reflected the operation of these several elements. At the end of that period occurred the break in the continuity of the system which has been referred to. The feudal struggle for the chief power had thrown up military chiefs, the last and greatest of whom was Hideyoshi.

Seeking a parallel in European history modern Japanese writers have called him the Napoleon of Japan. A policy of unification by force welded the clans and made Japan a nation. Hideyoshi then turned his gaze outwards and aimed to conquer Corea and China. With a seasoned army in being it was a good opportunity to avenge the unsuccessful attempt made in the twelfth century by Genghis Khan's grandson Kublai Khan, the first Emperor of the Mongol Dynasty in China, to conquer Japan. A great force of men and ships was based on the southern island of Japan near Karatsu, a place whose name indicates its early connection as a point of communication with China. Building himself a great castle on a headland looking across to the island of Tsushima which forms a stepping-stone to Corea, Hideyoshi settled down to the direction of the campaign. But although Japanese arms were successful in the early stages, Hideyoshi's generals never got beyond the river Yalu, the northern boundary of Corea. After seven years, faced by powerful Chinese armies and with their communications threatened, the Japanese were glad to make peace. But the results of the war for Corea had been disastrous. 'The complete devastation wrought wherever the Japanese armies had penetrated,' says Mr. Gubbins, 'left traces which have never been effaced. Nor did Japan come out of the struggle with any profit. When the final accounts were balanced all she had to show for her lavish expenditure in lives and money was the establishment in Japan of a colony of Korean potters, who were the first to make the well-known Satsuma faience, and the doubtful privilege of keeping a small trading port at the southern end of the Korean peninsula.' [1]

Thus ended Japan's first and only adventure on the mainland of Asia, excluding merely piratical raids, until modern times. Similarly Kublai Khan's expedition in the twelfth century was China's only attempt to reduce Japan to a tribute nation.

In 1598 Hideyoshi died. He had destroyed one Shōgunate and he did not found another. His sons were minors and the military government which he had established was carried on for a time by a Council. In 1603, however, Hideyoshi's son-in-law, Tokugawa Iyeyasu, founded what was destined to be the last of the Shōgunates.

The Tokugawa Shōgunate lasted rather over two hundred and fifty years. It was chiefly remarkable for adopting a deliberate policy of seclusion. Japanese were forbidden to leave the country and foreign intercourse was banned. Hitherto Japan had not lacked her adventurers who had found their way to the South Seas and seen something of the colonial expansion of western states. Nor had she been illiberal in her attitude towards western contacts whether in the matter of commerce or religion. In the early days the Dutch in particular developed a considerable trade. As regards religious activity Francis Xavier, who has already been mentioned in relation to Macao, introduced the Christian faith. Rather strangely for a people under the dual influence of Buddhism and its own native Shinto, Christianity made great headway. In 1614, however, a decree was issued ordering the expulsion of missionaries which was followed by twenty years of persecution. Many missionaries and converts fled to Macao. There they built a church which more than two hundred years later was to inspire Sir John Bowring [2] to write

[1] *The Making of Modern Japan*, by J. H. Gubbins, C.M.G., p. 30.
[2] *Ante*, p. 209.

a hymn, which is better known in the United States than in England.[1]

The decree of exclusion of all foreigners was issued in the year 1638, but it was not of universal application. Chinese and Dutch traders were allowed to remain, although under conditions of even greater humiliation and restriction than prevailed in the factories at Canton. Japan became, as Corea had always been, a hermit kingdom. When in the middle of the nineteenth century America and Europe made a new approach, 'a mystery,' as Michie says, ' hung over the Island Empire which had been sealed against foreign intercourse for two hundred years, and its mere seclusion apart from the weird romance which gilded such fragments of its history as were known, invested the efforts to reopen the country with a romantic charm.'

It was not long before the pleasant prospect visualized by Michie was rudely disturbed. The days of the Tokugawa Shōgunate were numbered. For years it had with difficulty maintained itself in power. The Court party, reinforced by powerful clans, had been gradually asserting itself. The grant of Treaty rights to foreigners by the Shōgun sealed his doom. As in China attack on foreign rights has at times been used to bind the people together or to deflect the course of agitation, so in Japan the cry of ' Expel the Foreigner ' was one of the chief rallying-cries of the enemies of the Shōgunate seeking to restore the Mikado's prestige and power. It was unreasonable enough since the Shōgun had had no alternative. But it served its purpose. The ' children of the Gods,' as the Japanese still thought and spoke of themselves, were of no mind to have foreign relationships thrust upon them. There were many and grave outrages against foreigners which were productive of serious embarrassment to the Government and made necessary the use of foreign force. Gradually the Court party gained the upper hand. In 1868 what was called ' The Restoration ' took place involving the final disappearance of the Shōgunate.

[1] ' In the Cross of Christ I glory
Towering o'er the wrecks of time.'

Chapter 36
The Meiji Era
1868–1912

At the Restoration Japan adopted the Chinese custom of choosing a name to cover the period of each reign. The name now chosen was Meiji, meaning ' era of enlightened government.' Events were to justify the choice. The duration of the period was forty-four years. In that time Japan developed from an obscure Asiatic people, with limitations imposed on her Sovereignty by treaties with America and many European states, to a world power.

Broadly speaking this extraordinary achievement was due to three main causes. In the first place the Japanese have a great pride of race coupled with a sense of realism. After the first fierce outbursts it began to be recognized that the rights which had been ceded to foreigners could not be eliminated by any policy of violent anti-foreignism, but only by raising Japan herself to a position of equality. This attitude of mind supplied a driving force which prepared the country to proceed along a path of development on western lines. Secondly, the feudal system had created a people who in a certain sense were docile and easily led. There was a tradition of service and loyalty. There was also leadership. Feudalism had developed an hereditary hierarchy which greatly facilitated the change over to the new order. Thirdly, there was no such vast upheaval as would make the transition unduly difficult. There was in fact much less change than superficial observers might think. Under the Shōgunate the country had been ruled by the Shōgun with the Mikado in the background. The Restoration did not actually create direct control by the Sovereign, who ruled through the government which was then established. The destruction of the Shōgunate had been accomplished in the main by the combination of four of the most powerful clans, of which the most influential were Satsuma and Choshiu. The government which was formed was a bureaucratic government, the heads of which were composed of the more influential members of these clans. There was thus substituted for the Shōgun's direct rule an equally direct rule by a cabinet or committee. The chief difference lay in the fact that in pursuance of the policy of those who had attacked the Shōgunate the Mikado was no longer a lay figure. It was rather as though a new Shōgunate in commission had been established inspired with a sense of loyalty to the Emperor and an ambition to secure to him his rightful position as head of the State.

The new Government established eight departments of state, one of which concerned itself with the study of the things required to be met by legislation, while five others concerned themselves with the ordinary business of government. In addition there were two departments which ranked above the remaining six, namely the Department of Supreme Administration and the Department of Shinto. The latter, concerning itself with ceremonial and religious observances, reflected the importance attached to the old religion of the Country. The former was intended to exercise general control of the various government activities, but it was soon abolished, its place being taken by a Council of State.

The new system was given form in the eyes of the people on April 6, 1868, by what was called the ' Charter Oath.' This was a decree by the Emperor addressed to the people at large. As was to be expected in a country whose literary form and moral sentiment was borrowed largely from China, this document was characterized by dignity of phrase and nobility of aspiration. But in addition to vague abstractions two important principles were laid down. One was that knowledge should be sought throughout the world, a phrase indicating intention to draw on the resources of European civilization. The second point was the promise of a deliberative assembly and the decision of all matters by public opinion. In the realization of the first part of this programme Japan deliberately put herself, as it were, to school in western things. Special missions were sent to foreign countries composed of men drawn from the ruling classes who were required to make studies of methods of government, systems of law, industrialism, and in any other fields of outstanding importance to a modern state. Students were sent to foreign schools and universities. Foreign instructors and advisers were brought to the country to assist in drawing up modern laws, in the organization and training of the army and navy, for assistance in the construction and development of communications, and generally to help in the industrial and commercial fields. Thus, under the fostering care of the Government, the change took place. Modern ships of war found their home in Japanese waters. The swords and armour of the Samurai yielded to modern arms. The methods of the factory invaded the craftsman's domain.

In the vigorous prosecution of this policy much was owed to men who had already been abroad. Although, as we have seen, the order of the Tokugawa Shōgunate two hundred years before excluding foreigners also made it an offence for Japanese to leave the country, some of the younger men, recognizing the need of progress, had gone abroad secretly and at considerable risk in order to familiarize themselves with what to them was the new learning. Such men were Hirobumi Ito, afterwards to be known to fame as Prince Ito, the greatest figure in the rise of modern Japan, and Tsuyoshi Inouye, known to later generations as Marquis Inouye, whose services to the State were hardly less remarkable.

As regards representative government, although the first effort in the direction of constitutionalism in discharge of the Emperor's obligation under the ' Charter Oath ' included the establishment of an assembly with one representative from each of the clans, it was not a success and in 1873 it was abolished. Two years later a Senate was established with legislative authority. This body, however, was only representative to the extent that theoretically its members were nominated by the Emperor from the different classes of the people. At the same time the Supreme Court of Justice was formed designed to establish the ' Rule of Law.' But it was not till the following decade that substantial steps were taken towards completion of political and legal institutions.

To record these briefly, in 1880 a Criminal Code and Code of Criminal Procedure, based on the French model, were promulgated ; in 1881 in response to political agitation by Press and political parties the Constitution was promised for 1890 ; in 1884 a new order of nobility was created, gratifying alike to the feudal houses, the old Court nobility, a select number of ex-Samurai and other commoners. In 1888 a Privy Council was formed and immediately charged with the task of completing the draft constitution. Finally in 1890 the Constitution was promulgated. This last event may be said to have marked the close of the first half of the Meiji Era. During this period had been laid the main foundations of a modern state. The remaining twenty-two years were to see the restoration of Japan's full sovereign rights and her evolution to the point of Empire.

It must not be supposed that these things were accomplished without much trial and tribulation. The Tokugawa House had yielded readily its ancient rights. But the clans who had led the Imperialist campaign against the Shōgunate were set against anything that looked like compromise. In the fighting which ensued the supporters of the Tokugawa House with their weak leadership could do little against the powerful combination against them. When hostilities came to an end early in 1869 the Government wisely imposed lenient terms. Such a departure from the ordinary policy of *vae victis* was a source of annoyance to the conservative elements in the victorious clans, notably the Lord of Satsuma. This clan was also aggrieved in the matter of the distribution of office. Furthermore it disapproved of the course which was being set. Traditional sentiment was dying hard and those who believed that the time had come to break with the past had uphill work before them. With the exception of a small liberal section amongst the Satsuma leaders the clan withdrew its support of the new government, which had not been established at Tokio, and watched events from its feudal stronghold.

Attempts to placate the chiefs of Satsuma were unsuccessful. The discontent represented by them was increased amongst the Samurai class throughout the country by the abolition of feudalism. This measure represented a fine effort of self-denial which well illustrates an element in the Japanese character which makes for the subordination of individual interests to the claims of the State. It is true that in form, much as in the case of the abolition of the Shōgunate, there was no overwhelming change. In accordance with the logical demands of the principle of the Restoration, means had to be devised to ensure centralization. The sentiment of veneration amounting almost to worship of the Mikado helped the transition through. The fiefs became prefectures and the feudal lords their heads. The revenues were paid to the State while the former chiefs drew salaries, allowances and pensions. Only the Samurai, the professional fighters, were deprived of their occupation and had some cause for discontent. The cessation too of the Samurai practice of wearing swords marked the beginning of class fusion and the abolition of class privilege. They also suffered humiliation in seeing a system of universal conscription which put the lower orders on the same footing as men of birth and social status.

Things came to a head in the Satsuma rebellion. In the circumstances of the times the Government may be considered fortunate in having quelled it. Once again it showed a wise foresight. Satsuma defeated was still too powerful morally, intellectually and traditionally to be ignored. The liberal group of the clan had remained supporters of the Government and through them the resources of Satsuma could still be availed of. In conjunction with the powerful Choshiu clan who had shared with Satsuma the leadership in the Restoration, they retained the real rulership of the country. This state of affairs continued for the next twenty years until the formation of political parties which began to assert themselves. Even so the influence of these two clans remained, and still is, supreme as regards the armed forces.

The Satsuma Rebellion cleared the air. Thenceforward the plans for progress proceeded without serious hindrance. But how much was owed to the restrained liberalism of Prince Ito and the men of his time who led the van of progress and in their later years as 'Genro' or 'Elder Statesmen' gave wise authoritative counsel, can never be determined. Only in retrospect it stands out clearly that, mainly because Japan had leaders, her travail, compared to that of China, was comparatively easy.

Chapter 37
Modern Japan and her Needs

From the end of the Meiji Era to September 18, 1931, was a period of nearly twenty years. During that time important developments in the political world and in the industrial field, coupled with the problem of a growing population, produced political and economic reactions of a far-reaching character.

If we are to understand them, it is not so much the details of Japan's development which must engage our attention as the spirit which has informed them. Writing in 1922, ten years after the Meiji Era, Mr. Gubbins concluded his book on the *Making of Modern Japan* with the question, How much in Japan has been changed? He answers it thus:

> ' Outwardly, of course, the effects of the wholesale adoption of much of the material civilization of the West are very plain. Whether these effects extend much deeper is another matter. Japan, it must be borne in mind, is in a state of transition. The new ideas imported from abroad exist side by side with the old, so that the former balance of things has disappeared.'

A Chinese student, Dr. Hu Shih, writing comparatively recently, expresses much the same view:

> ' The rapid cultural transformation in Japan has been achieved with too great a speed and at too early a date to allow sufficient time for the new ideas and influences to penetrate into the native institutions and attain a more thorough cultural re-adjustment.'[1]

Many travellers and students gain much the same impression. The mechanical and formal side of western civilization, as it were ' the letter,' would seem to have been acquired with but little of ' the spirit.' On the other hand, so far as this conclusion may involve an apparent criticism, there is no logical reason why a nation bent on securing equality should not limit its adoption of an alien civilization to that end. This at least has been achieved.

The machine of government is based on the Prussian model.

[1] *The Chinese Renaissance*, p. 24.

The Cabinet is responsible to the Emperor and not to Parliament. The spirit of the British conception of ' no taxation without representation ' finds no place in the Constitution. The payment of taxes is the constitutional duty of the subject. Although Parliament has in theory the right to control finance it has only a consultative function as regards legislation. Amendment of the Constitution lies solely with the Emperor. The armed forces claim to be independent of the Government. In Japan the Emperor, as was the Kaiser in the Imperial German system, is not only the titular head, but the direct source of authority.

As in the case of the Constitution so for the organization of the Army recourse was had to Germany. For the Navy Great Britain supplied the model. French ideas, as we have seen, inspired the Criminal Law, while in Civil Law the code of Saxony is said to have been followed.

It is easy to see that the Spirit of Japan had no time to release itself from the ideas of the feudal age. Until 1877 the grim two sworded man was still a familiar figure. Clearly the country could be more easily controlled by bureaucratic methods of government and the development of militaristic sentiment. This conclusion is emphasized by a comparison of the principles of Shinto reinforced by the code of Bushido, to the personal devotion of the people of Germany in 1914 to the Kaiser and the ideals of war.

The Japanese system has not crystallized without strong opposition from sections of public opinion. Even in the early days not a few pressed keenly for the realization of the Democracy promised by the ' Charter Oath.' But what in essence is the oligarchic principle of Government has on the whole contrived to maintain its sway. Qualified observers have thus summarized this aspect of conditions in the Japanese Empire as they exist to-day :

' The essential liberty in a democratic community has been expressly hampered by the new Police Peace Preservation Laws with their intolerant applications of police regulations not only in the restriction of expression and association, but also in the application of torture to persons suspected of these offences. There is little more academic liberty, or freedom of Press, of speech or of association in Japan than in reactionary Italy or Germany, not merely as a result of the Police Peace Preservation Law enacted by the legally constituted authorities, but also as a result of the " Lynching Law " of the fascistic or chauvinistic societies which venture to commit arson and murder when dealing with people alleged to be animated by sentiments less patriotic than their own.' [1]

From this imperfect impression of modern Japan in the light of political science, we must now turn to a brief survey of the Empire and its present needs.

We have already recorded the consequences of the war with China which broke out in 1894, and the war with Russia ten years later. As a result of these wars and of some earlier friction with China which was adjusted in favour of Japan, the Empire of Japan includes the whole of the island group from a mid-line drawn across the island of Saghalien to Formosa. In addition there are a large number of islands in the Pacific which are controlled by Japan under mandate of the League of Nations in accordance with the Treaty of Versailles. On the mainland Japan is lessee of what is called the Kuantung Peninsula which includes Port Arthur and Dairen. Since 1910, contrary to the earnest advice of Prince Ito and in defiance of treaty obligation, she has asserted sovereignty over Corea.

The area of the Japanese Empire thus defined is 261,180 square miles of which little over half, 147,641 square miles, represents Japan proper. The population of the Japanese Empire in round figures is ninety millions of which some sixty-five millions are living in the original ' Land of the Rising Sun.' It is estimated that this population is increasing at the rate approaching 1,000,000 each year.

Of the area of Japan proper but little over one-sixth is cultivable, giving a total of 2,500 people who have to be supported from every square mile of country. As matters of interest and not necessarily for argument Britain's population to the arable square mile exceeds 2,000, while that of Belgium is nearly 1,700. At the other end of the scale the figures in round numbers for the United States and Australia respectively are 190 and 170.[2]

[1] *The Problem of the Far East*, by Sobei Mogi and H. Vere Redman, p. 60.
[2] For detailed statistical information reference should be made to the *Economic Handbook of the Pacific Area*, by F. V. Field.

During the period of Japan's development, particularly in later years, there has been enormous industrial progress. At the beginning of the century, ' secluded in the Far East,' as Mr Kawakami, Japan's foremost publicist wrote in *Foreign Affairs* a year or two ago, ' hers was still a land of fragile pretty things, of the cherry blossom and the dancing girl.' To-day in various fields she is a serious competitor. Coupled with this industrial advance an industrial population has grown up which is not always so acquiescent in the militaristic adventures of Japan as might be supposed from the news which is allowed to come from the country. As elsewhere seeds of Communism have been sown. Although the growth may be checked there is at least criticism of the dangerous finance to which we shall have later to refer.

One way and another the problems of Japan are difficult and complicated. Her needs fall into two groups. Of these the first is the question of the steps which may justifiably be taken to ensure security, which includes protection against the insidious ravages of Communism. The other group embraces three inter-dependent economic problems ; how to provide for the maintenance of an increasing population ; the maintenance of old or the establishment of new markets for industrial products ; the question of how far it is necessary and possible to control the sources of essential raw materials.

In seeking a solution of her problems there is little doubt but that the country is divided. The soldiers see salvation in the prosecution of Imperialist designs on the mainland of Asia. The Navy believes the future lies on the sea and looks to dominion southward. The civilian element pins its faith to diplomacy and business sense.

Chapter 38

Russia, China and her old Dominions, and Japan

The circumstances under which the last five years of Japanese policy and action in respect to the mainland of Asia were begun, imposed upon her before the forum of international conscience a line of defence based primarily on events in Manchuria prior to September 18, 1931. The wider issue of security could only be developed in general support of action alleged to have been provoked by local events.

Thus the chief strength of the Japanese case could not be presented in such a way as to secure to itself adequate recognition. If, however, a correct appreciation is to be formed of the forces in the Far East which have gone to create the present situation the question of security cannot be overlooked. Consciously or unconsciously, in the last resort, it is the governing factor in relations between Japan and the mainland of Asia. Japan cannot afford to be indifferent to the conditions, strength and policies either of China or of Russia.

In the Customs hall of the wayside station of Nigoreloya, which lies just inside the Russian frontier in the West and is the starting-point of the great train journey across Russia and Siberia, one of the walls was filled until recently with a map of Russia in Europe and Asia. Vast and impressive she looks as she sprawls from the Baltic Sea to the Pacific Ocean, flanked on the one side by a striking bronze bust of Stalin, the ' Man of Steel,' and on the other by the head of the mystic Lenin.

The great buff-coloured map was studded with innumerable flags and other signs of military depots, aerodromes, factories, mines of all kinds, oil wells and other points of material value or activity. On the extreme eastern side there is an arm, as it were a left arm, coming inwards and running south. It is what is known as Primorsk or the Littoral province. At its base is Vladivostock within air-cruising distance of the capital and industrial centres of Japan.

The question which arises is whether there is any difference between Czarist Russia, whose Far Eastern policies culminated in the war with Japan in 1904, and the Russia which has grown up since her revolution. Under the Czars the ideal of Russia's empire builders was control of Asia. ' To the Russian mind,' wrote Senator Albert J. Beveridge in 1904, ' China is to be Russian, Persia is to be Russian, India is to be Russian.' [1] In 1909 a Chinese project to build a railway from Chinchow in Manchuria to Aigun on the Amur River was objected to by Russia as menacing her strategic position. [2] In 1916 a scheme for railways in Inner Mongolia was opposed by Russia on the ground that it would open up Mongolia to Chinese colonization, whereas Russia wished Mongolia to form a buffer state. [3]

Russian ideals, once the Soviet system of government had established itself, reasserted themselves. But ideas, Moscow's ideology, rather than force of arms, were to be the medium of conquest. We have traced in some detail the attempt of the Soviets, which so nearly succeeded, to secure control of China through the medium of money and arms supplied to Chinese communists, the reorganization and subtle reorientation of the Kuomintang and the Nationalist armies by Russians under the direction of Michael Borodin, and the thinly disguised Communist drive.

Again, if the vast former dominions of the Chinese Empire under the Manchus be looked at, the tale is the same with the difference that there the Russians have achieved success.

In the far north-west the old maps show the vast area of Chinese Turkestan, called by the Chinese Hsinchiang, better known to foreigners as Sinkiang, or the New Dominion. It is now the subject of Russian economic penetration and influence. Strategically, should need arise, it is dominated by the Turk-Sib Railway, which would appear to have determined its destiny. Already, in 1931, the writing was on the wall.

Coming farther west is the still greater expanse of territory, Outer Mongolia, which we shall look at in greater detail later on. Though not, in fact, Russian territory, it is controlled by a Soviet organization under the Mongol princes, called the Mongolian People's Republic, and is a fertile field for Russian ideas. This hostile influence has made itself felt so far away as Tientsin,

[1] *The Russian Advance*, p. 368.
[2] *Foreign Relations of the United States*, 1910, pp. 249–50. Japan also opposed the construction of this line on the ground that it competed with the South Manchurian Railway.
[3] *Foreign Relations of the United States*, 1916, p. 199.

the sources of whose wool supply for the former great north-west trade, have long been in Russian hands. The facts had been communicated as far back as 1927 by the British community at Tientsin to the British authorities. There was nothing imaginary therefore about the situation in 1931. While China was engaged in alienating the sympathies of her friends at the Treaty Ports and elsewhere these vast territories were allowed to slip from her grasp.

In China herself in 1931 the Chinese Communists were established in vast areas south of the Yangtze, with a highly organized Soviet form of government estimated to dominate a population of ninety millions, in the province of Kiangsi. The threat to Nanking was grave. Even to-day recent campaigns of Chiang Kai-shek have failed to destroy the main Chinese Red Armies, important sections of which escaped from Kiangsi and reformed in the western provinces, Szechuen, Shensi and Kansu.[1] There they are within easy touch with the Red Armies of Russia and occupy territory that might well form a Russian corridor to the Yangtze. Read in the light of Russia's ideal of world revolution, such events have a relentless and sinister aspect.

It is true that as a result of the triumph of Stalin over Trotsky Russia's programme of World Revolution was claimed to have been discarded in favour of limitation of her principles to her own territories. But can anyone predicate with certainty that her vast project is other than in abeyance for internal economic or external political reasons ? Moscow was and still is the home of the Comintern.

On the great map at Nigoreloya the islands which constitute the Empire of Japan were coloured grey. In contrast to the vast Russian domain they suggested nothing more than a coral fringe to the Asiatic continent set in the eastern sea. Recalling once more that Vladivostok is within cruising range by air of the industrial cities of Japan, the Island Empire seemed at the least to be precariously situated.

Lord Salisbury, who was Queen Victoria's Prime Minister, once said, ' Politics should be studied with large maps.' The map at Nigoreloya was certainly a large one. Japan may be forgiven if, in the light of Russian history, the conditions it

[1] The latest developments in those regions, occurring as this book goes to press, are dealt with in Chapter 47.

reflected had for her alarming implications. Such could not in 1931 justify her invasion of Manchuria, but they entitled her to call upon China either herself to devise measures, or to concert with Japan in devising measures, to stay the oncoming tide.

Chapter 39

Japan in Manchuria and at Shanghai

We now return after necessary digression to the night of September 18, 1931.

The central event has already been briefly chronicled. The more detailed reference called for by the narrative is best made by quoting the account in the *Report of the Commission of Enquiry of the League of Nations*.

'Tense feeling undoubtedly existed between the Japanese and Chinese military forces. The Japanese, as was explained to the Commission in evidence, had a carefully prepared plan to meet the case of possible hostilities between themselves and the Chinese. On the night of September 18–19 this plan was put into operation with swiftness and precision. The Chinese in accordance with the instructions referred to on page 81 had no plan of attacking the Japanese troops, or of endangering the lives or property of Japanese nationals at this particular time or place. They made no concerted or authorized attack on the Japanese forces, and were surprised by the Japanese attack and subsequent operations. An explosion undoubtedly occurred on or near the railroad between 10.0 p.m. and 10.30 p.m. on September 18, but the damage, if any, to the railroad did not in fact prevent the punctual arrival of the south-bound train from Changchun, and was not in itself sufficient to justify military action. The military operations of the Japanese troops during this night, which have been described above, cannot be regarded as measures of legitimate self-defence. In saying this the Commission does not exclude the hypothesis that the officers [1] on the spot may have thought they were acting in self-defence.'

Soldiers will appreciate the justice of the reservation contained in the last sentence, but ordinarily they would not expect a general action to develop from a local alarm. The fact that all the Japanese forces ' in Manchuria and some of those in Corea were brought into action almost simultaneously on the night of September 18 over the whole area of the South Manchuria Railway from Changchun to Port Arthur,' [2] constitutes a serious piece of evidence against the Japanese claim of good faith. Similarly the fact established by the Commission that the Chinese were taken by surprise and put up resistance at but few points, has strong evidentiary value in support of the Chinese denial of knowledge and responsibility. It may also be pointed out in this connection that in the previous year the best of the troops in Manchuria, nearer 150,000 than 100,000 men, had been moved inside the Great Wall in support of Chiang Kai-shek. They were now disposed at strategic points in Chihli holding the country down to the Yellow River in allegiance to Nanking. Although, therefore, it is possible that the explosion was caused through the medium of some Chinese anti-Japanese agency, no impartial student of the evidence could fail to be satisfied that the Chinese administration in Manchuria was free from blame.

The Japanese plan having been put into operation on the night of September 18, events rapidly followed. Next morning Mukden awoke to find itself occupied by Japanese forces. The Chinese police had been easily overpowered. Simultaneously the Chinese garrison at Changchun was attacked. With an estimated strength of 10,000 men and 40 guns there was some resistance, which however, was overcome in the course of the night and during the next day. At almost every place in the railway zone the Chinese forces allowed themselves to be disarmed without any fighting taking place. Kirin was occupied three days later, and was proclaimed semi-officially by the Japanese to complete

---

[1] Page 83 of the edition published by the Waichiaopu at Nanking. The Report became known as the Lytton Report and for convenience is hereafter so referred to.
[2] *Ibidem*, p. 84.

precautions deemed necessary to secure the protection of the railway.

High-handed and apparently unjustifiable as these proceedings were, a tenuous argument might perhaps have been based on the terms of the railway agreement, which entitled the Japanese to ensure the protection of the line, had not its validity almost immediately been vitiated. Alleged incidents of an anti-Japanese character were deemed by the chiefs of the Kuantung army to compel them to undertake further operations.

It is convenient to explain at this point that the Japanese troops in Manchuria have their headquarters in the leased territory known as the Kuantung Peninsula, which includes Port Arthur and Dairen. They are organized as an army. In the light of subsequent events it seems probable that the Kuantung army having got on the move became a law unto itself, and that the weight of the General Staff in the councils of the nation in Tokio compelled the Government to endorse its actions.

The alleged incidents of anti-Japanese character which were considered to justify further operations carrying them outside the South Manchurian Railway zone, seem to have been conjectured rather than experienced. On September 19 Japanese troops occupied Yingkow, a terminus of the Peiping–Liaoning railway opposite Newchwang. On September 20 Japanese aeroplanes raided Hsinmin station some forty miles from Mukden and on the following day went farther afield, dropping bombs on Tahushan station some eighty miles from Mukden. Two days later a Japanese armoured train shelled Tungliao, the terminus of a branch line from Tahushan, and on the same day Japanese troop trains made their appearance on the Chinese railway. On September 24 the town of Chinchow, a hundred and fifty miles from Mukden, where the Provincial Government had established itself provisionally, was made the object of aeroplane attack. On the same day Koupangtze, the point at which the original railway to Yingkow branches in a more northerly direction to make connection with Mukden, was also bombed. Between September 20 and the end of the year there were no less than twenty-eight attacks by air at various points on the section of the Peking–Mukden railway outside the Great Wall. Meanwhile the Japanese had been advancing south along the railway. Early in the New Year the occupation of southern Manchuria was complete. On January 3, 1932, Japanese troops entered Chinchow. Three days later Japanese trains reached Shanhaikuan and on January 7 the ' Mukden Shanhaikuan Railway Administration ' was established under Japanese control.[1]

The Japanese invasion had taken China not only by surprise but caught her unawares. Nanking and Canton were on the verge of Civil War.[2] Chang Hsueh-liang, the 'Young Marshal' as he was familiarly known, was in Peiping where he had had his headquarters since the previous year when with the pick of his troops he had come inside the Great Wall in support of Chiang Kai-shek. Though there was ample time for him to mobilize in defence of Chinchow, he hesitated first on grounds of lack of funds for a campaign and when these were supplied he still delayed for reasons presumably of policy. It was not to be supposed that Japan would come inside the Great Wall and certainly he could not hope to eject the Japanese from Manchuria. On the other hand a strong front might well have limited the field of Japanese action. It would also have had a good moral effect. It would have shown at least that China was prepared to help herself and not rely entirely on the League.

Chang Hsueh-liang's failure to risk his army and his own position, unsupported as it appeared he would have to be by troops from Nanking, reflected the personal attitude of many Chinese leaders in face of national crisis. In the present case it was surprising, for the Japanese were treating him with the utmost hostility and contumely. Flying over Chinchow as soon as it had been established as the temporary seat of the Chinese Government over the Three Eastern Provinces, handbills were dropped assailing him in grossly insulting terms. Later on when the Japanese had occupied his Mukden quarters his ' bag and baggage ' was reported to have been sent after him in the form of 437 cases containing household furniture and personal effects with a notification that his return was not desired. Few commanders in history with troops behind them have failed in such circumstances to strike a blow. It can only be supposed that Marshal Chang lacked confidence in his troops and equipment and feared to involve China in war.

[1] *Japan Speaks on the Sino-Japanese Crisis*, by K. K. Kawakami, pp. 116, 117.
[2] *Ante*, p. 154.

Simultaneously with these events important operations had taken place in northern Manchuria tending to indicate the existence of a Japanese plan of far-reaching design which could by no means be mistaken for a protective measure limited to the South Manchuria railway. By the end of November Japan controlled the remaining railways of Manchuria outside the Russian sphere.[1]

All this time strong feeling against Japan had been generating throughout China. It came to a head in Shanghai. The boycott which had long been China's favourite defensive and even offensive weapon against Foreigners had been applied so effectively after the Manchurian incident that Japanese export trade to China had dropped by the end of 1931 to insignificant proportions. Except, however, for the illegal destruction of Japanese goods when found by the Anti-Japanese Association, there was no clash until January 18, 1932. On that day, according to a Japanese official account, a party of Japanese priests and their companions, in all five persons, was the subject of an unprovoked attack by Chinese desperadoes. Three of the Japanese were wounded and one was killed. China admitted a number of street brawls between Chinese and Japanese in Shanghai, in one of which a Japanese monk was seriously wounded and later died.[2]

On January 20 demand was made to the Mayor of Greater Shanghai by the Japanese Consul-General for an apology. Immediate arrest of those responsible for the alleged attack was also called for together with payment of damages and hospital bills, control of anti-Japanese activity and dissolution of anti-Japanese organizations.

Of these five demands the first three were acceded to next day. But the last two were said to present difficulties. Thereupon Admiral Shiozawa gave public notice through the Press that ' should the Mayor of Greater Shanghai fail to give a satisfactory reply to the Japanese and fulfil their demands without delay he

[1] See *Report of Peiping–Liaoning Railway*, prepared by Mr. W. O. Leitch, Engineer-in-Chief, who with Mr. W. H. Steele, C.B.E., Traffic Manager, and other British officials and one Swedish subject, at considerable personal risk, did what they could to stem the tide in Manchuria and protect Chinese railway officials from outrage.

[2] *China Speaks on the Conflict between China and Japan*, by Chih Meng, p. 97.

was determined to take the necessary steps in order to protect Japanese Imperial rights and interests.'

The Mayor, though still unwilling to stultify himself by giving what he regarded as an impossible undertaking, was nevertheless doing what he could to check anti-Japanese activities and did in fact cause to be seized by the police several offices of the Anti-Japanese Boycott Association.

Unfortunately these measures failed to satisfy the Japanese authorities and on January 27 the Japanese Consul-General notified the Mayor that unless he received a satisfactory reply to the demands by 6 p.m. next day 'the Japanese would take the necessary steps to enforce them.'

Early on January 28 the Japanese Commander notified the other foreign commanders that such action as might be required would be taken on the following morning.

The Japanese had now assembled at Shanghai two cruisers, an aircraft carrier and sixteen destroyers, with a landing force of between two and three thousand marines. By an unfortunate coincidence in the Chapei district bordering the International Settlement on the north side was quartered a considerable Chinese force known as the XIXth Route Army.

In the circumstances it became necessary to declare a state of emergency in the International Settlement and French Concession and for the foreign troops to take up their positions for defence should need arise.

With the exception of the Japanese, the sectors assigned to the various foreign units were occupied by 4 p.m. on January 28, that is to say in daylight. The Japanese, whose sector was the Hongkew area contiguous on one side to Chapei, not only elected to delay taking up their position till several hours later, but at 11 p.m. notified the Mayor of Shanghai of their intention to include a portion of Chapei where there were resident a number of Japanese. This not only represented a departure from previous practice but could hardly fail to bring Japanese forces into direct and provocative contact with the troops of the XIXth Route Army. Moreover, Japanese marines began to move into position at 11.45 p.m. before there had been sufficient time for any adjustment in the Chinese police or military dispositions in that neighbourhood to be made. As, therefore, Mr. Stimson says, 'the fair-minded historian must reach the conclusion that

258

when Admiral Shiozawa began his movement, he, to put it mildly, was not at all reluctant at the prospect of having an armed clash with the Chinese forces in the district into which he was moving. In fact he was courting such a clash and must have known it.' [1]

The inevitable happened. According to the Japanese official account, when Japanese marines were proceeding to their assigned sector the Chinese opened fire on them, precipitating a conflict. The Chinese contention, on the other hand, was that shortly after midnight Japanese marines invaded Chapei in disregard of previous official Japanese assurances that no military steps would be taken without twenty-four hours' notice through the Consular authorities. The Chinese troops, it is admitted, offered resistance, which resulted in the Japanese Admiral sending his planes over and bombing the ' unwarned and helpless civilian native quarter of Chapei.'

' It was an act of inexcusable cruelty,' as Mr. Stimson has written, ' and has stained the Japanese record at Shanghai for all time. Not only were bombs dropped upon the positions held by the Chinese troops, but incendiary bombs were used which soon had the whole quarter in flames.' [2]

Nevertheless the XIXth Route Army maintained their position in Chapei for several weeks until an enveloping movement from the Yangtze coupled with a strong frontal attack compelled their retirement. This, however, was effected in good order before a Japanese force which had increased to one mixed Brigade and the IXth and XIth divisions, supported by fire from the Japanese naval contingent in the river.

On March 3 it was announced that the Japanese military and naval authorities having accomplished their object, namely the protection of Japanese lives and property, and secured the safety of the International Settlement, had decided that their military operations should be stopped forthwith. A short time later the Japanese forces were withdrawn except for an important contingent which was left in the Chapei district in Shanghai, where they established an imposing headquarters of reinforced concrete capable of sustaining a moderate siege.

So much for the official winding up of this operation. Far

[1] *The Far-Eastern Crisis*, by Henry L. Stimson (Secretary of State 1929–33), p. 123.
[2] *Ibidem*, p. 124.

from protecting the International Settlement it might easily have involved it in disaster. A multitude of poor people had been rendered homeless. A populous district had been reduced to a smoking ruin. The Commercial Press, the leading printing and publishing house in China, which its valuable records which could never be replaced, had been utterly destroyed. The Shanghai terminus of the Shanghai–Nanking railway had been reduced to a thing of twisted girders and crumbling walls.

No conceivably useful purpose had been served by the operation. Its only effects had been to increase the bitterness of the discord between Japan and China, to show that under favourable circumstances the modern Chinese soldier may hold his own, and to distress and alienate the sympathy of Japan's best friends.

Meanwhile the position had become crystallized in Manchuria. Early in October it was found that the ex-Emperor P'u Yi, who had been living in the Japanese concession at Tientsin, was no longer in the Treaty Port. Rumour in some quarters had it that he had been forcibly removed to Dairen. The leading figure in this alleged kidnapping was said to have been Major, now Major-General Doihara, a man apparently with aspirations to soldier-statesmanship, who has been styled by his friends ' the Japanese Lawrence.' According to other accounts the ex-Emperor was no unwilling participator in a plan to proclaim Manchuria as an independent state with himself in the position of chief executive. Sir Reginald Johnston seems to confirm this. The epilogue to his book *Twilight in the Forbidden City*, bears the title ' The Dragon goes Home.' Nor did some Chinese see anything amiss in such a proceeding. As long before as 1925 the veteran statesman, T'ang Shao-yi, saw Manchuria as still the rightful heritage of the Manchus.'[1] The ex-Emperor P'u Yi certainly owed nothing to China who had broken faith with the Ta Ch'ing House. The plan materialized in March 1932, the new state being known as Manchoukuo.

In his book, *The Case for Manchoukuo*, Mr. G. Bronson Rae sees in this action a legitimate case of self-determination. Basing himself on a saying of Thomas Jefferson which declares that ' the will of the nation is the only thing essential to be regarded,' and the modern doctrine in accordance with which the map of Europe

[1] *North China Herald*, October 26, 1925, quoted in *Twilight in the Forbidden City*, p. 436.

was re-drawn in 1919 at Versailles, he urges the right of peoples to revolt against intolerably bad government. In the present case he claims that the declaration of independence reflected the sentiment of the thirty-odd millions, mainly Chinese, which made up the population of the Three Eastern Provinces. In support of this conclusion he points to a number of statements, bearing all the marks of being inspired, which emanated from public bodies throughout the territory.

The truth is that the plan was part of a policy carefully conceived and deliberately executed. Some three months before it was carried out a Japanese friend, with whom the writer had been for many years in close and confidential touch, informed him under the seal of confidence that the installation of the ex-Emperor as the Chief Executive of the new state was in contemplation. Rightly or wrongly the writer observed the confidence. But realizing that he had been approached in this manner in order to ascertain probable British reaction, he did all in his power to impress the unwisdom of spoiling a case, which in some respects was a good case, by endeavouring to crystallize the situation on lines which would make compromise difficult and might involve a break with the League of Nations. Apart from this piece of evidence, no one could suppose that the Chinese masses which went to make up the bulk of the country were capable of exercising any right of self-determination any more than the masses of China inside the Great Wall had been able to exercise any influence on the course of events during the twenty years which went to the forging of Nationalist China.

Chapter 40
Japan and the League of Nations

Before the forum of public opinion Japan's defence was undertaken by her leading publicist Mr. K. K. Kawakami to whose book, *Japan Speaks*, with a preface by Mr. T. Inukai, a former Prime Minister of Japan, reference has been made.

As regards Japan's activities at Shanghai Mr. Kawakami frankly admitted that this was at least a blunder which it would be idle to waste time in discussing. The extent of the blunder, if that is the right word, may be gained by a perusal of Mr. Stimson's book already quoted.

The action in Manchuria is put by Mr. Kawakami on a different plane. Apart from considerations of security, the case is based on a long series of alleged breaches of treaty culminating in the explosion on the railway.

China's defence was a denial. In the alternative, if any action of hers could be construed as constituting a breach of any treaty such treaty, she said, had been entered into under duress. She denied categorically all knowledge of, or responsibility for, the alleged attack on the railway.

Japan further claimed that a number of hostile actions had been perpetrated by Chinese justifying intervention, which, of course, China could not admit. Japan also pointed to the new harbour at Hulutao designed to compete with Dairen and to a number of infringements of an alleged undertaking by China that railway lines parallel to the South Manchuria Railway should not be constructed. China denied any such undertaking. She said that a demand to embody such a provision in the treaty between China and Japan negotiated in December 1905, which recognized the transfer to Japan of the Russian rights in South Manchuria, had been refused. At Japan's request the circumstance was recorded in the minutes without creating any obligation.

Such was the broad issue. A study of the documents and the facts of the case compels the conclusion that Japan's action was not justified. In the circumstances of the times, however, limited intervention was understandable on the assumption, provided it was well-founded, that there had been an attempt by

Chinese to blow up the railway. Feeling was running high throughout the ranks of the Kuantung army. A short time previously a certain Captain Nakamura had been killed by Chinese soldiers in an out-of-the-way part of Manchuria. To quote again from the Lytton Report :

'While passing through Harbin, where his passport was examined by the Chinese authorities, he represented himself as an agricultural expert. He was at that time warned that the region in which he intended to travel was a bandit-ridden area, and this fact was noted on his passport. He was armed, and carried patent medicine which, according to the Chinese, included narcotic drugs for non-medical purposes.

'On June 9, accompanied by three interpreters and assistants, Captain Nakamura left Ilikotu Station on the western section of the Chinese Eastern Railway. When he had reached a point some distance in the interior, in the direction of Taonan, he and the other members of his party were placed under detention by Chinese soldiers under Kuan Yu-heng, the Commander of the Third Regiment of the Reclamation Army. Several days later, about June 27, he and his companions were shot by Chinese soldiers and their bodies were cremated to conceal the evidence of the deed.

'The Japanese insisted that the killing of Captain Naka-mura and his companions was unjustified and showed arrogant disrespect for the Japanese army and nation ; they asserted that the Chinese authorities in Manchuria delayed to institute official inquiries into the circumstances, were reluctant to assume responsibility for the occurrence, and were insincere in their claim that they were making every effort to ascertain the facts in the case.

'The Chinese declared, at first, that Captain Nakamura and his party were detained pending an examination of their permits, which, according to custom, were required of foreigners travelling in the interior ; that they had been treated well ; and that Captain Nakamura was shot by a sentry while endeavouring to make his escape. Documents, including a Japanese military map and two diaries, they stated, were found on his person, which proved that he was either a military spy or an officer on special military mission.' [1]

Coming on top of a series of anti-foreign outrages throughout

[1] Lytton Report, p. 74.

China, the killing of this party, whatever may have been the right or wrong of the case, inevitably aroused strong passion.

But apart from this disputable matter Japan could have made a good case on many issues. In connection with the threat to her security, attention might have been drawn to the fact that the Nine Power Treaty [1] concluded at Washington in 1922, designed to secure the integrity of China and maintain the *status quo*, did not include Russia. In International Law self-defence transcends treaties. She was entitled to claim the right to intervene in the affairs of China in order to stay the Russian advance if her security required it.

Again in the matter of the alleged breaches of treaty by China and the building of lines parallel to the South Manchuria Railway, a case for a reasonable protection of the economic interests of the railway could have been made out, supported in a measure by the precedents created by acquiescence in the Japanese protest against the building of what was known as the Fakumen Railway in 1907 and the Chinchow–Aigun railway in 1909. The Chinese contention that the treaties made in pursuance of the ' Twenty-one Demands ' had been made under duress could also have been disposed of. One of them, the treaty as regards Shantung, had been recognized by the Allies in the Treaty of Versailles. Apart from this the circumstances under which many treaties are negotiated can hardly avoid the implication of duress. International Law ' regards all compacts as valid, notwithstanding force or intimidation, which do not destroy the independence of the State which has been obliged to enter into them.' [2]

It was unfortunate that the Kuantung army took charge. On the other hand, though its methods were deplorable it can scarcely be denied that it reflected Japanese sentiment. As one looks back over the history and considers the bearing of events since 1931 the conclusion cannot be avoided that Japan has regarded Manchuria almost as her own. The Russo-Japanese War was fought primarily in Japan's defence, though theoretically in China's interest also. Manchuria was well on the way to becoming a Russian province.[3] Japan may not have intended,

[1] The terms of this instrument are summarized in Chapter 12 on pp. 88 and 89.
[2] Hall's *International Law* (8th Edition), p. 381.
[3] *Ante*, p. 33.

and under the influence of Prince Ito it is probable that she did not intend, to absorb Manchuria as she subsequently absorbed Corea. On the other hand she did not mean to do herself any injustice or to forget her soldiers who had died at Port Arthur and in the Manchurian plains. Deep and legitimate sentiment was involved. Her loss in men had been 200,000 and in treasure 2,000 million yen. She meant to secure economic domination of the Three Eastern Provinces. The ' Twenty-one Demands ' in 1915 were designed primarily to strengthen her position against the growing power of Yuan Shih-k'ai who had no love for Japan. It cannot be supposed that her sympathy was increased towards China when she learnt for the first time at the Washington Conference in 1921, that China was in secret alliance with Russia under the terms of the Li-Lobanov Treaty of 1896 at the time of the Russo-Japanese War. It would have been valuable knowledge in the negotiations at the end of 1905 for recognition of the transfer of the Russian rights. It might have been used as a weapon with which to have enforced her demand that lines should not be constructed parallel to the South Manchuria Railway, at least within defined distances.

The results of the Washington Conference must also have made for a sense of disappointed isolation. It was a triumph for America and had a far from satisfactory outcome for Japan, or so far as can be seen for Great Britain. At the time Japan made no comment. She was influential in Peking and Manchuria. But as the years passed Chang Tso-lin became less amenable. After his assassination Japan doubtless expected easier times. Yang Yu-t'ing, his chief of staff, was pro-Japanese and would work in conformity with Japanese views. But Chang Hsueh-liang, the ' young Marshal', did not see himself in leading strings and Yang Yu-t'ing and his henchman Wang Yi-t'ang were invited to a party and sent to join their old chief at the ' Yellow Springs.' This was early in 1929. At the end of 1929 Marshal Chang flew the Nationalist flag and, as we have seen, in the following year threw in his lot with Chiang Kai-shek. Up to that time Japan had been able to have her own way, but the last year or two of the Chang Tso-lin regime followed by that of his son made Japan uneasy. She could no longer carry on in the old way and had to find a new technique or yield in part her claims.

China with her sound case in principle early appealed to the League of Nations.

The Council met to consider China's communication on September 22, and after hearing statements by representatives of both parties addressed an urgent appeal to the two governments to abstain from any act which might aggravate the situation or prejudice the peaceful settlement of the problem. On September 29 a report was made to the Assembly, and on the following day the Council again met. The situation was then recorded in a resolution which *inter alia* recognized the importance of the Japanese Government's statement that it had no territorial designs in Manchuria, noted its conviction that both governments were anxious to avoid taking any action which might disturb the peace and good understanding between the two nations, and requested both parties to do all in their power to hasten the restoration of normal relations.

This expression of confidence was soon seen to be misplaced. China officially assumed the early withdrawal of Japanese troops and arranged for representatives to take over the areas to be evacuated. Japan, on the other hand, remained in occupation, protesting strongly against anti-Japanese agitation and proposing direct negotiations with China on what she called the ' Fundamental Points.' On October 9 China protested vainly against the bombardment of Chinchow by aeroplanes and fresh ' aggressive ' operations. Hope, however, of a satisfactory solution was inspired by a proposal of the representative of Japan on November 21, that a Commission of Inquiry should be sent to the spot in order that the Council might obtain an impartial view of the situation. Although this proposal was accompanied by a statement that the Japanese Government was anxious that the resolution of September 30 should be observed in the spirit and the letter, critics of Japan and those who had a deeper insight into the situation, doubted if not its sincerity, the power of the Cabinet to resist the pressure of the Army. Unfortunately this doubt proved to be well-founded. The Commission was appointed on December 10, 1931, and had hardly arrived in the Far East when the independence of Manchoukuo was proclaimed. Subsequently by the time the Commission's report was published, towards the end of September 1932, Japan had already signed a protocol with the Prime Minister of Manchoukuo according recognition to the new state. Japan in fact had long since prejudged the issue. Her view had already been made clear both by the blunt announcement of General Araki, the War Minister, and in the more diplomatic language of the Foreign Office. 'The General, whose utterances are not without an attractive simplicity,' as a writer in the *Round Table* observed, had gone so far as to say that ' Japan had no wish to ruin the League by seceding, but, if it refused to take the Japanese point of view, then Japan could co-operate with it no longer.' [1]

Diplomatically these actions by Japan constituted not the least flagrant offence. Japan herself had proposed the sending of a Commission of Inquiry. On January 7, 1932, the United States Government, who had been co-operating closely with the League, had formally notified Japan and China that it could not recognize any situation, treaty or agreement in violation of the Nine Power Treaty or Pact of Paris, more familiarly known as the Kellogg Pact.[2] Two months later the Assembly of the League had declared that ' it was incumbent upon the members of the League of Nations not to recognize any situation, treaty or agreement which may be brought about by means contrary to the Covenant of the League of Nations or to the Pact of Paris.'

The Japanese procedure, therefore, had created a virtual impasse. Nevertheless the League felt constrained to follow the course which had been set. There was in fact little if any choice. Although in February 1932, Mr. Stimson had proposed a joint representation by America and Great Britain, with any signatories who might be willing to participate, under the Nine Power Treaty, the matter had not proceeded further. Short of forceful intervention or application of economic sanctions there was nothing else that could be done. The same still remained true.

Inferentially Great Britain's failure to fall in with Mr. Stimson's suggestion is made subject of criticism by Mr. Stimson of British policy. If, however, the Foreign Secretary, Sir John Simon, doubted the wisdom or efficacy of such a course at that

[1] *Round Table*, March 1933, p. 307.
[2] The Pact of Paris (Kellogg Pact) dated August 27, 1928, outlawed war and provided that the settlement of all disputes and conflicts between the signatories should never be sought except by pacific means. The High Contracting Parties were Germany, United States, Belgium, France, Great Britain, Italy, Japan, Poland and Czecho-Slovakia. Amongst those subsequently adhering to the Pact was China.

time, he was not alone in that opinion. Those near to events saw no hope of inducing the retirement of the Kuantung army or checking the operations at Shanghai by a statement ' whose main purpose was to make clear our faith in and intention to live up to the covenants of the Nine Power Treaty respecting the future sovereignty and integrity of China.' [1] Japan was in desperate mood. To borrow a metaphorical phrase occurring in an editorial notice of Mr. Stimson's book in the *Peking and Tientsin Times* of September 26, 1936, ' She might have announced her readiness to commit hara-kiri on our doorsteps.'

The findings and recommendations of the League Assembly followed the view of the Commission as to the principles to which any satisfactory solution should conform. These took liberal regard to all Japanese claims and were as follows :

' 1. Compatibility with the interests of both China and Japan.

2. Consideration for the interests of the Union of Soviet Socialist Republics.

3. Conformity with existing multilateral treaties.

4. Recognition of Japanese interests in Manchuria.

5. Establishment of new treaty relations between China and Japan.

6. Effective provision for the settlement of future disputes.

7. Manchurian autonomy.

8. Internal order and security against external aggression.

9. Encouragement of an economic rapprochement between China and Japan.

10. International Co-operation in Chinese reconstruction.' [2]

The condemnation of Japan, *nemine contradicente*, and her resignation from the League, are facts which have become history. Japan's actions had ruined her case. Apart from this the Japanese representatives failed to impress the League Assembly with the spirit of history which went so far to support their country's view. The case for China, on the other hand, was brilliantly presented by two of her foremost dialecticians.

Japan left Geneva in a mood of defiant isolation. The World saw her go with grave regret and not without sympathy. She now set herself seriously to the tasks of consolidating her position

[1] *The Far Eastern Crisis*, by Henry L. Stimson, pp. 162–4.
[2] *The League from Year to Year* (1931–2), p. 173.

in Manchoukuo, protecting her flank in relation to Outer Mongolia, and expanding her influence southward into North China. As the story of the next four years will show, she went on her way regardless of world opinion and consequences.

Chapter 41

The Empire of Manchoukuo [1]

On March 1, 1934, the constitutional form of Manchoukuo was changed by the enthronement of the Chief Executive. Thus the last occupant of the Dragon Throne of China, the ex-Emperor P'u Yi, regained his Imperial state. A reign name was chosen, K'ang Te, meaning ' Vigorous Virtue.' At the same time the moral principles of Wang Tao, or the ' Princely Way,' [2] were adopted for the spiritual and moral guidance of Emperor and people.

Behind this political façade has been completed under the direction of what are euphemistically called Japanese advisers an efficient administration, the foundation of which was laid on the declaration of Manchuria's independence, followed shortly by the seizure of the Chinese Customs and Salt Revenues in Manchuria, two years before. In this field Japan's achievement has been remarkable, distracting attention from, if it does not obscure, her moral obliquity. Concurrently steps have been taken towards the realization of Japan's policy designed to satisfy her sense of security and to meet her economic needs.

Early in 1933 the Province of Jehol, the eastern-most of the

---

[1] This is often spelt ' Manchukuo,' which, however, does not reflect accurately the sound of the middle Chinese character.

[2] Wang Tao is a quasi-Confucian doctrine evolved in military circles in Japan comparable to Bushido, the product of feudal days. It professes to aim at peace and security by means of government conforming to the wish of the people.

four provinces into which Inner Mongolia had been divided in 1928 for purposes of more effective administration by China, was brought under the control of the new state. Affording a strong natural political boundary, its occupation was deemed essential to security in the south-west. Despite its strength it was yielded by the Chinese without serious opposition.

For this Chang Hsueh-liang, as the Commander in North China, must bear the chief responsibility. Admittedly his position was a difficult one in the earlier phase in view of the suddenness of the Japanese action. Without attempting to excuse his failure in regard to Chinchow, his best troops were inside the Great Wall. The remaining troops amounting to about 100,000 men were dispersed throughout Manchuria. In the absence of support from Nanking apparently he saw no reason to oblige his political enemies by courting destruction.

But Jehol was a different matter. Attack on Jehol constituted invasion of China in a sense quite different to the invasion of Manchuria which had already been a cockpit of Asia. China now had a measure of cohesion.[1] There had been ample time to make dispositions. There should and could have been resistance. Political jealousies and sordid chaffering lost Jehol to China, and cost the ' young Marshal ' any reputation he had as patriot and soldier.

In North Manchuria the policy of Japan aimed to eliminate the influence of Russia. It will be recalled that by an agreement in 1896 between China and Russia, a concession was granted to the Russo-Chinese Bank to construct what became known as the Chinese Eastern Railway across North Manchuria to Vladivostock. Japan's victory over Russia nearly ten years later was not sufficiently convincing to enable her to demand the cession of Russian rights in northern Manchuria. Russia in consequence was left free to exploit the rich areas in that region. During the Great War the Allies undertook an expedition into Siberia by way of Vladivostock in order to keep open the Siberian Railway. When they retired management of the Chinese Eastern Railway was handed to China who subsequently agreed with Russia to the re-establishment of joint control and the restoration of Russian rights. It was now essential to Japanese policy to secure control of the railway.

[1] *Post*, p. 317.

The concession contract visualized a joint Russo-Chinese undertaking. The Russian interest was therefore limited to one half. The right was reserved in the contract to the Chinese Government to redeem the Russian interest in a period of thirty-six years which was about to expire. The Chinese Government rights in the railway could not, of course, be considered as having been rightfully acquired in contemplation of law by the newly constituted Empire of Manchoukuo. On the other hand a *de facto* situation existed which left little room for the operation of legal principle.

Despite protests by China, Russia took a realistic view. The determined attitude of the Japanese at that time, coupled with unpreparedness on the part of Russia, tended to make the Chinese Eastern Railway a source of weakness rather than of strength.

Prolonged and difficult negotiations resulted in March 1935 in the sale to Manchoukuo of the Russian interests in the railway at a price of 140 million yen at an agreed exchange. This sum in terms of sterling represented about six million pounds. The cost of the railway, including presumably land for its settlements and cities and a measure of development, is said to have exceeded the equivalent in roubles of the fabulous sum of 40 million sterling.[1]

A vigorous anti-bandit campaign, if it has not completed the establishment in Manchoukuo of conditions of reasonable tranquillity, has at least achieved remarkable results in that direction.

With the effective control of Manchuria, Japan completed an important step in her defensive measures. On the north and north-west her strategic frontier now marches with that of Soviet Russia ; farther south it runs in theory with Mongolia, Chahar and the Great Wall.

Meanwhile the development of the economic interests of Japan in Manchoukuo had been pushed with not less energy though with hardly so satisfactory results. Between September 1931 and September 1935, which was regarded as the first re-habilita-

[1] The change of railway control in North Manchuria has resulted in a change of the former Chinese Eastern Railway, now called the North Manchuria Railway, from the 5-foot Russian gauge to the English standard 4 foot 8½ inches which was adopted for China's railways. A streamline express called the ' Asia ' now runs from Dairen to Harbin, a distance of 670 miles in approximately 13 hours. A direct service, that is to say without change at Harbin, has also been established between Dairen and Manchuli, the border town in North-west Manchuria where connection is made with the Trans-Siberian Railway.

tion period, capital to the extent of upwards 700 million yen was poured into the country. By this means it was hoped that emigration from Japan would be stimulated, that the agricultural potentialities of Manchoukuo would be more fully realized, that wool production would be increased in quantity and improved in quality, and that important mineral developments would take place.

It is not to be expected that a far-reaching programme such as was contemplated could achieve early results. But perhaps sufficient time has elapsed to enable some conclusion to be formed as regards the outlook.

This on the whole cannot be regarded as promising. There has been no considerable settlement of farming families and such settlements as have been established have been a source of expense to Japan rather than of profit. The Japanese are not good colonists. The environment of Manchuria is strange to them. Instead of the mild climate of Japan they have to endure the hard continental climate with its great extremes of heat and cold. Cultivation has to be carried on on dry soil presenting difficult problems of irrigation. Finally, the Japanese works in competition with the Chinese whose scale of life is definitely lower.

In the absence of emigration from Japan the food problem has been stressed as one of primary importance. In defence of the 'needs must' theory it has been consistently urged that the control of a food supply outside Japan was essential to meet the needs of Japan's growing population. When the figures come to be examined, however, it appears that the volume of imports by Japan of food stuffs from Manchuria has shown little change in the last five years. According to a recent article dealing with the effects of the occupation of Manchuria on Japan's national economy, which appeared in the *Nankai Social and Economic Quarterly* of October 1936, ' the import of food stuffs into Japan from Manchuria now is on the same level as in 1929–31, for no reason other than that Japan has no need of foreign food supply. The statistics of import and export in 1935 show that even the import of rice into Japan is balanced by its exports from Japan. The Empire has become almost self-sufficient in this respect, due to the intensification of agriculture, and in a lesser degree to the difficulties of rice consumption by some groups of the population.' [1]

[1] p. 61.

Statistics show that Japan proper supplies 85 per cent of her needs. The balance is satisfied from Corea and Formosa. ' It is a common error,' says Mr., now Sir, G. B. Sansom, ' to suppose that Japan is to a considerable extent dependent upon foreign food supplies. This is only true if supplies of rice from Korea and Formosa are treated as foreign.' [1]

If, therefore, the time is approaching which is foreseen by some authorities on population when a fall of birth-rate begins, this aspect of Japan's problems is perhaps not quite so acute as for political and Imperial purposes is sometimes made to appear.

Amongst the agricultural possibilities of Manchuria on which hopes were built is that of increase of the cotton area, which would help to meet one of Japan's basic needs. But ' experiments with cotton in Manchuria have not given favourable results and the crop harvest in 1935 was less than that of 1933. Moreover climatic conditions in South Manchuria allow cultivation of cotton of only very inferior quality.' [2]

As regards iron ore, another of Japan's basic needs, the iron content in ores so far found in Manchuria are estimated as ' from 29 to 36 per cent of iron in comparison with 60 per cent in Malayan ores, so the pig iron produced in Manchuria and imported into Japan costs more than that cast in Japan from Malayan and Australian ores.' [3]

It also appears from Japanese estimates that reserves of iron ores in sight amount to rather over 800 million tons, which may be expressed comparatively as ' barely enough for ten years of the United States' production of steel at its present rate.' [3] Nevertheless this would help Japan's steel industry materially for many years but for the increasing demand of Manchuria for iron due to the growth of railways and requirements in other directions.

Some claim has been made for an important gold supply yet to be developed. The opinions of experts, however, has not put the value of these fields at more than about 1,300 tons, say four times the average annual output of the Rand in South Africa.

Summarizing the export position of Manchoukuo to Japan, the

[1] *Economic Conditions of Japan*, 1933–34, Report by G. B. Sansom, C.M.G., Commercial Counsellor, His Majesty's Embassy at Tokio, p. 46.
[2] *Nankai Social and Economic Quarterly*, October, 1936, p. 62.
[3] *Ibidem*, p. 63.

writer of the article above referred to expresses himself in the following terms :

'We have come to some curious but meaningful conclusions. Manchuria as a granary is not of any greater importance to Japan now than before the occupation. Manchuria does not for the most part export to Japan now more raw materials than she did before the occupation. Those materials which Manchuria exports now in greater quantity, it would supply anyway even if no occupation had taken place. The occupation, in other words, has brought no advantages to Japan in this respect.' [1]

On the other hand exports from Japan to Manchuria show a rise from 6·6 per cent in 1931 of Japan's total export to 17·1 per cent in 1935. This is due, however, to causes of a temporary character. Clearly increase in exports from Japan to Manchoukuo can only depend either on raising the standard of living in that country, involving a demand for better goods, or on the continued flow of capital into Manchoukuo for the establishment of factories calling for the purchase of machinery. But there is at present no sign of an improvement in the conditions of life of the people, while the late Mr. Takahashi, Finance Minister, is reported to have informed his colleagues barely two years ago that investment in Manchuria would require to be curtailed if serious financial disturbance was to be avoided.

That these pessimistic conclusions represent the result of scientific investigation and are not dictated by pro-Chinese sentiment is borne out by an article which appeared in the *Japan Advertiser* in September 1935 by Dr. S. Washio, a foremost Japanese authority. The view he expressed was as follows :

'As far as can be judged from the development of the past four years, the economic prospect of Manchuria has been disillusioning to the high hopes entertained in the early days of the Manchurian affair. The speedy restoration of peace and order in the new state and especially the balancing of the budget and stabilization of the currency have been feats to be proud of. But they have been performed at the expense of Japan. The control of bandits is a credit to the Japanese army. The balanced budget of the new state has been made possible by relief of Manchuria from the military

---

[1] *Nankai Social and Economic Quarterly*, October 1936, p. 65.

expenditure of the old Mukden regime. Whatever re-habilitation and development works that have progressed have been made by Japanese capital. The new state itself has hardly grown. Its chief asset, the agricultural industry, has been very discouraging. The standard of 90 per cent of its population has sunk instead of rising. Proportionately the incomes of Manchuria have decreased.'

Again :

' Manchuria's value for Japan as a source of supply of raw materials beyond what she was getting before the Man-churian incident has still to be looked for in the future, and not in the very near future. As far as can be seen in the past four years' experience, no great promises have been opened up. The essential things which Japan needs seem mostly to be lacking at present. There is no oil, except that Fushun coal may be used for the extraction of oil. Cotton and wool are not produced at present and there is not a particularly encouraging prospect of their being produced. In prospects of wheat production, too, North China seems to be better. Most manufacturing industries that may be attempted profitably in Manchuria are in danger of com-peting with home industries in Japan. It seems Japan's settled policy that textile and other light industries shall not be encouraged in Manchuria. Even in coal, iron and fertilizer, complaints of competition have been repeatedly raised.

' In short, so far as the past four years' prosperity of this country has been related to the development of Manchuria, it has been largely due to Japanese capital released by in-flationary finance and used for rehabilitation of the new state. The new state itself has practically made little economic contributions. Now that this rehabilitation is coming to a close such economic limitations of Manchuria as are here reviewed in the light of the past four years' experience will practically come to tell on the trade figures between the two countries.'

Turning, in conclusion, to the position of international trade in Manchuria, it has to be recorded that its interests have suffered in many directions. Long before 1931 it used to be said that if the door was still open in Manchuria it was at the best only ajar. Since 1931 Japan's policy in Manchuria has been still more nationalistic. With the exception of Banks, whose credit facilities are welcome, such insurance as has not been transferred to Japanese Companies and shipping at Dairen, the tobacco industry, some long-established bean-exporting houses at Harbin and a modest import of what are called luxury goods, foreign business is negligible. There is no room for much that is not of Japanese origin.

The dread of Communism and the brutal methods of the Army and Gendarmerie have resulted in many cases of savage treatment. Even though such incidents should be based on genuine suspicion and be not aimed at foreign business firms, the methods that are employed can only engender distrust and lack of confidence in the Administration. Terrorism, whether of foreigners of other than Japanese nationality, or of the Chinese employees of foreign firms, whatever its cause, can only be calculated to drive business out.

Again, from the earliest days since the Russo-Japanese War it has always been believed despite official denials that Japan's control of the South Manchuria Railway has enabled a system of freight rebates to come into existence which could only be availed of by the large shippers to and from Japan. Since the new state was established an oil monopoly has had the effect of dispossessing important oil interests which wisely or unwisely did not see their way to submitting to what appeared to be Japanese exploitation under the guise of legislation of the Government of Manchoukuo. The British American Tobacco Company, on the other hand, realizing that expansion was impossible under the old conditions, boldly embarked on a new policy and established a company in conformity with the laws of Manchoukuo. In consequence they have continued to do a flourishing business. It must be recalled, however, that from this company an immense revenue is derived. It would, therefore, in most circumstances be favourably regarded. It is not so clear what the position would be if the Japanese Tobacco Monopoly were able to supply the needs of this field.

Chapter 42
Mongolia

The march of events has made the tableland of Mongolia, with an area of a million and a half square miles and a population of possibly two to every three square miles, a region of strategic importance.

The second group of the ' Twenty-one Demands ', which called for the opening of suitable places in Inner Mongolia to foreign trade and residence, evidenced the importance attached by Japan to the stretch of country lying along the Great Wall. Her interest in Outer Mongolia was the consequence of the creation of the new state of Manchoukuo and the spread of Bolshevist ideas. Russia, on the other hand, has also been interested in Mongolia, at least from the last decade of the nineteenth century. It was then that she visualized a connection between the Siberian Railway, in the neighbourhood of Lake Baikal, and Peking by way of Urga, which would have reduced the Trans-Continental journey from Peking to Paris to less than eight days. Since the Russian Revolution it has become a fertile field for the spread of Bolshevist ideas. To-day it represents an outlying defence to Japanese ambitions of Asiatic conquest.

China, of course, has been interested in Mongolia through the ages. It was primarily Mongol incursions which caused the building of the Great Wall. If the Mongol clans were ever regarded by China as included in the vast loose-knit empire of the T'angs (A.D. 618–907) their successors remained the prey of border ravages until Genghis Khan turned his attention to China. Of his famous campaigns one of the earliest laid the foundations for her conquest. His last campaign completed it. Genghis himself died in China as the campaign neared its end, his grandson Kublai Khan becoming the first emperor of the Mongol or Yuan Dynasty (A.D. 1280–1368). As the empire of Genghis Khan became disintegrated, the link which bound the Mongol clans was weakened. As time passed a re-grouping took place which may be traced to-day in the broad differences which exist between the inhabitants of Sinkiang, Outer Mongolia, Inner Mongolia and the western portion of Manchuria.

Mongolia began to count again in world affairs in the seventeenth century when the Manchus, busy with their empire building, brought the Mongols into alliance on the basis of Manchu suzerainty. When in 1911 the Chinese Revolution broke out and the Manchus shortly abdicated, although Inner Mongolia considered her interests lay with China, Outer Mongolia declared her independence.

To Czarist Russia this was a welcome development. China, however, claimed Mongolia as a dominion, and when in 1917 the Revolution took place in Russia, the Chinese seized the opportunity to assert their claim. In November 1919 the Mongols were compelled to yield to the Chinese demand for cancellation of Outer Mongolian autonomy.

But the success of China was short-lived. In the following year, as will be recalled, the Anfu party were driven out and the Chinese hold relaxed. For a time Outer Mongolia became the base and to some extent the field of operations of the White Russians. A strong revolutionary element, however, in Mongolia was sympathetic to the Soviet Government with whom an agreement was made on November 5, 1921, in which the parties undertook to oppose the activities of hostile 'governments, organizations, groups and individuals' on its territory, and to refuse to allow importation or transportation of arms by 'organizations struggling directly or indirectly' against either government.

Thus was established in favour of Russia the first defence measure against any power challenging Soviet Russia's influence. Four years later, in May 1924, as part of the arrangements in connection with Chinese recognition of Soviet Russia, Outer Mongolia was recognized by Russia as an integral part of the Republic of China. But this view did not receive the endorsement of the Mongols themselves, and in the following month Outer Mongolia declared itself a republic under the name of the Mongolian People's Republic. Since then Outer Mongolia with Russian assistance has developed steadily on Soviet lines.

Meanwhile Inner Mongolia had been the subject of gradual penetration by Chinese. In 1928, with a view to strengthening the Chinese position in that region, Inner Mongolia was divided into four administrative provinces in which were incorporated in some cases portions of the neighbouring Chinese provinces.

These four administrative areas from west to east were Ninghsia, Suiyuan, Chahar, and lastly Jehol which has already been referred to.

The policy of Japan, being directed to weakening Russian influence in Outer Mongolia, naturally interests itself also in Inner Mongolia, while Russia is deeply concerned to resist Japanese encroachment in a region which she regards as a buffer state against Japanese further advance.

The last five years have seen Japanese plans materially advanced at the expense of China in Inner Mongolia. It will be recalled that in February 1933, Japan moved westward from Chinchow, and without resistance from China, extended the boundaries of Manchoukuo to include the Province of Jehol. The process of absorption has continued till Chahar is under substantial Japanese control. Although the Japanese assert, and possibly truly, that they have no troops in Chahar, they have military missions at Kalgan and other places in the province. They also hold the passes of Kupeikou and other places along the Great Wall north and north-east of Peiping.

In the neighbouring province of Suiyuan the Japanese also have military missions, and have been endeavouring for some time to secure the retirement of General Fu Tso-yi, a subordinate of Yen Hsi-shan, the Governor of Shansi Province. Fighting to that end has been even now (December 1936) in progress, though at the moment reverses have been suffered owing to Chinese resistance under General Fu Tso-yi, a man of stout record. The Japanese also control in effect the Peiping–Suiyuan railway, a factor of great strategic importance. No observer doubts that Japanese influence will be extended at least as far west in the near future as to include this province. By this means there will be established an area between China and Communist Outer Mongolia which will be under Japanese control. Strategically, it then becomes necessary for Japan to have some understanding with China or to be in a position to assert control in North China to prevent this stretch of territory from becoming a source of weakness through an exposed left or southern flank.

Further north, in order to strengthen the western marches of Manchoukuo, Japan has caused a new administrative province to be formed consisting of the eastern portion of the Province of Heilungkiang and the northern part of Jehol. These districts are Mongol and uncolonized by Chinese. Their inhabitants are conservative in their instincts and politics, and it was thought might form a useful buffer state against the Mongolian People's Republic. For this purpose it was granted a semi-autonomous system. In addition to forming a protection to Manchoukuo, it was designed to push forward the western boundaries into territories which politically remained undefined. Hence there have been numerous border incidents.

A study of the map shows, on the one hand, the importance of Outer Mongolia to Russia primarily as protecting her lines of communication with Eastern Asia, and on the other hand, the nature of the threat of the constant pressure by the newly-formed Mongol province of Manchoukuo which has been referred to and is known as Hsingan, and by the Japanese progressive domination of Inner Mongolia. 'One thing is clear,' ran an official Russian pronouncement at the beginning of the present year, 'the playing with fire along our Far Eastern borders has not ceased and the Japanese military authorities are creeping towards our frontiers both directly and across other territories.'[1]

But it is not only just now that the ultimate implications of Japanese domination of Manchuria had presented themselves to the Russian mind. In recent years the danger has been kept steadily in view. With Russian assistance the Mongolian People's Republic has been strengthened by important communications with Soviet territory. A Mongolian army has been trained and equipped by Russia, and a conservative estimate puts them at 50,000 men and not less than 250 or more aeroplanes. 'The pilots,' says Sir William Oudendyk, 'are exclusively Soviet Russians.' He adds that 'in February last, after a visit to Moscow of the Mongolian Prime Minister, it was decided that the military forces and equipment would be largely increased, with more Russian instructors, and that a loan of 50,000,000 roubles would be made to the Government, while that part of the

[1] Quoted by Sir William Oudendyk, K.C.M.G. in an address on Soviet policy in the Far East, published in *International Affairs*, Nov.–Dec. 1936, p. 37. In addition to this address a reference may be made in connection with this subject to *Outer Mongolia : A new danger shown in the Far East*, by T. A. Bisson, *American Foreign Policy Report* of Nov. 20, 1935 ; *Russo-Japanese Relations*, an address by Owen Lattimore reproduced in *International Affairs*, July–Aug. 1936, and an article by the same writer in *Pacific Affairs*, Sept. 1936, *The historical setting of Inner Mongolian Nationalism*.

proceeds devoted to military purposes would be expended under the direction of the Soviet authorities.'[1]

Russia also has not been neglectful of her own defence. Her frontier posts have been multiplied and fortified on modern lines. During the last two or three years in particular she has made strides which have astonished and alarmed Japan, whose general staff would appear to have made some miscalculations. At the Pacific Conference held last August at Yosemite Park, the Japanese delegates demanded to know if it was not a fact that the Russian forces in Eastern Russia exceeded the entire Japanese Army. The Soviet representatives admitted that it was likely. They lacked, however, the precise figures which they said they would try to obtain later. They maintained, however, that their army was purely defensive, and for the purpose of pursuing pacific policies and maintaining peace in Asia. This was also the contention of Japan. It must be mentioned, however, that when it became clear that Japan in effect had invaded Manchuria and did not propose to withdraw, Russia proposed a security pact which Japan refused.

Clearly the outlook of the two countries is fundamentally different. Russia intends to see that the *status quo* is maintained in Outer Mongolia. It is her protection of the Baikal region. The Japanese view regards Mongolia as ' a territory belonging to the East,' to adopt the language of General Araki when Minister of War in Tokyo. ' It cannot be left,' he said, ' in the position where other countries spread their aggressive policies with respect to it. To leave Mongolia in its ambiguous position means to maintain a centre of disorder in the East.'

' Ambiguous position ' is perhaps a good description. Outer Mongolia is still claimed as a dominion of China and that position has been recognized by Soviet Russia in a formal treaty. Outer Mongolia herself has declared her independence and for more than twelve years has been building up an independent state. In that state Russia has not only shown a keen and helpful interest from the point of view of the policies of the Mongolian People's Republic, but has also, on March 15, 1936, signed a protocol with her Government providing that ' in the event of a menace of attack upon the territory of the U.S.S.R. or the Mongolian People's Republic by a third state, the two governments under-

[1] *International Affairs*, Nov.–Dec. 1936, p. 832.

take immediately to consider jointly the situation that has arisen and take all measures which should be necessary for protection and security of their territories.' This provision is complemented by an undertaking by each party ' to render to the other every assistance including military assistance in the event of military attack upon either one of them.' On this protocol becoming known, China, of course, entered a strong protest.

Thus China keeps open her claims to Outer Mongolia and reminds Moscow that the recent protocol involved an infraction of the 1924 Treaty. At the same time she conveys diplomatic assurance to Japan that she was not allowing to pass unchallenged an instrument directed against a power with whom, in the language of treaties, she is on terms of ' amity and friendship.'

Chapter 43
Japan and North China

Keeping pace with steps taken elsewhere towards consolidation of the Japanese position on the mainland, Shanhaikuan was bombarded by Japanese troops on January 1, 1933, on the alleged ground that the Chinese garrison had fired on Japanese troops on the Manchoukuo side of the Great Wall. Military operations followed on an important scale, during which Japan occupied the Peiping–Mukden railway as far south as Tangku. At that point an agreement was made under date May 31, 1933, known as ' the Tangku truce,' the effect of which was to disarm the north-eastern triangle of North China as defined by the Great Wall, the sea and a line running roughly from a point to the north-west of Peiping to Lutai a few miles north of Tangku. Under the agreement all Chinese troops were to be withdrawn to a point to the west of this line. The maintenance of peace and order in the area thus disarmed was to be undertaken by a Chinese police force, which should not ' be constituted of armed units hostile to Japanese feelings.' The Japanese for their part undertook ' not to cross the said line and not to continue to attack the Chinese troops,' and to withdraw voluntarily to the Great Wall. At the same time the right was reserved to the Japanese Army at any time ' to use aeroplanes or other means to verify carrying out the Chinese undertaking.'

The justification given by Japan for this further encroachment, involving the establishment in effect of a neutral zone at the further expense of China, was that the pacification of Manchuria had been much retarded by the activities of Chinese bands of volunteers who combined with bandits to unsettle the country.

It was not surprising that in the absence of mobilization by China to protect the Three Eastern Provinces, strenuous local resistance was offered to the Japanese advance. It is certainly true that volunteers from within the Great Wall participated, and it would be strange indeed if disorganized remnants of troops, volunteers and bandits had not co-operated in the common cause. Such operations necessarily partook of the nature of guerrilla warfare, but by now volunteering had died down. In any case this could not justify invasion of China proper. It was not open to Japan having created conditions of warfare in Manchuria to treat the inevitable consequences as giving rise to legitimate grievance.

Nevertheless this was the position which had to be accepted. It could only be hoped that with the establishment of a neutral zone, the occupation of Jehol which we have already recorded, and the general steps that were being taken to suppress banditry and establish conditions of law and order in Manchuria, while at the same time taking military and economic measures to protect the new state from Russian advance, Japanese ambitions would be satisfied. But two years only were to elapse before the inference became justifiable either that this halt merely represented a stage in the Japanese programme in north-east Asia, or reflected the suspicion that Manchuria without domination of North China would fail to satisfy even in part the primary needs of Japan.

Tenseness of feeling also played its part in ushering in the new phase.

On May 4, 1935, there appeared in the *New Life Weekly*,

a Chinese periodical published in Shanghai, an article on the subject of emperors. A reference to the Emperor of Japan gave offence to the Japanese. However, the responsible officials of the Shanghai Censorship Bureau and the publisher having been duly punished, the latter with fourteen months' imprisonment, the incident was considered closed. Meanwhile Tientsin had provided an opening in a more convenient field. Two Chinese editors of newspapers of alleged pro-Japanese sentiment, published from the Japanese Concession in Tientsin, were murdered. As in the case of the Manchurian incident of September 18, 1931, the Japanese professed to see in this the culmination of a long series of anti-Japanese activities in China which justified them in demanding that measures be taken for the better security of Japanese interests. It began to be hinted that North China, insufficiently controlled and developed, as was alleged, from Nanking, should form an independent economic area.

This solution, it was suggested, would be in harmony with the existence of a strong autonomy movement on the part of the Chinese in North China which Japanese agents professed to have discovered. The provinces of China, north of the Yellow River, had certainly some cause for grievance. Prior to the Japanese advent local government and economic life had for years been grossly interfered with by branch offices of the Kuomintang, known as Tang Pu, who were charged with maintaining the dictatorship of the party and thwarting foreign enterprise. Although as will hereafter be seen there have been important developments in China in recent years, they have been mostly in the valley of the Yangtze, especially in the neighbourhood of Nanking. Very little government money has been spent farther north. It would not be surprising, therefore, if there was dissatisfaction with the Nanking Government. But nowhere in the opinion of those in close touch with Chinese thought was there any idea of autonomy or secession. The plan seems to have been a product of the fertile brain of the ' Japanese Lawrence.' Nevertheless, about the time when Europe was anxiously occupied with the affairs of Italy and Abyssinia, the idea began to take rather definite shape. The five provinces of Chahar, Suiyuan, Shansi, Hopei, and Shantung, it was intimated, should become an autonomous unit.

At this stage the Chinese Goverment put forward certain proposals aiming at adjustment of the differences between the two countries. While indicating that these proposals were not unacceptable in principle, Japan's foreign minister, Mr. Hirota, laid down certain fundamental principles which his Government considered should be agreed to.

These principles as stated in the *China Year Book*, 1936, are as follows :

' 1. China must abandon the policy of playing one foreign country against another.

2. China must respect the fact of the existence of Manchuria.

3. China and Japan must jointly devise effective measures for preventing the spread of Communism in regions in the northern part of China.' [1]

The first of these principles was one in which all foreign nations would readily concur. One of the difficulties in time past has been the exploitation by Chinese statesmen of international jealousies. The other two points, however, were of a different complexion. Recognition of Manchuria could not as yet be expected in view of prevailing Chinese sentiment. As regards the prevention of the spread of Communism, while all would recognize the desirability of this, the admission of Japanese co-operation might easily lead to a thinly disguised military control of the vast territories of North China, in area some 400,000 square miles with a population of 83 millions, on which Japan was casting covetous eyes.

Mr. Hirota's statement was made in September 1935, and remains to-day a cardinal point of Japanese policy. It was a broad statement of the Government's views. At the same time presumably it was not intended to modify the basic idea of closer economic co-operation between China and Japan. If, on the other hand, it reflected the sound Japanese business instinct to refrain from anything which would widen the breach between the two countries and thus was designed to check the economists of the Kuantung army in the plan of the five autonomous provinces in North China, it failed of its object. For it was shortly followed by a pronouncement made at Tientsin by Major-General Tada, commanding Japanese troops in North China. This statement, after making a fierce attack upon foreign policies of the West,

[1] *China Year Book*, 1936, p. 176.

expatiated on what was described as ' Japan's sacred mission,' and claimed that ' Japan alone has, as a national policy, throughout advocated the preservation of Chinese territory for the Chinese.' [1]

A correspondent of the *Peking and Tientsin Times*, writing on September 28, 1935, under the name of ' Observer,' reflected the view taken by Chinese and foreigners alike of the claim by Japan to be actuated by motives of altruism.

' The preservation of the integrity of Chinese territory has been amply exemplified by the seizure of 360,000 square miles of territory in Manchuria, whose population was in 1933 estimated at 30,000,000, Chinese representing 29,000,000 of this number ; and is further exemplified by the stranglehold Japan has, and is rapidly increasing, over the whole of North China.

' The publication of the Statement adumbrates the tightening of this stranglehold in the near future in a territory where the unfortunate Chinese officials have no longer any free will, but must proceed in all things at the dictation of their Japanese saviours.

' The peaceful nature of Japan's policy is indicated by a further extract. " She (Japan) should exterminate anyone who tries to obstruct her work."

' Yet one more extract, and a comment thereon : " she is working to make their (the Oriental Races) living safer and happier, for the maintenance of their *dignity*, with *due respect for their independence*." We all know how much dignity and independence have been left to the Koreans, and to the inhabitants of Formosa, and also to the Chinese inhabitants of Manchuria, and this is, I think, sufficient comment.'

As General Tada's statement also contained grave criticisms of the alleged corruption of the Nanking Government and a violent personal attack on General Chiang Kai-shek, it was hardly to be supposed that negotiations, if seriously initiated, could proceed with that smoothness which might be expected from a more diplomatic approach. But possibly the Japanese military party were relying more on the efficacy of deeds in the North China theatre.

When the matter of autonomy of the five northern provinces was seriously broached with the rulers of these provinces, there

[1] See Appendix 7.

was found a strong disinclination on the part of practically all of them to fall in with the suggestion. But the Japanese were not to be thus deflected from their course. When, therefore, on November 4, China without reference to Japan went off silver and adopted a managed currency,[1] the opportunity was taken to forward Japanese policy. The omission to consult Japan was regarded as an affront. The alleged linking of the currency with sterling was assumed to indicate an increase of British influence in Nanking, and immediate steps were taken by Japan to prevent the application of the scheme to North China. The pseudo-autonomy movement was pressed on. Japanese troop trains were moved down the railway to within a few miles of the Great Wall. The gravest developments seemed imminent.

But in the event the blocking of the currency measures proved only temporary and the autonomy project was not proceeded with. Somehow or other Japanese intentions became known with some exactness. Whether representations were made which added the extra weight necessary to enable the Cabinet to persuade the Army, or whether some other reasoning at the eleventh hour influenced the situation, can only be conjectured. ' Foiled in their larger purpose,' as Mr. E. M. Gull wrote in the *Nineteenth Century* of August last, ' Doihara and his friends induced an adventurous nonentity, Yin Ju-kêng, who is a Chêkiang man with a Japanese wife, to declare the autonomy of Eastern Hopei. When Yin's arrest was ordered by Nanking, they declared their intention of protecting him and seized strategic points on the railways. Chiang Kai-shek, on the other hand, agreed to the institution on December 8 of a semi-autonomous Council for Hopei and Chahar, comprising their chairmen, the mayors of Peiping and Tientsin, and other Chinese officials.'

Meanwhile smuggling, which with a long coastline is inevitable up to a certain point, attained in North China unprecedented proportions. Originating in effect in circumstances unconnected with China, it ended by becoming a political weapon in the hands of Japan.

When the United States adopted a programme of buying silver the price of silver rose, with the result that there was shortly established a steady drain of silver from China which threatened to

---

[1] Reference to the principle of the scheme is contained in Chapter 50, *post*, p. 336.

deplete the necessary silver reserves of the country. In order to counteract this tendency the Chinese placed a tax on the export of silver which absorbed the profit. Then was the chance for the smuggler. Working chiefly through Coreans, who as Japanese subjects enjoyed the protection of extra-territoriality, for the early smugglers seem to have been mostly Chinese, silver was smuggled out through Shanhaikuan and at other points in the Great Wall, where the operation of the Tangku truce hampered Customs officials and prevented them from being armed. In order to pay for the silver an inward smuggling trade was developed, notably in sugar, silk, kerosine oil and rayon.

Japan, appealed to for the better control of her subjects, was not only disinclined to interfere but seriously hampered the operations of the preventive service at sea by their interpretation of the Tangku truce as extending the neutral zonè to include the three-mile limit. The Customs cruisers were thus compelled to operate at long range while in addition the strongest exception was taken to searching suspected vessels under the Japanese flag.

Space forbids any detailed account of the state of lawlessness which has prevailed in North China during the past two years. It may perhaps be mentioned, however, that Peitaiho, a well-known summer resort in North China about twenty miles south of Shanhaikuan and therefore within the so-called autonomous district of Eastern Hopei just referred to, became as it were a free port. At the mouth of the small river from which Peitaiho derives its name even warehouses have been erected for the storage of smuggled goods and fly the Japanese flag.

But this is not all. The Administration of Eastern Hopei levies for its own revenue purposes an import duty on smuggled goods coming into the area. The amount of this duty being approximately one-eighth of the Chinese Customs duty, legitimate import of goods in the classes of those being smuggled has become impossible. Not only so, but the imposition of this duty, as is reliably reported, has been used to discriminate in favour of goods of Japanese origin. It follows, therefore, that British sugar, for example, cannot be imported directly into North China because it cannot compete with smuggled sugar. Nor can it compete in the Dairen market because the dealers can buy Japanese sugar, if destined for the North China market, at a lower price. The same is the case in relation to kerosine oil.

Exact figures are not available, but the loss to the Customs revenue has been relatively enormous. If the revenue has not been reduced to a point where the Administration cannot maintain its loan services, at one time the danger-line was not far off. In consequence the usefulness of the Customs as the chief agency for the maintenance of Chinese credit threatened to be impaired.

Thanks to the courage and ingenuity of the Customs' staffs in North China, a check was placed for a time upon the activities of the ' free-traders.' The course of events had made possible a system that, while not relaxing preventive measures, has been largely successful in restricting distribution. The extent of the smuggled goods was bound in time to glut the market of Eastern Hopei. Smugglers found themselves with an accumulation of goods on their hands which must be disposed of elsewhere. Many seizures have been made, and some of those occupied in this nefarious trade are faced with heavy loss. Their latest answer has been an increase of violence and the adoption of a place called Chikow, on the coast about midway between Tangku and Chefoo, as their port of entry with a view to operating farther south.

This then is the Customs position in North China at the end of 1936. The political position remained broadly speaking the same as at the end of the previous year. For the moment the economists in Japan seemed to have got the upper hand. The past twelve months in particular have seen the forces of economic penetration set in motion. Japan has been making large investments in North China. Of eight cotton mills, formerly Chinese-owned, which had been unable to stand up against depression and competition owing in the main to unscientific management and unsound finance, six are now in Japanese hands. Of the remaining two, one is closed and its sale is already under negotiation to Japan. At Chinwangtao, Japanese glass interests have acquired the Belgian share of a Sino-Belgian factory known as the Yao Hua Mechanical Glass Company Limited whose output of glass by the Fourcault process competes seriously with the Japanese product.

In the electrical field an enterprise is planned on a scale which may one day rival the Victoria Falls Power Company and the vast organization controlling electrical supplies in the Union of South Africa. Much resented in recent years by some Chinese, under Chinese Law such utility enterprises are no longer allowed to be undertaken by Foreigners and are in process of being taken over by Chinese.[1] But legal difficulties fade away before the forceful backing of the Kuantung army, although in this case there has been a temporary check in apparent deference to Nanking. A suggestion of British co-operation is understood also to have been made. Without approval of the appropriate Chinese authorities British co-operation is not of course possible. Furthermore, although British co-operation with China in conjunction with Japan might solve the problem of North China, it has to be considered how far this particular proposal is influenced by the fact that the British Municipality at Tientsin owns and operates an important power plant, as does also the Kailan Mining Administration, the Sino-British mining enterprise in the Kaiping coal-field.

Unfortunately Japanese activities are not limited to open competition. Business advantages are secured and are likely to be secured to an increasing extent through the influence of Japanese advisers attached to Chinese administrative organs.[2]

Turning to the wider field, whatever might be said in palliation of Japanese action in Manchuria, certainly no argument can be advanced in defence of Japan's forward policy in North China. It represents nothing more than an attempt to compel North China to serve Japan's economic needs. Manchuria has proved a disappointment. Can North China be made to supply the deficiency ? Is it possible for an economic *bloc* to be established which should make Japan, Manchuria and North China to a substantial extent self-supporting ? Has North China the raw materials to meet Japan's needs in peace and war ?

The answers which must be given to these questions are definitely encouraging, from Japan's point of view. It is true that there is no rubber, while the existence of oil in the Province

[1] A recent case is that of the Tientsin Native City Waterworks Company Limited, a British Company which gave the Tientsin City its first supply of running water. Prior to 1901 water was baled from the river, the City's drainage sump, and distributed in water-carts.

[2] Applicable to the whole of China is the unfair competition in foreign products by the wholesale imitation of foreign trade-marks. A grave indictment by the League of Nations has also to be recorded in the matter of the manufacture of narcotics and their uncontrolled distribution outside the Japanese Empire. Their disastrous effect during the worst period of smuggling, especially on labour conditions in North China, became matter of deep concern.

of Shensi in commercial quantities has still to be proved. Again, a need of Japan is wool, more than 90 per cent of the Chinese production of which comes from the North. It has been thought that if the market could be controlled and the quality were suitable Japan could become largely independent of Australia. But it must be pointed out that in 1935 Japan drew 95 per cent of her needs from Australia and a negligible quantity from China. Moreover, wool from Mongolia and North China is of a quality which is only possible for rougher textiles. It is quite unsuitable for cloth and finer articles. For various reasons attempts which have been made in time past to improve the quality have failed, and there is no indication that substantial improvement can be effected.

But in other directions North China holds out promising prospects. Formerly North China drew beans from Manchuria in large quantities. There is no reason why that trade, which was frightened away by hostility to Japanese policy, should not be re-established. In other fields also some export from Manchuria might be made to North China. North China, on her part, could certainly pay for such imports in raw material which could be usefully employed in Japan.

North China is an important cotton-growing area, and much of the cotton is suitable for manufacture of explosives and certain textile purposes. Other classes of cotton of different staple can be improved so as to take the place of Indian and Egyptian cotton for the finer textile industries. With extension of area under cotton possibly a large proportion of the cotton needs of Japan could be supplied from North China in the fullness of time, but at present North China's contribution in the best of recent years has been only 4 per cent of Japan's needs corresponding roughly to 70 per cent of China's export.

Coking coal is also a requirement of Japan, and that can certainly be supplied from North China which produces 70 per cent of the total coal production of the whole country. Of the total coal reserves estimated at 248 billion tons, 54 per cent are in North China and much is coking coal.

Iron is also a need of Japan, and nearly half of the iron reserves of China estimated at 250 million tons are found in Chahar, Hopei, Shantung and Shansi, though not generally speaking in the neighbourhood of coal.[1] Another estimate puts it at 381

[1] *Economic Handbook of the Pacific Area*, by F. V. Field, p. 504.

million tons. But this need not be stressed. As Mr. Hubbard points out, ' the deposits which for centuries supported a native iron industry have no significance under modern conditions.' [1]

Some of these provinces forming part of the great North China plain, with its fertile loess formation, are also rich in cereals, particularly wheat and rice. It is not surprising that Dr. Franklin L. Ho, one of China's leading economists, recently wrote that ' the provinces of Hopei, Shantung, Shansi, Chahar and Suiyuan, formed the cultural centre of this country in olden days, and the fertile soil and rich natural resources added to this importance. Following the Mukden incident in 1931 these provinces have become China's frontier region the defence of which is vitally important to the existence of the nation. From an economic point of view North China is really the control centre of the whole nation without which the whole national economic structure will be shaken.' [2]

Nevertheless in 1929, prior to the time when trade relations were disturbed, the whole of China absorbed only 16·1 per cent of Japan's exports and contributed but 9·5 per cent of Japan's imports. These figures, by a curious coincidence, both represented the same proportion of China's export and import trade, namely 25·2 per cent or one-fourth.[3] Thus raising the standard of living and other important economic changes will be called for in China before she can make a substantial contribution to the solution of Japan's needs. Against such a consummation China's own needs and unrestricted development will be a potent factor. The struggle then between China and Japan will be for economic domination of this vital region. It follows, therefore, that inherent in the Japanese demands are threats to China's political and economic independence which cannot safely be ignored. Autonomy, even in the sense of semi-autonomy, in North China would almost certainly lead to independence of Nanking and the creation of a state which

[1] *Eastern Industrialism and its effect on the West*, by G. E. Hubbard, assisted by Denzil Baring, p. 64.

[2] ' The Economic Importance of North China,' by Dr. Franklin L.Ho, *Eastern Miscellany*, Vol. 33, No. 7.

[3] *Trade and Economic Conditions in China*, 1933–1935, Report by A. H. George, Acting Commercial Counsellor at Shanghai, p. 7. The figures for Japan's trade will be found at p. 77 of the *Report on Economic and Commercial Conditions in Japan*, *June* 1936, by Sir G. B. Sansom, K.C.M.G., Commercial Counsellor, His Majesty's Embassy, Tokyo.

must inevitably become a buffer state between the China ruled from Nanking and Manchoukuo, or be absorbed by Manchoukuo, involving a re-seating of the Emperor P'u Yi on the Dragon Throne. Again economic relations such as Japan contemplates could scarcely fail to limit or prevent the industrial development of North China, since a highly industrialized China with its lower costs of production would be a matter of acute danger to Japan. Nor will industrialization of North China by Japan herself bring large employment to her people, and consequently will not assist in the solution of her agrarian problem which partly consists in finding factory employment for the surplus population not required on the land.

The year is closing on an obscure and complicated situation. There is some reason to suppose that in the late summer the aggressive intentions of the Kuantung army were checked by Imperial command. Towards the end of August Mr. Shinji Sogo, formerly a Director of the South Manchuria Railway and now President of a concern known as the Shingchung Kungssu (China Development Company), a Japanese organization which it is generally supposed is an offshoot of the South Manchuria Railway Company established to undertake in North China the type of economic development undertaken by the railway company in Manchuria, published his views in a Chinese newspaper of pro-Japanese sentiment. These went to the length of admitting that the present strained relationship was ' unquestionably the fault of Japan's China policy.' He pointed out that a generation had grown up in China, including many of the rulers of China, which had been brought up on anti-Japanese sentiment. In his view ' Japan should reconsider all her past methods and treat China anew as the first step in the creation of a new atmosphere towards friendship.' [1]

Clearly Mr. Sogo could not have made such a pronouncement without knowledge and private official backing, and it is possible that a more reasonable attitude was on the eve of adoption. Unfortunately about this time there were a number of outrages in China involving the deaths of Japanese. Although it is generally agreed that these merely represented the intolerable sense of outrage developed amongst Chinese and could not have been prevented by any means at the disposal of the Government,

[1] *Peking and Tientsin Times*, September 8, 1936.

Japan insisted on negotiations between her Ambassador to China and the Generalissimo, accompanied by the stern assurance that if a reasonable solution was not found Japan would not delay longer taking serious action.

After a preliminary discussion between the Japanese Ambassador and the Generalissimo, negotiations between the Japanese Ambassador and the Chinese Foreign Minister were opened in Nanking.

By this time, for reasons dealt with hereafter,[1] the Nanking Government was able to feel that the country was behind it. Events had also tended to engender a measure of military confidence should Japanese demands prove impossible of acceptance. On the Chinese side, therefore, negotiations could be carried on with reasonable firmness.

It appears that economic co-operation in North China was accepted in principle and definite agreement was claimed by Japan to have been reached on the suppression of anti-Japanese agitation, employment of Japanese advisers, and the reduction of tariffs. No progress seems to have been made in the direction of securing China's consent to two of Mr. Hirota's points, namely, the co-operation for suppression of Communism and of some sort of recognition of Manchoukuo.

At this stage Japan demanded a formal agreement on the points which she considered had been accepted. But meanwhile border pressure had developed into serious military operations in Suiyuan in which it was alleged Japanese troops were engaged in support of Manchoukuo troops who were pushing their boundary westward. China refused, therefore, to implement the understandings which she denied had reached the concrete shape claimed by Japan, and negotiations were suspended.

That Japan did not at this juncture adopt a forcing attitude is susceptible of explanation perhaps on one or other of two theories. One would like to believe that while China felt herself able to adopt a firmer attitude, the civilian element in the Government of Japan had also begun to find itself strong enough to adopt a more considerate attitude and to insist on the impossibility of diplomatic achievement so long as the Kuantung army persisted in its independent adventures. In such case the atmosphere would be definitely more promising. Some support was given

[1] *Post*, Chapter 47, pp. 322–4.

to such hope a day or two before the close of the year by news of the settlement, without political conditions, of two of the more important of the outstanding incidents which had involved the death of Japanese. On the other hand the possibility cannot be ignored that a sense of security and added strength rather than a change of heart may be responsible for anything in the nature of apparent acquiescence by the Army in a less forward policy. Long-standing rumours of an understanding between Japan and Germany against Russia crystallized on November 25 in an agreement ostensibly directed against the Comintern. If Japan realizes, as she must, that if pressed too far China would fight, the desire in the present state of international affairs to avoid being committed to military operations in China which might be long and lead far afield is likely to have been an important factor.

Chapter 44

Pan-Asianism

In recent years Japan has enunciated a policy which has been called Pan-Asianism. It has been sometimes described, rather inadequately, as the Monroe doctrine of the Far East. But apart from scope and definition, the question which arises is whether it is the result of far-reaching design or the consequence of political circumstances. In other words, have developments on the mainland of Asia been inspired by a policy consciously aiming at the hegemony of Asia, or was the Pan-Asia Doctrine expounded to explain and further them?

Certainly a Japanese Pan-Asia policy is not traditional. We have seen that with the exception of the invasion of Corea by Hideyoshi with a view to ultimate attack on China, no attempt was made by Japan until modern times to establish herself upon the mainland. But with the extension of European activities in the Far East, Japan could not remain indifferent to developments in neighbouring countries. The seizure by Russia of the island of Saghalien and later on Russia's attempt to establish herself on the island of Tsushima,[1] the cession by China to Russia of the Maritime Province including the important harbour of Vladivostock and the building of the Trans-Siberian Railway, compelled Japan to look outward.

A Corea under the suzerainty of China, which still persisted in regarding Japan as a tribute race and was subjected to Russian pressure, could not be tolerated. When Japan, therefore, defeated China in 1895 it was her aim once and for all to make her position secure. Corea was to be independent, which in effect put Japan's first line of defence on the River Yalu. The cession by China of the Liaotung Peninsula would give Japan marches on the mainland and at least one fortified harbour as the outworks of her defence.

To-day when we speak rather loosely and interchangeably of the Liaotung Peninsula and the Kuantung Peninsula, we think of Port Arthur and Dairen and the area leased originally to Russia, which now belongs to Japan. But geographically the Liaotung Peninsula is the much larger area lying south of a line drawn roughly from Antung at the mouth of the Yalu to Newchwang on the Liao River. It was the Liaotung Peninsula as thus roughly defined which was ceded by China to Japan by the treaty of Shimonoseki.

The war between Japan and China had a no less just foundation than most other wars. Japan was the victor. She was entitled to hold her gains. But not the least important of them was wrested from her at the instance, as we have seen, of Russia, France and Germany. She submitted with outward grace to the loss of the Liaotung Peninsula, but within was bitterness of heart. She was a new-comer into the family of Nations. A cartoonist of the day went to Lilliput to illustrate the Chinese giant caught slumbering and bound prisoner by hosts of midget men. Russia wanted a warm-water port and France was Russia's ally. Germany was feeling the 'Drang nach Osten.' She needed a naval base in Far Eastern waters and did not regard with equanimity the growth of Japan's power.

It was an international crime which time was to prove a grave blunder. But for this the course of events in the Far East might

[1] *Ante*, p. 34.

have developed less dangerously. Japan would have built up her new colony and been secure. Russia might still have obtained her railway across Northern Manchuria, though it cannot be certain. China freed from the menace of Russia would have carried her northern railway system to Mukden and beyond, creating possibly a stabilizing zone between Japanese and Russian spheres. Japan then could not have denied China a railway financed with British capital. Probably she would have welcomed a big British interest as a protective wedge between her new-won colony and Russia.

But the realization of such possibilities was not to be. Instead of a satisfied Japan there was to be a Japan with an anti-foreign heart. There came to life again the sort of sentiment that inspired Prince Ito when a young man to join with a dozen other young men in 1863 in burning down the new British Legation then being built at Yedo. A current story in the Far East was of a toast in the Japanese Army, a sort of ' der Tag,' to revenge on Russia, Germany and France.

The Anglo-Japanese Alliance removed this sense of being out-side the pale. Japan's achievements in the war with Russia re-established her self-respect. The surrender of Tsingtao by the Germans in the early stages of the Great War ministered further to her self-satisfaction. Unfortunately Japan could not resist the opportunity of putting herself in a stronger position still with China. She preferred to settle the Shantung question without waiting for the peace conference which would end the war. At the same time she took the opportunity to fortify her position in other directions, the whole making up the famous ' Twenty-one Demands.' The outlook for Japan then was favourable. Subsequently the refusal of the Chinese to be a party to the Treaty of Versailles, since it included what were known as the Shantung Clauses, and the outcome of the Wash-ington Conference, brought back the ' winter of ' her ' discon-tent.' Again she felt, not without reason, that the tide was setting against her. As we have seen negotiations under the mediation of Great Britain resulted in a settlement of the Shantung question on terms favourable to China, while the Anglo-Japanese Alliance was superseded by the Nine Power Treaty.[1] Despite the unpopularity of the alliance in Japan during the war, its non-

[1] *Ante*, p. 90.

renewal now looked to Japan as though so far as Great Britain was concerned she had served her turn. In 1923 the Lansing-Ishii agreement between Japan and America, which accorded Japan a measure of recognition of her special claim to interest in China in view of the fact that she was a near neighbour, was also terminated. America's Immigration Exclusion Act was passed in the following year.

The new diplomatic arrangements seemed designed to maintain the *status quo* more strictly than was consistent with Japan's needs. In later years tariffs were to add trade restrictions to those already imposed on her people by policies of exclusion. It is not surprising that Japan was aware of a sense of isolation, of definite separation from Europe and America. It was not unnatural that her thoughts should turn towards the mainland of Asia, and thus she began to think perhaps on lines of Pan-Asianism.

In 1927 there was a change of government in Japan. Three years before a series of oligarchical cabinets had yielded to the more liberal element in the country. Under Baron Kato a government was formed which in 1925 passed the manhood suffrage bill. Unfortunately Baron Kato died in 1926. An acute financial crisis in 1927 compelled his successor to resign. Way was made for a government headed by General Tanaka, a determined militarist. To him is ascribed a document which mysteriously appeared called the Tanaka Memorial. Cast in the form of a Memorial to the Emperor, dated July 25, 1927, it was a document which in translation runs to some 20,000 words. It envisages world conquest. But first there was to be conquest of Manchuria and Mongolia, to be followed by the conquest of China as a step to hegemony in Asia. It propounds vast railway schemes and the measures called for in order to secure economic domination.

Its authenticity has been denied on high authority, and the circumstances of its origin have not been sufficiently revealed to prove that it was not the work of enemy propagandists. On the other hand events since its publication have gone far to suggest, if not its authenticity, at least a reflection of the line of thought prevailing amongst the members of Japan's military caste who to-day are her virtual rulers. Subsequent declarations by Japan have done nothing to allay the anxiety roused by her alleged aims.

On April 17, 1934, the spokesman of the Japanese Foreign

Office issued a statement with reference to Japan's special 'position and mission' in the Far East. Explaining her withdrawal from the League of Nations through ' failure to agree on the fundamental principles of preserving peace in East Asia,' she claimed that only China was in a position ' to share with Japan the responsibility for the maintenance of peace in East Asia.' She pointed out that any ' joint operations undertaken by Foreign powers even in the name of technical or financial assistance ' could not fail to have ' political significance.' Japan, therefore, must object to such as a matter of principle. In brief it was a warning in the sense of ' hands off China.'

Mr. Hirota's subsequent explanation to the Chinese Ambassador at Tokio did nothing to soften the asperity of the statement. On the contrary it made it clear that Japan aimed to deal with China directly and without outside interference or suggestion in regard to outstanding matters.

From Great Britain the statement evoked a reminder of the Nine Power Treaty, to which Japan and Great Britain were both signatories. The British Foreign Secretary assumed that the Japanese statement was not intended to infringe the common rights of other powers in China and Japan's own treaty obligation. Mr. Hirota replied that this assumption was correct.

Statements by the United States and France also elicited indications that the true meaning of the utterance of Japan's official spokesman was somewhat other than appeared from the interpretation ordinarily placed on words.

There the matter was left. As the Foreign Secretary, Sir John Simon, was reported to have remarked under a barrage of logic in the House of Commons, Great Britain could not as a friendly nation very well reply, ' We don't believe you.'

The next *ballon d'essai*, or what appeared to be such, went up in the summer of 1935, that is to say rather more than a year later. It took the form of a vigorous article in the *Osaka Mainichi* on similar lines or even developing the idea further. When the reaction was unfavourable there was a denial, which the standing of the newspaper made somewhat difficult of acceptance.

Mr. Hirota's three principles, which could have far-reaching consequences, and General Tada's views on ' Japan's sacred mission,' which followed shortly afterwards, have already been referred to.

The agreement entered into between Germany and Japan, directed against the Comintern, marks the next phase. The text of this agreement, which was dated November 25, 1936, is as follows :

' The two Governments, wishing to co-operate in the fight against Communist deterioration, have agreed as follows :

' *Article* 1. The two Governments have agreed to inform each other about the activities of the Communist International, to discuss the necessary measures of defence, and to carry them out in close co-operation.

' *Article* 2. The two Governments will invite other Powers whose internal peace is threatened by the work of the Communist International to take measures of defence in the spirit of this agreement and to take part in this agreement.

' This agreement . . . comes into force with the seal of the signature and is concluded for five years. The two Powers will come to an understanding before the expiry of this term as regards future co-operation.'

There was also a protocol to the agreement in the following terms :

' The two parties have agreed :

' 1. The competent authorities of both States will co-operate in the exchange of news about the activity of the Communist International and as regards defensive measures against the Communist International.

' 2. The competent authorities of both States will, within their own laws, take severe measures against those who at home or abroad are working either directly or indirectly in the service of the Communist International or who further or promote the deteriorating work of this International.

' 3. In order to facilitate the co-operation of the competent authorities of both States as laid down in No. 1 of this protocol, a standing commission will be established.

' In this commission the necessary measures of defence against the deterioration work of the Communist International will be considered and decided.'

Consideration of the situation which this agreement produces is called for on realistic lines. We are asked to believe that it merely means what it says, that it does little more than draw the attention of states to a dangerous doctrine that has no regard

PAN-ASIANISM

for national boundaries and calls for unceasing vigilance and co-operation to resist it. Adherents have not yet been invited, but it is understood that they will be welcome.

The difficulty in accepting the agreement at its face value lies in the fact that the need of such a declaration is not obvious. Germany and Japan have long been recognized as the bulwarks in Europe and the Far East against the spread of Communism in Europe and Asia. Moreover competent observers are agreed that neither Germany nor Japan has a police system which would fail to cope with any internal situation.

Casting round for a more plausible explanation the economic aspect naturally presents itself. And here it may well be that Germany in some respects can be a more useful partner to Japan than Great Britain in the economic exploitation of North China. Even if the theory of an economic *bloc* between Japan, Manchoukuo and North China could be worked out, Japan would not be in a position to finance the developments in North China which would be called for. The warning of the late Mr. Takahashi against further capital expenditure in Manchoukuo applies equally to North China. But Germany has recently extended her trade connections with China by widespread development of her system of barter. And she can take much bean oil. Despite German inability to invest abroad, the idea of an economic *bloc* might prove a more workable proposition with the co-operation of Germany than with the co-operation of Great Britain. It would also suit Germany to have the support of Japan in pushing her trade in heavy industries in this important field.

The above considerations, without reading into the compact anything more sinister, would show sufficient advantages to both parties to justify an agreement. But here again we are met with the difficulty of fitting the terms of the compact to such an understanding. There is no reason why Germany should risk offence to China in order to secure economic co-operation which could be arranged in the ordinary course of business. With the best will in the world, therefore, it is difficult to attach to the agreement such an innocuous interpretation.

In these circumstances it would be unwise to act on the assumption that there is nothing more in the relationship created between these two powers than appears on the face of the compact or may be regarded as implicit within the field of legitimate inference.

Viewed in the light of Japan's forward policy in the Far East, the dreams attributed to her of Asiatic conquest, Germany's pre-war aspirations epitomized in the phrase ' Germany's place in the sun ' and the present demand for colonies, we can hardly resist the conclusion that the agreement contains at the least the seeds of alliance.

Such is the view taken in many quarters. China appears to read into the agreement support by her German friends of her not too friendly neighbour. Holland is unable to regard the pact with equanimity in relation to the Dutch East Indies. Russia frankly stigmatizes it as an offensive and defensive alliance and has replied with boasts of great military strength and patriotic demonstrations. Without attaching too much weight to allegations, even though made in quarters usually well-informed, of a secret agreement for technical military assistance by Germany to Japan and of a plan to divide up the Dutch East Indies and British possessions in the Pacific, it can hardly be doubted that it deals a further blow to collective security and involves an ultimate threat to the British Empire. While, therefore, we welcome the assurances which have been given by Japan of non-interference with our established interests, and by Germany of the public-spirited and pacific nature of her policy, we must not blind ourselves to the dangerous possibilities of those changes of policy which varying circumstances inspire.

Finally, as throwing light on Japan's attitude towards a Public Law common to all mankind, and thus indirectly on Pan-Asianism, we have her agreement with Italy in which these two powers seek mutually to legitimate actions which each in the other had formerly condemned.

What then is the answer to the question which we raised at the beginning of this chapter ?

It would appear to be this.

The seeds of Japan's Pan-Asianism were sown when Russia, France and Germany deprived her of not the least important of the spoils of victory over China little more than forty years ago.

Appreciation of the possibilities of a return to an anti-western policy came perhaps at the beginning of the Great War and was reflected in the ' Twenty-one Demands.'

The substitution of the Nine Power Treaty for the Anglo-Japanese Alliance at Washington in 1921 induced in Japan a deep and sore sense of isolation. This feeling was not decreased by the determination of the Lansing-Ishii agreement in 1923 and America's exclusionist policy in the following year. It was an easy step for Japan to the Pan-Asian concept.

But even this does not quite answer the question of cause and effect which has been raised. It is perhaps correct to say that the driving force of the Kuantung army created a position from which retirement was difficult. The statesmen of Japan are as likely to have been taken by surprise as China and the West. Japan's subsequent suggestion of an enquiry by the League would appear to reflect their failure to foresee their inability to control events. At that point Pan-Asianism was a sentiment rather than a policy.

History as revealed in these pages has shown that China's attitude towards foreigners had been one of provocation and repudiation of agreements. There was also general lawlessness throughout the country. If the truth could be determined, it would not improbably be found that Japan's actions in the autumn of 1931 in their inception represented a combination of resentment and determination to put an end to causes of friction in Manchuria. It must also be remembered that the Army has its own ideas on economics and national defence, and holds the view that a forward policy on the mainland affords the only solution to these problems. Again, the Army was restive foreseeing a reduction of military expenditure in harmony with the spirit of the naval treaty concluded in London in 1930. One view attributes military policy not less to the wish to commit the State to a mainland policy calling if anything for increase, certainly not reduction, of the land forces, than to Imperialist design. If these views are broadly correct, it would seem, in the light of subsequent events, that Japan's ' Hands off China ' statement of April 1934 partly was the result of what had happened and partly was designed to pave the way for further expansion. It is also a fair assumption that if the Anglo-Japanese Alliance, always a steadying factor, had still been in existence, Japanese action would have been localized.

In judging Japan insufficient weight has been attached to the history of Manchuria, dominated in turn through the ages by Mongol, Chinese, Manchu, Russian and Japanese. Nor has Japanese sentiment as regards Manchuria or eastern psychology been taken sufficiently into account. There can be little doubt that despite the disunion and chaos of China in 1931, direct negotiation would have resulted less disastrously.

The fault is somewhat unfairly attributed to the League of Nations and the attitude of the United States. Yet the Lytton Report displayed remarkable insight and America merely stood on the Treaties. Japan might be better off to-day in the Far East if her dignity had allowed a plan to be worked out in accordance with the recommendations of the Lytton Report which went so far towards meeting her point of view. Nor if blame is to be apportioned can China escape her share. She was nearest to Japan and knew her spirit best. World sentiment against armed intervention was plain for all to see. China's appeal to the League without making any serious sacrifice herself, so far, at least, as Manchuria was concerned, did her no good, and in the circumstances of the times placed the League in a false position and deprived its members of individual usefulness.

PART V

CHINA IN 1936

Chapter 45

Cultural Aspects

An account of China in 1936, a quarter of a century after the Revolution, even though avoiding excessive detail would demand at least a volume. During the past few years the various aspects of modern China's evolution have formed the task of many writers from different angles. An easily accessible foreign source of information is Mr. Woodhead's *China Year Book*. China herself has made her own contribution in the *China of To-day* series under the able editorship, and in some cases authorship, of Mr. T'ang Leang-li. Possibly these studies have been fettered to some extent by requirements of discretion, but for the discerning student they provide valuable material ranging over a wide field. If there is any propagandist tendency other than in the best sense, it can be corrected by reading in conjunction with them the works of such fearless writers as Hu Shih and Lin Yu-t'ang.

But the aim of this book is to present a picture that, however incomplete, at least may be suggestive. It would not be satisfied if no attempt were made to indicate the kind of China it is, intellectually, materially, morally and politically, which Japan to-day is so hardly pressing.

Moreover, the present writer is called upon to justify a profession of faith. Twenty-four years ago *The Passing of the Manchus* was concluded in the following not unhopeful terms :

> ' The West may well extend to China a patient and well-informed sympathy, remembering that if, like Pandora, the Revolutionaries have liberated a cloud of troubles, there also fluttered forth from the fateful box the radiant vision of Hope.'

305

Since then China has been in the crucible of civil war. We have seen the vaingloriousness of many of her leaders. We have followed her suffering people along thorny paths. The 'radiant vision of Hope' often seemed a Will-o'-the-Wisp. But for those who know China there was always the feeling that a pathway would be found some day out of the morass.

Time was passing. A new generation was growing up without knowledge of the old order, whose minds were being moulded on new lines. Dr. Hu Shih calls it the 'Chinese Renaissance.' He claims that despite its suspiciously occidental appearance, the stuff of which it is made 'is essentially the Chinese bedrock which much weathering and corrosion have only made stand out more clearly—the humanistic and rationalist China resurrected by the touch of the scientific and democratic civilization of the new world.' [1]

When in 1904 the old examination system as the path to office was abolished, there were many who felt, despite the general chorus of approval, that this drastic measure while securing the end in view undermined the foundations of China's moral structure. There was no substitute for the Confucian Ethic. Yuan Shih-k'ai, even in the hey-day of his dictatorship, realized the fundamental need of such a binding force. The extreme leaders of revolutionary thought have tacitly admitted it by their unremitting, almost frantic, efforts to invest Dr. Sun's teachings with the necessary moral and social force. The New Life Movement of Chiang Kai-shek emphasizes the value to the national life of the nation's priceless heritage from ancient times. China has stumbled over many stony places, but culturally her feet are at last set in the right way. The classical writings have come back, not as a subject of exclusive or even principal study, but to occupy something of their rightful place at once as Humane Letters and a great system of Ethics.

To-day the classics find a small place in the curricula of Chinese schools. The foreign municipal schools for Chinese in the International Settlement at Shanghai have never ceased to give some instruction in them. It has been already recorded that the British Municipal School for Chinese at Tientsin was the first amongst schools registered at the Board of Education in Nanking to recognize and meet the need of including an element

[1] *The Chinese Renaissance*, by Hu Shih, Preface, p. ix.

of the national culture. Finally, the Institute of History and Linguistics of the Academia Sinica in Nanking now devotes modern critical scholarship to historical and ancient literary fields.

In the matter of western education enough has perhaps been said in the chapter recalling the foreign contribution in the cultural field of China to indicate the strides which have been made in recent years. It is indeed a revelation to visit a Chinese middle school to-day which gives a higher scientific education than is to be found in many educational establishments in European countries. Nor in the same and many other respects do Chinese universities lag behind.

For the people at large a system of mass education has been developed which aims to raise the standard of intelligence throughout the country. As in so many other directions the inspiration came from outside. It will be recalled that during the war Chinese labour corps were organized for service on the lines of communication in France. Desirous of communicating with their families most of them could only do so through the time-honoured medium of scribes. The idea occurred to some of the British officers, most of whom were drawn from the ranks of language officers, consular and custom services, missionary and commercial fields, that it should be easy to select a comparatively small number of Chinese characters, say not more than a thousand, which would be sufficient to convey the simple ideas of such class of man. The idea was worked out and successfully applied. It was subsequently adopted in China with success in some of the cities. It was felt, however, that a still more important field offered in the country places, and now considerable work has developed on these lines. Associated with it has been some vocational training for the farming classes for which the need was strongly felt.

The foreign contribution to the cultural effort in China continues as before mainly through the medium of the Mission field. The anti-Christian spirit which under the influence of Borodin disfigured the nationalist campaign ten years ago has passed away. There is a realization that no source of culture should be neglected. On the other hand, so far as education is concerned the Chinese desire control and conformity to Chinese standards. In a sense, therefore, there are not quite the same opportunities for leadership and the practical question arises as to recruitment for the missionary services.

The Christian churches have supplied also a wide measure of spiritual inspiration. Nor should the value of club life in big cities provided by the Young Men's and Women's Christian Associations be overlooked, or again the vast charitable work of the Salvation Army in organizing relief for the destitute.

Finally, we come to the New Life Movement of the Generalissimo, Chiang Kai-shek. Although there has been a certain amount of lip-service to these ideals and in some of their sumptuary aspects they are unpopular and possibly unwise, there can be no doubt of the value of this contribution to the national life. Since the Revolution there has been a deliberate policy of weakening the bond of family which in China has had such deadening influence on social progress. The result in conjunction with the ideas derived from the wider liberty which is characteristic of modern education has produced a freedom which in many of the younger generation has degenerated into license. Foreign fashions, grossly travestied and misunderstood ideas, such as companionate marriage, which have been generally rejected, have led to social developments which have caused real alarm to the older generation of Chinese. To these developments the call to the new life has imposed an important check, while at the same time drawing the nation together in a common ideal. In laying down the principles Chiang Kai-shek has thus defined the aims which should be borne in view :

' If we want to avert the national crisis and to regenerate the race, the few who are already enlightened should lead the others in this common effort. . . . National regeneration does not depend so much on military strength as on economic and educational reconstruction . . . without the four cardinal principles of propriety, virtue, loyalty and discipline, no character-building is possible either for the individual or for the nation. True revolution is nothing but the universal adoption of these principles. . . . We must cultivate the spirit of bravery, alertness, hardihood and co-operation. When the nation calls us we must stand ready to sacrifice ourselves.'

Competent foreign testimony is not lacking to the value of the New Life Movement.

' New social goals have been set up and a new order of things is coming into being. Corruption and disloyalty have become unpopular. Technically trained men and women are replacing grafting politicians, and the farmers, workers and merchants are being given a square deal. All that the Communists could promise came to the people in a form more acceptable to those cradled in Chinese civilization. The effect upon the people has been electric. General and Madame Chiang Kai-shek through the inauguration of the New Life Movement fired the first shot in a great social revolution that will go down in history.' [1]

In other words a great step has been taken in China towards what Dr. Hu Shih has called the ' self-conscious reformation.'

Chapter 46

Progress

As we observe to-day the fruits of cultural influences in the national life of China we are amazed by a progress that a few years ago would have been unbelievable. Contemplating the country with its vast area, its prolific people, its urgent needs giving rise to far-reaching problems, we admire the courage with which this immense task has been undertaken. Fortunately it is not an unfavourable field.

China is a country primarily of village communities. Four-fifths of the people are on the land. Although there is illiteracy, ignorance and conservatism, on the other hand the people are endowed with a fine soundness and sense of practicability.

One of the ideals of the Revolution was to raise the standard of life and turn the attention of a substantial proportion of the

[1] *China Christian Year Book*, 1934–35, p. 95.

people to other things. But that has been found impossible and it has been realized to be a mistake. The agricultural basis of the country in the future as in the past has been recognized. Recently, therefore, the importance of vocational training for farmers, modernization of agricultural methods and improvement of crops have come into the foreground of the programme of National Reconstruction. Agricultural rehabilitation has been in three directions. Reclamation of land and bringing more land under cultivation has been perhaps the chief aim. In recent years the balance of trade against China has been increased by large imports of food-stuffs, to meet not only abnormal calls of flood and famine but also increasing normal requirements. This should not be the case since China has much reclaimable land and land which could be brought under cultivation. When it is recalled that Japan is in effect self-supporting in the matter of food, China should not fail in that respect even including a margin to meet the calls of famine and floods. Only with the absorption of areas for production of raw materials other than foods should China need to look abroad to supplement her food supplies.

Another agricultural interest which has called for attention has been deterioration in the quality of Chinese silk which has resulted in the decline of a once flourishing feature of the export trade. Sericulture has been pressed on in the form of establishment of sericultural schools, experimental stations and extensive mulberry plantations to produce in large quantities improved varieties of the silkworm egg. The revival of the tea trade, which once shared with silk pride of place, has been the subject of similar study.

Nor has the matter of public health been neglected. Such subjects as bacteriology and epidemic disease control, medical relief and social medicine, maternity and child health, amongst others, are developing on up-to-date modern lines.

But perhaps the achievements which from their nature are the most spectacular have been in the field of road-making and hydraulic engineering.

We have already remarked upon the lack of highways in China. In proportion to the highway systems of other countries there is still a serious shortage. But road-building was not seriously undertaken in China before 1921, and in the fifteen years which have since elapsed nearly 80,000 kilometres of roads have been constructed inside the Great Wall. It is true that 80 per cent are earth roads, but it will be appreciated that surfaced roads must take their turn in the satisfaction of their requirements by the National and the Provincial Treasuries. It should also be remarked without intending to detract from the valuable work done by Nanking, that over 10,000 kilometres are in Kiangsi, the recent stronghold of the Communists, and nearly 30,000 kilometres in the three provinces of Kwangtung, Kwangsi and Kweichow, the leading provinces in the South Western Federation which only this year gave their full allegiance to Nanking.

Unfortunately fears as to the future of North China have limited engineering activities in the main to the regions south of the Yellow River and in the far north-west. It would be misleading, therefore, to infer from the admirable road-system between the metropolitan province of Kiangsu and its neighbours, the provinces of Anhui and Chekiang, that the rest of China is equally well served.

Further in the field of engineering important results have been or are in process of being achieved in the matter of river conservancy, including the building of locks and dams, flood-prevention works and irrigation.

All these public works to which reference has been made have been within the province of the National Economic Council. This body, following the precedent set in other countries, was set up in 1933, after rather over two years' preparatory work. Its functions are to undertake ' a programme of economic reconstruction,' and to adjudicate upon ' all projects for economic reconstruction or development which are financed or subsidized by the National Treasury.' [1] It has received valuable help from a number of experts from the League of Nations.

Outside the field of the National Economic Council, outstanding progress has been made in the matter of hospitals, medical schools and educational establishments in general. But so vast is the task to be overtaken that although teachers are being turned out ' at the rate of over 10,000 a year, it has to be admitted that this is far from approaching the number really needed. At least 1,400,000 primary school teachers will be required during

[1] *Annual Report of the National Economic Council*, 1935, p. 1, and subsequent pages for statistical information.

the next twenty years if the plans of the Ministry of Education are to be fully carried out.' [1]

In the industrial field too there has been marked progress, notably in the matter of railways. Formerly under the Ministry of Communications, they are now the special province of a new Ministry of Railways.

Since 1930 China has wisely concentrated on the task of repairing the ravages to the railway system of the military operations which have already formed the subject of some detailed discussion and comment. At the same time construction has not been neglected. The most important work has been the completion of the southern half of the central trunk railway between Hankow and Canton which was rendered possible by funds made available from the British share of the Boxer Indemnity. Other developments have been extension of or connections between existing lines, and the construction of short lines of local importance in different parts of the country. Nevertheless, exclusive of Manchuria, the total mileage of the Chinese railways is less than 7,000 miles, which does not compare with that of foreign countries. It is to be expected, however, that rapid progress will be made in the near future. Amongst Sun Yat-sen's schemes was one for construction of 100,000 miles of railways with the assistance of foreign capital. Though this may be an inspiration it would not be wise to take it as a guide. Under existing conditions China's water-ways in many parts of the country form an adequate means of communication. Comparisons by length are misleading. The aim, it is suggested, should be judicious development of railways in conjunction with the water-ways. By pursuing this course China may be saved vast expenditure of capital which can be more usefully employed in other directions.

In the air progress has been remarkable. It is now possible to fly from Shanghai to Chengtu, the capital city of Szechuen, the most westerly province in China. Another route connects Shanghai with Canton. Regular connection also exists between Shanghai and Peiping by way alternately of Nanking and Haichow, Tsingtao and Tientsin. Other routes linking up Hsianfu and the north-west with Chengtu, Peiping and the Yangtze are also in operation. It is only right to say, however, that these results

[1] *China of To-day Series*, Vol. 3, ' Reconstruction in China,' edited by T'ang Leang-li, p. 79.

have been accomplished with American co-operation. This policy of using expert foreign assistance contrasts favourably with the railway policy in recent years which has been to dispense with that foreign assistance which has accomplished so much for China in connection with the foundation and development of the railway system from 1879 to the outbreak of the Revolution.[1]

In the field of Law considerable codification has been done. But much remains to be achieved especially in the matter of the spirit which informs legislation. At a time when China needs foreign help discriminatory features, whether direct or indirect, are bad policy apart from their objection in the theory of Jurisprudence. Again, as Lo Wen-kan when Minister of Justice pointed out, the Procurate system is unsuited to China, while Chinese conceptions of evidence involve frequent miscarriages of justice. On the other hand, the Civil Code is a remarkable piece of work, conforming to western ideas reflected by Young China however far removed from the Spirit of the People. Amongst other things it has three interesting features involving lines of attack on the family system. In the first place the universal succession which was a characteristic of Chinese law in olden times now yields not only to equal division, between children in the case of intestacy, but to compulsory portions in the nature of the Legitim of Scots and German law limiting the power of testamentary disposition. Provision is made for divorce on grounds appropriate to modern conditions and women's separate property is also recognized.

A law regulating the application of the Code to foreigners as regards marriage, succession and questions of status, goes far to protect the position in these important matters of Germans, Russians and other foreigners within Chinese jurisdiction.

No one will deny substantial progress. Administrative work is also making progress on western lines though still hampered by nepotism inherited from the old system. As pointed out, however, by Mr. Lin Yu-t-ang, in cynically humorous terms which may with advantage be quoted, this is inherent in the family system the spirit of which though attacked in many essential features still survives.

[1] With the exception of the Hankow–Canton railway, the main trunks were constructed prior to the Revolution with foreign capital under direction of foreign engineers.

' Every family in China is really a communistic unit, with the principle of " do what you can and take what you need " guiding its functions. Mutual helpfulness is developed to a very high degree, encouraged by a sense of moral obligation and family honour. . . . A successful man, if he is official, always gives the best jobs to his relatives, and if there are not real jobs, he can create sinecure ones. Thus sinecurism and nepotism developed, which, coupled with economic pressure, became an irresistible force, undermining, rather than being undermined by, any political reform movement. The force is so great that repeated efforts at reform, with the best of intentions, have proved unsuccessful. . . . The economic pressure and the pressure of overpopulation are so keen, and there are so many educated men who can write literary essays but who cannot repair a carburettor or set up a radio, that every new public organ of every official assuming a new post is daily flooded with literally hundreds of letters of recommendation. It is quite natural, therefore, that charity should begin at home. For the family system must be taken as the Chinese traditional system of insurance against unemployment. Every family takes care of its own unemployed, and having taken care of its unemployed, its next best work is to find employment for them. . . . And so, strange as it may seem, Chinese communism breeds Chinese individualism, and family-defined co-operation results in general kleptomania with an altruistic tinge to it. Kleptomania can go safely with the greatest personal honesty and even with philanthropy, which is nothing strange even in the West. The pillars of society, who in China are the most photographed men in the daily papers and who easily donate a hundred thousand dollars to a university or a civic hospital, are but returning the money they robbed from the people back to the people.' [1]

Summarizing China's progress in Law and Administration, tribute is due to the efforts which have been made to create machinery necessary to the establishment of a modern state. Encouragement tempered by sympathetic criticism is called for.

Turning to the question of personnel, here we find development in modern China which is in strong contrast to the intellectualism of ancient times. Whereas formerly philosophy and literature were the characteristic occupations of the Chinese

[1] *My Country and My People*, pp. 180 and 182.

mind, to-day its bent is largely towards law, science and economics. This has been particularly noticeable in recent years. It would appear to be the result largely of the changing conditions in the country, the appeal of these subjects to the practical side of the Chinese mind and the comparative uniformity of education.

Medicine and surgery, for example, are international. Although every country has its own school of thought there is a common pool of experience and knowledge. A young Chinese who becomes qualified in medicine in a foreign country returns to China able to undertake work irrespective of the administrative and technical methods of the hospital whose staff he may join. There is a directness of aim in medicine and surgery which ensures unity of idea and in ordinary practice does not leave time or room for substantial differences. It follows that those trained in medical schools in China receive the same class of instruction and absorb the same type of knowledge.

Much the same applies when we consider engineering or any other applied science. Moreover, these are fields offering satisfactory opportunity, since men can work without interference. Again apart from the human satisfaction in a definite task of which the result is a visible testimony to individual skill, there is something in applied sciences which finds a peculiarly ready response in the Chinese character. The ages have made the Chinese an extremely practical and resourceful people. As a race too they have strong nerves, good heads and hands.

Economics is another subject the study of which opens up wide opportunity in banking and journalism. In recent years banking has made immense strides while the Press in China has achieved a position of great influence. The latter reflects indeed, as strongly as any other feature, the nation's progress.[1]

Unfortunately the more philosophical lines of education do not show the same advance. Though many study law an insufficient number would appear to be attracted to its practice. Leaving out of account the earliest students who went abroad and returned to play distinguished parts under the old regime, the earliest group that plays a substantial part to-day are those who went

[1] Apart from daily journalism much of which is of a high order, it is only necessary to glance at such quarterlies as the *Chinese Economic and Social Journal* and the *Nankai Social and Economic Quarterly* to realize the distinction and value of some of the work which is being done.

abroad after 1900, with the impetus of the national humiliation behind them. A number of them studied law. But most of them have been too valuable in connection with codification or in politics to be spared to devote their talents to Bench and Bar. Later students, with China's Laws being codified on Japanese lines based on continental codes, saw little profit in the Law Schools of America and England.

Another prejudicial factor has been the lack of independence and security of the judges which would appear to have discouraged young men when making choice of a career. With no special effort made by the Government to foster personnel it is not surprising that the Judiciary has not yet achieved a high standard. Furthermore the rewards of judicial office are so low that members of a Bar are not attracted to the Bench even if opportunity was offered them. But generally speaking the Bench is not recruited from the Bar, and men work their way up from the lower judicial offices. For one reason or another it is not surprising if the capacity and integrity of the Judiciary is not always of the standard which has been attained in those countries where incompetence and venality have been left behind.

Much more might be said, some things in criticism and others in sympathetic comment, on further analysis of conditions in China at the end of a quarter of a century since the Revolution. But it is perhaps sufficient to suggest that many will be found to agree with Madame Chiang Kai-shek, who on October 10 last wrote that ' the judgment at this anniversary of the Republic, taking all things into consideration, must be that great progress has been made in the face of heart-breaking internal obstructions, which have been aggravated by external interference of serious import and consequence.' [1]

[1] *North China Daily News :* Double Tenth Supplement, October 10, 1936.

Chapter 47

Constitutional and Political Developments

Those who have received a clear picture of conditions in China in 1931 [1] will recall that the action of Japan in Manchuria on September 18, 1931, found the country on the verge of civil war. Nor did this threat to the nation's security have any immediate consequence in causing Nanking and Canton to sink their differences. Of the two, Nanking was the more conciliatory. But nothing short of the retirement of Chiang Kai-shek would satisfy Canton. In order to prevent civil war, Chiang Kai-shek resigned. In November a new Government was formed, dominated by Canton, of which he was not a member.

But the threat to Shanghai and Nanking achieved what the invasion of Manchuria had failed to do. The ranks closed up. Wang Ching-wei who had been expelled from the Kuomintang in December 1929 had been reinstated. He now became president of the executive Yuan. Chiang Kai-shek returned to power as Generalissimo. Lo Wen-kan, a graduate of Oxford and a member of the English Bar, who had held office in northern militarist governments at Peking as Minister of Justice, Chief Justice and Foreign Minister, now became Minister of Justice in a Nationalist government. For a time he acted concurrently as Minister of Foreign Affairs until this office was taken over by Wang Ching-wei. Other appointments indicated a broader basis of government. Unfortunately the differences in principle between Hu Han-min and Chiang Kai-shek were too deep to be reconciled, and the former retired into opposition at Canton.

From this time onwards until the present time, politics in China have been dominated by the Japanese threat from without and the Communist danger and disunion within. Broadly speaking in the early years the Army and the anti-Communist campaign occupied the attention of Chiang Kai-shek, the strength of whose position imperceptibly increased although in the public eye Wang Ching-wei approached more nearly the position of being a politically active president of China.

Behind the scenes the same family group retained its influence.

[1] *Ante*, Chapter 23, p. 151 et seq.

There was also growing into a political force a number of men, former members of the Whampoa Cadet Corps, who have sometimes been described as ' Chiang's young men.' The Generalissimo's position was said to be further strengthened by control of a secret organization known as ' Blueshirts,' whose members are not entirely free from a reputation for terrorist methods.

Needless to say the enemies of Chiang Kai-shek accuse him and his political friends of most of the crimes in the political calendar. More particularly they are accused of having acquired vast fortunes and of having increased them by operating on the Shanghai exchange market with the benefit of inside knowledge.

It must be admitted, of course, that many of the leaders to-day like other revolutionaries began life as poor men and are now apparently wealthy in various degrees. On the other hand the emoluments of political office in China are insufficient to support the social demands of high position. Again some at least of these accumulations of wealth may be regarded as in the nature of war chests designed to maintain certain men in power in the honest belief that they promise the best hope of seeing the country through its difficulties. And there may be good grounds for that belief. For whatever may be said to the contrary no one can see any hope for China at present except under an authoritarian government on virtually oligarchic lines.

The standards of public life in China would appear to be improving. The history of other nations shows that progress in this direction is necessarily slow. One hundred and fifty years ago family fortunes were established by Army Pay-Masters. It is only just over a century ago that the Rotten Boroughs were abolished. Moreover, there is a certain inherited outlook in regard to these matters which still requires to be overcome. It is delightfully expressed by Lin Yu-t'ang upon whose book, *My Country and My People*, we have already drawn.

> ' In China, though a man may be arrested for stealing a purse, he is not arrested for stealing the national treasury, not even when our priceless national treasures in the National Museum of Peiping are stolen by the responsible authorities and publicly exposed. For we have such a thing as the necessity of political corruption, which follows as a logical corollary of the theory of " government by gentlemen."

Confucius told us to be governed by gentlemen, and we actually treat them like gentlemen, without budgets, reports of expenditures, legislative consent of the people or prison cells for official convicts. And the consequence is that their moral endowments do not quite equal the temptations put in their way, and thus many of them steal.

' The beauty of our democracy is that the money thus robbed or stolen always seeps back to the people, if not through a university, then through all the people who depend upon the official and serve him, down to the house servant. The servant who squeezes his master is but helping him to return the money to the people, and he does it with a clear conscience. The house servant has a domestic problem behind him, differing in magnitude but not in nature from the domestic problem of his master.'

And in another place:

' The most striking characteristic in our political life as a nation is the absence of a constitution and of the idea of civil rights. This is possible only because of a different social and political philosophy, which mixes morals with politics and is a philosophy of moral harmony rather than a philosophy of force. A " constitution " presupposes that our rulers might be crooks who might abuse their power and violate our " rights," which we use the constitution as a weapon to defend. The Chinese conception of government is the direct opposite of this supposition. It is known as a " parental government " or " government by gentlemen," who are supposed to look after the people's interests as parents look after their children's interests, and to whom we give a free hand and in whom we place an unbounded confidence. In these people's hands we place millions without asking for a report of expenditure and to these people we give unlimited official power without the thought of safeguarding ourselves. We treat them like gentlemen.' [1]

This quotation is also interesting from another point of view. China, of course, has a Constitution. The fact that Mr. Lin treats it as though it were non-existent shows how little have been developed in practice the sense and checks of constitutionalism.

Turning to the question of foreign politics in relation to

[1] Pp. 182 and 206.

Japan, Wang Ching-wei had no alternative but to adopt a friendly policy. It is not clear, however, that he received very strong support from the Generalissimo. When, therefore, during the summer of 1935 a crisis of importance arose which called for more definiteness of policy on the part of China than had hitherto been possible, Wang Ching-wei, suffering from ill-health, threatened resignation, and did in fact resign. Ultimately, however, he withdrew his resignation on receiving satisfactory assurances of co-operation and support from the Generalissimo. At the same time he secured an undertaking from the group of politicians sympathetic to British and American aims to refrain from opposition to his policy of active friendship with Japan.

Whether in face of the bluntness of Japanese policy the imaginative mind and agreeable personality of Wang Ching-wei, with his hand thus strengthened, could have achieved a solution of the situation acceptable to China, was not destined to be determined. For on November 1, just after he had delivered the inaugural address at the Sixth Plenary Session of the Kuomintang, an attempted assassination nearly ended his life. It was said that but for defective ammunition the wound from the automatic, which in these days has taken so largely the place of the assassin's knife, could hardly have failed to be fatal. It was characteristic of his wife, who had been one of his companions at the time of the attempt on the life of the Prince Regent, to recall the incident and in the darkest hour to proclaim her faith in his star.

The enforced retirement of Wang Ching-wei threw the main responsibility on Chiang Kai-shek. An attitude of even apparent aloofness from politics, which may and properly should characterize the commander-in-chief, could no longer be maintained.

The Fifth National Congress, consisting of delegates from branches of the Kuomintang throughout the country and a number of nominees of the Central Executive Committee and of the Government, met in Nanking a few days later to receive the report of the Central Executive Committee and to decide upon any necessary changes of Government.

During the Congress the Generalissimo took occasion to deliver an address in which he stressed China's claim for equality in the family of nations, the need for sincerity in international relations and internal progress. He made the following states-man-like reference to Japan :

> 'The Chinese race comprises one-fourth of the world's population. So the rise and fall of our nation must have a great effect upon world peace as well as the welfare of mankind, a fact which must have been well realized by all statesmen of the friendly Powers. It is natural, therefore, that our neighbour Japan should take a deeper interest in the peace of Asia as well as the common weal of the two countries. What we have been striving for incessantly is nothing more than our existence as a nation and co-existence with other countries in the family of nations. . . . If international developments do not menace our national existence or block the way of our national regeneration, we should, in view of the interests of the whole nation, practise forbearance in facing issues not of a fundamental nature. At the same time we should seek harmonious international relations provided there is no violation of our sovereignty. We should seek economic co-operation based upon the principle of equality and reciprocity. . . . We shall not forsake peace until there is no hope for peace. We shall not talk lightly of sacrifice until we are driven to the last extremity, which makes sacrifice inevitable. The sacrifice of an individual is insignificant, but the sacrifice of a nation is a mighty thing. For the life of an individual is finite, while the life of a nation is eternal. Granted a limit to conditions for peace and a determination to make the supreme sacrifice, we should exert our best efforts to preserve peace with the determination to make the final sacrifice in order to consolidate and regenerate our nation. I believe this is the basic policy of our Party for the salvation and upholding of our nation.' [1]

This declaration of policy, which was favourably received in Japan, generally speaking synchronized with the weakening of the forward policy in North China of the Kuantung Army and doubtless made its contribution to the improved prospect. Unfortunately the hopes with which the new year dawned were destined to be subjected to a series of grave shocks.

The first of these was a challenge to the authority of Nanking by the provinces of Kwangtung and Kwangsi.

It will be recalled that when we left our study of the machine

---

[1] Translation in *China Year Book*, 1936, pp. 169–70.

of government in 1928 the structure was without either foundation or coping-stone. The country was then in the second stage
of revolution, the period of tutelage. The representation of the
people, the foundation of Sun Yat-sen's democratic state, though
recognized, had not been defined. Neither was provision made
for a chief executive. At that time the constitution was only
provisional. In the following year it was decided that the period
of tutelage should come to an end in 1935. Owing, however,
to the external menace it was decided to postpone it for a further
year. A drafting committee was now appointed, and in due
course the Constitution was framed. Besides making due provision for the representation of the people on the basis of individual suffrage for all citizens over twenty years of age, rules
were laid down for the election of a president whose duties and
authority were defined. These latter involved command of the
forces of the whole country; authority to promulgate laws and
issue mandates, with the counter-signature of the president of
the Yuan concerned; the exercise of the power of declaring
war, negotiating peace and concluding treaties; and finally the
appointment and removal of civil and military officials in accordance with law. The establishment of a chief executive with
such a wide range of authority tended to create the impression
amongst the enemies of Chiang Kai-shek that he was paving
the way for a dictatorship. In point of fact the Generalissimo
to all intents and purposes was and is a dictator. For years
he had controlled the Central Government's armed forces combined with high political office. At the moment, in addition
to being Commander-in-Chief, he was in effect Prime Minister,
having been appointed President of the Executive Yuan owing to
the enforced retirement of Wang Ching-wei. He was also Vice-
Chairman of the Central Political Council of the Kuomintang,
as well as Vice-Chairman of its Central Executive Committee.

It is not perhaps surprising that the declarations which the
Generalissimo, now made, firstly that he was not a candidate
for the presidency and secondly that the authority of the office
of President followed constitutional lines, were not regarded as
conclusive. At any rate the principal provinces in the south-
west, Kwangtung and Kwangsi, which had been the dominant
provinces in the South Western Federation, refused to accept
this view. Their leaders believed that this was the last and

final step designed by Chiang Kai-shek to secure himself in the supreme power.

There were other causes of difference. The personal antagonism of Li Tsung-jen and Pai Chang-hsi, who were supreme in the Province of Kwangsi, has already been referred to. The ruler of the Province of Kwangtung, General Chen Chi-t'ang, was also estranged from the Generalissimo.

Again, although no opium was grown in the province of Kwangsi, it is understood that a considerable transit revenue was derived from the product of the neighbouring province of Kweichow on its carriage from the province. It was reported that this important revenue had recently been lost to Kwangsi owing to diversion of the route by way of the Yangtze.

In addition, the finances of South-West China based on Canton had been seriously disorganized by the policy of Nanking towards the end of the previous year.

On November 4, 1935, three days after the attempted assassination of Wang Ching-wei, China came off silver. This meant that the Government was embarking on a policy of controlled currency. Notes were to be issued by China's three principal banks, the value of which was to be maintained at about $1s.\ 2\frac{1}{2}d.$ in terms of the then value of the British pound note. All the silver in the country was called in for exchange for currency notes, the silver being retained by the Government as the country's reserve. The bearings of this policy will be discussed in a later chapter. In the present connection the point is that the southern provinces refused to fall in with the scheme, in consequence of which notes in Canton rapidly fell in comparison with the currency notes issued under orders of the Central Government.

In May 1936 Kwangtung and Kwangsi decided to make common cause against Nanking. The movement took the form of a patriotic design to resist the encroachments of Japan. Calling upon Chiang Kai-shek to adopt a strong policy, the South-West undertook itself to declare war on Japan should need arise and to put an end to the present equivocal and humiliating position. When this ultimatum to Nanking failed to produce the desired effect civil war appeared to be inevitable. Only the strong, skilful and conciliatory policy of the Generalissimo backed up by the Central Executive Committee of the Kuomintang, the Plenary Session of which took place in July in Nanking, was able to produce a settlement without the arbitrament of war.

For weeks the issue hung in the balance, but ultimately the threat from outside and the yielding policy of Nanking, which took into account the personal equation, went far to produce the unification of China on a broader basis than had yet been seen. At last negotiations could be carried on with Japan by the Government at Nanking with a real sense of the country's support. Similarly the machine of government devised by Sun Yat-sen could proceed to completion on the basis of a unified China.

In the course of a speech at Tientsin on September 29, 1936, on the occasion of a dinner in honour of the newly appointed British Ambassador, Sir Hughe Knatchbull-Hugessen, the writer ventured to state the conclusion to be drawn from these events by suggesting that they had ' flood-lit the fundamental conditions behind the political façade.' Unfortunately recent events in China have afforded a measure of justification of this somewhat pessimistic inference. The Nationalist failure to destroy the Communist organization and to allow its army to escape from the province of Kiangsi to the Western Provinces of China had still left the Communist problem open. When Marshal Chang Hsueh-liang returned from his visit abroad in 1933, which followed his resignation of office in the North after the fall of Jehol,[1] he had been appointed Deputy Commander-in-Chief of the forces detailed for the suppression of Communism and banditry in the North and North-West Provinces. He had occupied this position since February 1934 with varying fortunes. Clearly it was of great importance to China that she should demonstrate to Japan her capacity to dispose of the bandit menace. Unfortunately at this critical juncture there was not only no satisfactory news from the seat of war but such information as came through indicated fraternization between the Communists and the Government troops.

According to press reports the Generalissimo ordered that the troops of Manchurian origin should be transferred to posts in the South, which caused a revolt. Thereupon Chiang Kai-shek,

[1] This was the result of acute differences with Nanking and the charge of Wang Ching-wei that to the best of his knowledge he had not sent a single soldier or ' let loose a single arrow ' for the defence of the nation.

somewhat incomprehensibly, essayed to deal personally with the situation. He was, however, made prisoner by the 'Young Marshal' and detained at Hsianfu. Certain demands were made upon him, the chief of which, as was reported, was that an understanding should be reached with the Communist army with a view to the establishment of a united front against Japan. At the same time Chang Hsueh-liang sent out a circular telegram, such as we were used to in the old days of Civil War, calling upon the country to support this policy. It was a satisfactory sign of the improved health of the body politic that the only response was a series of telegrams of assurance of support to the Government at Nanking, and a gesture by Marshal Feng Yu-hsiang, the erstwhile 'Christian General,' who offered to take the place of the Generalissimo as hostage. The 'Young Marshal' was thus isolated. His military position was also threatened, involving indirect threat to the life of the Generalissimo, by a force of 150,000 Government troops.

The reported refusal of Chiang Kai-shek to negotiate with his captor and the attempts made by his adviser, Mr. W. H. Donald, his brother-in-law, Mr. T. V. Soong, and his wife to secure his release are matters of common knowledge.

In recording current political developments in China, it is wiser to allow the actual facts which emerge to speak for themselves, and not to occupy valuable time in endeavouring to probe the hidden mysteries. The present case is no exception to the rule. It is sufficient to say that on Christmas Eve what looked like a possible tragedy for the principal actors and also for China ended on a note of comedy. The Generalissimo was released and returned by air to Nanking. Before leaving Hsianfu he is reported to have published the following statement addressed to Marshal Chang and General Yang Yu-cheng, who was closely associated with him in making the *coup*.

'As you have shown regard for the welfare of the nation and have decided to send me back to Nanking, and as you no longer try to make any special demands or to force me to give any orders, it marks a turning-point in the life of the nation. . . . It is an ancient Chinese saying that gentlemen should correct mistakes as soon as they are realized, and, as you both admit wrongdoing, you are entitled to remain my subordinates.'

The same letter recognized that his own carelessness had made possible his detention, for which he professed to owe an apology to the Country.

The Generalissimo was shortly followed to Nanking by the 'Young Marshal' who wrote a letter to his chief in terms which follow.

> 'I am naturally rustic, surly and unpolished. Because of this I have committed this impudent and criminal act. Now I have penitently followed you to Nanking in order to await a punishment befitting the crime. I shall accept even death if beneficial to my country. Do not let sentiment or friendship deter you from dealing with me as I deserve.'

In accordance with Chinese custom the Generalissimo resigned his offices. His resignation, of course, was not accepted. At a meeting of the Political Council it was declared that he was more indispensable than ever. Towards the 'Young Marshal' clemency was extended on one of those easy assumptions so often made in China for the sake of compromise and peace. The slender evidence of a telegram to the Correspondent of *The Times* in Shanghai which had explained his action but unfortunately had miscarried, was accepted as proof that he was actuated by patriotic motives and at no time intended harm to his unwilling guest.

This fortunate issue was hailed with enthusiastic relief throughout the country. The danger of losing the Generalissimo had brought forth remarkable appreciation of the value of his services to the State. A further step was thus achieved towards that unity which is so essential to China's welfare. That such a striking event should have occurred so soon after the celebration on October 10 last of China's completion of twenty-five years since the outbreak of the Revolution, tended to transform it into a circumstance of happy augury.

But amidst the general rejoicing it must not be forgotten that the Communist problem in the West of China remains open coupled with disaffection amongst important sections of the Government's troops, festering sores threatening grave danger to the body politic.

PART VI

THE HOROLOGE OF TIME

Chapter 48

The Far Eastern Political Scene

If these pages have not failed of their purpose and something like a true ' perspective of events, cultural influences and policies ' has been achieved, the task of setting the ' Far Eastern Political Scene' should be a not too difficult one. It is a question of inference from fact. For in these disillusioning days of disregard of international obligation and unilateral denunciation of pacts and treaties, we dare not venture far in the direction of conclusions based on any less solid ground.

At the first sight the stage stretches from the Dutch East Indies to the Arctic Circle, from the Pacific slopes of Canada and the United States to Asiatic shores. But we must not overlook the islands just above the Equator, more than 600 of them comprised in the Marianne, Caroline and Marshall groups distributed in a wide area 1300 miles by 2700 miles, under Mandate of the League of Nations to Japan. Nor must we forget Australia and New Zealand. So in fact the stage extends until it becomes commensurate with the Pacific basin.

Of the principal actors, China and Japan struggle for the position of leading lady. But between Great Britain or the British Empire, the United States and Russia there is no competition for the position of leading man. Any of them may have the opportunity provided the part is not overdone.

But these are not all the players. Amongst the rest are France and Holland with their Asiatic possessions; and Germany with growing trade to-day with China, an understanding whatever it may amount to with Japan, and needs of which many could nowhere be so well supplied as in the Dutch East Indies.

A picture is conjured up reflecting the course of evolution which we have tried to describe.

We see China striving to secure unity, involving the suppression of Communism, cancellation of all limitations on her Sovereignty and development. Her chief need is time. Will she be given that time ? Let us look at the attitude of the Great Powers whose main concern it is. First, what is our own position ?

Unfortunately the British case in China is apt to be prejudiced by lack of appreciation of the fundamental principle of British policy. It seems to be considered by some people to be the result of an Imperialist policy of aggression at the expense of China instead of the inevitable consequence of the evolutionary process it in fact is. It has been represented that the so-called unequal Treaties were forced upon China in order to facilitate the exploitation of the Chinese for the benefit of the British. As we have seen, nothing could be further from the truth. The average Englishman in China is much the same as his fellow countrymen whose lines are more happily cast within sight or at least within reach of English fields. He is neither more grasping, less sympathetic nor more illiberal. The British commercial record in China is one of consistent fair dealing to which any independent Chinese of the great merchant class would testify. The so-called unequal Treaties were not forced upon China by Great Britain. In the early days of British intercourse there were no treaties. It has already been recorded how they became necessary by reason of the Chinese superiority complex. Even so liberal a statesman as Sir Austen Chamberlain, speaking in London at a lunch to British Delegates to the Chinese Tariff Conference on September 16, 1925, and making what was in reality a considered statement, could not avoid laying the foundation of his survey of Chinese affairs in the following terms :

' I wish that I could persuade some Chinese of historical knowledge, of statesmanship, and of authority with his own people, to explain that all this system of the unequal treaties was not of our choosing. We did not desire it, it was the minimum that we could ask of a China that repelled the foreigner, that would not give him justice in her own Courts, or secure for him the ordinary advantages of civilized and orderly government.'

To the correctness of this statement there is a ' cloud of

witness.' Since then our country has submitted to many indignities partly in order to avoid intervention and partly from the old spirit of liberalism and the new principle of self-determination which has held the Anglo-Saxon imagination. To-day a cardinal point in British policy is to extend every assistance to China in her great task.

American policy is on similar lines. Her great constructive contribution was the Declaration by John Hay in 1899 of the 'Open Door,' which in effect was subsequently enshrined in the Nine-Power Treaty at Washington in 1921. All America's China policy has been directed to securing equal opportunity, while culturally and materially she has been in a better position to help China in time of stress than any other people, a situation of which she has availed herself with generous liberality. No less than Great Britain she is China's friend. To-day there are only two questions of substance outstanding. Of these one is Extra-territorial Jurisdiction and the other the so-called 'Concessions,' the areas of foreign settlement. But the surrender of these rights at the present time could not be justified either on practical or political grounds. What would have been the position at Shanghai in 1932, it may be asked, if there had been no International Settlement and no Extra-territorial Jurisdiction? It was not only the accumulation of wealth in the Great Chinese Banks at Shanghai which was concerned, but the immense and vital foreign interests which nearly a hundred years of international endeavour has built along the banks of the Whangpoo. Questions of a sound body of law and efficient judicial administration apart, in the last resort practical considerations cannot be ignored. At the present time China cannot defend her own. Certainly she cannot defend the immense foreign interests which have grown up under foreign municipal government in the concession areas and the protection of extra-territorial jurisdiction.

We have seen something of the steps taken in the direction of development. In this field, as in other fields, China's chief need is time.

Of Russia it is not so easy to speak. The greatest caution is called for in assessing the forces that drive her on. She has declared her aim as World Revolution and has now retracted it. Yet in Moscow the Comintern still has its home. Ideological domination of the souls of people seems to be her inspiration rather than the land lust of Imperial Russia. But is there any true distinction ? Is not the one but the modern means to achieve the other ? Her ambition in the Far East has always been to reach warm water. She dominates Mongolia, and Sinkiang is ripe for her taking. If a Chinese Communist area were established in the western provinces of China, a Russian Communist corridor could well be established to the Yangtze at Hankow.

On the other hand, declarations of policy apart, indications point to the absence of desire on the part of Russia, at least for the time being, to interfere in the affairs of China. Since she made her great effort ten years ago and ultimately failed, despite great temporary success, she must realize that China is not favourable soil for Russian Communism. Apart from this she is sufficiently occupied with her own internal policies. It is an argument in her favour that though refusing to complete a new fisheries agreement with Japan in view of the agreement between Germany and Japan, directed as she sees it against herself, she has renewed the old agreement for a year. There was also the non-aggression pact which Russia offered to Japan some four years ago and Japan refused. On the whole the inference seems legitimate that apart from strong temptation or challenge she will not interfere in China's affairs at least for the time being.

Nor is there any other power that cannot afford to look with equanimity on the operation of the time factor in favour of China with the exception of Japan.

It is the tragedy of Japan that her needs in China must involve a contradiction. Although a strong China as a buffer state would protect her from Bolshevik Russia, on the other hand, a strong China would develop industrially and be in a position to defend an economic policy which might compete with Japan in world markets and deprive her of China's contribution to the raw materials she so badly needs. Despite her protests for the sake of orthodoxy to the contrary, Japan's policy aims to see China a house divided against itself.

The implication not much more than a year ago was that Japan, although negotiating with Nanking, considered that China was divided into three virtually autonomous parts. In the South were the provinces based upon virtually independent Canton. The Yangtze valley fell under the direct control of Nanking.

North China, north of the Yellow River, was autonomous, she claimed, in sentiment, and should be so in fact.

But this is not true. Although we have made no attempt to conceal the weaknesses of China and have in fact shown up the terrible fissures in the body politic and the element of self-seeking, the overriding factor in the end will be, as it also has been, Chinese sentiment. There is something in the Chinese soul which cannot endure the thought of disintegration. Many of the militarists have not worshipped only at the shrines of the Gods of Power and Wealth. The urge to unification whether by force or reason is there and at long last it must prevail.

When Japan says she wants to see a strong China, she means a well-ordered China, a China who will be a good purchaser, a China who will subordinate the development of her raw materials and industry to Japan's needs. Such a China should also be prepared, at least in Japan's estimation, to sacrifice her independence to the extent of allowing Japan to secure the frontiers on the mainland of Asia against the extension of Russian Communism.

As we have seen the spirit of China is not reduced to the acceptance of such a scheme. But the initiative is with Japan unless China can demonstrate in an effective manner, as it is believed she can do, her power to deal with her own Communists still in revolt against Nanking. It is timely to conclude our examination of the ' Far Eastern Political Scene ' with a brief reference to the internal political conditions of Japan, since on them depends her foreign policy.

It will be recalled that the armed forces derive authority from the Emperor and that although there has been considerable development towards party government, the Cabinet is independent of the Diet. In such a system conflict would appear to be inevitable between the armed forces and the Government, and since the Army took control in Manchuria in 1931 such conflict has become increasingly acute. It is difficult to believe that the Cabinet has approved all that the Kuantung army has done in Manchoukuo and China or appreciates its arrogance and disregard of the public and private interests of institutions and persons of other nationalities. In Japan itself things have been carried much farther. A number of grave incidents, including political assassinations, culminated on February 26, 1936, in the revolt of a group of young officers. Claiming to be actuated by purely patriotic motives and without personal interests to serve, they aimed ' to exterminate, at this moment of great crisis at home and abroad, the arch-traitors who were destroying the national policy, such as statesmen close to the Throne, financial magnates, military cliques, bureaucrats and members of political parties.' [1]

According to the finding of the Court Martial which tried them they were agreed on the following view :

> ' That the Government authorities were dealing with the critical national situation very ineffectually, that both domestic administration and foreign policy were slack, that the political parties were too devoted to partisan interests to think of the State, and that financial magnates were merely intent on the furtherance of selfish interests in utter disregard of the distress of the ordinary people. They particularly resented the circumstances connected with the signing of the London Treaty in the belief that there was an encroachment on the Imperial command of the navy. All this they attributed to the fact that privileged classes such as the Genro, important subjects close to the Throne, bureaucratic leaders, military cliques, political parties and financial magnates were acting in breach of the spirit of the national policy and in contempt of the Imperial prerogatives.' [2]

The execution of the plan involved the attempted murder of the premier, Admiral Okada, for whom Colonel Matsuo, his brother-in-law, was mistaken and killed ; the murder of Mr. Takahashi, the Finance Minister, and of General Watanabe, Inspector-General of Military Education ; the attempted murder of Admiral Suzuki, the Grand Chamberlain, who survived his wounds, and the murder of Admiral Viscount Saito, Lord Keeper of the Privy Seal, in the course of which Viscountess Saito was wounded. Prince Saionji and Count Makino were also marked down for assassination, but the plan against the Prince was abandoned at the last moment and Count Makino could not be found.

The victims of this crime had all rendered service to the State but none so signal as Mr. Takahashi, the Finance Minister, who

---

[1] *Far East in Ferment*, by Guenther Stein, quoted on p. 26.
[2] ' Official Statement by the War Department,' *Japan Chronicle*, July 8, 1936.

was at this time eighty-two years old. It was he who had persuaded financiers in London and New York to lend money to Japan without which she could not have carried through the later stages of the Russo-Japanese War. It was he who had opposed increases in the Army and Navy, and though he had been unsuccessful he was still a stumbling-block to those bent on expansion.

The revolt failed of its immediate object. A special Court Martial dealt with the ringleaders and those who had been prominent in their support. But the Army used the occasion to see that the members of the new government contained only men of whom the armed forces approved. In consequence foreign policy to-day is in effect dictated by the Army and it is only its failure which has begun to restore in some measure the Government's authority. Supporting the Government is the view of business men favouring, as we have seen, friendly instead of Imperialist approach to China. The internal condition of the country, calling for attention and sound finance, also adds weight to the scale opposed to military pretensions.

The issue of this conflict, so fraught with dangerous possibilities, will perhaps depend in the last resort upon the Emperor's command.

Chapter 49

Economic Aspects

The economic conditions of the countries predominant in the Pacific Area present wide differences. No great array of figures is called for to show that the commitments that could be undertaken by Great Britain and the United States are merely limited by political considerations, sentiment and a sense of fair-dealing. Unity of purpose can secure the great commonwealths that make the British Empire against economic attack. America could be made into a self-supporting economic unit. Russia is rapidly achieving economic independence and regaining the position of menace which she occupied along the boundaries of central Asia forty years ago. But there is this difference. Whereas the old threat was based on the unsubstantial foundations of Czarism, carried into modern times, the glitter of Grand Dukes and the pathetic little figures of ' Theatre Street,' to-day it is founded on labour organized to tear from the earth her treasures and to devote them to the making of a modern state. She is attacking her limitless forests. She is even building cities in the Arctic night. China and Japan alone provide serious food for economic speculation on vital things.

Reduced to its simplest terms the life of states depends on food and the raw materials of industry. The people must be fed. Since everywhere the gifts of nature have been turned to account standards of life have been established which must if possible be maintained, and even improved. The ideal state in a world from which covetousness had been banished would be that whose population bore reasonable relationship to its resources. It is the disproportion between these fundamental things which gives rise to barter buying and selling and differences between nations.

One of the major functions of the Science of Economics is to indicate the methods by which these fundamental matters may be adjusted with as little dislocation as possible of the international machinery. Nations protect themselves or redress the balance between themselves and the world at large by various means, notably managed currencies, tariff walls and trade agreements.

Let us first look at the question of currency.

In 1930 there was such a drop in world prices that in most countries acute economic depression set in. This is popularly supposed to have led to the abandonment of the gold standard by Great Britain in 1931, followed by Japan in December of the same year, and by the United States in April 1933.

As between China and Japan, the countries to which in effect we have reduced our consideration, the practical effect of these currency measures needs to be understood. Shorn of economic mystery what they amounted to was this. Formerly the Japanese unit, the yen, expressed in terms of sterling, was worth about two shillings. This was the gold yen. When Japan went off gold, the yen sank to a level of about 1s. 2½d. We may call this yen the paper yen. Amongst the people of Japan at large the purchasing power of the yen remained much the same since they are not dependent on imported goods. An article manufactured in Japan from imported raw material which formerly cost a gold yen would not under the new conditions cost anything like the difference between the value of the paper yen and the gold yen for the reason that only part of the cost of the article, namely the raw material, would have cost more, expressed in terms of yen, than formerly.

Meanwhile the silver dollar in China was worth about 1s. 6d. Formerly therefore an article costing a gold yen had to be sold in China at a cost of, say, one and a half dollars equivalent to 2s. 3d. If after the depreciation of the yen such article could still be sold for 2s. 3d. there would be a greatly enhanced profit which would enable reductions to be made to meet competition. This principle applied of course in all markets with the result that a tremendous boom ensued in Japanese exports, for although prices tend to follow Exchange this does not usually happen immediately and only where there is competition.

From China's point of view the position was not so satisfactory since Japan's desire to keep as much as possible of the profits from her export trade made her a reluctant adjuster of the new prices, expressed in paper yen, which she would have to pay for her imports.

China's export trade was also depressed for other reasons. The prolonged disturbances in the country had made for less production and uncertainty of deliveries. Prices had been increased by the impositions of War Lords. The quality of produce had deteriorated. There was a lack of standardization. China tea and silk no longer occupied their pre-eminent position. Wool, bought by weight, tended to arrive at the Treaty Ports with more than its usual proportion of sand.

The position of China's export trade was further handicapped by the American silver policy which was inaugurated on August 9, 1934. It will be recalled that under the influence of the silver states America decided on certain purchases of silver, defined as regards price, amount and the period within which they were to be effected. The result was to cause an immediate rise in the value of silver which made it necessary for China to obtain still higher prices, expressed in non-silver currencies, on export of her raw materials.

From the point of view of currency, the rise in the price of silver caused its export from China to a value which soon exceeded 150 million dollars and began to threaten the silver reserves of the country. To meet the danger a tax on silver on export was devised which absorbed all profit.

This, in its turn, caused the usual gap between the market value of silver and exchange rates to be widened to an abnormal extent. At the same time it became clear that the prospect of the removal of this embargo was so remote, that there was no reasonable prospect of a safe return to the currency. After centuries, therefore, the silver currency which had been admirably suited to Chinese needs was abandoned. On November 4, 1935, a managed currency was adopted which aimed to fix the Chinese dollar approximately at 1s. 2½d. Beneficial results to her economy were immediately achieved. Imports were checked and exports stimulated. The permanent success of the experiment, however, still depends on several factors. Of these the chief will be the ability of the Central Government to maintain sufficient funds abroad to support the value of the inconvertible notes which are now legal tender.

The effect of this change of policy was as unfavourable to Japanese exports to China as Japan's own policy of four years before had been helpful. On the other hand Japan profited by China's policy by being in a position to buy such of her imports as came from China at a cheaper rate, expressed in yen, as soon as the Chinese producer settled down to the new conditions.

As in 1935 Japanese exports to China were in nearly the same proportion, Japan was at no disadvantage. It is likely in time to be the other way. Even though Japan's full policy in relation to North China should not be realized, there will certainly be readjustment of tariff relationships in directions which will be helpful to Japanese trade. This brings us to the question of tariff protection which threatens Japan with serious consequences.

It was the Great War which gave Japan her opportunity. But for that Japan might have found it difficult to gain a foothold in foreign markets. As it was, industrially she developed during that period out of all proportion. More gradual trade expansion would have been less dangerous. Avoiding, on the one hand, the appearance of a challenge, on the other hand it would have involved less risk of economic disturbance in the event of its enforced curtailment.

The spectacular results achieved in the textile and light industries have been the cause of much anxiety to other industrial nations. The developments of the textile industry, for example, have resulted in an industrial war with Lancashire. In Japan the available labour in the country places, owing to the existing social conditions, facilitated the development in this field. As elsewhere much of the work is done by women operatives who are easily taught control of the machines. In a nation more than half of which is devoted to agriculture there is necessarily a surplus of the children of small farmers who are in a position to be spared from home to work elsewhere. The social system makes it easy for girls to be recruited for the mills and for their families to reap the benefit of their labours. A continuous stream of such labour is available for the reason that ordinarily such girls would work for two or three years in the fields at home or in carrying on the small home industries, which are so prominent in Japan, until they marry. Similarly as they reach marrying age in the factories they return home and the next generation takes their places. Such labour is easily controlled and works at prices which do not compare with wages paid in European countries.

Japan's enormous development in her textile industry with its advantages of cheap production made itself felt principally in the Indian market. The obvious British reply was the application of a tariff. Against this Japan has become a large importer of products of heavy industries from England. If she could not sell her textiles to India she would not have money to pay for her imports from Great Britain. It was also necessary for Japan to sell to India in order that she might be able to pay for the raw cotton which she bought from India for her mills.

A similar problem has arisen recently between Japan and Australia. In recent years Japan has satisfied her increasing demand for wool from Australia. In order to pay for it she has flooded Australia with cheap goods. A tariff placed by Australia to protect her home manufactures resulted in an attempt by Japan to boycott Australian wool. This was not felt so severely by Australia as Japan imagined would be the case, since Bradford which had been kept short of Australian shipments was a ready buyer at suitable prices. Something has already been said of the difficulties of improving the wool in China and of the failure of experiments on a small scale which have hitherto been made. The conclusion is ventured that it is most unlikely that Japan within any reasonable distance of time will be able to supply her wants from the mainland of Asia. In the long run she must be dependent on Australia for that part of her needs which calls for merino and higher-grade wool.

Much the same state of affairs exists between Japan and the Union of South Africa.

The answer has been trade agreements which enable some sort of reasonable adjustment to be made between the various economic requirements of the situation.

Within our present limits one can only indicate the general principles and some main applications.

The inference has been drawn as regards textiles that ' not only has the expansion of foreign markets reached its limits but there is danger of contraction.' [1] The same would appear also true of light industries.

Statistics show that more than half of Japan's total trade is with the British Empire, and the United States and Dependencies. The British Empire is Japan's most important buyer. The imposition, therefore, of economic sanctions by America and Great Britain, at a loss it is true but one which America and Great Britain could stand, would have the effect of disrupting

[1] *Report on Economic and Commercial Conditions in Japan*, June 1936, by Sir G. B. Sansom, p. 31.

completely Japanese economy within a relatively short space of time.

As one surveys this aspect of the economic field based in the last resort on exchange of commodities, it would appear that as between countries of similar economic systems but varying standards of living there can be no serious attempt to establish conditions of free trade. Countries with low production costs must ultimately be thrown back largely on their own resources. Japan, faced with ever-increasing restrictions upon the marketing of her manufactures, finds herself obliged in self-preservation to reduce still further the standard of living of her workpeople and to flood the markets of the world with still cheaper goods. Sooner or later she must reach the end of her resources. She will then be faced with the grim alternatives of a foreign war to force open the markets at present closed to her or revolution at home. It is to avoid one or other of these catastrophes that she seeks by economic penetration of other Far Eastern countries to break the bonds which bind her. If she could compel China and the Dutch East Indies to supply the major portion of her needs in raw material, to limit strictly industrial development and to satisfy their needs by manufactured goods from Japan, her problem might be near solution.

Regarding the position of China and Japan from this point of view and applying the last test of all, the budgetary test, to both countries, we get interesting and instructive results.

Looking to China first, it is true to say that if she is prepared to limit her needs and to advance slowly she can at least pay her way in the outside world. At the moment conditions are highly favourable. As late as November 24, 1936, Sir Frederick Leith-Ross, Chief Economic Adviser to the British Government, addressing the Royal Empire Society remarked as follows :

> 'Within a few months of leaving the silver standard, China's adverse balance of trade had been corrected, and remittance from over-sea increased. China was probably now, if anything, a creditor on current international account. This year she had had a " banner " harvest, which should enable her to dispense with imports of cereals and to increase her exports of agricultural products. This would give her larger resources for the purchase of manufactures of all kinds which she needed.'

Her budget position is not very promising. Expenditure in round figures for the year July 1, 1936, to June 30, 1937, is estimated at 990 million dollars. The revenue over the same period is estimated at less than this total by 125 million dollars which it is proposed to borrow. In other words the budget does not balance. Comment was made on the budget figures in the issue of *Finance and Commerce* of July 8, 1936, as follows :

' It seems obvious from these figures that China is paying her way, meeting Loan service out of revenue, and borrowing merely to finance a portion of necessary state undertakings. The result ought to be a steadily improving financial position, the trouble at the moment, of course, being that there are not sufficient funds for the efficient maintenance of the Administration. The sum of $162·6 million only is available for the whole of the Civil Government, which is an absurdly low figure for a country of this size.'

Attention, however, should be drawn to the fact that approximately one-third of the expenditure is for military purposes. It should also be remarked that no provision is made for dealing with arrears of payments due in respect of foreign loans. Capital and interest on railway loans alone had been allowed to reach a figure of more than 20 millions sterling.

The Ministers of Finance and Railways have been approaching the problem on the basis of discharging the obligations of the Government by payment, in effect, of a composition. In the case of the Tientsin–Pukow railway loans arrears amounted to £6,500,000. The proposal has been made to amortise capital, including amounts due in respect of drawn bonds, over a period of about forty years. Arrears of interest, on the other hand, have been scaled down to a point involving loss to bond-holders of over three million pounds. And there has been no alternative to acceptance. A similar procedure is envisaged and in some cases has been pursued in respect of other railway loans.

This would no doubt be a reasonable method of dealing with some of the loans which have been contracted since the Revolution, but it is not a just way of dealing with the old railway loans. With few exceptions they are secured on the railways themselves, while their proceeds are represented by public utilities, some of which are among the best revenue-earning assets of the country.

Turning now to Japan, notwithstanding her apparent pros-

perity and strong position in world politics the economic situation
is far from being sound. We have already shown how precarious
in truth it is. Put in a different way, Japan's main raw product
available for export is silk. This is exported in the raw state
to America, whose tariffs bar the finished product of Japanese
looms. The raw silk is paid for by raw cotton. American raw
cotton supplemented by purchases in India, Egypt and China is
turned into textiles which represent a value which would be
rather more than sufficient to cover the balance of her raw cotton.
The cost of her imports of wool, machinery and other requirements have to be met by silk and artificial silk tissues and a wide
range of other articles. Broadly speaking Japan's food supply,
as we have already seen, is enough. But she is deficient in coal
and iron. Of the former three-fourths of her requirements are
supplied by Manchoukuo and China. Of the latter only one-
fourth of the ore she imports is supplied by China which, however,
can be increased; Manchoukuo supplies roughly three-sevenths
of her pig-iron. But as iron and steel to a value double the
above has to be imported to satisfy Japan's total needs, the contributions of Manchoukuo and China are so far not considerable.

As regards oil, ' over 80 per cent of the crude oil supply comes
from sources outside Japanese territory, and about 93 per cent
of the supply of petroleum products is either imported or manufactured from imported crude oil. The extent of Japan's depend-
ence upon foreign supplies is slightly diminished if account is
taken of production which, though not in Japanese territory, is
in Japanese hands.' [1] The amount of such diminution may be
put at rather over 2 per cent. It includes shale oil from the
Fushun mines in Manchoukuo.

For rubber Japan is entirely dependent on outside supplies.

If a nation's aspirations are towards peace and she is unthreat-
ened by other Powers, these deficiencies need cause no alarm.
But if she is in danger or herself has aggressive designs they
necessarily give rise to grave anxiety. It is not only a question
of keeping open the supply of raw material but the means of
paying for amounts which, compared to normal peace-time
demands, are excessive.

In 1935 there was a trade balance against Japan of only 14

[1] *Economic Conditions in Japan, 1933–1934,* by G. B. Sansom, C.M.G.,
now Sir G. B. Sansom, K.C.M.G., p. 82.

million yen. But the average amount of excess of imports during the four preceding years was over 100 million yen. In the first six months of 1936 it was 315 million yen, which however might be expected to be less taken over the whole year.

These may not represent absolutely large amounts, but they are large for a country whose invisible exports barely cover the deficiency. It follows therefore that Japan is involved, largely through her militaristic policy, in a terrible struggle to survive in the strict economic sense. There is no margin for error or failure of her economic machine.

Her budgetary position reflects still more clearly the economic state of the country dominated as it is by militaristic policies. In the budget for 1935-6 estimated expenditure on armaments and service of the national debt accounted for 68 per cent of the total. Only 32 per cent was left for general administrative purposes. There was a balance of expenditure equal to 35 per cent of the budget which was not covered by revenue and had to be covered by borrowing. The budget figure for the year 1936-7 amounted to 2,800 million yen, and as usual the big items were the naval and military estimates which amounted to 1,300 million yen, or nearly half. The budget for 1937-8 has recently been approved by the Cabinet at just over 3,000 million yen. Of this sum the Army and Navy absorb 47 per cent. The estimated deficit is 800 million yen, which together with a sum in round figures of 150 million yen required for railways and other productive works, will be covered by borrowings.

Since the year 1931, when the Manchurian adventure was embarked upon, the expenditure on armaments has amounted to 4,000 millions, which is a large sum for a country of Japan's economic resources. At that time the national debt of Japan in round figures amounted to 6,400 million yen. To-day it amounts to 10,400 million yen, the increase being the equivalent of the amount expended on armaments.

Such a debt amounting probably to something between 600 and 700 millions expressed in sterling, is considerable when compared with China's national debt which is about 225 millions expressed in sterling. On the other hand it compares favourably with England's national debt after the Napoleonic wars which had only been decreased to 700 millions by the time of the outbreak of the Boer War.

Such a debt can easily be dealt with provided the country is on a sound economic and political basis. But that, it is submitted in all friendliness, is not the case at present. Military adventure, disproportionate industrial production to pay for abnormal needs, subsidized shipping aiming to displace the established shipping of other countries, can at the least result in trade war, which in the long run must result disastrously for Japan.

How far this is a correct conclusion may be gathered, it is suggested, from the facts which have been marshalled in elucidation of the tangle of events in Eastern Asia.

Miss Freda Utley, at any rate, has formed a definite opinion as regards the basic conditions, for she begins her book, *Japan's Feet of Clay*, with the following outspoken paragraph :

> ' Japan is putting up a big bluff to the world. She started the game of politics and military aggression with the scantiest of resources, but unless her bluff is soon called she may actually achieve the success which could still easily be prevented.' [1]

Sir George Sansom expresses what is probably not far behind the same conclusion in more conservative terms :

> ' A slight turn of the wheel of fortune can easily falsify calculations as to the future course of trade and finance, and more than once in the past, when the situation looked unpromising, some unforeseen development has relieved it. It is therefore better not to prophesy, but to confine oneself to pointing out that the present margin of safety is rather small.' [2]

[1] The writer's attention was drawn to this book too late for it to be of assistance to him, but it confirms in a remarkable manner lines of thought which have been indicated. Readers will find Miss Utley's book not only a mine of information but of intense interest.

[2] *Report of Economic and Commercial Conditions in Japan*, June 1936, p. 13. See also Mr. G. E. Hubbard's book, *Eastern Industrialism and its Effect on the West*, and *Economic Handbook of the Pacific Area*, by F. V. Field.

Chapter 50
The Pacific Problem

The position of the great protagonists on the Far Eastern political stage is reflected in terms of Naval and Military strategy in what is called the Problem of the Pacific or more shortly the Pacific Problem. This does not mean, of course, that the Problem of the Pacific is a problem independent of all else. It is true that from the physical and strategical aspects it is independent. But the forces on which its solution depends vary from time to time in strength and effectiveness according to their commitments or the threats to which they are submitted elsewhere. At present this means the position in Europe which is still either directly or indirectly the dominating influence over events elsewhere. If Europe is engaged in her own affairs to the exclusion of all other considerations she can play no part in the moulding of events in the Far East. The nations whose territories, apart from European colonial and imperial interests, fringe the Pacific basin are then, for the time being at least, free to follow what they conceive to be their own destiny. In such circumstances what may be regarded as the Western view can only be represented effectively by the United States of America. It is true that Russia on the mainland is an all-important factor, but neither historically nor sentimentally has she been a subscriber, save as a matter of diplomatic form, to the ' Open Door ' and equal opportunity. And that, in conjunction with the maintenance of the territorial integrity of China, is what constitutes the Western view. But this is only a part of the problem. There are many other factors : the basic needs of Japan and her ideas as to the means which may legitimately be taken to satisfy them ; the help and time required by China to achieve stability ; and Russian ambitions whether offensive or defensive.

Involved in these conflicting forces would be the ultimate fate of the interests of the Imperial and Colonial Powers in the Pacific area, Great Britain, France and Holland, should immobilization in Europe render them impotent.

The trend of events in recent years has been towards defini-

344

tion of the Pacific Problem as the question whether or not Japan shall control at least the western half of the Pacific to the virtual exclusion, as she may think fit, of all other Powers. Taking a broad view of the situation to-day, it is found that the chief interests in the Pacific are ranged on one side, against Japan on the other.

Great Britain, France, Holland, the United States, China, subject to the Manchoukuo problem, and apparently Russia are all interested in the maintenance of the *status quo*. Japan alone in the Pacific feels that she must expand or break down economically. In the West must not be forgotten Germany who maybe is experiencing once more the ' Drang nach Osten ' of forty years ago.

On October 30, 1934, a spokesman of the Japanese Navy, remarking in Tokyo on the acute difference between the United States and Japan at the naval talks in London, stated the foregoing view of the Pacific Problem, perhaps unintentionally, in a few words. ' The Japanese plan,' he was reported to have said, ' is based on the idea of making disarmament so effective that no single Power could threaten or invade another.'

Japan claims she merely asks for security. Other countries also merely ask for security. Much depends on what is meant by security. The security of the British Empire calls for a larger protective force than is needed for the protection of the Empire of Japan. The United States, with her two seaboards and Pacific Island possessions, needs a larger protective force than Japan.

An American definition of security may be drawn from the demand of Rear-Admiral Stirling, Commander of the Navy Yard in New York, speaking a day or two after the Japanese spokesman.

> ' We must be capable of exerting our sea power in the Orient in order to maintain equality in the markets there. We can do this only with an adequate fleet, fully manned and securely based in the area of possible conflict, and a large modern merchant fleet capable of carrying the greater part of our trade and acting as auxiliaries to the war fleet in emergencies.'

On the same day Mr. Williams Phillips, Under-Secretary of State in Washington, said that the United States had no intention of relaxing her efforts to maintain the principle of the ' Open Door ' in the Far East.

In these American pronouncements also can be found the essence of the Pacific Problem as it stands to-day north of the Equator. However it may be disguised by words, the essence of the problem is whether or no Japan is, in the last resort, to have a free hand on the mainland of Far Eastern Asia.

The adjustment of this conflict need not prove beyond the capacity of those charged by the various countries with their foreign interests. The function of this chapter, however, is not to try to point the way, but to state in brief compass and in lay terms the factors going to make the strategic position that would appear to arise in the event of its settlement unfortunately being put to the arbitrament of arms.

According to press reports of the Pacific Conference held at Yosemite Park in August 1936, a conflict on the Pacific was regarded as technically impossible, as America's range of effective action is the Hawaiian Islands, Britain's range is Singapore and Japan's range is her home bases.

From San Francisco to Honolulu is 2100 miles. From Honolulu to the Philippines is 4840 miles. West of Honolulu, roughly two-thirds of this distance, is the island of Guam which belongs to the United States. Described as ' the key of the Western Pacific,' [1] Guam has the makings of a first-class naval base. Unfortunately the opportunity for its adequate fortification and development was not taken by America before the fortification of islands in the Pacific became no longer possible in view of the agreement come to at Washington in 1921. For the same reason the Philippines, American withdrawal from which is in sight, also fall short at present of the requirements of a first-class naval base.

Great Britain has her base at Singapore, with Hongkong, 1430 miles off, as an advanced base but also suffering from the non-fortification clauses in the Washington agreement. The nearest fortified harbour in Australia is Port Darwin, 1800 miles distant from Singapore.

In relation to Japan the southern end of Formosa is 1625 miles from Singapore and less than a day's steam from Hongkong. Sasebo, the great Japanese naval station in the Yellow Sea, is roughly 900 miles farther north.

From Sasebo to the Philippines is 1318 miles and to Guam 1466 miles. From Honolulu by the most direct route to

[1] *Sea-power in the Pacific*, by Hector C. Bywater, Map 2.

Yokosuka, Japan's chief naval base on the east side, is 3374 miles.[1]

The Dutch and French fortified harbours are not of strength to provide adequate naval bases.

Since, as Mr. Bywater says, ' the factor of distance dominates the whole question of Pacific strategy ' it is not difficult to understand how the representatives of America, Japan and England reached their conclusion. It in fact reflected the old lessons in distances and bases which were re-affirmed in the Great War. It is to be supposed, however, that such a view has to be read in terms of difficulty rather than of impossibility. In an imaginary history of a war between Japan and America, called *The Great Pacific War*, Mr. Bywater tells a story of a conjectural naval war which ultimately resulted in favour of the United States. Again in a book entitled *Japan Must Fight Britain* a Japanese naval officer visualizes the strategy of a war aimed to enable Japan to take Great Britain's place. In the strategic sense also, the developments in the air and in the matter of aircraft carriers have shortened distances.

The expiration at midnight on December 31, 1936, of the Washington Treaty and the London Naval Treaty of 1930 will also change the position in the matter of the bases. Great Britain suggested renewal of article 19 of the Washington Treaty which governs fortifications in the Pacific. But so far Japan's only reply has been a broadcast from Tokyo on December 30, 1936, saying that the Naval Treaties would be allowed to expire. It was explained by the same agency that the British proposal called for further consideration.

The attitude of Japan in this matter can hardly be considered promising and no doubt America and England will duly consider and act upon its implication.

Turning to the distribution of forces, Great Britain, under existing conditions in Europe, must be considered to be partially immobilized though she would still be a valuable ally in a long-range blockade. Germany would appear to be entirely immobilized at present so far as the Pacific Area is concerned, while

[1] Reference is purposely omitted to the Panama Canal and the possibilities of a canal through the isthmus of Kra, the narrow neck of land, part of Siam, which divides Burma from the Malay States. America may be relied upon to safeguard the former, while the latter would hardly appear within the bounds of practical politics and finance.

France so far from being able to influence seriously the issue must be considered in the same position. The naval power of Holland would also be negligible against the power that could be brought to bear by Japan. Similarly, Australia would have but slight powers of resistance against a Japanese Squadron and aeroplane attack.

Such would not be the case, however, with Russia. In the event of conflict between Japan and America or Japan and Great Britain, there is little doubt but that Russia would seize the occasion to weaken Japan and strengthen her own position on the mainland of Asia. Russia is under no illusion as regards Japan. Japan's strategic conception of the possibilities envisages, or at least was believed by some observers to envisage, a wide prospect. About half-way between Manchuli, the border town of Manchoukuo in the North-West, and Lake Baikal, are the Yablonoi mountains, a region of great strategic importance. In the event of a land war between Japan and Russia considerable military support is found for the view that Japan's aim would be to secure permanent control of that region. By this means Japan would secure a strong geographical boundary and deprive Russia of the whole of Eastern Siberia. Incidentally her food problem so far as fish is concerned would be solved. Japan's situation in other respects would also be improved. The menace of Vladivostock, which still justifies its name of ' Lord of the East ' and blocks the path of Empire, would also be removed. But Russia has no intention of yielding anything to Japan and it is for this reason, as we have seen, that she gives support to Mongolia. The opportunity of a war between Japan and a third power would offer Russia the chance of settling once and for all the modern threat to the supremacy, whether imperialist or ideological, at which she may appear to aim. Nor in the circumstances of such a war is Russia to be despised at sea or in the air. She has submarines and light torpedo craft based on Vladivostock where she maintains an air force which might be strong enough to inflict irreparable damage on Japan in the course of a few hours.

At the Pacific Conference in the lovely environment of the Yosemite Valley there was much plain talk. The Japanese delegates charged Russia with maintaining a force in the Far East which was in excess of the total strength of the Japanese peace-time establishment. The Russian delegates replied coolly that they had not the figures but would inquire for them if necessary. Meanwhile they thought it very likely that the Japanese contention was correct. An American delegate commented caustically on Japan's unsatisfactory reply to questions on her building progress. Neither America nor Great Britain left any doubt that their response would be larger building still.

What do we all want ? And how is it to be achieved ?

Certainly no one desires to see Japan go down before Russia any more than they would welcome Japanese hegemony in the Far East. Nor is opinion unanimous that Germany could defeat Russia on her European front. Many remembering Russian history and knowing something of the condition and spirit of her people to-day, believe she could not. It would seem that given good faith peace should be assured. It is true that a 'blue-water' school of thought in Japan attaches little importance to England. And any weakening on our part may only serve to strengthen this view which has been stated thus :

> 'Two conditions are essential to the successful development of British strategy in the Pacific. One is the completion of the base at Singapore, the other the presence there of a fleet at the critical moment. The base will shortly be finished, but without a fleet there at the right time and in a condition to operate, the Japanese fleet would have a free hand, and Australia, New Zealand, India, and the other possessions, together with the command of the sea in the Indian Ocean, would fall into the hands of the enemy.
>
> 'But England is not in a position to station a fleet at Singapore in time of peace, on account of conditions in Europe, and there can be no doubt that the problem of getting one there at the appropriate time is extremely difficult. Should the fleet fail to arrive in time, England would lose Hongkong, Singapore, her Self-Governing Dominions and her other possessions. That is one of England's troubles of which her enemy can take advantage.' [1]

If, however, it should be found in any crisis that Great Britain at sea was too immobilized to meet Japan at least on equal terms, it is difficult to suppose that America could risk the

---

[1] *Japan Must Fight Britain*, by Lt.-Comdr. Tota Ishimaru, translated by Instructor-Capt. G. V. Rayment, C.B.E., R.N. (Retired), p. 179.

danger to herself which would result from the substitution of Japan for Great Britain in the Pacific with the probability of a German-Japanese, or purely German, domination of the Dutch East Indies. Nor could Russia under the joint threat of Germany and Japan stand by and watch such a fatal extension of Japanese power.

This does not mean a British policy hostile to Japan or that England will not recognize the needs of Japan and try by all means within her power to meet them. It is not British policy but Japanese policy which forces upon Great Britain the consideration of her Imperial defence.

It is a commonplace in Japan that given a few years her position will be strong enough to defy any force that could be brought against her in the Far East, and it would be the height of folly to disregard this warning. It is our bounden duty to provide for our defence. We should not rely on the sentiment or self-interest of any other Power. We can face the task with equanimity if we will and justify the vision of Stamford Raffles when he planted the British flag at Singapore more than a hundred years ago.

Chapter 51

' *Within the Four Seas*———'

In the days before geographers the world was conceived of by the Chinese as continuous land bounded by four seas. Once in ancient times when a disciple of Confucius was mourning the loss of a brother, a fellow disciple sought to comfort him. According to the records he quoted ' the Master ' as having said, ' Within the four seas all are brothers.'

Unhappily the perspective of events and policies in the Far East during the Twentieth Century is far from reflecting the

Confucian philosophy. Nor looking farther afield is the prospect more encouraging. The Christian nations, a conception of whose faith is also the brotherhood of man, have failed even amongst themselves in the centuries that lie between Genghis Kahn and Modern Japan.

Until a nearer approach is made in international affairs to the implications of this pagan and Christian ideal, it is only possible to take a realistic view of the possible operation of world forces.

When this book was begun some two years ago, it seemed, broadly speaking, that the future of the world in our time would be expressed in terms of the resultant of three opposing forces : Communism, Pan-Asianism, and the world leadership of Europe.

To be taken into consideration, of course, were the cross-divisions between individual or group dictatorships on the one hand, and the great democracies on the other. These, however, appeared to be matters of internal policy which would be subordinate to the needs of a common cause. There was some kinship of race between France and Italy, a sentimental affinity between Germany and England.

Clearly the future in the Far East will be settled, in effect, in Western Europe with such co-operation as America may see fit to give. A gesture would be sufficient to gain China that time she so sorely needs and to save her from being pressed beyond a point at which the economic demands of Japan transgress the bounds of reason. Save in the case of some unfortunate heat-generating accident in the political field, the strength of possible combinations in the last resort, for it is in terms of the last resort in which we have to think and plan, would, it seemed, deter even the Japanese military party.

On the other hand if events in Europe were to immobilize Great Britain the situation might well be otherwise. China might have to choose between Japanese hegemony, in terms wholly incompatible with her pride of race, or war.

It has been said that China would not fight. That is not true. The belief has already been expressed that in certain contingencies China would choose war. The resistance she would put up against Japan might come as a surprise to many. But war between China and Japan would bring in Russia, for Russia cannot afford to see a Japanese hegemony either. Supposing, as two years ago might have been supposed, the rest of the world observing a strict neutrality, this would be too much for Japan. Russia would be left as the dominant power in the Far East. Communism would inevitably spread. It follows that the policy of Western Europe should be directed to harmonizing the interests of Japan with those of China and thus keeping Communism at bay. But the keynote to such a policy must be at least a measure of solidarity in Western Europe. Hence the ' Foreword,' which actually was written before a line of the book in order to define its object and scope, concluded with these words :

> ' The problems of Europe have obscured far-away processes of evolution charged with Fate. Europe has led the world too long to see before her any other destiny. National rivalries are sapping her strength. She forgets that she invaded the seclusion of Eastern Asia, however inevitably, with consequences which can neither be avoided nor delayed.'

But since those words were written much has happened to develop the cross-divisions based on political institutions to which reference has been made.

The Locarno Treaty has been torn up. Mr. Partridge's cartoon,[1] ' Trouble among the Locarno Quins ' with its Victorian nursery and text over the bed, ' Little children love one another,' may become as historic as ' Dropping the Pilot,' Tenniel's famous cartoon of the young Kaiser and the old Chancellor. However justifiable Germany's claim to the Rhineland, she has marched in under provocative circumstances to secure an end which could have been achieved by negotiation. Italy has gone into Abyssinia. Mussolini has at least dreamed of a modern Roman Empire designed to succeed the Empire of Britain, though at the moment it promises to yield to a Mediterranean Pact. Japan has become increasingly provocative in China, involving a challenge to Russia with the result that Russia's naval, military and air strength has been enormously increased. Events in Spain have roused the passions of rival ideologies. Pacts have been made between France, Russia and Czecho-Slovakia. Germany and Japan have entered into an agreement directed against Communism, and by an agreement between Italy and Japan each recognizes the other's acts of aggression.

[1] *Punch*, February 19, 1936.

Such are the main factors, some of them already referred to in greater detail, which have created an immeasurably more complicated and dangerous situation.

If pacts said all they mean or were respected by all the parties who enter into them, it would not perhaps be so difficult. But as international morality now stands in some quarters the true position becomes largely a matter of conjecture. It becomes unsafe to plan on any basis save that of those possibilities that involve dangerous consequences to ourselves.

We have therefore to admit that Germany, Italy and Japan tend at present to come closer together. Germany and Japan are military powers by modern tradition. Italy has made herself into a military power, and for the time at any rate apparently thinks in terms of empire. All three countries encourage population. They all demand colonies or political control of sources of raw materials. No one of them is economically strong.

The great democracies cannot contemplate the outlook with any sense of security. Though they make no alliance the British Empire, France and America cannot avoid being drawn more closely together. It is more than ever before a time for the New World ' to redress the balance of the old.'

As for Russia, she has an unique opportunity. She has declared her policies to be internal policies. She claims to be no longer desirous of conquering the World by means of her ideas. Her sincerity can well be shown by ceasing to give a home to the Comintern. Events favour, they even compel her, to draw closer to the great democracies.

What then is to be the policy in a world divided between Democracy, Fascism and Communism ?

We have first to realize that despite *The Great Illusion* politics which reflect national ambitions are a more potent cause of war than economics. This would appear to have two applications. One is in the matter of economic pressure which unskilfully applied might drive a nation to war in the hope of seeking to escape from economic disadvantage. The economists of the Kuantung army, for example, might not realize that in the long run they could not recoup themselves by war with China. The other is the matter of colonies which gives rise to conflict between economic sense and national pride. Nowhere has the position of colonies been a panacea for overpopulation. Japanese experiments in colonization in Manchuria both in the years following the Russo-Japanese War and since the establishment of Manchoukuo have been a failure. Formosa has also failed to absorb other than a small number of Japanese colonists. The Northern island of Japan which is climatically distasteful to the Japanese is still sparsely occupied. Italy prior to the operations in Abyssinia had done but little colonization. As Sir Norman Angell pointed out comparatively recently, ' after fifty years of ownership in the 2,000 square miles of territory in Eritrea most suitable for European residence, there were at the last census just about 400 Italians. Of the whole Italian population, numbering less than 5,000, over 3,000 were returned as residents of the capital, and when we have deducted government employees, children under ten, we find the total Italian population engaged in agriculture to be 84.'[1] The same authority pointed out that despite intense propaganda which had gone on for a generation about the need for a colonial outlet for Germany's redundant population, there were on the eve of the war more Germans earning their livelihood in the city of Paris than in all the German colonies in the whole world combined.

As to the matter of having sources of raw material under political control which is one of Japan's chief aims in relation to China, this is mainly a military argument and in the case of most parts of the world would not apply. Only in the event of command of the sea can communications with colonies or countries on which reliance is placed for raw materials be maintained. Apart from these considerations it has been abundantly demonstrated of late that some colonies are an economic burden rather than a source of profit.

It does not seem therefore that there is any need for colonial powers or powers administering territory under mandate of the League of Nations to approach this question under any sense of economic necessity or reason. Nor is it easy to discover any basis for colonial claims other than sentiment or strategy.

Amidst the plain talk at the Conference of the ' Institute of Pacific Relations ' which took place in the Yosemite Park in August last, it was stated, according to press reports, that if Japan insisted on a naval race, England would build perhaps

[1] ' Expansionism: Fact and Illusion,' by Sir Norman Angell, *The Spectator*, September 20, 1935.

even two to one. Statistics were produced on behalf of America showing that her trade was only 84 million dollars in the Pacific and her expenses in maintaining her Pacific Fleet were 600 millions of dollars. Nevertheless she would still use her resources to lose money in the Pacific ' because money isn't everything.'

These are important pronouncements. Though they suggest a just measure of prudence they are not informed by any sense of panic. They merely reflect a realistic view.

The best hope for peace is the clear enunciation of a definitely firm policy, realization of our own economic strength, and recognition of the fact that to allow Japan to exploit China in order to establish great economic and military strength is to conform to a policy of Pan-Asianism. On the other hand, there must be fair recognition of the Japanese position, both strategically and economically. But this Great Britain and the League of Nations has always been prepared to do.

Finally, China must be given that time which is necessary for her to establish herself on the lines of a modern state. She on her part, however, should be prepared to consider seriously either recognition or some compromise in the matter of Manchoukuo.

Historically Chinese influence outside the Great Wall from earliest times has been negligible. Certainly towards the close of the Ming Dynasty the Manchus controlled the country and were in armed offensive and defensive alliance with the Mongols and Tibet. It is true that there is now a large Chinese population which has grown up during the years of China's civil wars. But it does not give rise to quite the same position as would a population of long standing. Certainly there would appear to be room for readjustment of relations between China and Japan on a less hostile basis.

If Europe can be brought to grasp that the Far East is a part of the World's problem her suicidal tendencies might be checked. So far as Great Britain is concerned we need to realize that we must speak with no uncertain voice. We must be strong. We cannot afford to lag behind the pace which others set.

' The lesson of life,' wrote Emerson, ' is to believe the years and the centuries against the hours.' This has always been especially true of China, though as Lin Yu-t'ang has pointed out, ' the fact that China has absorbed her conquerors in time past is little satisfaction to suffering generations.' It also may be questioned whether it is true in a world that threatens struggle, with Russia perhaps a sardonic spectator, between the regimented and unregimented nations, the nations educated to plan and those left with intellectual freedom, the nations controlled by dictators and oligarchies and the nations who still retain democracy; struggle between conflicting social ideals; and finally struggle between East and West.

As long ago as 1915 a Japanese General is reported to have said, ' When China realizes that she can get no help against Japan she will fall into our arms.' It is even less of a possibility now than it was then, and it never was nor is a probability. Even so should not Europe begin to understand that the Kaiser's picture in 1900 of what he called ' the Yellow Peril ' was perhaps something more than a seer's vision ? And if, as many suppose, the recent agreement between Germany and Japan means that Germany will be outside the pale of Western Europe's interests, is there not food for grave thought by America ? We at least must be prepared to keep watch and ward.

Lt.-Comdr. Tota Ishimaru concluded his book *Japan Must Fight Britain* with an exhortation.

> ' Wake up, people of Britain ! Times have changed ! You cannot go on as you have done in the past.'

Wake up to what, and in what direction are we to mend our ways ? Lt.-Comdr. Tota Ishimaru gives us his answer.

> ' The British Empire is on the down grade, or perhaps at the parting of the ways that lead to salvation and destruction. To fight Japan is to court destruction. England had better swallow her pride and make way. This is the wisest thing she can do to protect herself.'

Lt.-Comdr. Tota Ishimaru and his book have been repudiated by the Diet in Japan. Still it does no harm sometimes to realize something of the ambitions that a section of opinion may form at the expense of the British Empire. Nor is it unwise to recall, to the deep regret of those who are friends of Germany, that the recent German-Japanese agreement might make of Germany at the best an unfriendly neutral. Nor perhaps is it untimely for the people of the United States to realize that a responsibility might be thrown upon their country which it would be unwise to evade.

Carlyle wrote of the French Revolution, ' the horologe of time struck and an old era passed away.' It was true of the Revolution in China a quarter of a century ago, though few would be persuaded to believe it. ' The horologe of time ' has perhaps again struck. Let us hope that its notes have not fallen on deaf ears.

Appendix I

Note on the pronunciation of Chinese, illustrated by simplified spellings of some of the more difficult names of persons and places which occur in the text.

The Chinese language is monosyllabic. It contains 420 sounds only. The process of representing these sounds in terms conveying a correct appreciation to European ears is called ' Romanization.' Systems of romanization differ owing to the different sound value of letters in different languages. The system adopted by the English was invented by Sir Thomas Wade, a former British Minister in Peking, assisted by Sir Walter Hillier, a former Chinese Secretary in Peking, who subsequently became Minister-Resident in Corea. It is based on the sounds of the official language of the Court at Peking, commonly called Mandarin. It has been largely adopted by China as the official method of transliteration.

Some of the Chinese sounds are very similar. In many cases they cannot be represented exactly by any English sound values, with the result that combinations of letters have been given specific values. Sometimes the Chinese monosyllabic sound can only be represented by what is in appearance a disyllable and requires to be pronounced as though it were a diphthong. In some of such cases the pronunciation tends towards being disyllabic although not completely so. This is chiefly when diphthongs and combinations of a vowel and consonants are preceded by ' i ' or ' u.' In such cases they are something between a separate syllable and ' y ' or ' w ' making a monosyllable of the whole combination. Thus ' iang ' often seems indistinguishably ' yang ' or ' iăng.' To most ears the disyllabic effect predominates.

The result of these various refinements is a highly artificial system which cannot convey a correct tone value to anyone who does not hold the key.

Although the purist ideas of the Wade-Hillier association were essential to secure the necessary accuracy, there has been difference of opinion as regards the method. Many think that for all practical purposes a more simple method would have met the case, while a slight sacrifice of purism would have been a help to many students who rely on the eye as well as the brain for memory. As, however, all names are spelt according to the Wade-Hillier system, except names of places such as Canton, Hankow, Peking, Nanking, the spelling of which has been long established by custom, no more simple method can be adopted. It is hoped that the following brief analysis of the

359

system, followed by illustrations limited to names of persons and places, will be of assistance towards approximate accuracy of pronunciation.

1. Consonants have their English value except in three cases where their characteristic is either emphasized or softened. To denote the difference Wade considered that the consonant required to be emphasized as undergoing a process of being as it were aspirated. In writing the process is indicated by an apostrophe after the letter in question. Thus:

(a) k'	as in	King
k	as in	Khedive
(b) p'	as in	Pay
p	as in	Pear
(c) t'	as in	Tarn
t	as in	Too

(*Note.*—In practice the soft *k*, *p* and *t* suggest such tone directions so slightly that they approach respectively hard *g* as in ' gain,' *b* as in ' boy ' and *d* as in ' don.' In the illustrations, therefore, these latter values will be adopted.)

2. Closely allied to the above idea there are certain consonants in combination to which an artificial value and differentiation is also attached. They are:

(a) Ch'	as in	Church
Ch	as in	Churn, but more near to ' J ' in James.
(b) Sh	as in	Shall
Hs	as in	Show

(*Note.*—Here again the distinction is so slight that many Chinese even do not feel that it is susceptible of expression.)

(c) Ss	as in	hiss
(d) Ts'	as in	Slats
Ts	as in	Tzar
(e) Tz'	as in	Metz
Tz	as in	Adze

3. There is no sound in Chinese which exactly corresponds either to *j* or *r*. *j* is adopted in the Wade-Hillier system to represent the intermediate sound which to many, including some Chinese, is much nearer *r* than *j*. In these notes *r* is adopted.

4. Vowel sounds are as follows:

a	as in	Ah
e	as in	Eh
ê	as aw in	Raw
i	as	' ee,' pronounced softly and shortly
o	as in	For
u	as in	German Jung

(*Note.*—This is reasonably well reflected in English by *oo* as in ' moon,' if care is exercised to give it a middle length. To avoid confusion *oo* is used for *u* in the example.

There is also a ' modified ' *u* as in the German *ü* or the French *u*. But it is a refinement which for present purposes may be neglected. Hillier gives as the nearest English equivalent the *u* sound of ' fool ' as pronounced in Devonshire ' vule.')

5. Diphthongs are :

ai	as i	in	high
ao	as ow	in	how
ei	as ay	in	hay
ia	as ya	in	yacht
iu	as you		
ou	as o	in	show
ua	as wa	in	wad
ui	as way		
uo	as uaw	in	squaw

6. Vowel and consonant combinations are given ordinary English values except the following :

an	like	arn	in	arnica
ang	between	{arng, the ' arn ' as in arnica / and ong	in	gong
eh	like	e	in	set
en	like	un	in	fun
eng	like	ung	in	sung
er	like	ur	in	burr
ih	like	ir	in	shirt
in	like	in	in	tin
un	like	German un	in	uns
ung	like	German ung	in	gesungen

Illustrations

Although at first sight the above analysis may suggest complications too difficult to master in passing, it becomes comparatively easy if illustrated by means of persons and places which occur in the text of the book. To save the reader from referring back, the sound value will be given in brackets where confusion might arise, as for example between the *ow* sound in ' how ' and ' show ' respectively. The reader must chiefly remember (*a*) that *arn* and *iarng* though given the open *a* sound are pronounced crisply with only a suggestion of the *r*, and (*b*) that the parts of words in form disyllabic are both short and tend to run into each other. *i* is always short except where marked long.

Names of Persons

Chang Fa-kwei   Jarng Fah-gway
Chang Hsueh-liang   Jarng Shooeh-leearng

APPENDIX

Names of Persons

Chang Tso-lin	Jarng Tsor-lin
Chiang Kai-shek	Jeearng Kī-sheck

(*Note.*—Sheck is a sound in the Cantonese dialect. The combination ' eck ' has the sound value of ' ec ' in ' dialect.')

Feng Kuo-chang	Fung Guaw-jarng
Feng Yu-hsiang	Fung Yoo-shearng
Hsiung Hsi-ling	Sheoong She-ling
Hsu Shih-ch'ang	Shoo Shir-charng
Hu Han-min	Hoo Harn-min
Hu Shih	Hoo Shir (' ir ' as in ' shirt ')
Huang Fu	Hwarng Foo
H. H. K'ung	H. H. Koong
Kuo Sung-ling	Guaw Soong-ling
Kwang Hsu	Gwarng Shoo
Liang Tun-yen	Leearng Toon-yen
Li Tsung-jen	Lee Tsoong-ren

(*Note.*—The *e* in ' Jen ' should strictly be affected with a circumflex accent which makes the pronunciation nearer to ' run,' but it is not very important. The correct mandarin pronunciation is between the two.)

Li Yuan-hung	Lee Yooarn-hoong
Pai Chung-hsi	Bī Joong-she
P'u Yi	Poo Yee
Charles W. Soong	

(*Note.*—Many Chinese, especially those educated abroad, have as a matter of convenience adopted a foreign ' Christian ' name in addition to their Chinese personal names. Such is Mr. Soong. He and his family have also adopted the spelling ' Soong,' for the family name of ' Sung ' pronounced ' (*ge*)*sung*(*en*).' Presumably Mr. Soong, the first of the family to seek education abroad, found himself called by so many variations in America that he adopted the *oo* instead of the *u*. This was also in accordance with practice in the South where the nearest English sound was adopted. Apart from this when Mr. Soong went abroad the Wade-Hillier system had hardly passed beyond the walls of Peking.)

Soong Mei-ling	Soong May-ling
Sun Ch'uan-fang	Soon Chwarn-farng
Sun Fo	Soon For
Sung Chiao-jen	Soong Jeeow-ren (' ow ' as in ' how ')
Sun Yat-sen	Soon Yat-sen

(*Note.*—This is also Cantonese. The middle name does not have the long *a* sound, the ' at ' being as ' at ' in ' hat.')

T'ang Shao-yi	Tarng Show-yee (' ow ' as in ' how ')
T'ang Sheng-chih	Tarng Shung-jir (' ir ' as in ' shirt ')
Ts'ao Jui	Tsow Ruay
Ts'ao K'un	Tsow Koon (' ow ' as in ' how ')

APPENDIX

Names of Persons

Tuan Ch'i-jui	Dwarn Chee-ruay
Tsu Hsi	Tzoo She

(*Note.*—Yehonala, the clan name of the Empress Dowager by which she was known in the early days, is Manchu and is pronounced approximately Yay-hor-nah-lah, with emphasis on the third syllable.)

Wang Ching-wei	Warng Jing-way
Wang Ch'ung-hui	Warng Choong-way
Wu P'ei-fu	Woo Pay-foo
Yuan Shih-k'ai	Yooarn Shir-kī

(*Note.*—The shortness of the *ar* sound when ' an ' is preceded by another sound must be borne in mind. It is something between *an* in ' antidote ' and *un* in ' under.')

Yu Hsien	Yoo She-en

Names of Places

Chahar	Chah Hah
Fengtien	Fung Tee-en
Hopei	Hor Bay
Hsinchiang	Shin Jiarng
Hsuchoufu	Shoo Jow-foo (' ow ' as in ' show ')
Jehol	Reh Hole

(*Note.*—Although not so far removed from the Chinese as Peking, Nanking, Canton and other places, the romanization is not accurate. It should be Jê Ho, pronounced approximately Răw Hor, meaning ' Hot River.')

Liaotung	Leeow Doong (' ow ' as in ' how ')
Manchoukuo	Marn Jow Guaw (' ow ' as in ' show ')
Shihchiachuang	Shir Jeeah-jwarng
Talienwan	Dah Lee-en Warn (' arn ' as in ' arnica ')
T'ungchow	Toong Jow (' ow ' as in ' show ')

Appendix II

Extract from the translation of the Mandate of the Chinese Emperor Ch'ien Lung to George III of England sent by the hand of Lord Macartney in 1793.

'You (George III), O King, live beyond the confines of many seas, nevertheless, impelled by your humble desire to partake of the benefits of our civilization, you have despatched a mission respectfully bearing your memorial. . . . I have perused your memorial: the earnest terms in which it is couched reveal a respectful humility on your part, which is highly praiseworthy.

'In consideration of the fact that your Ambassador and his deputy have come a long way with your memorial and tribute, I have shown them high favour and have allowed them to be introduced into my presence. To manifest my indulgence, I have entertained them at a banquet and made them numerous gifts. . . .

'As to your entreaty to send one of your nationals to be accredited to my Celestial Court and to be in control of your country's trade with China, this request is contrary to all usage of my dynasty and cannot possibly be entertained. . . . If you assert that your reverence for Our Celestial dynasty fills you with a desire to acquire our civilization, our ceremonies and code of laws differ so completely from your own that, even if your Envoy were able to acquire the rudiments of our civilization, you could not possibly transplant our manners and customs to your alien soil. Therefore, however adept the Envoy might become, nothing would be gained thereby.

'Swaying the wide world, I have but one aim in view, namely, to maintain a perfect governance and to fulfil the duties of the State: strange and costly objects do not interest me. If I have commanded that the tribute offerings sent by you, O King, are to be accepted, this was solely in consideration for the spirit which prompted you to despatch them from afar. Our dynasty's majestic virtue has penetrated into every country under Heaven, and Kings of all nations have offered their costly tribute by land and sea. As your Ambassador can see for himself, we possess all things. I set no value on objects strange or ingenious, and have no use for your country's manufactures.'

Appendix III

Measures for Treaty Modification as communicated by the British Minister at Peking to the Chinese Authorities on January 27, 1927.

1. His Majesty's Government are prepared to recognize the modern Chinese law courts as the competent courts for cases brought by British plaintiffs or complainants and to waive the right of attendance of a British representative at the hearing of such cases.

2. His Majesty's Government are prepared to recognize the validity of a reasonable Chinese nationality law.

3. His Majesty's Government are prepared to apply as far as practicable in British courts in China the modern Chinese Civil and Commercial Codes (apart from Procedure Codes and those affecting personal status) and duly enacted subordinate legislation as and when such laws and regulations are promulgated and enforced in Chinese courts and on Chinese citizens throughout China.

4. His Majesty's Government are prepared to make British subjects in China liable to pay such regular and legal Chinese taxation, not involving discrimination against British subjects or British goods, as is in fact imposed on and paid by Chinese citizens throughout China.

5. His Majesty's Government are prepared as soon as the revised Chinese Penal Code is promulgated and applied in Chinese courts to consider its application in British courts in China.

6. His Majesty's Government are prepared to discuss and enter into arrangements, according to the particular circumstances at each port concerned, for the modification of the municipal administrations of British concessions so as to bring them into line with the administrations of the special Chinese administrations set up in former concessions at Hankow or for their amalgamation with neighbouring concessions or former concessions now under Chinese control or for the transfer of police control of the concession areas to the Chinese authorities.

7. His Majesty's Government are prepared to accept the principle that British missionaries should no longer claim the right to purchase land in the interior, that Chinese converts should look to Chinese law and not to treaties for protection, and that missionary, educational and medical institutions will conform to Chinese laws and regulations applying to similar Chinese institutions.

Appendix IV

Extract from Memorandum 22 of the Tientsin British Committee of Information, reproducing a supplement to the ' Peking and Tientsin Times ' on June 17, 1927, by kind permission of the Editor.

Document ' O '

FENG YU-HSIANG'S RECEIPTS

A certified copy of the obligation signed by Feng Yu-hsiang in 1926 while in Moscow. This copy was on file in the office of the Soviet Military Attaché in Peking.

OBLIGATION

I, Marshal Feng Yu-hsiang, undertake hereby a solemn obligation before the Government of the U.S.S.R. that for all military as well as all other supplies whatever they may consist of, which I have received from the Government of the U.S.S.R. or its organs, I pledge myself to compensate their value to the Government of the U.S.S.R. at its first demand and in the manner prescribed by the Government of the U.S.S.R.

By the supplies mentioned in the present obligation I understand the supplies received by me personally in the capacity of the Commander in Chief of the Kuominchun as well as the supplies received by the Commanders or duly authorized officers of the individual National Armies.

As acknowledgment of the present obligation I set my hand and seal thereto.

Moscow

August 1926.

....

Translator's Note :

Under the above obligation the following pledge (in Chinese) has been given by Feng Yu-hsiang :

' I hereby undertake the obligation and give my assurance that for all military and other supplies received by me in the capacity of the Commander in Chief of the Independent National Armies from the Government of the U.S.S.R. I am obligated to repay their value to the Government of the U.S.S.R. which I certify by my signature.

Signed : FENG YU-HSIANG.

15 August, 1926.

Translated by K. Kraff.

16 August, 1926.

A TRUE COPY :

Signed : V. ROGATCHEFF.'

APPENDIX

A certified copy of a receipt which was on file in the Office of the Soviet Military Attaché in Peking. It is for the amount of roubles 6,395,642, signed by Feng Yu-hsiang while in Moscow in 1926. Attached thereto is a list of arms and munitions covering that amount. The copy is certified by Rogatcheff, who in September, 1926, came as Assistant Military Attaché to the Soviet Embassy in Peking.

RECEIPT

The present receipt is given to the Government of the U.S.S.R. in token that, in accordance with the obligation entered into by me, I have received supplies to the amount of six million three hundred and ninety five thousand six hundred and forty-two roubles, according to the list attached hereto.

(August 1926, Moscow).

ROUBLES, 6,395,642

I have received the supplies in accordance with the list which I certify hereby.

Signed : FENG YU-HSIANG.

15 August, 1926.

Translated by K. Kraff.

16 August, 1926.

A TRUE COPY :

Signed : V. ROGATCHEFF.

Very Secret.

LIST AND VALUE OF THE PROPERTY DELIVERED TO THE KUOMINCHUN UP TO 1 JUNE, 1926

Names of Articles	Quantity	Cost of a unit Roubles	Total value Roubles	% of discount	Total reduction Roubles	Total reduced value subject to payment Roubles
Rifles . . .	27,970	55.25	1,545,342.50	5	77,267.12	1,468,075.38
Cartridges . . .	27,350,545	82.23	2,249,031.62	5	112,451.58	2,136,580.04
Machine guns (Maxim)	90	1,552.12	139,726.80	30	41,918.04	97,808.76
Machine guns (St. Etien) . . .	50	1,880.75	94,037.50	30	48,211.25	65,826.25
Machine guns (Vickers)	3	1,260.00	3,600.00	30	1,080.00	2,520.00
Machine guns (Lewis)	4	1,086.75	4,347.00	30	1,304.10	3,042.90
Guns (3-in.) . .	42	7,956.00	334,158.00	30	100,245.50	233,906.50
Limbers . . .	42	751.40	31,558.80	30	9,467.64	22,091.16
Gun carriages . .	84	1,502.80	126,236.20	30	37,870.56	88,364.64
Artillery harness .	126	859.15	108,252.90	30	32,475.87	75,777.03
Panoramic sights .	63	442.00	27,846.00	30	8,353.80	19,492.20
Shrapnel (for field guns) . . .	11,346	39.07	443,288.22	5	22,164.41	421,123.81
High explosive shells (for field guns) .	11,346	52.08	590,899.68	5	29,544.98	561,354.70
Hand grenades . .	10,000	4.63	46,300.00	100	46,300.00	—
Chemical shells . .	640	38.56	24,678.40	5	1,233.92	23,444.48
Trench mortars .	10	400.00	4,000.00	100	4,000.00	—
Shells for bombthrowers . . .	1,000	15.00	15,000.00	100	15,000.00	—
Swords . . .	1,000	12.75	12,750.00	30	3,825.00	8,925.00
Spears . . .	500	9	4,500.00	100	4,500.00	—
Engineer materials .	—	—	93,488.00	25	23,372.00	70,116.00
Aeroplanes . .	3	—	300,291.16	25	75,072.79	225,218.37
TOTAL . .	—	—	6,199,325.78	—	675,658.56	5,959,276.70
Cost of transport .	.	.	.	.	.	436,365.61
GRAND TOTAL .	.	.	.	.	.	6,395,642.31

367

APPENDIX

This document, found in the Office of the Military Attaché, Soviet Embassy, Peking, is a certified copy of an original receipt signed by Feng Yu-hsiang for the amount of roubles 4,501,999, while in Moscow in 1926. Attached thereto is a list of arms and munitions covering that amount.

RECEIPT

The present receipt is given to the Government of the U.S.S.R. in token that, in accordance with the obligation undertaken by me, I have received supplies to the amount of four million five hundred and one thousand nine hundred and ninety-nine roubles, according to the list attached thereto.

Roubles 4,501,999.

August 1926, Moscow.

I have received the supplies according to the list which I certify hereby.

Signed : FENG YU-HSIANG.
15 August, 1926.
Translated by K. Kraff.
16 August, 1926.
A TRUE COPY :
Signed : V. ROGATCHEFF.
Very Secret.

LIST AND COST OF ARTICLES TO BE DELIVERED TO THE KUOMINCHUN

Names of Articles	Quantity	Price	Total Cost	% of discount	Discount	Total cost discount deducted
Rifles . . .	3,530	552.25	195,032.50	5	9,757.62	185,280.88
Cartridges . .	23,649,455	82.23*	1,944,451.69	5	97,222.58	1,847,229.11
' Maxim ' machine guns .	80	1,552.52	124,205.60	30	37,260.48	86,941.12
3-inch Field guns .	18	7,956.00	143,208.00	30	42,962.40	100,245.60
Limbers . .	18	751.40	13,525.20	30	1,352.52	12,172.68
Shell-cases . .	36	1,502.80	54,100.80	30	16,230.24	37,870.56
Field H.E. shells .	17,654	52.08	919,420.32	5	45,971.01	873,449.31
Field shrapnel .	17,654	39.07	689,741.78	5	34,487.08	655,254.70
Art. harness .	sets—54	859.15	46,394.10	30	13,918.23	32,475.87
Panoramic sights .	27	442.00	11,934.00	30	3,580.20	8,353.80
Chemical shells .	9,360	38.56	360,921.60	5	18,046.08	342,875.52
Trench mortars .	18	400.00	7,200.00	100	7,200.00	—
Powder charges .	1,800	15.00	27,000.00	100	27,000.00	—
Gas masks . .	30,000	8.00	240,000.00	—	—	240,000.00
Flammenwerfer .	10	200.00	2,000.00	—	—	2,000.00
Swords. . .	4,000	12.75	51,000.00	30	15,300.00	35,700.00
' Nagant ' revolvers	500	39.78	19,890.00	—	—	19,890.00
Cartridges . .	5,000	44.52	222.60	—	—	222.60
TOTAL . .	.	.	4,872,281.59		370,282.44	4,501,999.15

* Per 1,000.

Appendix V

Extract from Memorandum 20 of the Tientsin British Committee of Information, reproducing a supplement to the 'Peking and Tientsin Times' on May 12, 1927, by kind permission of the Editor.

Fragment of Instructions Drafted from a Resolution of Extended Plenary Session of Communist International giving Directions to the Military Attaché regarding Policy to be followed in China.

(Translation)

Very Confidential.

To the Military Attaché in China.

Enclosing a resolution on the Chinese question, carried . . . the extended plenary session of the Executive Committee of the Communist International, we send you an instruction drafted according to this resolution, which you will carry out.

(1) Every attention must be paid at present to lend to the revolutionary movement in China an exclusively national character. To this end it is necessary to carry on agitation in favour of the Kuomintang as of the party of the national independence of China. Use extensively the events at Hankow and the position taken up in them by England, as a proof, firstly, of the success of the Kuomintang in the national work and, secondly, of the indubitable weakness of the European Powers in the struggle against the Chinese revolution.

(2) It is necessary to organize anti-European disturbances in the territory occupied by the troops of Chang Tso-lin.

(3) It is necessary to discredit the activity of Chang Tso-lin, stigmatizing him as a mercenary of the international capitalistic . . . (currents ?), who hinders the Kuomintang in its work of liberating China . . . (foreign ?), control.

(4) It is necessary to organize agitation against European intrusion . . . (the rest has been burned).

(5) It is necessary to take all measures to stir up the mass of the population against . . . (the foreigners ?). To this end it is necessary to have the foreign Powers to resort . . . (to repressive measures ?) in the struggle with the mob. In order to provoke the intervention of foreign . . . (troops ?) do not shrink before any measures, even such as looting and mass . . . (massacre ?). In case of collisions with European troops use largely these cases for agitation.

(6) Be careful not to carry out at present the communistic programme. This might strengthen Chang Tso-lin's position and

augment the split in the Kuomintang. (We have categorically ordered Borodin to abstain) [1] for the present from too strong pressure on the capitalistic elements, having in mind the aim to keep in the Kuomintang all classes of the population, including the bourgeoisie, until the fall of Chang Tso-lin.

(7) While carrying out the present anti-European movement it is most important to keep up the present antagonism among powers. It is especially important to isolate Japan as the country which can within the shortest time move into China a large number of troops. To this end it is necessary to pay strict attention that Japanese residents should not suffer during any riots. However, as regards agitation against the foreigners, the exclusion of Japan might produce an unfavourable impression. It is therefore necessary to carry on the agitation against foreigners in the form of an anti-British movement. . . . immediately send to all chiefs of sections and follow . . . (this instruction ?) . . . (the rest has been burned).

[1] The words in brackets had been erased in the original, but when photographed with a special lens the indentations of the typewriter were clearly visible.

Appendix VI

Extracts from full translation of statement by Major-General Tada, Commanding Japanese troops in China, to Japanese journalists on September 24, 1935.[1]

Introduction

The attitude of the western powers towards China has always been to endeavour to bring the partition of the country. Sometimes they have been advocating the setting up of a joint administration with themselves as leaders, at other times they have been engaged in enlarging their own sphere of influence or struggling to get a monopoly of the markets, privileges and concessions that China has to offer. Such aggressive methods have it must be admitted at times been changed in order to be more in keeping with the times, but the final result has always been that foreign countries have treated China as the victim and tried to get as much out of her as they could in order to increase the prosperity of their own country. During this time our imperial Empire alone has as a national policy throughout advocated the preservation of Chinese territory for the Chinese, and moreover striven to bring about a friendly alliance between Japan and China in order to facilitate mutual help and mutual prosperity between the two countries. . . .

In order to carry out its sacred mission Imperial Japan must first of all ensure that its own nation itself is steady and strong, otherwise how will it be able to take into consideration and reflect on the affairs of others. While being steady and strong we must be sure that our steadiness and strength are founded on fairness and uprightness, otherwise there will be no permanency in it.

Our attitude towards China must be regulated to agree with and be in accord with both our own national policy and also with the execution of our missions outlined above. That is to say, the main object of the continental policy of Japan is to aim at the development of the home country and at the same time and concurrently with this to rescue the oppressed Far Eastern nations, give them peace and happiness, whilst ensuring that they retain their sense of honour and dignity. By

[1] In translation the whole statement involves about 10,000 words. The extracts which have been selected are designed to illustrate fairly Japan's criticism of foreign powers, her criticism of the present-day rulers of China, the sympathy she claims to have with the people of China, and her ' sacred mission.' Although necessarily of some length they will well repay perusal.

this means and, in addition, by respecting their independence we must establish such peaceful relations and co-operation between ourselves, and create such close political, economical and military connections that the two nations will become absolutely inseparable.

Such a course is without doubt an upright one in accordance with heaven's decree and must be correctly followed without opposition both at home and abroad. We feel no shame in professing before the world that we have a sincere faith and belief that this is our heaven-sent mission.

We Japanese in carrying through our lofty mission must in order to carry out our imperial decree advance steadily and bravely and endeavour to help our meeker neighbours and bring about permanent peace in the Far East. The realization of the above-mentioned mission is really the touchstone for solving the Chinese problem and already the first stone has been thrown. We must cease following old customs and playing about with petty ideas and in a straightforward and impartial manner investigate methods to bring happiness to all the people. Whilst bringing forward these noble and praiseworthy ideas we must get rid of anything that prevents putting them into practice. Thus must we have a fixed determination to rescue the 400,000,000 people. . . .

The Basic Principles of our Chinese Policy

It is obvious that our Chinese policy is based on our national policy to maintain permanent peace in the Far East, and on our mission to rescue the eastern nations who are groaning under the suppression of the white races. . . .

At the present time China is as a result of the insatiable squeeze of the various military cliques in power since the Revolution, and also coming to more recent times of the suppression by the military party formed by the union of Chiang Kai-shek and the Chekiang military leaders, now groaning under unprecedented burdens of squeeze and extortion and is floundering about in the lowest and most abject state of existence. Owing to this therefore and also to a continual succession of unavoidable natural calamities due to lawless soldiery and disasters caused by the hands of bandits, the agricultural villages find themselves groping along the road to disaster and things have got to such a state that the farmer is owing to the condition of things all around him placed in a position whereby he must think out whether it would not be better for he himself to become a bandit.

This pitiable state of affairs is without a doubt the work of Chiang Kai-shek's party and the political leaders at Nanking, who for their home policy have nothing to show but squeeze and destruction, and for foreign policy instead of getting down to it and selecting some definite line of action which is calculated to enable them to attain successfully their object, spend their time trying to control one foreign country through another, a most ridiculous policy which in the end gets them nowhere and which is equivalent to digging their own grave.

Not only do they forget their good fortune in having been able to avoid their country being divided up or jointly administered by others, owing to the existence of Japan, a strong and determined country, as their neighbour, but on the contrary they look upon Japan as an enemy, infringe upon our legitimate rights and privileges and both secretly and openly plot with other foreign countries for our downfall. To harbour such underhand plans is despicable from every point of view. Not only is such conduct against her good neighbour Japan from the point of view of international moral inexcusable, but also from China's point of view too it breeds more and more ill feeling amongst the Chinese and in particular brings on anti-Japanese boycotts which in the end do nothing more than increase many times the miseries of the Chinese people.

Thus Chiang Kai-shek and his clique, failing to realize that without Japan, China would be unable to exist at all as an independent country and acting at all times in order to fill their own bellies at the expense of the people, are not only enemies of close co-operation between the Chinese people and Japan but can also be said to be enemies of humanity. Consequently they cannot be entrusted with the work of saving China and if China is not saved now the 400 million pitiable people will be thrown into such terrible chaos, that they will eventually be beyond saving. If such a thing should happen it is as clear as daylight that the effect on Japan owing to its close and mutual relationship will be very great. This fact is the root of the danger to peace in the Far East and a thing that must be most regretted by both the Japanese and Chinese people.

Looking at things in this light, it is clear that the fundamental basis of our China policy is to weed out thoroughly these evils and at the same time to save China and plan for the happiness and prosperity of both peoples. Some say that the internal situation in our country at the present time is serious and ask how we can afford any of our power and strength for use abroad, but it must be remembered that if our Chinese policy is correctly pursued no very great sacrifice will be necessary, also that the direct effect on our homeland of our policy in Manchoukuo and China is very great. . . .

The necessity to follow a definite and determined line of action

In destroying everything that is unjust and unrighteous or in punishing the obstinate and immoral it is of course necessary to use power and authority reasonably and fairly. This is especially so in dealing with the so-called ' Intelligentsia ' Chinese as they have very little public moral sense and are given to intrigue and finesse. . . .

Abolishing the principle of ' squeeze ' and substituting the principle of ' giving '

The fundamental basis of economic co-operation between Japan and China lies in mutual existence and mutual prosperity, and the basis of this mutual existence and mutual prosperity lies in the abolition of the system of squeeze. Now the system of squeeze is a legacy of the capitalist system of Europe and America. At the present time western materialism and civilization are at a standstill and it goes without saying therefore that to follow a policy of licking their leavings is worse than foolish. How very right and correct is therefore surely Imperial Japan's continental policy, based as it is on righteousness and uplift and relief.

It is clear that Japan in carrying out her mission must select a method which is peculiar to herself and this peculiar method can be said to be to carry out thoroughly the principle of ' giving.'

It is obvious that in order to help and relieve the Chinese people who live in surroundings of abject poverty and who are worn out with difficulties and trials the first necessity is to give them happiness and nourishment. That is to say we must first of all give them capital, technical knowledge and peaceful surroundings and happiness in their work, in order to enable them to live a satisfactory life. It is necessary also to give them a margin over and above the absolute bare essentials for life and to increase the purchasing power of the individual. In giving happiness to the people the feelings between the two nations will be improved, economic relations will become so close and linked together as to be inseparable.

China can become a market for our products whilst she on her part can supply us with raw materials and in this way the two countries can go along together increasing in happiness and prosperity. This is what is meant by ' mutual existence and mutual prosperity.' If China fails to realize the actual conditions prevailing in this ever-changing world and purposely sticks to her old customs and her system of squeeze, or is foolish enough to continue in carrying on the mistaken policy of each man looking after himself and thinking only of what private gains he can get, she will go along the same road as she has done before, will become despondent and pessimistic. It will be foolish indeed if she does so. If, however, on the contrary she comes forward as suggested above with a desire to improve she will become the object of admiration of all the smaller nations of the world and without even demanding it herself will be installed as one of the world's leading powers.

The so-called magnanimity of a great power is based on a recognition of this system of ' giving ' in substitution of a system of ever thinking of one's self and of looking upon others merely as another means to procure personal gain. It demands the important quality of calmly and unostentatiously placing one's self in a position to be able to respect others and understand their point of view. In other words it is the art of being able to bring happiness to others.

The necessity to respect the independence of others and to maintain their honour and dignity

The desire of every nation in the world to maintain the honour and dignity of its own race, in other words its ideas regarding independence, are instinctive. . . .

A continental policy which aims merely at increasing our territory would on the contrary weaken the whole country and this is the reason for adopting the principles upon which the state of Manchoukuo has been built. In this case a new principle has been adopted which allows for the maintenance of independence whilst at the same time enabling the two countries to grow up alongside each other and develop such close relations with each other that they will become inseparable. Although the government and people of Japan, who are humane and kind-hearted, should not fall into the error of talking about annexing China or conquering it, there are many examples of our people being so ignorant as to go about carelessly talking and acting as if we were going to make Manchoukuo a second Korea. Such talk and actions have created doubt and anxiety in the minds of the people of Manchoukuo and have had a very bad effect and created difficulties in the administration of the country. Such people by their conduct have given opportunities to Chinese statesmen and officials to try and disseminate anti-Japanese propaganda amongst the ignorant masses and increase their enmity towards our country. It is very important therefore to explain in a clear and straightforward manner the sincerity of Japan and her earnest wish for the improvement of the happiness of the people, and to get the people to realize that for their own happiness the determination to get rid of anyone preventing us carrying out our object and of all the enemies of co-operation is fair, upright and unbiassed. . . .

The necessity to abolish our mistaken superiority complex

One of the things that the Chinese complain of in our dealings with them is that we look down on them and are for ever trying to show off airs of superiority. Of course if we compare ourselves with the Chinese it is natural enough that we should feel superior. We will however not get them to respect us by showing off and adopting a boasting attitude. No one will approve of and certainly it is not in accordance with the attitude to be adopted by a great country to carry on in a way that some low-class Japanese sometimes do such as trading in forbidden articles, riding on trains without buying a ticket or such similar unlawful acts. By adopting a boastful attitude towards Chinese we on the contrary actually put ourselves on an equal with them. It is natural for a people who are in fact of superior quality, being what they are, to be able to show great generosity to others, to be able to befriend and protect them and at the same time to treat them with dignity and honour ; in other words it is natural for them to act in the way that is expected of a great country. When such an attitude is adopted the other people without even being asked naturally look upon us as teachers and come to yield to our wishes.

The shallow superficial airs adopted by some Japanese in Manchoukuo have acted as a definite obstruction in the friendship of the two peoples and caused difficulty in the work of government, and are a stumbling-block in the way of carrying out our continental policy. They must be carefully guarded against.

To sum up, the fundamental ideas regarding our Chinese policy are with our great mission to rescue the people of the world as a basis to aim at relieving the Chinese people and enable them to advance along with the Japanese nation to wealth and prosperity. By this means, in the belief that we are bringing about permanent peace in Asia we must have a fixed determination, fair, honourable and unbiassed, to advance courageously and steadily forward in our mission, brushing aside all opposition in our way.

The Nationalist Party and Chiang Kai-shek

When making a review of China with the above-mentioned impartial object in view it is clear that the obstruction in the way of attaining this object is due to the existence of the Nationalist Party and the political power of Chiang Kai-shek. Recently there have been persistent reports that Chiang Kai-shek has become pro-Japanese and is regretting a great many of his past acts, and there are some people who believe this to be true. Are these people not however mixing up dreams with actual facts owing to being under the illusion that the central authority of Chiang Kai-shek has been successful up to a certain point and that he has been able to change radically the ideas of the party leaders.

Admittedly abstract ideas and arguments cannot be carried out completely and conclusively as if they were just mathematical problems, and although it is impossible always to force one's will upon others it is reasonable to expect that a man's ideas about definite factors upon a conclusion will for the most part be in accord with the conclusion itself. That such should be so is a very important point concerning the consolidation of the policy of the imperial country, and as this is a cause why Japan and Chiang Kai-shek's Nationalist Party cannot exist alongside each other, we will investigate the matter in order to endeavour to provide material for general information purposes. . . .

The unprecedented way in which Chiang Kai-shek, that is to say the new military clique created by the union of the Nationalist Party and the Chekiang military, has suppressed and squeezed the 400 million people has already been given above. It is quite clear that there can be no union or co-operation between a country like Japan which has as its aim the happiness of the people and a body of men who squeeze the people in this manner. It is said that there are people who look upon Chiang Kai-shek as an opportunist who is able to change in accordance with the times. This however is taking a very blind look at things because this change round of his really signifies defeat and the leaving behind for posterity of a dishonourable and ignominious reputation, whilst at the same time the principles and aims that have brought about this change must invite a result which will in the end be equivalent to committing suicide.

When taking into consideration the influence acquired through their wives by Chiang Kai-shek, Mr. Ch'en Li Fu, Mr. H. H. Kung and Mr. T. V. Soong and their relations with the Chekiang financiers, and remembering the connections established by all these with England and the United States, especially the private money invested in British and American banks, it is quite clear as to whether there is ever any possibility of them co-operating with a country like Japan whose interests lie in quite the opposite direction. It is obvious that such co-operation cannot on any account be hoped for.

Despite the fact that the result of the recent incidents in North China, judging from actual facts, was that the Nationalist Government was forced to issue instructions for a change-over to a pro-Japanese policy, these people have not ceased carrying on in an underhand way anti-Japanese work. There are many proofs to show that those members who belong to the Blue Shirt Party and are still remaining in power are carrying out in an underhand manner movements against Manchoukuo, and also many proofs that in the commercial, railway and financial branches of the Nanking Government instructions and guidance calculated to hinder the creation of a Sino-Japanese alliance are being issued.

Although we recognize that just at the present time when they have been forced to change temporarily their attitude towards us it is difficult for them all at once to alter everything in order to conform to this policy and also recognize that a certain amount of time is required to eradicate completely anti-Japanese ideas that have been disseminated and are now thoroughly sunk into the minds of the lower classes, even then when we consider the actual evidence available regarding their anti-Japanese movement and actions in North China, regrettable as it is, it is quite impossible to acknowledge any form of sincerity in them.

In other words one can say that their change of heart is useless unless it produces some definite and concrete action. As seen from what is stated above the present change of heart is merely a temporary expedient to tide over the present difficult time. Therefore even if by any chance they give way to us now and in return for some form of compensation recognize Manchoukuo and concede to us in a few other purely formal matters, as soon as the international situation changes and a good opportunity arises for them to return to their so-called revenge policy they will surely again follow blindly in the wake of the European and American and once more bring forward their plea for the abrogation of the unequal treaties and restoration of lost territory. We must anticipate them doing this and returning to us evil for good. . . .

The Red Movement in China

The red menace in China began with the incorporation of the Communist elements in the Nationalist Party and gradually spread all over the country. Chiang Kai-shek has often since 1927 endeavoured to bring about movements for the expulsion of communism but communistic ideas still prevail among the lower ranks of the Nationalist Party. Although all Chiang Kai-shek's principal assistants have combined with the Chekiang plutocrats and degenerated into a clique of capitalist bandits the organization, constitution and activities of the body are not very different from those of the communists. This is obvious from a study of their past record. Although Chiang Kai-shek has been carrying on an anti-red campaign for many years now, he had never been able to produce much of a result. To suppress entirely the communist movement is now quite impossible, and in actual fact the red menace will probably tend to become more serious with the possible threat of the realization of the North-Western link of Szechuan, Tsinghai and Sinkiang which is one of the hoped for schemes of the 3rd International. There is no doubt at all that Chiang Kai-shek is not really earnest in his campaign to suppress the Reds. . . .

It is but natural and reasonable that the Soviet communist party should use this movement with a view to increasing their own prestige and power in China. It is clear that so long as the selfish and tyrannical policy of the Nationalist Party continues so will the condition of the farmers and peasants get worse and worse and the worse their condition becomes so much will their desire for communism increase. . . .

The existence of a communist party in China is as stated above due primarily to the bad government of the Nationalist Party and the way to save the Chinese therefore lies in the reform of this latter party.

In other words, we must lighten the burden of the people, eradicate suppression and guarantee everyone a sure and reasonable livelihood. Therefore looking at things either from the point of view of getting rid of communism or of trying to relieve the people a complete reorganization of the present administrative system in China must be the united object of both the Chinese and Japanese peoples. As stated above, the Chinese Nationalist Party has an organization and constitution not unlike those of Soviet Russia and therefore in time of great distress it will be more likely to look for help from the Soviet communist party than from Japan.

A perusal of the latest reports confirm that there is some truth in this and there is very positive proof that Chiang Kai-shek is seeking an alliance with and has already endeavoured to obtain assistance from the Soviet in his work of preventing Japan from successfully carrying through her natural policy.

To sum up it may be said that although the Chinese communist party is not in itself anything to fear it might some time be used by the Soviet in such a way as to effect adversely our country and for this reason must be closely watched.

The main point to remember in trying to suppress the Reds is to destroy the people's desire for such a kind of thing as Bolshevism and this is only another way of saying that it is necessary to reorganize and reconstruct the present incompetent and inefficient form of government in China.

APPENDIX

Conclusion

On looking back at our history ever since the remote ages, no matter how many times we have set foot on the continent, we have always met with failure, have been forced to retire, and have gone on and done the same thing over again. It was thus in our campaigns at Tsingtao and in Siberia. Nothing now can alter the past but now at the present day in the work of building up Manchoukuo and developing North China shall we go on and again repeat our former mistakes ? Surely let us hope not. This time not only will it mean just a retirement from the continent, if we fail, but it will in very truth also mean a very great deal more as the very existence of our country and fate of our nation is at stake.

For this reason therefore it is to be hoped that everyone will study our past history, see where we made mistakes and search out their cause so that we may avoid them in future.

INDEX

381

Manchoukuo, independence of, 260 ; empire of, 269 et seq. ; purchase of Chinese Eastern Railway, 270–1 ; economic prospects in, 272–5 ; international trade and open door, 275–6 ; terrorism in, 276 ; oil monopoly, 276

Manchuria, Russian activities in, 24, 25 ; Russian railway rights and construction in, 26, 27 ; cession of southern section Harbin–Port Arthur Railway to Japan, 36 ; Chang Tso-lin regime (*see* Chang Tso-lin), September 18, 1931, and events following (*see* under Japan), theory of self-determination, 260–1

Manchus, *see* Abdication of Manchu Dynasty

Maritime Province, *see* Littoral Province

Mass Education, 307

Maxwell, Dr. J. Preston, 229

May 30, 1925, incident at Shanghai on, 100 et seq.

Medicine and surgery in China, 229, 311, 315

Meiji Era, 241 et seq.

Mencius, quoted, 38, 142

Middle Kingdom, 21

Ming Dynasty, 66, 67, 355

Missionary effort, *see* Christian Missions

Mixed Court, at Shanghai, 189

Mongol Dynasty, 277

Mongolia, strategic importance of, 277 ; Japanese and Russian interest in, 277 ; alliance with Manchus, 278 ; claims of China in, Russian policy in and assistance to, and conflict between China and Russia in regard to, 278 et seq. ; Japan's border policy, 279–80 ; ambiguous position of, 281

Mongolian People's Republic, establishment of, 278 ; protocol with Russia, 281

Morrison, Dr. Robert, 172

Muddy Flat, battle of, 186

Mukden incident, September 18, 1931, 253–4 ; subsequent events, 254 et seq. ; *see also* Manchoukuo

Muraviev, Count, 23

Nakamura, Captain, 263

Nanking Government, *see* National Government at Nanking ; fight of, for supremacy, 126 ; struggle of, with Communism, 154, 317, 324 ; outrage against foreigners, 123–5 ; settlement of, 133

Treaty of, 30, 174

Na Tung, 20

Napier, Lord, 170, 171

National Council, 66

National Economic Council, 311

National Government at Nanking, machine, 137 et seq. ; personnel of first government, 143, 144 ; coalition in 1932, 317

Naval Ratio, 87

Nerchinsk, Treaty of, 23

Newchwang, Treaty port of, 255

New Life movement, 308–9

Nine-Power Treaty, terms of, 88, 89 ; proposed to be invoked, 267–8 ; Russia not a party, 264

XIXth Route Army, 258–9

Ningpo, 180

Nishihara loans, 85

Noa, U.S. Destroyer, 123

Nogi, General, 35

North China, Japanese military operations in, 282–3 ; alleged autonomous sentiment in, 284 ; threat to enforce, 287 ; autonomy of Eastern Hopei, 287 ; Chahar-Hopei political council, 287 ; smuggling in, 287–9 ; Japanese economic projects, 289 et seq. ; negotiations between Japan and China in regard to, 294

Oil, 275–6, 290

O'Malley, O. St. C., 121, 122

'Open Door,' 329 ; in Manchuria and Manchoukuo, 275–6

Opium question, 172–5

Organic Law, The, 137

INDEX

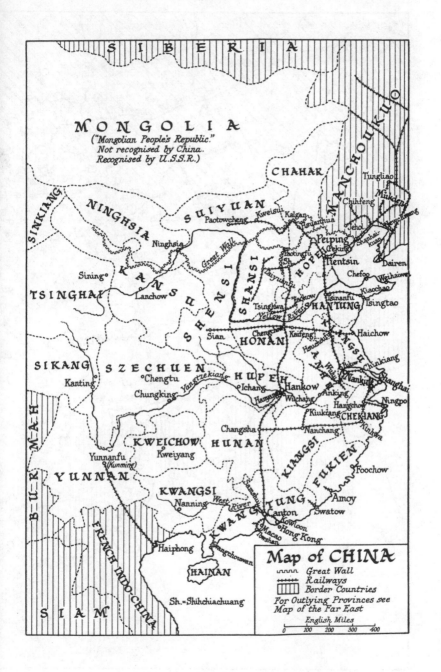

MONGOLIA
("Mongolian People's Republic."
Not recognised by China.
Recognised by U.S.S.R.)

S I B E R I A

SINKIANG

NINGHSIA

SUIYUAN

CHAHAR

MANCHOUKUO

Tungliao

Chihfeng

Mukden

Paotowcheng

Kweisui

Kalgan

Hsuanhua

Jehol

Shanhai-
kuan

Ninghsia

Great Wall

Peiping

Chinwangtao

TSINGHAI

Sining

KANSU

Lanchow

SHENSI

SHANSI

Paotingfu
Sh.

Choking

HOPEH

Tientsin

Dairen

Chefoo

Weihaiwei

Taiyuanfu

Tsinghwa

Yellow River

Hankow

Tsinanfu

Kiaochao

SHANTUNG

Tsingtao

Sian

Chengchow

Kaifeng

HONAN

Haichow

KIANGSU

SIKANG

Kanting

SZECHUEN

Chengtu

Chungking

Yangtzekiang

HUPEH

Ichang

Hankow

Hanyang
Wuchang

Hsuchow

Whuhu

Chinkiang

Nanking

Shanghai

Anking

Hangchow

Ningpo

Kiukiang

Changsha

Nanchang

CHEKIANG

Kinhwa

KWEICHOW

Kweiyang

HUNAN

KIANGSI

Yunnanfu
(Kunming)

YUNNAN

B U R M A H

KWANGSI

Nanning

West River

FUKIEN

Foochow

Amoy

KWANGTUNG

Canton

Swatow

Kowloon
Hong Kong

Samshui

Macao
Kwangchowwan

Haiphong

FRENCH INDO-CHINA

HAINAN

Sh.=Shihchiachuang

SIAM

Map of CHINA

〰〰〰 Great Wall
╪╪╪╪ Railways
▥▥▥ Border Countries
For Outlying Provinces see
Map of the Far East

English Miles
0   100   200   300   400

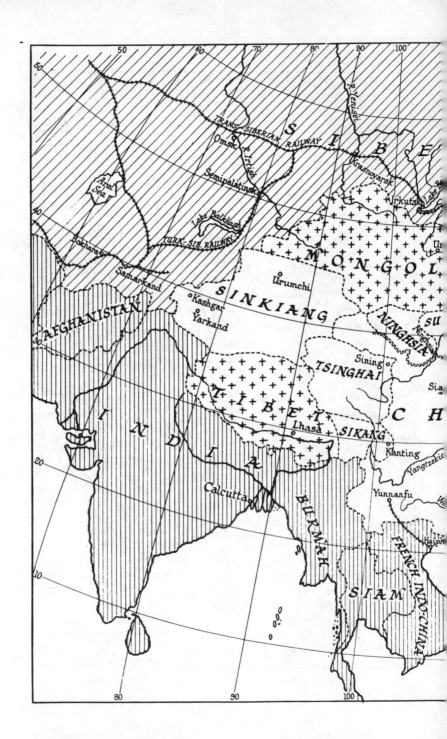

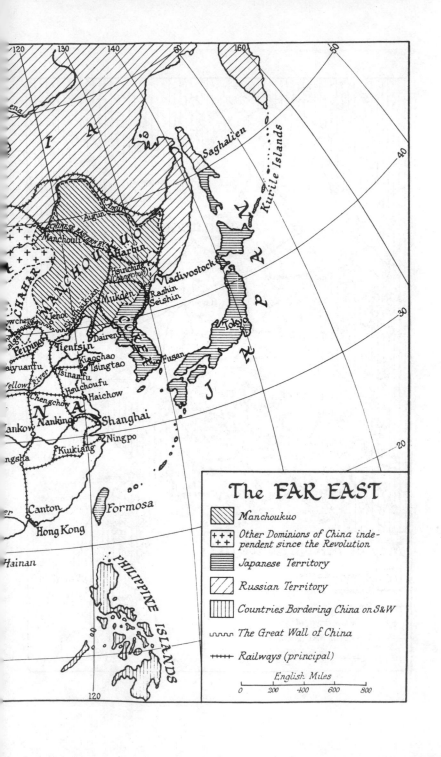

The FAR EAST

⧄	*Manchoukuo*
+++ +++	*Other Dominions of China inde-pendent since the Revolution*
▤	*Japanese Territory*
⧄	*Russian Territory*
▥	*Countries Bordering China on S&W*
ᨠᨠᨠ	*The Great Wall of China*
++++	*Railways (principal)*

English Miles

0   200   400   600   800

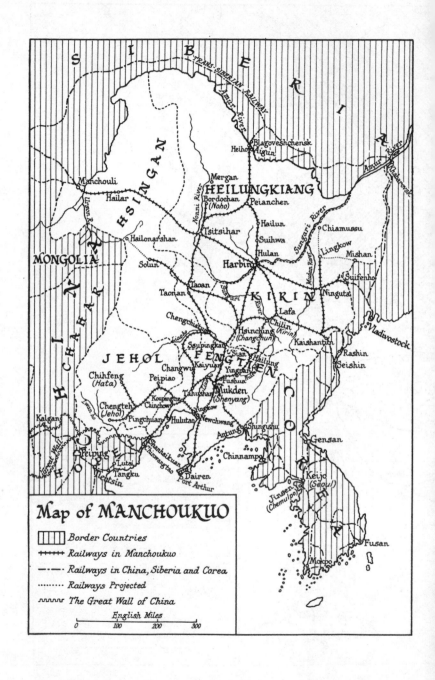

Map of MANCHOUKUO

|||| Border Countries
++++++ Railways in Manchoukuo
─·─·─ Railways in China, Siberia and Corea
········ Railways Projected
∿∿∿∿ The Great Wall of China

English Miles

0   100   200   300

Labels on map:

S I B E R I A

MONGOLIA

HSINGAN

CHINGAR

CHAHAR

JEHOL

FENGTIEN

KIRIN

HEILUNGKIANG

COREA

TRANS-SIBERIAN RAILWAY

Amur River

Sungari River

Nonni River

Mudan River

Liaon River

Shara-mur

Yalu River

Great Wall

Manchouli
Hailar
Hailonarshan
Solun
Taonan
Taoan
Mergan
Bordochan (Noho)
Peianchen
Hailun
Tsitsihar
Suihwa
Hulan
Harbin
Heiho
Aigun
Blagoveshchensk
Chiamussu
Lingkow
Mishan
Suifenho
Ninguta
Lafa
Chilin (Kirin)
Hsinching (Changchun)
Chengchiatun
Ssupingkai
Sian
Kaishantih
Vladivostock
Rashin
Seishin
Changwu
Kaiyuan
Yungpan
Hailing
Fushun
Peipiao
Chihfeng (Hata)
Chengteh (Jehol)
Kouangtze
Chinchow
Tahushan
Mukden (Shenyang)
Yingkow
Newchwang
Hulutao
Pingchuan
Kalgan
Peiping
Lutai
Tientsin
Tangku
Shanhaikuan
Chinwangtao
Dairen
Port Arthur
Shungishu
Antung
Chinnampo
Gensan
Keijo (Seoul)
Jinsen (Chemulpo)
Fusan
Mokpo
Khabarovsk